PUBLIC SCHOOLS
AND THE
GREAT WAR

To Mike Bushby and Dennis Silk,
friends and mentors

PUBLIC SCHOOLS AND THE GREAT WAR

The Generation Lost

by
Anthony Seldon and David Walsh

Pen & Sword
MILITARY

First published in Great Britain in 2013 by
PEN & SWORD MILITARY
An imprint of
Pen & Sword Books Ltd
47 Church Street
Barnsley
South Yorkshire
S70 2AS

ISBN 978-1-78159-308-0

Typeset in 10.5/12.5pt Palatino by
Concept, Huddersfield, West Yorkshire

Printed and bound in England by
CPI Group (UK) Ltd, Croydon, CRO 4YY

Pen & Sword Books Ltd incorporates the imprints of Pen & Sword
Archaeology, Atlas, Aviation, Battleground, Discovery, Family History,
History, Maritime, Military, Naval, Politics, Railways, Select, Social
History, Transport, True Crime, and Claymore Press, Frontline Books,
Leo Cooper, Praetorian Press, Remember When, Seaforth Publishing
and Wharncliffe.

For a complete list of Pen & Sword titles please contact
PEN & SWORD BOOKS LIMITED
47 Church Street, Barnsley, South Yorkshire, S70 2AS, England
E-mail: enquiries@pen-and-sword.co.uk
Website: www.pen-and-sword.co.uk

Contents

Acknowledgements

We would like first to give a very sincere thanks to all the people, organizations and, particularly, schools, who have made this book possible. In acknowledging below the many people who have helped, we are more than conscious that some will have been left out, so many apologies if your name does not appear below. We are, of course, very grateful.

The bedrock of this book has been the material supplied in the questionnaires, and in much supplementary material, by school archivists, teachers, and some headmasters. The archivists are an under-recognized part of school life and we would like to thank them very much indeed, particularly those who have responded many times to what must have become tiresome requests for information. Preserving the history of our schools presents many challenges of competing for scarce resources and time, and those challenges will not diminish in the digital age, but we hope that schools will continue to consider the importance of acknowledging and prioritizing their heritage. The list below also includes archivists from overseas schools, and it has been a great pleasure, in the context of this book, to unite public schools in many corners of the world. Most of the following have either full- or part-time roles as school archivists, but the individual questionnaires have also been returned by headmasters, teachers, bursars, alumni relations officers and CCF commanding officers. To all of the following, therefore, we are very grateful:

Susanna Schofield (Alleyns), Andrea King (Ardingly), K. Shenton (Arnold), A. Barker (Ashville), T. Harkin (Bablake), Jeremy Bromfield (Bancrofts), David Greenaway (Bangor GS), Dorothy Jones (Barnard Castle), Jane Kirby (Bedales), Leslie Harrison (Bedford), Richard Wildman (Bedford Modern), Rachel Guy (Berkhamsted), Maggie Garrett (Bishops Stortford), Paul Murray and Basil Bey (Bishops), Simon Batten (Bloxham), Mike Sampson (Blundells), Jenny Woodland (Bootham),

Tom Robertson (Bradfield), Sue South (Bradford GS), Godfrey Thomas (Brentwood), Joyce Heater (Brighton), Anne Bradley (Bristol GS), Philip Bowen (Bromsgrove), Mark Hone (Bury GS), Keith Haines (Campbell), Colin Bagnall (Caterham), Kay Moore (Cheadle Hulme), Christine Leighton (Cheltenham), Rachel Roberts (Cheltenham Ladies College), M. Delfgou (Chigwell), G. Clarke (Churchers), Tony Chew (Clayesmore), C. Knighton (Clifton), Margaret Doyle (Clongowes Wood), Catherine Smith (Charterhouse), Felicity Kilpatrick (Christ's Brecon), David Miller and Mike Barford (Christ's Hospital), Freida French (Christ Church), Jane Teal (Christs NZ), Terry Heard (City of London), Joe Cassells (Coleraine AI), Andrew Whittaker (Colfe's), Martin Williamson (Cranleigh), L. Robinson (Culford), J. Hind (Dame Allans), Calder Benzies (Daniel Stewarts), Ben Sandell (Dauntseys), Fiona Atkinson (Denstone), Janet Carolan (Dollar), P. Barry (Dover), Calista Lucy (Dulwich), J. Malden (Durham), Michael Partridge (Eastbourne), Sarah Heintze and Andrew McMillan (Edinburgh Academy), D. Carruthers (Elizabeth Guernsey), John Harvey (Ellesmere), Mark Stickings (Eltham), Tony Jones (Emanuel), Alan Scadding (Epsom), Penny Hatfield (Eton), Kevin White (Exeter), Christopher Dawkins (Felsted), Andrew Murray (Fettes), Sue Coates (Forest), Robert Montgomery (Foyle) Mark Robinson (Framlingham), Melissa Campbell and Michael Persse (Geelong GS), Fraser Simm (George Heriots), Fiona Hooper (George Watsons), Barbara Gent (Giggleswick), Simon Wood (Glasgow Academy), Elaine Mundill (Glenalmond), Liz Larby (Greshams), Keith Cheyney (Haberdashers),Toby Parker (Haileybury), Angharad Meredith (Harrow), Henley Henley-Smith (Highgate), Bev Davidge (Hilton), Ian Holt (Hulme GS), Martin Williams (Hurstpierpoint), Bridget Renwick (Hymers), Melissa Joralemon (Ipswich), Michelle Gascoine (John Lyon), John Bean (King's Auckland), Andrew Leach (King's Bruton), Paul Golightly (KES Birmingham), Peter Henderson (King's Canterbury), Ros Harding (Kings Chester), Rebecca Davies (KES Bath), David Evans (Kings Gloucester), Jenny Pearce (King's Parramatta), Alison Mason (King's Taunton), Marilyn Wilkes (KES Witley), Stanley Kitt (KES Lytham), Simon Hyde (Kings Macclesfield), Bryan Stokes (KCS Wimbledon), Michael Hoy (KWIOM), Vanessa Bowles (Kelly), Michael Over (Kent College), Marion Bradnock (Kingston GS), Zoe Parsons (Kingswood), Kate Ramsay (Lakefield Canada), John Fidler (Lancaster RGS), Anne Drewery (Lancing), Malcolm Smith (Latymer), Meenaskshi Solomon (Lawrence, Pakistan), Penny Wallington and John Allinson (Leighton Park), John Harding (The Leys), Susan Bamber (Liverpool), William Durran (Loretto), Roger Willson (Loughborough GS), Rebecca Roseff (MCS), Ian Quickfall (Malvern), Rachel Kneale (Manchester

GS), Terry Rogers (Marlborough), Stewart Brook (Melbourne CEGS), Geoffrey Brown (Merchant Taylors), Trevor Hildrey (MT Crosby), Nick Blair (Merchiston Castle), Alison Weir (Methodist Belfast), Robyn Gruiters (Michaelhouse), Peter McDonough (Mill Hill), Pat Davitt (Monmouth), David Bowden (Monkton Combe), Tricia Halley (Morrisons), John Walker (Norwich), Yvette Gunther (Nottingham HS), Jon Wills (Oakham), Clive Dytor (Oratory), Stephen Forge (Oundle), David Jones (Perse), Chris Robinson (Plymouth), Paul Bennett (Pocklington), John Sadden (Portsmouth GS), S. Ryan (QEH Bristol), G. Bisson (Queens Taunton), Joanna Lavelle (QEGS Blackburn), E. Merckx (QEGS Wakefield), Clare Sargent (Radley), Nigel Cave (Ratcliffe), Peter Burgess (Reigate GS), Paul Stevens (Repton), Dean Templeman (Ridley Canada), Sharon Potts (Rossall), Brian Todd (RBAI), Oliver Edwards (RGS Newcastle), Bernard de Neumann (RHS), A. Dodd (RGS Guildford), Andrew Rattue (RGS Worcester), Rusty MacLean (Rugby), Richard Aldrich (Ruthin), Robert Tickner (Rydal), Nigel Wood-Smith (St Albans), Lin Andrew and Marguerite Poland (St Andrew's SA), A. Reeve (St Bees), Morgan Dockrell (St Columba's), Sue Brown (St Dunstans), Martin Clifford (St Edmunds Canterbury), Chris Nathan (St Edward's), A. Alexander (St George's) John McCarthy (St George's Zim), Sally Todd (St John's), Jenni Millward (St John's SA), Tom Moulton (St Lawrence), Richard McQuade (St Michael's Canada), Alexandra Aslett (St Paul's), Howard Bailes (St Paul's Girls), Pat Chandler (St Peter's), Paul Mishura (Scotch Aus), Katy Iliffe (Sedbergh), Sally Robbins (Sevenoaks), Rachel Hassall and Patrick Francis (Sherborne), Kate Riseley (Shore), Mike Morrogh (Shrewsbury), Louise Leach (Silcoates), John Loynton (Solihull), John Craddock (Stamford), Stuart Helm (Stockport GS), David Knight (Stonyhurst), Richard Fitzsimmons (Strathallan), David Pickard (Sutton Valence), Gordon Cooper (Sydney GS), John Brown (Taunton), Bev Matthews (Tonbridge), David Pinney (Trent), Viola Lyons (Trinity College School Canada), Annie Fairley (Trinity Croydon), Jo Wood (Truro), Andrew Wilkes (UCS), Jill Spellman (Upper Canada College), Jerry Rudman (Uppingham), G. N. Frykman (Warwick), Elizabeth Wells (Westminster), Neil Lyon (Wellingborough), Patrick Mileham (Wellington), Juliet Handley (Wellington School), Berwick Coates (West Buckland), William Wood (Whitgift), Suzanne Foster (Winchester), Russell Charlesworth (Wolverhampton GS), Richard Thornton (Wood-house Grove), Wendy Bain (Worksop).

Some schools and their archivists have been particularly helpful in allowing us to explore their wonderfully interesting records, have sent through additional information in a second questionnaire, and been extraordinarily kind in responding to requests for information: Leslie Harrison (Bedford), Rachel Guy (Berkhamsted), Paul Murray and Basil Bey (Bishops), Simon Batten (Bloxham), Joyce Heater (Brighton), Mark Hone (Bury GS), Keith Haines (Campbell), Catherine Smith (Charterhouse), Rachel Roberts (Cheltenham Ladies), Felicity Kilpatrick (Christ's Brecon), Jane Teal (Christ's NZ), David Miller (Christ's Hospital), Margaret Doyle (Clongowes), Sarah Heintze and Andrew McMillan (Edinburgh Academy), Tony Jones (Emanuel), Penny Hatfield and Roddy Fisher (Eton), Andrew Murray (Fettes), Simon Wood (Glasgow Academy), Liz Larby (Greshams), Toby Parker (Haileybury), Angharad Meredith (Harrow), Paul Golightly (KES Birmingham), Peter Henderson (KSC), Jenny Pearce (King's Parramatta), John Allinson (Leighton Park), John Harding (The Leys), Rachel Kneale (Manchester GS), Terry Rogers (Marlborough), Stewart Brook (Melbourne GS), Robyn Gruiters (Michaelhouse), Nigel Cave (Ratcliffe), Paul Stevens (Repton), Rusty Maclean (Rugby), Katy Iliffe (Sedbergh), Rachel Hassall (Sherborne), Kate Risely (Shore), Mike Morrogh (Shrewsbury), David Knight (Stonyhurst), Chris Nathan (St Edward's), Sally Todd (St John's Leatherhead), Jenni Millward (St John's SA), Gordon Cooper (Sydney GS), Bev Matthews (Tonbridge), Jill Spellman (Upper Canada College), Jerry Rudman (Uppingham), Patrick Mileham (Wellington), Neil Lyon (Wellingborough), Elizabeth Wells (Westminster), Suzanne Foster (Winchester).

We would also like to thank all those schools who have given us access to and allowed us to quote from school magazines, school histories and war memorial books, which are listed in the bibliography. These have provided much of the subject matter in the book.

We are also very grateful to the Governors and Headmasters of the following schools for allowing us to quote from official papers in their archives: Berkhamsted School, Charterhouse School, Eton College, Harrow School, Gresham's School, Manchester Grammar School, Sherborne School, Tonbridge School, Wellington College, Winchester College.

We are also very grateful to the Governors and Headmasters of the following schools for allowing us to use photographs from their archives: Charterhouse School, Cheltenham Ladies College, Christ's College, Eton College, Fettes College, Geelong GS, Glasgow Academy, Gresham's School, King's School Canterbury, King William's College, Isle of Man, Kingston GS (and the Surrey History Centre), Marlborough College, Michaelhouse, Rugby School, St Paul's School, Sherborne School, Shrewsbury School, Tonbridge School, Wellington College, Winchester College.

We would like to give particular thanks to Professor Sir Michael Howard for his historical insights and for kindly writing the Foreword to the book.

Dr William Richardson, General Secretary of the Headmasters' and Headmistresses' Conference, has been enormously supportive and helpful throughout this project. He has not only allowed us to use the records of HMC Annual Conferences and Committee meetings covering this period, but has also read through the draft and given us the benefit of his profound knowledge and reflection.

We would also like to thank all those others who have read and commented on drafts of the book for their knowledgeable and incisive comments, which have resulted in a much improved text: Dr Andrew Bamji, Robin Brodhurst, Christopher Everett, Sir Anthony Goodenough, Peter Henderson, John James, Louise James, Patrick Mileham, Christopher Moore-Bick, Joanna Seldon, Professor Gary Sheffield, Philip Stevens, Professor Sir Hew Strachan, Patrick Tobin.

Other heads or teachers, past and current, in HMC schools have been very generous with their help and advice, including John Allinson, Simon Batten, Patrick Francis, Keith Haines, John Harding, Neil Lyon, David McDowell, Mike Morrogh, David Raeburn, Martin Reader, Andrew Robinson. John Witheridge, Headmaster of Charterhouse, should be especially thanked for sharing with us his outstanding research and writing on Frank Fletcher, and allowing us copious access to the school archives.

We have also been aware of our limitations as military historians of the Great War and have been very grateful for advice from many distinguished historians writing in this field, including Jeremy Archer, Richard Carr, Nigel Cave, Stephen Cooper, Professor Eric Grove, Charles Messenger, Patrick Mileham, Christopher Moore-Bick, Professor Gary Sheffield, Professor Peter Simkins, Keith Simpson MP, Philip Stevens, Professor Sir Hew Strachan.

We also acknowledge the help and support given to both of us by many colleagues past and present in the History Department at Tonbridge, with whom teaching has always been fun and who helped with so many Great War battlefield trips. They include: Mike Bushby, Francis Cazalet, David Cooper, Joe Davies, Fiona Dix Perkin, Jonathan Harber, Ceri Jones, Robert Oliver, Luke Ramsden, Melanie Robinson, Paul Taylor, Patrick Tobin, and Anthony Wallersteiner.

Anthony has also greatly appreciated advice and help given on this book by colleagues at Wellington, including James Breen, Alastair Dunn, David James, Julian Jeffrey, Ben Lewsley, Robin Macpherson and Patrick Mileham. He would also like to thank the Wellington

Governors, his Senior Leadership Team and the Common Room for their ever cheerful support.

Others who have given valuable help include Dr John Ford, Nicholas Hellen, Father Tim Novis, Piers Storie-Pugh, Brigadier Johnny Walker.

We could not have written this book without the huge help given us by Conor Turley, who has visited many archives on our behalf and coped with all kinds of jobs put his way. We are also very grateful to Jonathan Meakin for his help on the text, particularly his work on the index, and to Lara Bradban for her clerical assistance.

Angela Reed and Paula Maynard, in Anthony's office, have also been very supportive and helpful, as has Lucy Atherton in the College Library.

The editorial staff at Pen & Sword have been immensely professional and helpful, as befits a great publishing house. In particular, George Chamier, our editor, has been meticulous in his work and always ready to respond with advice. Henry Wilson has developed the project from the outset and his forbearance and advice during its course has been vital. Matt Jones has produced the finished work with great care and professionalism.

Finally, we should acknowledge that this book is the result of a friendship which goes back many years. Anthony left Tonbridge as a boy just as David arrived to teach there in 1972. Anthony's roots with Tonbridge were deep, nourished by the many inspiring figures who taught him there, especially Jonathan Smith and Mike Bushby; he came back to teach there for four years from 1989 to 1993, running the history department in which David taught, and building a family friendship which has deepened ever since; both Joanna and Judy, our wives, have been enormously supportive of this project. Together we developed at Tonbridge the battlefield trips which have now become a staple of school life; one particularly memorable event was the walk for over 200 boys, parents and colleagues along the old front line of the Somme, in 1992, which raised substantial funds for Leonard Cheshire's World Disaster Fund.

We are conscious much of value has been missed out in the writing of this book, but we had to draw the line somewhere. We leave it to other and better historians to write a longer and more penetrating book about this extraordinary episode in the history of the great public schools of Britain and her Commonwealth. We very much hope that this book will help schools to develop their own initiatives for commemorating the centenary of the Great War. The opportunities that this centenary gives to deepen and humanise our young people is almost beyond limit.

Foreword

by Professor Sir Michael Howard
OM, CH, CBE, MC, FBA, MA

The British 'Public Schools' were established, mainly in the nineteenth century, to instil into the new middle classes the values of the old gentry. These assumed the rights of a ruling elite, but also the obligations that went with them; not least responsibility for leadership in war. This involved unquestioning obedience to higher authority; care for those under one's own command; and where necessary a readiness to sacrifice one's own life in fulfilment of both.

Until the end of the nineteenth century war had been for the British a distant affair, conducted by a small professional army bred to the task. But with the dawn of a new century it soon became clear that war was now a matter for the entire nation, and that a massive army would be needed to wage it. Such an army would need officers on a scale far exceeding the tiny elite that had sufficed earlier generations, and in 1914 the public schools stood ready to supply them: Rupert Brooke was not the only public-school man who thanked God for having matched him with His hour.

The year 1914 was thus a moment of high drama for the public schools, but one that rapidly turned to tragedy. The qualities of leadership they so successfully instilled were tested almost to destruction. The new 'industrial war' that their pupils encountered was not to be won by heroic courage alone: it demanded a new kind of professionalism that could master the complex interaction of weapons, many of which had barely been invented. That professionalism could be learned only by a ghastly process of trial and error. Without it, the heroic courage instilled into the pupils of public schools was simply suicidal, and to demand it of troops under their command all too often murderous. Whether there could have been any short-cut to the creation of the highly professional force that ultimately delivered the promised victory, we can never know.

Anthony Seldon and David Walsh have done a brilliant job in describing that 'doomed generation'; how it was moulded, how it performed and not least, how it has been remembered. This book should be read by anyone tempted to make instant judgements about the quality of the leadership of the British Army in what it still seems appropriate to call 'The Great War'. But let me add a footnote.

I was brought up, at the school of which Anthony Seldon is now Master, in the shadow of that generation. We could not escape the implications of those sad memorials, those tragic lists of 'the fallen', above all the sombre remembrance services every November with their message, spoken or unspoken, that we in our turn must be prepared, if need be, to follow the example of our predecessors and make our own sacrifice. But when that time did come, my experience was rather different. The officer who welcomed us when I joined my officer train-ing unit, a colonel with a DSO and two MCs, told us bluntly, 'If any of you are thinking of laying down your lives for your country, forget it. It's not your job to get yourself killed: it's to kill the other chap, and you are here to learn how to do it'. I have to admit that this cheered us up enormously.

That was the lesson my generation carried away from our own experience. There was nothing noble about war. It was a difficult, dis-agreeable and dangerous job, no business for amateurs. But sometimes it had to be done.

Michael Howard

Maps

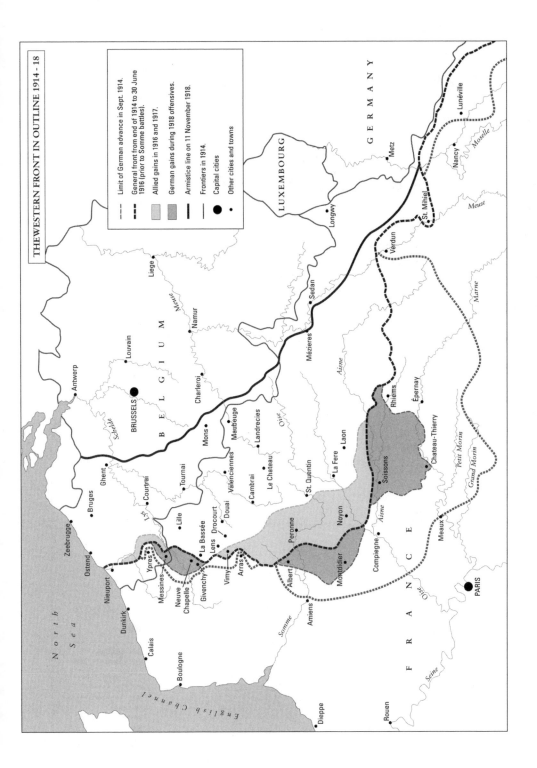

THE WESTERN FRONT IN OUTLINE 1914 - 18

Limit of German advance in Sept. 1914.

General front from end of 1914 to 30 June 1916 (prior to Somme battles).

Allied gains in 1916 and 1917.

German gains during 1918 offensives.

Armistice line on 11 November 1918.

Frontiers in 1914.

Capital cities

Other cities and towns

North Sea

English Channel

GERMANY

LUXEMBOURG

BELGIUM

FRANCE

BRUSSELS

PARIS

Liege
Louvain
Antwerp
Namur
Ghent
Bruges
Charleroi
Zeebrugge
Ostend
Courtrai
Tournai
Mons
Maubeuge
Landrecies
Mézières
Sedan
Nieuport
Dunkirk
Calais
Boulogne
Lille
Valenciennes
Cambrai
Le Chateau
St. Quentin
La Fere
Laon
Soissons
Rhiems
Épernay
Chateau-Thierry
Ypres
Messines
Neuve Chapelle
Givenchy
La Bassée
Lens
Drocourt
Douai
Vimy
Arras
Albert
Peronne
Montdidier
Noyon
Compiegne
Meaux
Amiens
Dieppe
Rouen
Verdun
St. Mihiel
Metz
Nancy
Lunéville
Longwy

Scheldt
Meuse
Oise
Somme
Seine
Aisne
Aisne
Marne
Petit Morin
Grand Morin
Meuse
Moselle

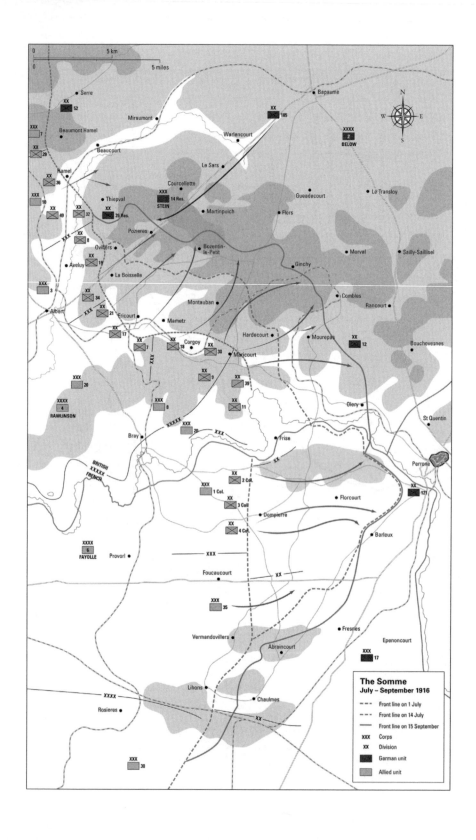

The Somme
July – September 1916

--- Front line on 1 July
-- - Front line on 14 July
— Front line on 15 September
XXX Corps
XX   Division
▓   German unit
▒   Allied unit

0   5 km
0   5 miles

N
W   E
S

Serre
52
7
Beaumont Hamel
29
Beaucourt
Hamel
36
49 32
Thiepval 26 Res.
8
Ovilers
19
Aveluy
3
La Boisselle
Albert
34
21 Fricourt
17
7
Corgoy
18 30
Maricourt
20
4 RAWLINSON
8
Bray
BRITISH
XXXXX
FRENCH
20
6 FAYOLLE Provorl
35

Mirsumont
Warlencourt
Le Sars
Courcellette
14 Res. STEIN
Martinpuich
Pozieres
Bozentin-le-Petit
Montauban
Mametz
9
39
11
XXXXX
Frise

Bapaume
185
2 BELOW
Gueadecourt
Le Transloy
Flers
Ginchy
Morval
Saily-Saillisel
Comblas
Rancourt
Hardecourt
Mourepas
12
Bouchovesnes
Olery
St Quentin
Perrone
121
Florcourt
Barleux

1 Col.
2 Col.
3 Col
4 Col.
Dompierre
XXX
Foucaucourt
XX
Vermandovillers
Abraincourt
Fresnes
Epenoncourt
17
Lihons
Chaulmes
Rosieres
XX
30

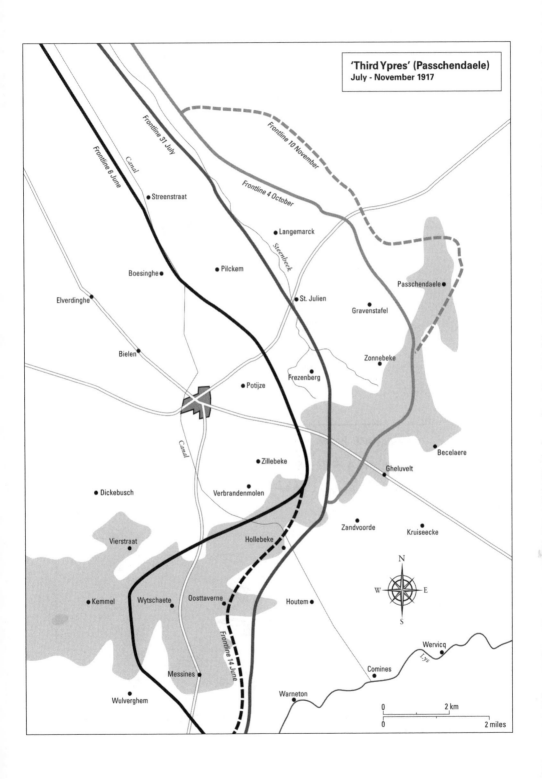

'Third Ypres' (Passchendaele)
July - November 1917

Streenstraat

Langemarck

Frontline 31 July

Frontline 10 November

Frontline 4 October

Frontline 6 June

Canal

Steenbeek

Boesinghe

Pilckem

Passchendaele

Elverdinghe

St. Julien

Gravenstafel

Bielen

Zonnebeke

Potijze

Frezenberg

Canal

Becelaere

Zillebeke

Gheluvelt

Dickebusch

Verbrandenmolen

Zandvoorde

Kruiseecke

Vierstraat

Hollebeke

N

Kemmel

Wytschaete

Oosttaverne

Houtem

W   E

S

Frontline 14 June

Wervicq

Lys

Messines

Comines

Wulverghem

Warneton

0   2 km

0   2 miles

Wilfrid Willett from Henry Williamson
Christmas 1928.
With Best Wishes.

Be merciful to these small essays:
they are the work of a boy
who had great hopes
but very little
knowledge

Ploegsteert wood 1914. Ha-ha!
I got out of that place alive!
Ha ha! Ha ha!! ha ha!!!

Enough.
The night cometh...

aerymore

Henry Williamson's inscription in his book *Lone Swallows* (1928) to Wilfred Willett, his comrade-in-arms in the Great War.

Introduction

Why a book about the Great War and the Public Schools? Some 35,000 old boys of these schools in Britain and its Dominions died in the war out of a total of 900,000 dead. They constituted just over 3 per cent of the total fatalities, and less than 2 per cent of those who fought. Yet, small though these figures are, public school alumni exercised a disproportionately heavy influence on strategic decisions throughout the war, on how the battles were fought on the ground, and on the way the war has been portrayed by subsequent generations. This in part explains the need for the book, though many other factors led us to write it.

Public schoolboys were to die at almost twice the average for all those who served. Whereas some 11 per cent of those who fought overall were to die as a direct result of the fighting, the figure for public schoolboys was over 18 per cent. Those who left school between about 1908 and 1915 were to die at even higher rates, as they were the most likely to serve in the front line as junior officers, and as pilots in the Royal Flying Corps, which saw very high casualties. Those who died represented just the tip of the iceberg of the suffering that the war caused, measured in mental and physical trauma for the survivors and in a far wider circle of broken lives.

Over two million British servicemen were wounded in body or in mind, their lives never to be the same again. Untold numbers of all classes and backgrounds suffered grief and hardship through the loss of or debilitating injury to fathers, brothers, sons and friends. The long shadow of the war extends right up until the present day. Many families across Europe, and indeed the world, will still be affected through psychological and physical scars. We can underestimate too the difficulties that returning servicemen found, coming back to a country that they scarcely recognized, picking up the threads of relationships damaged by long separations and by the unbridgeable chasm of experience that language could not bridge. The understanding of

1

trauma, pioneered by public school alumni, was still in its infancy. For many who served, their harrowing experience was even worse after the war ended than during it.

We describe the experience of old boys of public schools who fought in all three services. Because the scale is so vast, we follow one particular figure, Wilfred Willett, who left St Paul's School in 1909 for Trinity College, Cambridge, an idealistic young man whose dream was to serve his fellow human beings by becoming a doctor. As soon as war was declared, he saw it as his duty to volunteer, dropping his medical studies for the duration of the fighting, and hurriedly marrying his fiancée Eileen before he left for the front. A gregarious and impulsive young man, he made many friends at the front, one of them Henry Williamson, the author of *Tarka the Otter*, whose inscription 'To Wilfred Willett', in his book, *Lone Swallows*, precedes this introduction. Willett survived the war, but at what cost to him and his family?

The public schools have not emerged well in representations of the Great War, the predominant impression being one of callous staff officers who operated a long way behind the lines, and bumbling junior officers. Such impressions were powerfully shaped by *Oh! What a Lovely War*, the musical and film which appeared in the 1960s, and the final series of the television programme, *Blackadder Goes Forth*, first screened in 1989. General Melchett, Captain Darling, Lieutenant George and Captain Blackadder himself are very obviously public school officers, played by public school types. They are portrayed as men lacking brains, leadership or courage. Blackadder, with his 'cunning plans' vainly tries to find an escape route from the trenches, while Melchett shows his disdain for human life, planning his attacks in order to move his 'drinks cabinet six inches closer to Berlin'.

Contrast *Oh! What a Lovely War* and *Blackadder* with the portrayal of public school officers in a piece of writing which much more faithfully reflects the multi-textured truths of the war, R. C. Sherriff's *Journeys End*, a play first produced in December 1928 and based directly on the author's experience in the front line. Nowhere in either *Oh! What a Lovely War* or *Blackadder* can be found characters like Captain Stanhope, the hero of *Journey's End*, who, though ground down by the pressures of war and its losses, remains professional and caring of his men to the end. Nor are there characters to compare to the young subaltern Raleigh, who follows Stanhope, his hero from his boarding house at public school, to his company on the Western Front; nor any figure akin to Lieutenant Osborne, the avuncular public schoolmaster who cares devotedly for the soldiers under his command, as he does for his much younger company commander, Stanhope. Our book, indeed, has much to say about the contribution to the war by the teaching and support staff of public schools and the toll it took on them. Several headmasters and housemasters were broken by the losses of so many of their young men.

Images of public schools since the fiftieth anniversary of the Great War have thus been overwhelmingly negative. One book to appear on the subject, Peter Parker's well-written and thoughtful *The Old Lie: The Great War and the Public School Ethos* (1987), blames the schools for inculcating and glorifying a culture which led directly to the wasteful sacrifice of so many men. *The Donkeys* by Alan Clark (1961), had earlier popularized the image of incompetent public school senior officers. As historian Stephen Badsey has written, albeit with some exaggeration, 'It is doubtful if any British play, film or television programme of the Western Front since perhaps 1950 has depicted what was actually a commonplace of the war: a competent officer bravely and successfully leading his troops'.[1] Much of this disdain flowed from the pens of former public schoolboys.

Our book praises the character development by the public schools, which provided the young men leading their soldiers with codes of service, courage and loyalty, meriting our respect more than derision. This book, drawing heavily on research from across the public schools, is full of examples of admirable character traits of old boys, qualities which could well be accentuated more in schools of all kinds today. The importance of duty, service to others and personal responsibility, as well as courage and loyalty, grounded in classical philosophy and religious codes, are as needed today as in any age. The book also shows that public schoolboys of the era were not all the bluff, anti-intellectual sporting hearties of the popular image. The products of these schools were as varied as Edward Thomas and Paul Nash, Ralph Vaughan Williams and Anthony Eden, Siegfried Sassoon and Noel Chavasse.

We are not saying that some public schoolboys were not cowards; we are not saying that some were not snobs; we are not saying that some were not heartless. Some, an unknown number, were these and worse. But the evidence in this book indicates that the great majority were not like this. We are not saying that only public schoolboys displayed courage, loyalty, and other laudable values, nor do we believe that public schoolboys had a monopoly of excellent character. We are expressly not saying that the lives and deaths of former public schoolboys were any more valuable than those educated elsewhere. Finally, the book is not saying that those officers not educated at public schools were any less brave or courageous than those who had the benefit of a public school education. The prevailing social and economic reality, as well as the organization of the military, meant that almost all officers, particularly in the first years of the war, were from public schools. Significant numbers of public schoolboys equally chose to fight in the ranks, including left-wing intellectuals like R. H. Tawney from Rugby, while others, often driven by conscience, chose non-combat roles, like stretcher-bearing, with no less bravery.

The book focuses on junior officers, though it contains many examples of more senior officers from the rank of major to general, who were compassionate and courageous, and surprisingly large numbers of whom, contrary to popular belief, were to die in action. Senior officers, however, tended to be more remote from the lives of the ordinary soldiers and junior officers, and some were certainly guilty of being indifferent to the lives of men under their command. R. C. Sherriff portrayed one such figure in *Journey's End*, the Colonel, himself pressured from above, who orders Stanhope to mount a trench raid which Stanhope knows will end in tragedy. Senior officers were often long out of their public schools, and the influences that governed their actions were far more the codes of the professional soldier than those of the public school.

The public school model and ethos spread far beyond the shores of the British Isles and was replicated across the Dominions. Public schools in Australia and South Africa, for instance, were already long established and thriving institutions by 1914. Alumni from such schools, and those in Canada, New Zealand, and even more far-flung places, responded just as positively as their counterparts in Britain to the call of duty and patriotism and were to fight bravely on the Western Front, in Italy, the Middle East, and in the war in the air and at sea. The contribution of these public schoolboys has again received little attention, and where it has, the attention has often been critical. The powerful Australian film *Gallipoli* (1981) is perhaps the most telling example, in its portrayal of callous officers, both British and Australian. Public school politicians and staff officers were far more to blame in the strategy and execution of the Gallipoli campaign than arguably in any other, but the overall contribution of officers who participated in the campaign was far more positive and subtle than the simplistic but influential film suggests.

In the face of the shocking losses of the Great War, it is natural to seek easy stereotypes and figures to blame, and what easier and more risible target can there be than the public school buffoon? But few at the time or since have suggested ideas for conducting the Great War in ways different to the ones which were pursued. There was indeed little contemporary criticism and few alternative strategies on offer, other than suing for peace. The simple truth is that nine million soldiers were to die on all sides in the Great War because technology had reached the state of advance whereby it could transport and deploy mass armies

4

with weapons of such devastating effectiveness that they caused mass casualties. The power of artillery and the machine gun, allied to barbed wire, trenches, dugouts and 'No-Man's-Land', created a static killing-ground which only changed with the development of the tank and the aeroplane. The book does not seek to justify the war into which public school alumni led the country and subsequently directed. We believe that no one nation was responsible for starting the war and that it settled little or nothing. Blame and triumphalism are equally irrelevant. What matters to us is *lived* history, not the abstract theorising of historians and commentators.

We thus offer *Public Schools and the Great War* in an attempt to redress a gap in historical scholarship and an imbalance in popular perceptions. The war was the single greatest tragedy in the history of public schools. A far higher number were killed in it than in any other war in history, including 1939–45, many of them dying on three of the most terrible days: 25 April 1915 at Gallipoli, 25 September 1915 at Loos, and 1 July 1916 on the Somme. The Great War is deeply imprinted on the sense of history and identity of every public school, its inescapable presence felt in the many familiar places which commemorate it – memorial chapels and halls, plaques, photographs and statues. It is felt too in the rituals to which schools still subscribe today with a sense of reverence and awe: Armistice Day, Remembrance Sunday, the wearing of poppies and battlefield trips.

The schools, and the nation, should feel as proud of the part they played in the Great War as they did in the Second World War. Representations of the public schools and their alumni in the latter, whether in films of the 1950s such as *The Dam Busters* (Wing Commander Guy Gibson VC from St Edward's School, Oxford, led the raid) or *Colditz* (often perversely thought of as a jolly public school boarding house full of naughty boys), or more recently in *The Battle of Britain* (many of 'The Few' came from public schools in Britain and her Dominions), have been much kinder, with the public school ethos treated at worst as a subject of gentle parody rather than derision. Yet the strategy and conduct of the Second World War, whilst still heavily influenced by the former public schoolboy, was much more democratic, with products of the inter-war state schools rising to positions of prominence in far higher numbers. It was not, unlike the First, a 'public school war'.

It is time for the contribution of the public schoolboy to the First World War to be properly reappraised. Such reappraisal should also extend to girls' public schools and their alumni, on whom we only briefly touch. They made major contributions in a war which had such

5

a profound effect on the role and status of women in society. The centenary is the opportunity indeed for schools of all types to research and celebrate their past pupils who fought, and examine why they fought. Most state secondary schools were established after 1918, but many more primary schools were already in existence and each has its own history to research. As Professor Sir Hew Strachan has written of the coming centenary, 'The main challenge is to produce an educational legacy'.[2] Children need to be taught that the war continues to raise more questions than provide answers, just as those who went to war in 1914 knew neither what they faced nor when their ordeal would end. Research into the role played by past pupils of state schools is every bit as important; after all, the fallen from public and state schools lie side by side under equal gravestones in the war cemeteries left behind by the Great War.

The Great War was the catalyst for much social, economic and scientific change in Britain. But it had surprisingly little impact on the public schools. Exhausted and traumatized by over four years of war, the schools returned to a curriculum and way of life that was reassuringly familiar. Not until the 1960s did the schools significantly change many customs and approaches that would have not been out of place in the Edwardian era. The schools thus had a far greater impact on the war than the war had on them. Understanding that impact is extraordinarily complex. It begs a counter-factual question: how might the war have been differently conducted had the public schools not existed? The answer can only be a surmise, but the pages of this book repeatedly show that the former public school boys were imbued with a set of values and beliefs, implanted by their home backgrounds as well as prep and senior schools, which gave them a resilience and courage, a loyalty to orders, and an ability to inspire others to follow them through months and years of hardship and acute anxiety. Some may call that example folly and worse; that is their choice.

Anthony Seldon
David Walsh

Chapter 1

Public School Men

The years leading up to the First World War were 'the golden age of the public school system', according to classicist and writer Rex Warner.[1] The hundred plus public schools of those years powerfully shaped the character, thinking and attainment of the ruling class in Britain. These schools, almost without exception, educated only boys, although a parallel system of girls' public schools developed from the nineteenth century. Those who were to fight and die in the Great War were shaped of course by more than just their schools. But, for the social elite who attended them, the public schools exerted a conditioning, for better or worse, of such power that their old boys were incapable of freeing themselves entirely from its spell. This chapter examines the nature of these schools, and the experiences that young men had within them, in the tranquil years before the summer of 1914.

Speech Day 1914

Imagine a scene replicated countless times in public schools across Britain and her Dominions. The summer term was ending and the schools were gathering for their final grand send-off, 'Speech Day'. The scene at Tonbridge School in Kent that summer was repeated in well over a hundred schools. That day, 25 July 1914, was 'Skinners' Day' at Tonbridge, the annual governors' visitation by the Master, Wardens and Court of the Skinners' Company; this had taken place every summer since the school's foundation in 1553. All schools had their unique rituals and ceremonies for Speech Day: at Tonbridge this included a speech in Latin by the Captain of the School to welcome the governors, and a response by a Fellow of All Souls, appointed by the governors as an examiner for their prize exhibitions. In 1914 the All Souls don was Charles Cruttwell, a distinguished historian who was to be badly wounded in the war and wrote the well-regarded *History of the Great War 1914–18*, published in 1934. The Captain of the School was George Cressey, already the recipient of an Open Scholarship in Classics to Christ's College, Cambridge.

After the reception of the governors *ad portas* (at the school gates), the day continued with the service in the parish church to commemorate the school's benefactors, picnic lunches and an afternoon prize-giving. The Skinners' Company gave the top five scholars, on the recommendation of the All Souls' examiner, exhibitions worth £75 each, named after the founder of the school, Sir Andrew Judde. The recipients that day in July 1914, when not a hint of the gathering international crisis penetrated the day's celebrations, were Edward Hale, Edward Newbery, Michael Topham, John Greenway and Kenneth Moore – all Oxbridge scholars. Like George Cressey, they were looking forward to entering their chosen colleges that autumn.

For these six boys, as well as for hundreds of other eighteen-year-olds winning prizes at similar speech days that July and eagerly anticipating going up to university, life was about to take an unexpected direction. Instead of Oxford or Cambridge, all six elected to put their futures precariously on hold as they volunteered to serve their country. George Cressey, the son of a local surgeon, had made a powerful speech as Captain of the School at the Old Tonbridgian dinner in London earlier that July, when he spoke of the duty to support the Tonbridge School Mission, a boys' club in the deprived area of Holy Cross, St Pancras in London. His headmaster, Charles Lowry, gave him high praise in his speech at prize-giving on Skinners' Day, and just two weeks later, as headmasters were doing for their boys all over the country, he signed Cressey's application for a commission. After training at Sandhurst, Cressey proudly took command of his platoon of the 2nd Battalion, The Yorkshire Regiment in France at the end of August 1915. Four weeks later he was dead. On the second day of the Battle of Loos, 26 September 1915, he was shot through the head while holding a captured trench. His company commander described him in a letter to Cressey's father as 'the most exceptional young officer I have ever met'.

Michael Topham, the son of a railway engineer based in India, had reached the Science Sixth at Tonbridge at the age of only fifteen. He was also captain of the Shooting VIII, which had done well at Bisley in 1914. He won an Open Scholarship in Science to Downing College, Cambridge, but chose to become one of the first recruits in the Public Schools Brigade which gathered at Epsom that September. He served in the ranks of the infantry in France from the middle of 1915, using his marksmanship skills to pick off enemy snipers, until he was commissioned and transferred to the Royal Flying Corps in August 1916.

8

After all too brief a training, he joined his squadron in France in March 1917 and was shot down in flames on a bombing raid just a month later.

Kenneth Moore, an only child who benefited from a generous scholarship to allow him to come to Tonbridge, won an Open Scholarship in Classics to Emmanuel College, Cambridge in December 1913. He was a prominent gymnast, debater and editor of *The Tonbridgian*. Only seventeen when war broke out, he stayed on at school until Easter 1915 before being commissioned into the Dorset Regiment, serving in France from December 1915. He was one of thousands of public schoolboys to be killed on the Somme, on 7 July 1916 near Mametz Wood; his commanding officer wrote that, 'he was leading his platoon against an enemy trench, was hit in the head and killed instantly'. He is buried in the large military cemetery at Serre Road No. 2.

Even the survivors among the six scholars that Skinners' Day were not untouched. Edward Hale was wounded so badly near Neuve Chapelle in December 1915 that he was left permanently lame, but took up his place at Oxford after the war, emerging with first class honours and going on to a distinguished career at the Treasury and in the Cabinet Office. John Greenway left as Captain of the School in March 1915 and then served continuously in the front line, from August 1915 until the end of the war, in France and Salonika. He went up to Oxford in 1920 and followed a career in the Diplomatic Service, but, like most who fought, he found it hard to distance himself from his war experiences and did not reach the career heights his youthful promise suggested. Edward Newbery served with the Royal Garrison Artillery through all the major battles on the Western Front from 1915 to 1918, winning the Military Cross on the Somme for courage in a forward post. He ended the war with the rank of Major, abandoned his Cambridge maths scholarship to study engineering at Glasgow University and then had a long-term career with the General Electric Company; he was one of the lucky ones – of the twenty-five boys who joined Tonbridge with him in the summer term 1910, seven were killed and another five wounded.

Seven dead out of twenty-five may not approach the fifty per cent death rate of the six Tonbridge scholars that Skinners' Day, but it mirrors what happened in public schools at large, a fifth of whose former pupils were killed, mostly those just out of school. The fate of these schoolboys, on the brink of their adult lives in August 1914, shows in microcosm that sense of a generation lost in the Great War, not just in the fearful toll of young lives from the public schools, but also in the deep physical and emotional scars it left in the survivors.[2]

What was a public school?

Close your eyes and make a list of the great public schools of today, and you might think you were back in 1914. The most prestigious then and now would certainly have included Eton and Harrow, Winchester and Westminster, Charterhouse and Rugby. Alumni of such elite public schools still dominate the upper echelons of politics, business, the law, the military, journalism and the arts, much as they did in 1914. In 2014 Britain has an Etonian Prime Minister in David Cameron, with many other Etonians as his closest advisers, and a Deputy Prime Minister from Westminster School in Nick Clegg. In 1914 Herbert Asquith (City of London School) was Prime Minister, and with him at the helm of government in the lead-up to war was the Foreign Secretary, Sir Edward Grey (Winchester). Through the upheavals of two World Wars, the end of the British Empire, the rise of the welfare state and scientific change beyond the imagination of anyone in 1914, the continuities in the social and educational structure of the country are as striking as they are shocking.

In the three centuries following the Norman Conquest, advanced schooling available to the public was supervised by the Church or overseen by other bodies such as boroughs or by the local lord. Such schools were urban, charged fees and were meeting a steadily growing demand for a literate, secular education. From the 1380s new schools, also teaching grammar, began to be endowed by patrons, while others were re-founded, so increasing the spread of such education and, in time, catering to a new rural gentry class. Prominent examples included Winchester (1382), Eton (1440) and St Paul's (re-founded in 1509). The schools were 'public' in the sense that places were not the preserve of trainees for the Church. However, most pupils still paid fees, the endowment usually contributing to the salary of the master. Among these ancient schools and newer foundations, some began to recruit regionally or even nationally, and to act as channels to the universities. The term 'public school' emerged in the early nineteenth century and was applied to these influential institutions shortly before the most prominent became the focus of public concern over their finances, the state of their buildings and the quality of their management.

In 1861 the Clarendon Commission was set up by parliament to investigate these concerns, the focus being on nine of the leading schools. Two day schools, St Paul's and Merchant Taylors', both in London, were selected alongside seven boarding schools: Eton, Harrow, Westminster, Winchester, Charterhouse, Rugby and Shrewsbury. Clarendon reported in 1864 and the report bore legislative fruit in the Public Schools Act of 1868. The growing social exclusivity of these schools did not seem to have troubled the Commission, indeed some of its recommendations, including competitive exams for entry, served to place them even further out of the reach of poor children. The Act defined a 'public school' as one open to the paying public from anywhere in the country, as opposed to religious schools open only to members of a certain church, local schools only for nearby residents, or private education at home (common still amongst aristocratic and royal families). The Act recognized all nine schools as having 'public school status' but did not restrict this appellation solely to them.[3] As a result, a second commission, the Taunton Commission, also concerned with the management of school finances, was established in 1864, dealing with almost 800 endowed schools, a small proportion of which the commissioners intended to label as of the 'first grade' due to their clear links to the universities.

In 1869, responding to the fear that their independence was under threat from government, Edward Thring, the celebrated headmaster of Uppingham, asked sixty fellow headmasters of schools of the first grade to meet at his school house to consider the formation of a 'School Society and Annual Conference'. Thirteen schools sent heads: Bromsgrove, Bury St Edmunds, King's Canterbury, Felsted, Lancing, Liverpool College, Norwich, Oakham, Repton, Richmond, Sherborne, Tonbridge and Uppingham.[4] These founder members of the 'Head Masters' Conference' (HMC), as it came to be known, did not include most of the grander public schools – although all these joined in the years immediately following – and contained one, Richmond, which no longer exists as an independent school today. In 1889 the first *Public Schools Yearbook* was published. HMC numbers steadily rose, and by 1914 membership stood at 114.[5]

Demand for quality schools from the expanding business and professional classes, aided by the new railways which made it much easier for parents to send their children away from home, fuelled their growth. Cheaper fees at these new schools compared to the older public schools helped to further their popularity. Many were modelled on the ideas of the greatest reforming headmaster of them all, Thomas Arnold of Rugby (1828–41). His regime included prefects to keep order, the virtues of community life, character-building activities and the paramount importance of the classics. The new schools emerged almost annually during Victoria's reign (1837–1901), including those as diverse as Marlborough College (1843), Brighton College (1845), Glasgow Academy (1845), Radley (1847), Liverpool College (1840), Wellington College (1859), Clifton College and Malvern (1862), Leighton Park (1890) and Campbell College, Belfast (1894). Haileybury, founded in

11

1862, saw a particularly swift growth in numbers. Housed in the grand buildings the East India Company vacated after 1857, it opened with 54 boys, but had grown to 475 by 1914. This new breed of Victorian school featured prominently in the 1893 publication *Great Public Schools*.[6]

The first fourteen years of the twentieth century saw the schools blossom in size and confidence. Tonbridge, founded in 1553, expanded from 175 in the 1890s to 436 in 1914. Gresham's in Norfolk grew from some 50 boys in the nineteenth century to 230 the year the Great War broke out, helped by a charismatic headmaster, George Howson. The school was included for the first time in 1903 in the *Public Schools Yearbook*, a status much sought after.[7] The schools listed were predominantly Anglican, with Catholic and Nonconformist schools battling for recognition as full 'public schools'. Day schools fared better, with Manchester, Leeds and Portsmouth Grammar Schools all deemed to be 'proper' public schools.

Schools at the top of the pecking order differed markedly from those lower down, a hierarchy most evident in sport. When in 1866 the captain of the 1st cricket XI at Shrewsbury wrote to his opposite number at Westminster to ask for a fixture, he was told that, 'the Captain of the Westminster XI is sorry to disappoint Shrewsbury, but Westminster plays no schools except Public Schools'.[8] Before 1914, Eton only played cricket against Harrow and Winchester, while Harrow only played Eton. Other matches were played against gentlemen's clubs. The privilege of being invited by the Marylebone Cricket Club (MCC) to play at Lord's was one reserved strictly for the elite: Eton first played Harrow there in 1805, followed by Marlborough against Rugby, Cheltenham against Haileybury and then, for the first time in the summer of 1914, Clifton against Tonbridge.

The Ashburton Shield for shooting further reveals the character of the sporting hierarchy. Founded in 1861, for its first forty years the competition was open only to those twenty schools that had a 'Volunteer Corps'. When Winchester won the Ashburton in 1904, George Mallory, the Everest mountaineer, wrote to his sister: 'We badly beat Eton at cricket, and now we have won the public schools shooting, which is really the best of the lot, as every decent school goes in for it'.[9] School colours were another source of great pride.

Though academic success appears to have played little part in distinguishing the more from the less glamorous schools, an early form of 'league table' existed, with schools publicizing their Oxbridge scholarships (rather than mere places). The powerhouses of Winchester, Eton, Westminster and other grand schools had their chances further bolstered by the existence of 'closed scholarships' for their pupils at certain colleges.

The age of the school was no guarantee of public school status. R. C. Sherriff, author of *Journey's End*, attended Kingston Grammar School, founded in 1567, where he distinguished himself as a scholar, notably in the classics, as well as being captain of games. When he attempted in August 1914 to gain entry to the Army as an officer, he watched alumni of two 'top' schools walk away with commissions after cursory interviews. When his turn came, the adjutant asked him his school. On hearing the answer, the officer shook his head apologetically: 'Our instructions are that all applicants for commissions must be selected from the recognized public schools, and yours is not among them'.[10]

Public school life on the eve of war

'These schools', declared the Clarendon Commission, 'have been the chief nurseries of our statesmen; [they and] the schools modelled after them ... have had perhaps the largest share in moulding the character of an English gentleman'.[11] Few would deny the powerful influence of the public schools on their pupils; but many have been heavily critical of that conditioning. Rudyard Kipling let rip at the games culture of the schools: 'Then ye contented your souls/With the flannelled fool at the wicket or the mudded oafs at the goals'.[12] In 1917, most famously, the young Alec Waugh attacked public schools in his novel *The Loom of Youth*. In 1932 Bernard Shaw wrote perhaps the most damning indictment: 'Eton, Harrow, Winchester ... and their cheaper and more pernicious imitators should be razed to the ground and their foundations sown with salt'.[13] In 1945 Rex Whistler attacked the public school ethos for its hypocrisy and exclusivity: 'Religion has often been exclusive, discipline either slack or oppressive, culture neglected, athletics over-emphasized and service to the general community rather a sham.'[14] Noel Annan was sniffily dismissive of their reactionary influence in *Our Age* (1990), while more ferociously, Peter Parker attacked the impact of the ethos in his book *The Old Lie: The Great War and the Public School Ethos* (1987).

Public schools were self-confident places, with the public school model widely admired and emulated by schools across the world, notably in the British Dominions and the United States. Attendance at a public school gave a young man a clear identity, social status and set of precepts for the rest of his life. What was this formative experience? The school day began typically at 6.45 a.m. At Charterhouse it began with a glass of milk, while at Shrewsbury boys rose at 7 a.m. to a cold shower.[15] Carthusians then dashed off to chapel, where the doors closed at 7.30 a.m., with punishments for late arrivals. First lesson was at 7.45 and breakfast at 8.30. Much depended on the generosity of the housemaster, but the meal usually consisted of bread, butter and tea. Younger boys were back in class at 9.30 a.m., seniors at 10, with a fifteen-minute break at 10.30. Lessons continued till 12.30, with some free time before lunch at 1.15. As water was then considered not always safe, beer could be served. Two further lessons were then followed by games, with Wednesdays and Saturdays as half-holidays. 'Tea' was at 6.30, followed by 'prep' in houses and 'prayers' at 9.00 p.m. Younger boys would then go to bed, monitored by the prefects and less regularly by their housemaster. Senior boys would have their lights out at 10.30 p.m., and prefects, who ran the house, would go to bed when they chose.[16] Day schools such as Manchester Grammar had shorter days, with lessons beginning at 9.05 and finishing at 3.10 p.m., the school day consisting of five one-hour lessons. Games were less important at day schools, with sport for roughly two hours fortnightly. After lessons the boys might attend a variety of activities including a drama society, debating and a 'glee club'.[17] At Edinburgh Academy in 1913 the school day lasted from 9.00 a.m. to 3.00 p.m., with extra science classes, drawing and painting workshops and clubs and societies after the school day was over.

Chapel was a dominant feature of life for every public school boarder. Older public schools and many newer ones had fine chapels. Two services were a staple on Sundays, in addition to a morning service each weekday. At Winchester daily services lasted thirty minutes, with an additional service every Saturday evening. Haileybury boys had three compulsory services on Sundays, at 8.00 a.m., 11 and 6.30 p.m. Warner considered public school religion something of a sham, but it is doubtful if the piety of the public school pupil has changed much over the past hundred years, with a spectrum from the ardent believer to the cynical atheist.

Neither the headmasters nor the establishment at large seem to have been unduly troubled by the fact that the public schools served only a very narrow section of British society. The Clarendon and Taunton Commissions were entirely content to separate the leading schools into a rationed cadre of 'the first grade', accessible, in the main, only to families able to afford substantial fees. The hierarchical nature of Victorian and Edwardian society led to acceptance of the status quo. Charity and Christian service to those less fortunate found fullest expression in the establishment by public schools of a series of 'charitable missions' to support the poor and sick. Many schools had such missions in large cities, with Marlborough establishing theirs in Tottenham in 1882, while Rugby had an overseas mission in India from 1848 and a club in Notting Hill from 1884.

The hold of classics on the curriculum remained strong in 1914 and beyond. At King's Canterbury a fourth form boy (typically aged fourteen or fifteen) might have experienced seven and a half hours each week of Latin, five hours of Greek, German or science, four hours of maths, three hours of French, but only two hours of English, which included history and geography, and one and three quarter hours of divinity.[18] At Sherborne the classics-heavy curriculum was supplemented by each class except the sixth form undergoing compulsory physical drill and gymnastics an hour a week.[19] In the days before public exams at sixteen and eighteen, pioneering headmasters had ample curricular freedom, if they chose to exercise it. Rugby thus pioneered science education, appointing its first teacher as early as 1851 and building a science laboratory in 1859. Praised by the Clarendon Commission for being far-seeing, headmaster Frederick Temple nevertheless argued that 'the real defect of maths and science as instruments of education is that they have not any tendency to humanize. Such studies do not make a man more human but simply more intelligent'.[20] Frederick Sanderson, headmaster of Oundle (1892–1922), was another pioneering head of his era, a member of a fairly select club who stressed the importance of science alongside the development of the whole child.[21]

The dominance of classics at a time of such rapid scientific and technological advance in the world at large was a matter of increasing public concern. At Winchester, Greek was only made voluntary in the lower and middle schools in 1911. Curriculum change was not facilitated by generally conservative heads and staff, with their classical education and heavy clerical dominance. At Winchester in 1914 six out of the thirty-eight teachers were clergy, all Oxbridge-educated (overwhelmingly in the classics) bar the music master. Even at lesser academic schools like Sedbergh, all but two staff had been students at Oxbridge. Many heads were themselves clergy: William Vaughan, the first lay headmaster of Wellington, was not appointed until 1910, while Marlborough appointed its first lay head in 1903. In 1914, of the 114 headmasters in HMC, no fewer than ninety-two were classicists.[22] The hold of the classicist continued at public schools long into the twentieth century: as a schoolboy Anthony had two classicist headmasters at Tonbridge, while the heads that he taught under at his first three schools (Whitgift, Tonbridge and St Dunstan's) before becoming a head in 1997 were all classicists.

15

The 'school year' was more fluid a hundred years ago. Radley's experience was not unusual, with boys arriving and leaving in all three terms, and only half joining in September and leaving in July. Our research suggests that only a third of boys left boarding school at eighteen; twenty-two per cent left at younger ages, while fifteen per cent stayed on beyond their nineteenth birthday, particularly if they were top games players. Only thirty-five per cent of leavers from Marlborough, Radley and Tonbridge went on to university, almost all to Oxbridge, while fifteen per cent took up positions across the empire, and six per cent enlisted in the army.[23] At Manchester Grammar, in contrast, only ten of the fifty-six leavers in 1913 whose destination is known went to Oxbridge, while eighteen went to other universities, and twenty-three directly into professions.[24]

Progress through school was based more on academic merit than mere age; very bright boys found themselves promoted at speed. Harold Roseveare, who won a scholarship to Marlborough in 1908, thus reached the sixth form at the age of fifteen, and was head of his house for two years.[25] The upper sixth form at Tonbridge in 1913 included boys of both fifteen and nineteen; a majority of school leavers never reached the sixth form at all.[26] Taking public exams before leaving was very far from the norm. For the minority destined for university, the Higher Certificate examination would be sat, as well as scholarship exams set by Oxford or Cambridge, or by other long-established universities, including London.

The public school experience featured a heavily male, regimented and hierarchical environment. Teachers were all male, and the female presence within the school was generally limited to house matrons or 'dames', servants in the houses and elsewhere, and the wives of teachers. A Marlborough boy remembered his dame as having 'her favourites among us and two large bottles, labelled "cough mixture" and "cold mixture", with which we were dosed indiscriminately for every internal ailment'.[27] The prevailing school culture was dictated by the older boys, with traditions handed down year on year, rather than by teachers, who were less conspicuous presences in the lives of the young men. While each school had its own time-honoured traditions, boarding schools had much in common with each other, including pressure on individuals to conform. Every minute of a boy's life was monitored and overseen by others. These were somewhat illiberal institutions.

The house, consisting of perhaps thirty boys, was the fulcrum of each boy's life. Housemasters often owned their houses, charged fees for board separate from the school's academic fees, and ran the house according to their own principles and sense of fair play. Control was delegated largely to the prefects. The housemaster might only emerge from his house or 'private side' to take roll-call, for to be seen too often on the boys' side could be deemed an 'insulting lack of trust' in his prefects.[28] 'Fagging', the running of errands for older boys, was ubiquitous, and also included making toast, cleaning shoes and uniform, or more demeaning tasks. Discipline was underpinned by a strict regime of punishments, including beating by older boys, often for trivial and personal reasons. By 1914, governors in many schools were providing money for houses to be purchased by the schools themselves, though the system of the house essentially being run by the older boys survived the change of ownership. Convention prevented younger boys from consorting with older boys in houses, mainly because of fears of 'vice'. The future diplomat and Labour politician, Harold Nicolson, complained that, at Wellington, 'the authorities in their desire to deprive us of all occasion for illicit intercourse, deprived us of all occasion for any intercourse at all. We were not allowed to consort with boys not in our house ... during those four years my training in human relationships was confined to the ten boys who appeared more or less to be my contemporaries'.[29] Alumnus Sebastian Faulks clearly thought conditions at Wellington had changed little by the 1970s, judging by the thinly disguised portrait of the school he presents in his novel *Engleby*, published in 2007.[30]

The centre of each boy's life was his dormitory, where he slept on an iron bedstead among others laid out in double rows as in a hospital ward. Some boys in more spacious houses would benefit from 'common rooms', and as they moved up the school they might even acquire a study, or very rarely a private bedroom. At Eton, however, single rooms were the norm, even for younger boys. Living conditions were spartan for all. Dormitories lacked central heating, lighting was dim, hot water never guaranteed and the lavatories were a mean and intimidating experience for the young and anxious. John Betjeman's horror of the 'law of the jungle' at Marlborough was vented in his autobiographical poem *Summoned by Bells*.[31] Homoerotic thoughts and activity were commonplace features of house life, although 'homosexual affairs were much rarer at public schools than is often made out'.[32]

A. A. Milne recalled of Westminster that, 'in all my years, I never ceased to be hungry'.[33] A boarder at Bloxham in Oxfordshire recalled: 'The whole four years [1903–7], lunch never changed once. Monday was hash, Tuesday was roast mutton, Wednesday the remains of the mutton made into a pie, Thursday roast beef, Friday cold beef salted –

hard, tough and very salty'.[34] At Rugby, a 'stodge rule' specified which food the boys were able to eat over and above house provisions, to help preserve their fitness for house games. One junior boy was beaten in 1912 for being found eating a cake sent by his mother.[35] Poor nutrition contributed to frequent outbreaks of infection, with school registers recording, on an almost annual basis, the deaths of pupils. When in 1891 two boys died at Wellington from diphtheria, all pupils were sent home to allow the buildings to be disinfected, and the following term was spent at a hotel in Malvern.[36]

Sport filled much of the boys' waking hours when they were not in lessons, house or chapel. Rugby or football in the winter, and cricket or rowing in the summer, were the staple activities, alongside 'minor sports' including rackets, fencing, shooting, boxing and swimming. Keeping boys busy was the main preoccupation of the system. In 1889 Rector Mackenzie of Edinburgh Academy wrote: 'If I was asked what was the most dangerous occupation for a boy's hours of leisure, I should at once name loafing'.[37] Schools were usually represented just by a first team at the various sports, with much of the organization undertaken by the boys themselves through 'games committees'. House matches and competitions occupied many afternoons, with inter-house rivalry being every bit as keen as that between schools. Sporting prowess was how status and privilege were achieved, the relative priorities of sport and scholarship being as controversial then as they are a hundred years later. Robert Graves recalled bitterly that, 'the eleventh man in the football eleven, though he might be a member of the under-fourth form, enjoyed far more prestige than the most brilliant scholar in the sixth'.[38]

Intellectuals or aesthetes could, however, carve out their own niche. The poet Charles Sorley described a summer day at Marlborough in 1913 thus: 'Yesterday after Chapel, the weather being perfect, I went on the best walk I have ever had ... along the downs almost to Swindon, but turned off into Liddington, and made a life-long friend of the publican ... then returned in the evening across the Aldbourne downs'.[39] Such forays were, however, the exception, because when not playing sport, the Officer Training Corps (OTC) and other organized activities filled idle time. For sensitive, individualist and home-loving boys, the schools could be torture. But for the mentally and physically robust, who were good at sport and happy to suppress their individuality, school could represent 'the happiest days of their lives'. How exactly did the schools shape the minds and sensibilities of those who attended them?

The public school ethos

George Orwell, educated at Wellington College briefly and then Eton during the war, argued that the middle classes 'are trained for war ... not technically, but morally'.[40] Public schools can indeed be seen as well-oiled machines, very successful at filing down individuality and machine-tooling young men ready for elevated positions in society in Britain, the empire, or the battlefield. Orwell's fellow Etonian, General Herbert Plumer, captured another truth when he said at an Old Etonian dinner in 1916: 'We are often told they taught us nothing at Eton. It may be so, but I think they taught it very well.'[41] Eton certainly taught Plumer wit: on the eve of the Battle of Messines in June 1917, for which nineteen large mines had been placed underneath German trenches, he remarked, 'Gentlemen, we may not make history tomorrow, but we shall certainly change geography.'[42]

Plumer's and Orwell's words suggest one of the main charges against the pre-1914 public schools, that they were more interested in building character than developing intellect. The perception that public schools were philistine places, widely aired at the time and since, is at least partly disproved by the quality of the intellects which emerged from these schools. Among the third and more leaving the older schools for Oxford or Cambridge each year there were many brilliant pupils, not just confined to the scholars at Eton and Westminster. Luminaries such as Rupert Brooke from Rugby, or Raymond Asquith from Winchester, the latter described as 'the most brilliant and remarkable of all those who lost their lives [in the war]',[43] were far from unique. The prize-giving at Uppingham the summer term before the war, described so movingly by Vera Brittain in her diaries and in *Testament of Youth*, was a scholarly celebration repeated across the public schools. Vera's eyes were firmly fixed on the young man with whom she was to fall in love, Roland Leighton, but one senses a wider adulation from his peers at his haul of prizes, for English, Latin prose, Greek prose, Greek epigram and Latin hexameters.[44] The experience of Stephen Hewett from Downside similarly calls the 'philistine' tag into question: he went up to Balliol College, Oxford, in 1911 and won successively the Craven, Hertford and Ireland Scholarships, and was also a hockey blue. The memorial book assembled by his grieving parents after his death on the Somme was entitled *A Scholar's Letters from the Front*. Many public school alumni were to make their names across all fields of the arts: novelist E. M. Forster (Tonbridge), composer Ralph Vaughan Williams (Charterhouse), artist Paul Nash (St Paul's), and poet Ivor Gurney (King's Gloucester). The public schools' syllabus may have been narrow, but many found sympathetic staff who nurtured their interests.

The Common Rooms of public schools were indeed full of brilliant and earnest scholars, drawn to teaching by the excitement of imparting their knowledge and enthusiasms to a new generation. The deliberations of headmasters at their HMC Annual Conferences were equally dominated by the academic life of their schools; even as the war raged in 1916, they resolved unanimously, if not before time, to give more support to the teaching of science in public schools. There were many philistine teachers in public schools, and much boorish anti-intellectualism, as there is today. But it should not blind us to the many boys and teachers cut from a different cloth.

Many sought to combat anti-intellectualism head-on. Frank Fletcher, a Balliol classical scholar, was the first layman to head a major public school when he became Master of Marlborough in 1903 at the age of thirty-four. Appointed headmaster of Charterhouse in 1911, he smartly introduced a more academic curriculum, but found he had to fight 'a war against both philistine sportsmen and sour intellectuals'.[45] One of his pupils, Robert Graves, may have exaggerated when he wrote that 'the school consisted of about 600 boys, whose chief interests were games and romantic friendships. Everyone despised school work'.[46] In 1904 A. C. Benson, son of the first Wellington head, an Eton master and later Master of Magdalene College, Cambridge, wrote in an equally jaundiced tone about seeing 'these well-mannered, rational, manly boys all taking the same view of things, smiling politely at the eccentricity of anyone who finds matter for serious interest in books, art or music'.[47] Cyril Norwood, head of Bristol Grammar, and later of Marlborough and Harrow, wrote in 1909 that, 'boys from public schools are ignorant of life, contemptuous of all outside the pale of their own cast, un-interested in work, never desiring nor revering knowledge.'[48] Julian Bickersteth, a boy at Rugby, and later chaplain of Melbourne Grammar in Australia, had this to say, in a letter home in September 1918, on his experience of public school officers he met while serving as a military chaplain: 'The failure to educate is more and more brought to me as a fair criticism of the public schools. The knowledge of the world, too, of the ordinary public school man is extraordinarily limited. Of great labour movements they know nothing, except what the press intends them to know.'[49] His words echo the despair today of many Oxbridge admissions tutors, and not just about the narrow knowledge of candi-dates from public schools.

Historian of education John Honey wrote that the public schools aimed to produce 'an identifiable elite, a community of men who shared a similarity of outlook, values and code of honour, because they shared a similar type of boyhood experience'.[50] But the similarity of schooling and experience should not blind us to the fact that the range of schools was enormously wide in terms of social status, academic standards, priorities and facilities. The gap between a boarding school in the south-east and a day school in the north-west were as wide then as in 2014. Even within a school the boys differed greatly. Raymond Asquith said of one Etonian officer he defended in a court martial in 1916 that he was 'a perfect man of his type – insolent, languid, fearless and of a virile elegance which is most engaging'.[51] Yet Eton in the same era produced prize-winning physicist, Henry Moseley; a leading composer, George Butterworth; a committed social reformer, Stephen Hobhouse; several distinguished headmasters; and many others for whom the terms 'insolent' and 'languid' could not be less apt.

Most public schools nevertheless regarded the development of character as of at least equal importance to intellectual development. Character was imparted through the traditions and hierarchies implicit in the public school system. The unwritten code of behaviour in public schools included ingredients such as unquestioning loyalty to the school and house, subordination of self to the team and school, reverence for 'manliness', stoicism in the face of physical and emotional pain, and the requirement to be self-effacing. Much of this groundwork was in place before the boys joined at thirteen, with many boys attending preparatory schools, whose core purpose was to mould their charges for the public school experience. Long before they left these incubation pens, boys had learned to avoid trouble, that the people who mattered were the senior pupils, far more than the teachers, and not to 'grass' on fellow pupils. Schools could be cruel places for boys who stepped out of line and did not show 'respect for their superiors'. Any indications of precociousness or 'cheek' were dealt with harshly and peremptorily, out of the sight or earshot of adults. The future art scholar Kenneth Clark, on the train down to Winchester for his first day at the school in 1916, had the temerity to venture some of his opinions to older boys; he was beaten by a prefect that evening for breaking a rule he did not know existed.[52] The powers given to prefects to inflict corporal punishment, virtually on whim, were matched by the expectation that boys would accept such punishment without flinching or squealing.

Character was imparted further through organized games, which enhanced physical strength and fitness, and taught boys to overcome pain and fear. Boys learnt to 'lay their bodies on the line', to put team above self, to remain calm under physical danger and uncomplaining at injury, even when severe. Rugby and cricket were the highest expressions of schoolboy sport, teaching differing physical and moral qualities, the one more team-based, the other more individual. The phrase 'playing the game', with its inducement to chivalric and unselfish behaviour, is often associated with the public school ethos: it was even uttered by the American millionaire Benjamin Guggenheim in justifying his decision not to enter a lifeboat on the *Titanic* before all the women and children. It is telling how in *Journey's End* the young subaltern Raleigh pays far greater heed to his fellow officer, the schoolmaster Osborne, when he discovers he has played rugby for Harlequins and England.[53] The power of cricket to shape character has never been caught better than in the poem by Henry Newbolt, *Vitaï Lampada*, about a future soldier learning his selfless commitment to duty in cricket matches while at Clifton: 'And England's far, and Honour a name,/ But the voice of a schoolboy rallies the ranks:/"Play up! play up! and play the game!"'[54] 'Playing the game' became a much less appropriate concept for the Western Front, where it mattered very much if you won or lost; it was not heard much after 1916. Sending gas shells over for the enemy to choke agonisingly to death on inhalation was not a school cricket or rugby match.

In a debate at Eton in 1914 on the importance of games the proposer argued that they were 'a relic of barbarism, when the theory of the survival of the fittest had as yet not been superseded', and were to the detriment of literature, art and academic study. These arguments were readily mown down by other boys, retorting that 'the Battle of Waterloo was won on the playing fields of Eton' and asserting that a healthy body was essential to a sane and well-ordered mind. The motion, which was hardly revolutionary, was defeated by a factor of over three to one.[55] That keen arbiter of human conduct, Douglas Haig, was in no doubt about the importance that sport played in the war. He said in 1919 that, 'the inspiration of games has brought us through this war, as it carried us through the battles of the past'.[56] Brigadier-General Adrian Carton de Wiart VC (The Oratory) thought similarly: he believed school sport had been vital because the skills it imparted allowed boys to develop 'the ability to deal with and handle men in later years'.[57] Professor Spencer Wilkinson was a comparatively lone voice when he raised the question during a 1904 Royal Commission whether sport might 'distract boys' attention from the cultivation of their intelligence'.[58]

Service in the OTC became by 1914 virtually compulsory across every public school, with boys learning military skills such as drill and rifle-shooting, as well as the need to obey orders and endure hardship. Historian Brian Bond believes the public-school ethos prepared young men well for the deprivations of army life: 'It was a completely male-dominated, authoritarian world with strict hierarchies of power and a culture of homoerotic yearnings and shame which would be transported, unchanged in essentials, to the womanless world of military ranks and regimental traditions of the Western Front.'[59] Kipling's short stories, especially *Stalky & Co*, can be seen as epitomizing these public school notions of manliness, stoicism, self-denial, loyalty to others and a sense of adventure.[60] To a large extent pre-war public schools were thus 'militarized institutions', although the OTC training bore little resemblance to the reality of war when it came. Many boys held in 1914 a very chivalric attitude to war. Gilbert Talbot (Winchester) wrote about the death of a man in his platoon: 'I think I felt in him for the first time by personal experience how fine a soldier's death is.'[61] Such beliefs would be gradually undermined as the slaughter intensified.

The Clarendon Commission's description of the public school as 'the nursery' of future leaders in the 1860s applied every bit as much fifty years later. In the words of Old Etonian Sir Ralph Furse, 'We could not have run the show [the British Empire] without public schoolboys. In England, universities train the mind: the public schools teach character and leadership.'[62] John Wynne-Wilson, Master of Marlborough from 1911, believed that, 'But for our public schools, you would never get the successful administrators of empire which England produces in such numbers.' The system of prefects was the key: 'The older boys, having to exercise a certain rule over their juniors, gain in experience which is distinctly good for them.'[63]

Leadership lay at the heart of the qualities in which public schoolboys were trained for a life in public service, the armed forces, in commerce or the British Empire. The training and expectation of leadership would cost them dearly on the battlefields of the Great War, with the casualty rates for officers so high. We should also not overlook the many public schoolboys who did not aspire to leadership either at school or in the army. The future Prime Minister, Anthony Eden, 'never came within a mile of being elected to Pop', the self-electing oligarchy of prefects who were the real rulers of Eton.[64] Some certainly eligible for commissions in the war deliberately refused, including left-wing intellectuals like R. H. Tawney (Rugby) and Frederic Keeling (Winchester). Courage, leadership and example were not of course the prerogatives solely of the officer class, still less of public schoolboys.

If character training, however, was integral to the public school ethos, the question remains as to what kind of 'character' was being developed. Richard Aldington (Brighton College), and an infantry officer in the war, became a critic of the public schools. In *Death of a Hero*, published in 1929, he damned his fellow public schoolboys as ignorant, prejudiced and philistine. In faint praise he conceded that the public

23

schoolboy 'could obey orders and command obedience in others, he took pains to look after his men, he could be implicitly relied on to lead a hopeless attack and to maintain a desperate defence to the very end'.[65] This image of the public schoolboy as the bluff, unquestioning, anti-intellectual hearty, inspired by simple ideals of loyalty, duty and patriotism, certainly captures part of the truth. Many of them died gallantly on the battlefield, revolver in one hand, whistle in the other, unquestioningly leading their men over the top in some hopeless attack. But at the other end of the spectrum were those who questioned, but saw the futility of such questioning. These were men of the calibre of Charles Sorley, poet, and George Butterworth, musician, intellectuals and artists, deeply cultured young men whose lives had been enriched by their contact with inspiring teachers and who themselves enriched the intellectual life of their school.

But perhaps Wynne-Wilson was right: in some respects, this training did have positive features. The leadership which public schoolboys assumed, and the character which schools taught, were instrumental in helping their alumni to stand up to the exacting battlefield test to come. In *Journey's End*, Raleigh's hero from his house at school, Captain Stanhope, inspires him with a vision of service and a desire to join his company. By the end of the play, Raleigh is shocked by Stanhope, not because he is leading men to their deaths unquestioningly but because he no longer acts with the decorum he displayed when leader in his house. The harrowing experience of the war has led Stanhope to drink, and he has become a pale shadow of his former self. But even if Stanhope has strayed from the public school ideal of 'upright, manly, good and true', he still conducts himself as a caring officer and a courageous and compassionate leader, qualities which contributed significantly to the successful outcome of the war.

The Officers' Training Corps

'I look to you public schoolboys to set an example. Let it be your ambition to render yourselves capable of becoming leaders to others who have not had your advantages, should you ever be called upon to fight for your country.' So said Field Marshal Lord Roberts, hero of the Boer War, to the boys at Glenalmond in Scotland in 1906.[66] Roberts visited the school as part of a national tour, presenting prizes and inspecting the schools' corps. The Boer War had been a rude wake-up call to the British governing classes. In 1900, when the war was at its height, a meeting of HMC headmasters was convened at Bradfield College. The headmaster of Charterhouse declared that it was part of the duty of all HMC headmasters to consider 'how best they could lay the natural foundations of participation in national defence through the boys in their schools'.[67]

Heads took their patriotic duty very seriously. At the 1904 HMC conference, held at Christ's Hospital, the headmaster of Cheltenham College proposed compulsory military service for all boys over thirteen. The headmaster of The Leys, Cambridge, argued against: 'To make it compulsory would exclude from public school life all such as Quakers and those who, mistakenly as I think, certainly conscientiously, object to war under any conditions, and fear Cadet Corps as making for militarism.' The meeting adopted a milder resolution, to set up a committee 'to consider the desirability and feasibility of making training in the use of arms compulsory on boys in public schools'.[68] HMC schools were eager to take their responsibilities to the nation seriously. To have taken so long to subdue the Boer farmers in South Africa had provoked a national debate about the state of military preparedness in Britain. Lord Haldane, Secretary of State for War, introduced in 1907 wide-ranging reforms aimed at creating a modern national army, backed up by the Special Reserve and Territorial Force.

In the public schools this new energy resulted in the establishment of the Officers' Training Corps (OTC), replacing the 'Rifle Volunteer Corps' which had existed in some schools since the 1860s, when they were set up to counter the perceived threat posed by Emperor Napoleon III of France. Unlike the Volunteer Corps, the OTCs came under direct War Office control, with the clear purpose of overcoming the current shortage of officers in the army. Senior OTCs were to be established at universities, and a junior division at schools, mostly though not exclusively at public schools (by 1914, only a third were not at public schools). Keir Hardie, the Labour leader, protested that the OTCs were resulting 'in the training of officers from the ranks of the rich and well-to-do to the practical exclusion of the capable sons of the working classes'.[69] Few heeded Hardie's complaint.

By 1914 eighty per cent of public schools boasted an OTC, so the institution extended far beyond the ranks of the grander schools. Smaller and newer establishments saw it as a way of emulating the most prestigious schools, and thereby enhancing their reputation and social standing. Bury Grammar School had raised a Volunteer Corps in the 1890s under the inspiration of the school's headmaster, the Revd W. H. Howlett, which then became its OTC contingent in 1907. Edinburgh Academy's OTC was established at the same time. Haldane, an old boy of the school, carried out its first official review, praising the boys for their smart Seaforth tartan kilts. He told the massed ranks: 'We thought that if we could get boys sufficiently early to take a serious

25

view of their future as citizens . . . to fight and, if necessary, to die for the empire . . . then we should have given them a piece of idealism and we at the same time should have given to the nation a reserve of officers'.[70]

Not all participants shared his lofty ideals. Charles Sorley made light of passing the OTC exam at Marlborough in 1912: 'I entered with fear and trembling. Twenty questions I was asked, and I looked sheepish and said "Don't know" to each one. "Is there anything you do know?", the officer asked, and I gave him the only two pieces of knowledge I had come armed with – the weight of a rifle and episodes in the life of a bullet from the time it leaves the breech until it hits its man. Then I saluted really smartly and the gentleman gave me sixty out of 100 . . . We left the barracks about 2.30 pm: only three people had been ploughed – they must have been really bad'.[71] A similar note was sounded by the Inspecting Officer for Fettes' summer 1914 inspection: 'A good many cadets wanted their hair cut . . . and during the exercise there was a good deal of laughing and talking which rather spoilt the whole thing'.[72]

Even if some cadets did not take the OTC seriously, the army did. Mindful of stirrings across the English Channel, it insisted on absolute military efficiency of OTCs, subjecting their size, training and finance to rigorous inspection, and publicizing its powers to disband any school's OTC which failed to meet its exacting requirements. Headmasters felt under considerable pressure to ensure that their OTCs were of the highest standard. Boys were generally compelled to join the OTC: often only good medical reasons would suffice for not doing so. At Sherborne in 1914 only seven boys avoided the OTC, and one house was publicly congratulated for having one hundred per cent membership.[73]

The more intellectual and independent-minded boys found the weekly chore of parades, kit cleaning and rifle practice an ordeal; but for others it provided a welcome outlet for physical exercise, obedience and leadership. One such OTC cadet at Bablake School, Coventry in 1913 exhorted his fellow pupils to join thus: 'If all the men in a team insist on playing forward, very few matches will be won. If all men in a nation were as individuals, each living selfishly, that nation will not be strong. That is why I should join.'[74] Only one afternoon a week was usually given to the OTC, with the time being divided between drill, rifle shooting, map reading and fieldcraft. At Uppingham no pupil was allowed to win a school prize or even to take part in an inter-house competition without first passing the marksmanship test.[75] However, Alec Waugh described the Sherborne OTC as 'a hell on earth', a view apparently endorsed by at least one master who regarded it as a 'bally sweat and piffling waste of time.[76]

The boys generally looked forward to 'field days', a termly opportunity to get away from school for a few blessed hours. In November 1913 a special train was organized to take 235 cadets, from Tonbridge and other Kent schools, to Folkestone for a day of activities. Boys deemed to be particularly promising were scouted by regular soldiers to apply for commissions in the army.[77] At a joint field day, cadets from Catholic Downside charged the Malvern cadets with fixed bayonets, resulting in one being wounded in the hand. In retaliation, the Malvern cadets seized the Downside rifles during the tea interval and stuck them upside-down in the mud, crying out, 'To hell with the Pope.'[78]

Annual camp provided similar opportunities for boys to 'have a lark' and let off steam. At the beginning of the summer holidays many schools sent contingents to military centres across the country, including Tidworth on Salisbury Plain and Hagley Park in the Midlands. Camp lasted up to ten days and, though masters attended as officers of the OTC, the training was overseen by regulars, often from the Guards Division or Rifle Brigade. Schoolmasters complained then as now that too many boys produced 'pathetic' excuses for missing camp, such as preferring to play in school matches in the holidays. 'Holiday cricket', wrote one, 'might well follow the example of that good bird the grouse and enjoy a close time until the tents are struck.'[79] At Westminster in June 1914 a letter to *The Elizabethan* complained about the relatively low numbers attending annual camp, regretting that it gave the school a bad name among others 'to many of which Westminster considers herself superior'.[80]

The OTC movement might have fallen short of the high ambitions Haldane articulated in 1907, and it may not always have been taken as seriously by boys as the army, headmasters and masters would have liked, but its impact was felt. It broadened the range of public schools from which the army was to draw its officers: in the Boer War, Eton provided eleven per cent of officers, but between 1907 and 1914 4,000 boys were to receive commissions from OTCs, drawn from a wide range of public schools, with Wellington (324) and Cheltenham (309) being the biggest single contributors. Increased international tension was also making an impact. Lord Roberts stoked fears with a letter to all public school headmasters stressing the importance of service and military preparedness. In 1912 the commanding officer of the OTC at Eton sent the parents of leavers a letter urging them to ensure that their sons continued to be involved in military training after they left. If the crisis came, he said, trained officers would be required and 'there is no doubt that the public schools can supply the type of officer which is needed'.[81]

Summer 1914

For public schools, the summer of 1914 was much like all earlier summers stretching back to the beginning of the century and before. Boys were looking forward to a long holiday, as were their teachers. 'It all seemed gaiety, sunshine and good food,' wrote future Foreign Secretary and Prime Minister, Anthony Eden, of his time at Eton that summer.[82] Term had still another month to run when, on 28 June, the Archduke Franz Ferdinand, heir to the Habsburg Empire, was assassinated in Sarajevo. One Fettes pupil recalled that, 'while the murder of the Archduke was noticed, on the whole, like most healthy people, we didn't worry much. The possibility of a war had never been far from us and most of these political businesses got smoothed over one way or another.'[83] Boys were much more preoccupied by what was happening at school, with exams to be sat and prizes to be won, cricket matches and rowing regattas, and house tournaments. For the marksmen, the Ashburton Shield at Bisley was a far more imminent prospect than shooting at any enemy in Europe. A rare note of urgency was injected when on 15 June at the annual inspection of the Harrow OTC, old boy General Horace Smith-Dorrien reminded cadets that, 'the future of Britain and her empire depended on whether her young men would, or would not, be ready to serve her'.[84] School magazines and letters home from boys barely mentioned the impending crisis. Eden himself, more attuned perhaps to international affairs than some, recorded that 'Sarajevo sounded ominously'. But his family still let his older brother remain studying in Germany.[85] Amongst the 38,000 attending Lord's for the two-day Harrow and Eton cricket match, the state of the wicket ranked higher in the conversation than that of Europe. Vera Brittain was attending her brother Edward's final speech day at Uppingham on 11 July. She recorded 'the one perfect summer idyll that I ever experienced ... the lovely legacy of a vanished world'. The pupils in chapel were in OTC uniform and were brought up short in 'breathless silence' when they heard the headmaster intone, 'If a man cannot be useful to his country, he is better dead.' His words created a 'queer, indescribable foreboding' amongst those present.[86]

For the next two weeks, until the Austro-Hungarian ultimatum to the Serbian government on 23 July, school life continued much as before. On 24 July speech day was held at Campbell College in Belfast, founded just twenty years before on 'Arnoldian principles'. Not a hint of events in Europe appears in the record of proceedings; of far more interest was that on the platform stood a Campbell College Governor, Fred Crawford, chief gunrunner for the Ulster Volunteer Force (UVF), while the guest of honour was the Brigadier-General in command of the

British forces sent to Ulster to subdue them.[87] On Saturday, 25 July, 'Skinners' Day' was held at Tonbridge. The school magazine records events of that day in minute detail; not a word about events in Europe is mentioned.[88]

The pace quickened sharply when on Tuesday, 28 July, Austria-Hungary declared war on Serbia and the Russians began to mobilize. Foreign Secretary Grey's efforts to resolve the crisis had failed, but schools, many in their final week, carried on regardless. 'In my diary I can find no mention of war until 27 July ... Again on 31 July, bad war rumours. We may be involved', wrote Dallas Wynne Willson, a housemaster at Gresham's in Norfolk. On Sunday, 2 August, his diary recorded, 'great European tension – grave sermon by the Rector'. But his diary equally records, 'tennis parties and a cricket match, family news ... and little household details – in fact, the last dregs of the full cup of those vanished Victorian-Edwardian pre-war years'.[89]

On Monday, 27 July many schools had embarked on their OTC annual camps. *The Marlburian* records : 'On board the trains bound for the tents we discussed the situation ... and unanimously dismissed the whole affair as one of midsummer madness'.[90] Wellington joined Marlborough in Wiltshire: 'We had hardly got to Tidworth before the international crisis became acute. The excitement grew daily, but it was purified by the knowledge that many of those leading us would soon be at the front.'[91] Shrewsbury travelled south to Rugeley for their camp: 'Exactly 200 strong being, with the exception of Repton, the largest contingent there, supervised by officers from Sandhurst. Besides the drills and route marches, there was also time for football.'[92] On Friday, 31 July, a Gresham's boy wrote to his mother: 'Very many thanks for the fruitcake: it was nicer than ever before. How very serious the war outlook is!'[93] The next day, 1 August, 'things began to look serious, and Sunday morning broke in a torrential downpour and news that the fleet was mobilising'.[94] Cadets were told in camps across the country that on 1 August Germany had mobilized against Russia, and on Monday, 3 August Germany had declared war on France.

That Monday afternoon, orders were received for cadets to strike camp, causing problems for the staff officers, who had to pedal around cadet tents on bicycles, their horses having been requisitioned. Shrewsbury staff had run out of money, but 'Mr Kitchin saved the situation by dashing to Shrewsbury by night, returning in the early hours laden with gold.'[95] At Tidworth that Monday evening, the 300 Wellington boys on their last night executed 'manoeuvres with battalions in attack and defence ... [and] found ourselves singing "God Save the King"'.[96] On Tuesday, 4 August, as members of the OTC contingents somehow arrived back in school to be collected by their parents, Britain declared war on Germany. Much grumbling was heard: 'Camp was largely spoilt this year, by war and the rumours of war', recorded one magazine.[97]

The prevailing mood was well captured by Alan Haig-Brown, Lancing OTC commanding officer: 'In the first place there was a not ill-founded dread that Great Britain must stand apart. As that dispersed, there was an intensely serious appreciation of the task that awaited her. Amongst the boys, there was not the slightest hint of jingoism or flag-waving. Even they did not want a war.'[98] Eden thought similarly, recalling there was no eagerness for war and certainly no conception of what any war would be like, except that it was likely to be over quickly. As the Eton contingent left the camp, they marched to the station singing 'Long Way to Tipperary.'[99] Desmond Allhusen had a totally different recollection, remembering 'scenes of wild enthusiasm' as the boys returned to school and onward to their homes. Wynne Willson recalls a cheering crowd at midnight in the streets of Holt outside Gresham's as news came that the British ultimatum to Germany expired. The school doctor cautioned: 'Don't cheer, you don't know what you are in for.'[100]

Headmasters experienced mixed emotions: pride at the role that old boys of their school would soon be playing, anticipation of plaudits for the way that their school had prepared them, but also fears for the future. Apprehensions of casualty lists were trumped by more pressing concerns, above all the loss of staff to the army and consequent fear of classes being without teachers when term resumed in September. War breaking out at the beginning of the long summer holidays at least offered some respite. At Kent College in Canterbury, headmaster Alfred Brownscombe recorded in his logbook: 'Mr J. A. Ward B.A., who had only been with us for one term, enlisted during vacation in the Royal Horse Artillery. Mr Groom, who was to have filled the place of Mr Norman, was gazetted a Lieutenant in the East Yorkshire Regiment ... Mr Oldacre left and enlisted in the East Kent Mounted Rifles; his place was difficult to fill'.[101] In that first week of the war alone, Sedbergh saw three masters join up out of only sixteen permanent staff. At Wellington ten masters promptly left, as well as twenty college servants, leading to worries about how boarding houses were to run when the boys returned.

Then came a new activity: writing recommendations for school leavers to obtain commissions. In the first seven months of the war commissions were awarded to at least 21,000 who had served in their OTCs, on top of those who had been commissioned between 1907 and the outbreak of war. A further 13,000 enlisted in the ranks. The bigger schools had a much higher proportion of officers: Marlborough, for instance, provided 506 officers and 39 other ranks, while Hurstpierpoint College in Sussex had 64 officers and 205 joining the ranks.[102] Robert Graves, who had recently left Charterhouse, secured his commission in the Royal Welch Fusiliers with his headmaster's recommendation and another from the secretary of the Harlech Golf Club.[103] Some older boys jumped on the war as an opportunity to leave school earlier than their parents might have wanted. The headmaster of Winchester wrote of 'an unusually large number of leavers – 112, of whom 95 are in the army'.[104]

Young men desperate to join up at the earliest opportunity milked old boy and other social connections for all they were worth. On 6 August Arthur Behrend, who had recently left the Sedbergh OTC, telegraphed the adjutant of the 4th East Lancashires, a family friend. The reply came crisply back: 'Come tomorrow, prepared to stay. Bring all necessary kit.'[105] Douglas Wimberley, a promising eighteen-year-old who had just left Wellington, received a letter shortly after the outbreak of war from the commanding officer of the Wellington OTC to say that an old boy was raising a battalion of the Devonshire Regiment. 'As I had been an NCO in the OTC, he thought I would be suitable and he enclosed an application form for a commission.'[106] Ulric Nisbet had left Marlborough at the end of the summer term, to be told by the commanding officer of the Queen's Own Royal West Kent Regiment, 'to try to get other Old Marlburians to apply for commissions in it'. The commander was an old Rugbeian, and Nisbet wrote: 'During that first winter, Old Rugbeians and Old Marlburians were numerous enough to field a rugger side against officers in the battalion from other public schools.'[107]

Advertisements appeared in the press on Sunday, 7 August asking for 2,000 junior officers to join the New Army being formed by Lord Kitchener, now Minister of War. The 'Pals' Battalions' initiative was also taken up by public school men. In late August a committee of North London businessmen approached the Middlesex Regiment with a proposal to form a battalion open only to public school and university men, to become the 16th Middlesex (Public Schools) battalion. A similar venture was the formation of the Universities and Public Schools Brigade, comprising four battalions of Royal Fusiliers. Recruiting for this brigade took place all over the country, with several headmasters directly involved, such as John Paton of Manchester Grammar.[108] Old boys of some schools tried to form their own battalion or company, including those from Glasgow Academy, who formed their own company within the 17th Highland Light Infantry. Worksop College old boys similarly joined together in the 10th Lincolnshire Regiment (the 'Grimsby Chums'), alongside boys from several state schools.

Headmasters were torn throughout the summer holidays between their patriotic loyalty and their need to open a functioning school in September. A special meeting was convened of HMC on 15 September 'to answer questions and suggest lines of common policy in regard to various emergencies created by the war'. Chaired by Frank Fletcher of Charterhouse, the heads agreed that where a boy currently in school joined up with the full consent of the headmaster, fees should be remitted, but that governors should share the loss in income which otherwise would fall on housemasters. The HMC endorsed 'the principle, laid down by the War Office authorities, that the first duty of masters who are OTC officers is to the OTC of their school, and that, unless they can be spared from this, they should not go away'.[109] Boys were in little mood to settle down to work once the schools reopened in late September. An editorial in *The Meteor*, the magazine at Rugby, aired the pride the school felt in being so well represented in the 'armies of the Empire', noting that 'many of us now here will take their places in one or two or three terms' time: nor so long as men are needed will Rugby fail to send her sons'.[110] Cyril Alington, headmaster of Shrewsbury, was not alone in composing a poem encapsulating his thoughts, called *To the School at War*: 'We don't forget – while in this dark December/We sit in schoolrooms that you knew so well.'[111]

The cause

The early summer crisis of 1914 seemed at first not unlike the previous European crises which had been successfully calmed by sensible diplomacy, as in the Bosnian Crisis of 1908 and the Balkans in 1912–13. The assassination of Franz Ferdinand in Sarajevo on 28 June 1914 by Bosnian Serb extremists, however, was to initiate a chain reaction which proved beyond the realms of diplomatic pacification. The starting-point, Austria's declaration of war on Serbia on 28 July, was not only revenge for the crime; it also sought to weaken the influence in the Balkans of Serbia's main ally, Russia. When Russia duly mobilized her army in support of Serbia, Germany mobilized in support of her ally, Austria. German strategy in the event of war was known as the Schlieffen Plan, which committed Germany first to attack and defeat France within six weeks, before turning on Russia. To pull off this feat Germany believed it had to attack France through neutral Belgium. Mobilization, and the rigid thinking of the high commands of their respective armies, left politicians and diplomats with too little room for negotiation, and, within a week of the original Austrian attack on

Serbia, Germany had declared war on France. Continental Europe was at war.

If Sarajevo was the spark that lit the tinder, the war's origins go back much further into the complex web of European political, economic and imperial rivalries that had developed since German unification in 1871, and before. The main debate among historians ranges those who see the war as a result of deliberate German intent, as the 'war guilt clause' in the 1919 Treaty of Versailles stated, against those who see it as a tragic accident, blame being shared among the belligerents, and European statesmen doing insufficient to defuse the tensions following Sarajevo and failing to comprehend the full scale of the forces which they were unleashing.

Britain herself faced a dilemma as the crisis unfolded. She had no rigid treaty commitments to be invoked beyond an 1839 agreement to protect Belgian neutrality and an Entente with France in 1904. Relations between Britain and Germany had, however, been compromised by commercial, imperial and naval rivalries, with Germany regarded increasingly as a threat to Britain's world power status. If Germany were to defeat France, Britain worried she might find herself isolated in Europe, while Germany would be able to use her European hegemony to challenge Britain's interests worldwide.

Britain responded to the evolving crisis in Europe with little political unity or indeed popular enthusiasm. Liberal newspapers like the *Manchester Guardian* were against British involvement right up until 4 August, and most of the provincial press similarly supported British neutrality in the event of European war: on 31 July the *Oxford Chronicle* said Britain's first duty was to localise the conflict and 'our second duty is to preserve our own neutrality'.[112] As the crisis deepened, conviction grew in the Liberal government that it was in Britain's interest to support France and prevent a German victory. But the Cabinet itself was by no means united. The German invasion of neutral Belgium made it easier for Prime Minister Asquith to persuade his own party, Parliament and the press to support a belligerent line, while also fanning the flames of popular enthusiasm to support France and help defend 'little Belgium'. Declaration of war at midnight on 4 August followed.

For the boys, and all who worked in the public schools, the final countdown came days after term ended and took most by surprise. The attitudes of those on OTC camp between 27 July and 4 August changed from cavalier dismissal of just another European crisis to preparation for war. How much public schoolboys understood of the wider geo-political factors and the moral issues at play can only be surmised, but politics and modern history beyond 1832 or 1878 did not feature on the curricula of most schools. Nor was it likely that many had any real idea of the horrific nature of modern war, although even a passing knowledge of the American Civil War in the 1860s or Russo-Japanese war of 1904–5 might have alerted them to the horrors which would unfold. The response of most was dominated by the largely unquestioning belief that, if their government decided war was necessary, it was their duty to serve.

Many reasons for volunteering were given by the young men. A single-minded sense of duty led the impulsive young Wilfred Willett, fresh out of St Paul's and Cambridge and studying to be a doctor at the London Hospital, to join up. He had loved the OTC life and shooting at school, and volunteering was simply the natural thing for him to do.[113] 'The path of duty was the way to glory', poet Alfred Lord Tennyson had written in his *Ode on the Death of the Duke of Wellington*, and such thinking was deeply imbued in almost all. An editorial in Wellingborough's magazine stressed that England had been obliged to go to war out of a sense of honour, which should be the motive for its young people to fight.[114] Duty inspired Donald Hankey (Rugby) to fight: 'His whole training, the traditions of his kind, had prepared him for that hour. From his earliest schooldays he'd been taught that it was the mark of a gentleman to welcome danger and to regard the risk of death as the most piquant source of life.'[115]

A Wellington headmaster, Frederick Malim, later wrote that a public school emphatically should 'inculcate the duty of public service'.[116] This, together with loyalty learned to house and school, also translated easily into patriotism. Ulric Nisbet, a Marlburian, recorded his feelings in August 1914: 'We were fighting for King and Country and Empire ... We had been taught to worship God one day a week but to worship Country and Empire seven days a week'.[117]

Duty was closely allied to patriotism. Robert Graves (Charterhouse) recalled that 'I was outraged by the Germans' cynical violation of Belgian neutrality and atrocity stories ... My father felt proud that I had done the right thing'.[118] Up and down the country, young men were equally told by their fathers and grandfathers, headmasters and housemasters, vicars and godparents, that they were 'proud of them' for joining up. Sholto Douglas (Tonbridge) recorded how, 'At the mention of patriotism, we all felt an instant quickening of the pulse ... I had no hesitation about deciding as soon as war was declared just what I was going to do'.[119]

The prospect of excitement, a break from routine and a wish not to miss out on a great adventure were all part of the rich cocktail of factors which led many to volunteer. Alfred Pollard (Merchant Taylor's

Northwood), bored with his clerical job in insurance, recorded how on 7 August he had watched a big crowd file past on their way to war. He decided, 'he wanted so much to be one of them'. At 5.00 pm on 8 August, he left work for good, and queued outside a recruiting office, pushing his way to the front because, 'What if the numbers were limited or it was all over before they got to the front?'[120] In 1917 he went on to win the Victoria Cross at Gavrelle in France, leading a successful counter-attack, with only four men, to recover lost ground. Future Prime Minister Harold Macmillan, who had just left Eton, echoed Pollard's initial impulse: 'Our major anxiety was by hook or by crook not to miss it.'[121]

Others were in agonies over whether to join up. Guy Chapman (Westminster) described in his war memoir how he had been 'loath to go. I had no romantic illusions. I was not eager or even resigned to self-sacrifice and my heart gave back no answering throb to the thought of England. In fact I was very much afraid and afraid of being afraid, lest I show it.'[122] Fear of being thought a coward was a factor that would propel many to join, while not a few joined in the hope that it would impress their loved ones, or a girl they desired to become a loved one. For Robert Nichols (Winchester) a complex of factors explained his decision to volunteer: a sense of patriotism and sympathy for Belgium and France, 'the desire existing within every youth to suffer for others', allied to 'the vague feeling that it was the right thing to do'.[123] The fact that enlistment peaked in early September rather than in August suggests that for some the decision to join was a considered and a fraught one.

The spirit of the institution – the school, university or club – was a powerful motive for many. Sam Paget took comfort and pride from the fact that all Winchester's cricket eleven joined up, apart from those too young and still at school. Even the most longstanding of public school rivalries were set aside for the duration of the war. Addressing the boys at Harrow in October 1914, Lord Curzon apologised for having been educated at Eton but said, 'In the present crisis Eton will not be one whit behind Harrow, nor Harrow one whit behind Eton in the final fight that we are waging for the honour of our country.'[124] Attendance at Oxford and Cambridge, or the other universities in London and the major provincial cities, similarly inspired and emboldened many to go off and fight.

Rupert Brooke famously wrote in 1914, 'Now God be thanked who has matched us with this hour', capturing the idealism which fired many tens of thousands of public schoolboys up and down the country to volunteer in 1914. That idealism was soon dampened by the reality of trench warfare and the realization that there would be a long, bitter struggle ahead. Once hostilities had begun, and casualties and the collateral costs began to mount, the paramount British interest became the imperative to win at all costs. To achieve it, no hardship or sacrifice was deemed too great, and public schoolboys, with their education and family upbringing instilling in them strong notions of patriotism, duty and service, were single-minded in their response. A very young man killed on the first day of the Somme, Second Lieutenant Jack Engall (St Paul's), wrote in his last letter that he would die doing his duty and asked his parents to consider it 'an honour that you have given a son for the sake of King and Country'.[125]

As the war progressed, such impulses for former public schoolboys remained strong, but other motives too emerged, including hopes of a better world order after the guns fell silent. Captain Robert Palmer (Winchester), a grandson of former Prime Minister Lord Salisbury, wrote home in September 1915, three months before he was killed in Mesopotamia, of his hopes that war might 'mark a distinct stage towards a more Christian conception of international relations'.[126] Lieutenant Malcolm White (Birkenhead School and Shrewsbury teacher), writing just before the Somme battle in which he was killed, believed that a re-assertion of the European status quo should be the right basis for a peace settlement: 'The greatest victory that could be won in this war would be, not the particular gain of one or a few nations, but the tragic realization by all nations that nobody has gained anything'.[127]

Attitudes of fighting soldiers to Germany were often at variance with the fiercer anti-Germanism of the home front. The Reverend Oswin Creighton (Marlborough), a military chaplain, complained in a letter of early 1917 about the anti-German invective of the government and the press: 'We are always being taught to hate Germans, and to refuse to think or speak of peace ... We all know we have to fight as long as we wear the uniform, and have thereby committed ourselves to slaughter as many Germans as possible, but I, for one, utterly refuse to hate the Kaiser or any of them or to believe that I am fighting for a glorious cause, or anything that the papers tell me'.[128] Even a senior regular officer, Brigadier-General Philip Howele (Lancing), could admit in September 1915 that he did not want to devote all his time to killing Germans, and he dreamed that, 'the ideal war would include long and frequent armistices during which both sides could walk across the trenches and discuss their respective points of view'.[129]

It is remarkable that there was so little overt protest against the horrific conditions of modern warfare and the carnage that all front line soldiers witnessed; even Siegfried Sassoon (Marlborough), who published an open letter against the war in 1917, eventually saw the imperative for him to return to the trenches. It all suggests that the concepts of duty and patriotism, blended with stoicism, were very deep-rooted in public schoolboys. Their mental worlds could not conceive any reality other than the need to finish the job which had been started in 1914; through the Somme, and beyond for the next two relentless years, it was the ability and requirement to endure which underpinned the former public schoolboys' leadership of the army and nation.

Chapter 2

Into Battle 1914–16

The expectation of a short war did not survive long. The opening months saw the involvement and destruction of Britain's professional army, officered almost entirely by public schoolboys. One of these, the poet-soldier Julian Grenfell, of Eton, Balliol and the Royal Dragoons, would survive the fierce battles of 1914, winning the DSO, only to be killed in May 1915. His poem 'Into Battle', published the day after his death, could still speak of 'the joy of battle',[1] an expectation of war not far from the thoughts of many young men volunteering. The extension of the conflict throughout 1915, bringing in soldiers from the Territorials and the New Army, on the Western Front and the Gallipoli peninsula, claimed, in the many costly and pointless battles, Julian Grenfell's brother Billy and so many of their public school and university friends. Billy Grenfell echoed his brother's romanticized view of war when he wrote to his mother on 1 June 1915, after hearing of Julian's death five days earlier and just two months before he was himself killed: 'The more I think of Julian, the more I seem to realise the nothingness of death. He has just passed on, outsoared the shadow of our night, and how could one pass on better than in the full tide of strength and glory and fearlessness.'[2] The dreadful slaughter of the Somme was to follow. The first verse of Grenfell's poem in early 1915 spoke of man's natural urge to fight: 'He is dead who will not fight, and who dies fighting has increase'. Few still subscribed to that view in December 1916.

The first blood is spilled: the battles of 1914
Twelve thousand officers were in Britain's regular army on the eve of the First World War, the vast majority of whom had been educated in public schools. Commissioned rank was not barred to those who had not attended them, nor indeed were public schoolboys barred from entering the other ranks. But their high fees, entrance exams and social status meant the schools were populated by those of privileged birth or

means who would not expect to 'muck in' with the masses. Sons tended to follow fathers into the military, including nearly half the cadets entering Sandhurst in 1910.[3] The 'old boy network' was based on the public schoolboy being trusted to know how to behave, in the mess and beyond. As historian Tim Travers noted, 'Group loyalty, deference, obedience to the accepted hierarchy, an aversion to political and intellectual discussion, and an emphasis on self-assurance and character', were the expected behaviours of true public school men.[4] Aspiring officers chose Sandhurst if they favoured the infantry, cavalry or the Indian army, and Woolwich if they wanted to join the Royal Artillery (RA) or Royal Engineers (RE). Technical demands for entry to both institutions became more exacting in the 1900s, with maths and science required. Some schools therefore offered an 'army class', as, for instance, at Cheltenham, Clifton, and Wellington. 'Military crammers' additionally offered crash courses to those whose schools did not give specialist preparation. Winston Churchill thus entered Captain James' crammer in London's Cromwell Road after leaving Harrow in the 1890s.[5] In 1910, mounting anxieties about the European situation led the army to propose the entry age for Woolwich be reduced to sixteen and a half, and seventeen for Sandhurst, to allow for longer and more specialized training. Headmasters saw this as a slight on the quality of their education. A deputation from HMC, including the headmasters of Eton and Harrow, marched in to complain to Haldane in January 1911. They succeeded in annulling the proposed policy, though all were left in no doubt about their duty to do a better job of preparing their charges to become officers.[6]

The British Expeditionary Force (BEF) which went to fight in France from August 1914 comprised some 100,000 men and some 7,000 officers. The officer corps was dominated not just by public schoolboys, but by the products of a very few schools. A sample of 700 senior commanders and staff officers shows that over half had been educated at just ten schools: Charterhouse, Eton, Harrow, Marlborough, Wellington, Clifton, Cheltenham, Haileybury, Rugby and Winchester. At a lower level, nearly half the cadets at Woolwich in 1913 came from Wellington, Cheltenham, Clifton, Marlborough and Winchester.[7] Another study, giving the biographies of sixty-nine senior officers of the rank of Brigadier-General and above, shows that at least fifty-seven were educated at public schools.[8] The grip of the grand public schools on the list of First World War generals remained tight throughout. Although Sir John French, the first Commander-in-Chief, was unusual in not having been at a public school because he entered first the Royal Navy, his two 1914 Corps Commanders were Haig (Clifton) and Smith-

Dorrien (Harrow). Seven of those who later reached the rank of Corps Commander on the Western Front were at Eton – Byng, Gough, Plumer, Cavan, Snow, Rawlinson and Pulteney. The rest were at other public schools, including Allenby (Haileybury) and Birdwood (Clifton).

By the end of 1914 4,000 of the initial 7,000 officers had become casualties, of whom 1,220 were killed. These early losses hit hardest those schools providing the most officers to the regular army. Some schools thus escaped lightly at first. Barnard Castle in County Durham, for instance, suffered 157 killed in the war but only one in 1914, while the Royal Belfast Academical Institution lost 133 of its old boys but only two during 1914.[9] On the other hand, Wellington suffered particularly grievously in that first year. In the five years leading up to the war, almost half the boys leaving Wellington were commissioned, either directly from the school's OTC or via their OTCs at university. When the BEF went to France, 845 Wellingtonians were serving, over 10 per cent of the BEF's total number of officers, with 482 holding the rank of major or above.[10] Eighty-five Old Wellingtonians were killed in 1914, and a further 191 wounded, representing a third of those who fought and 12 per cent of Wellington's total war dead of 707. The proportion of 1914 losses to total casualties in other public schools is nearer to 4 per cent.

The first Victoria Cross of the war was awarded to Lieutenant Maurice Dease of Stonyhurst, the first Catholic school to establish a military corps. One of many Irish boys at the school, his battalion arrived in France on 14 August and was sent to a village north of Mons, where on 23 August it came under overwhelming German attack. Dease was commanding the battalion's machine guns and covered its retreat. Hit five times, he stayed at his post before succumbing to his wounds.[11] He was not the first British soldier to have been killed; that is believed to be Private John Parr, at Oborg in Belgium on 21 August. Another early casualty was Lieutenant George Thompson (Wellington), who was killed in Togo, a German territory which possessed a powerful radio transmitter he wanted to destroy.[12] On some Remembrance Days, the British High Commissioner to Ghana takes part in a ceremony at the site of Thompson's grave, in the company of the German Ambassador to Togo, commemorating Germany's war dead.[13]

The death of Second Lieutenant Stewart Davison, a young professional soldier from Wellington in the King's Royal Rifle Corps, appears almost a caricature instance of public school 'pluck'. 'It was a rainy day and we were going through a cutting in the hillside when a terrible rain of bullets came among us', a soldier's contemporary account relates. 'I went with my platoon officer, Mr Davison, to the edge of a mangold patch. Then the Germans turned two machine guns on us from a haystack not ten yards to our front. Mr Davison seized hold of a man's rifle, stood up and fired ... He was shot through the eye immediately, and died a few minutes after. Before he died, however, he said, "Hold on to this position ... don't retire until you get orders"'.[14]

Harold Roseveare was a model school hero who had left Marlborough in July 1914 as 'Senior Prefect' (i.e. head boy) and Cadet Captain of the OTC. He was very unusual in holding a commission in the Special Reserve, and departed direct from Marlborough's OTC camp in early August to join his regiment, 1st Wiltshires; within just ten days he was in France. From the front on the Aisne in September he wrote to the school: 'I am now in a trench about 500 yards from goodness only knows how many Germans ... Shells sometimes whistle harmlessly overhead and some burst unpleasantly near our trenches and splinter the trees behind'.[15] Three days after writing these words he was shot in the chest leading his platoon in an attack on a German machine gun. He died the same night, as his fellow Marlburians returned to school for the new academic year. His obituary in the school magazine was written by his successor as head boy, Sidney Woodroffe: 'We knew he would manage to be in the thick of it (that was always his way) ... The news of his death here brought tears to the eyes of all the many masters and boys, and friends outside the college who knew him'.[16] Woodroffe was himself to die just a few months later, winning a posthumous VC in his final action.

Another young officer to die was the real 'Winslow Boy', George Archer-Shee, about whom Terence Rattigan wrote his celebrated play. After the famous court case, brought on by his father's attempt to clear his son's name of stealing a postal order at RNC Osborne, Archer-Shee was sent to Stonyhurst. He volunteered in August 1914 and was killed near Ypres on 31 October 1914, aged nineteen. His name, with 55,000 others, is on the Menin Gate.

Almost all the public school dead of 1914 were officers; very few public schoolboys would have served in the ranks of the old regular army. Harrow lost fifty-three old boys by December, all officers, out of about a thousand serving at this point.[17] Awareness of the toll came from school magazines. Robert Graves wrote to an old school friend in October 1914: 'You have probably seen the Charterhouse casualty list; awful ... I am in the special reserves which feed out two battalions in France. The 1st has been annihilated – except for two officers and a few men ... The chance against returning whole-skinned if we go out now is about 2–1 and I have consequently resigned myself'.[18]

A poignant memorial to the officer dead of 1914 is the 'aristocrats' cemetery' in the hamlet of Zillebeke outside Ypres, so named because of its unusual cluster of officers from the major public schools. Two of the fallen lying side by side encapsulate much of the history of those first months. Lieutenant Colonel Gordon Wilson (Melbourne GS in Australia and then Eton), aged 49, commanding the Royal Horse Guards, had served in the Boer War in the defence of Mafeking and was last seen alive on 6 November, horse discarded, rifle and bayonet still defiantly in hand. Next to him lies a much younger Etonian, Second Lieutenant Alexis de Gunzburg, a Russian aristocrat and an officer in the 11th Hussars. These are poignant reminders of Britain's old army and its public school officers.

The Christmas truce 1914

Few episodes have become more iconic in the memory than the events that took place along the Western Front on the first Christmas of the war. What occurred did so with the overt or tacit consent of many officers, the great majority from the regular army. By December the Western Front was in stalemate, neither side able to outflank the other, and with trenches extending some 500 miles from the English Channel in Belgium to the Swiss Alps. In those early days, with the armies on both sides struggling to defend themselves in inadequate trenches and cold weather, an official policy of 'live and let live' had been adopted, with periodic ceasefires to allow both sides to recover their wounded and dead. On Christmas Day 1914 some 100,000 officers and men from both sides fraternized in No-Man's-Land, a truce that lasted all day and in places longer. This was despite Smith-Dorrien, Commander of the BEF's Second Army, giving strict instructions on 5 December that temporary ceasefires damaged the 'offensive spirit' of troops and were firmly prohibited. Disciplinary action was to be taken against any who ignored his instructions. The message certainly got home. Captain Stockwell, serving with the 1st Royal Welch Fusiliers near Ploegsteert, Ypres, recorded that, 'strict orders had been issued that there was to be no fraternising on Christmas Day.'[19]

The instinct of officers was to ignore Smith-Dorrien. Edward Hulse (Eton), serving with the Scots Guards near Ypres, wrote to his mother on 28 December: 'We stood to arms as usual at 0630 hrs on the 25th, and I noticed there was not much shooting ... At 0830 hrs I was looking out and saw four Germans leave their trenches and come towards us; I told two of my men to go and meet them unarmed and to see that they did not pass the half-way line. My fellows were not very keen so I went

42

out alone … They were three private soldiers and a stretcher bearer and their spokesman started off by wishing us a Happy Christmas, and trusted us implicitly to keep the truce'.[20] Another Etonian, Lionel Cohen, a future Law Lord serving in the 1/13th (County of London) Battalion (Kensington), wrote home in a letter: 'Christmas Day was a farce in the trenches. Neither side fired a shot. They met in the middle and talked. A German gave our adjutant a photo to post to his sister in Birmingham. Cigars and cigarettes were exchanged and bully beef for a glass of German beer.'[21]

Captain Mervyn Richardson (Radley), whose death in April 1916 is described in Robert Graves' *Goodbye to All That*, wrote: 'On Christmas Eve we had a sing-song with the men in the trenches and put up a canvas sheet, with "Merry Christmas" and a picture of the Kaiser painted on it, on the parapet. The next morning there was a thick fog and, when it lifted about 1200 hrs, Saxons began to shout across and beckon to our men to come halfway and exchange gifts. Then they came out of their trenches and gave our men cigars and cigarettes and two barrels of beer, in exchange for tins of bully beef … Another officer and myself went out and met seven of their officers, and arranged that we should have an armistice until the next morning … We gave them a plum pudding, then saluted and returned to our respective trenches … Not a shot was fired all day, and the next morning we pulled our card down, and they put one up with "Thank you" on it'.[22]

Private Henry Williamson (Colfe's), author of *Tarka the Otter*, serving at Ploegsteert with the London Rifle Brigade, a Territorial battalion, wrote: 'On Christmas Eve, both armies sang carols and cheered and there was very little firing. The Germans (in some places 80 yards away) called our men to come and fetch a cigar and our men told them to come to us. This went on for some time … until a bold Tommy crept out and stood between the trenches and immediately a Saxon came to him. They shook hands and laughed and then sixteen Germans came out'.[23] Guy Cave had been a schoolboy at Tonbridge and was serving with the Royal Fusiliers as a second lieutenant. He wrote to his parents on 31 December: 'Christmas Day will go down in history as a day absolutely unique … On Christmas Eve, the Germans had their Christmas trees blazing all night and we had our photos taken in a group. The Germans and Tommies together and officers … One of them said "You are Anglo-Saxons, we are Saxons. Then why should we shoot?"'[24]

The fraternization can be understood as a symptom of mutual respect between regular officers from Germany and Britain. It also speaks of a deep humanity and comradeship that the young men learned at school, which transcended even the reality of war. Smith-Dorrien was irate, and gave express orders that there was to be no repetition in 1915. Artillery barrages were to be fired throughout the day. By then, another twelve months of slaughter had hardened the hearts of many. Some carol singing across the trenches and brief ceasefires to allow the dead to be buried nevertheless occurred.

The Territorials arrive on the Western Front

The extensive slaughter of the regular army meant that the high command needed to look to the Territorials to take their places. Haldane had been prescient in 1907 in establishing the Territorial Force (TF) and a Special Reserve (SR) directly under the War Office's control, to back up the regular army. There were differences in the social composition of TF battalions, with some having a higher proportion of public schoolboys. John Reith, the future BBC director general and a pupil at Glasgow Academy, recalled joining the Territorials: 'I was commissioned into the 5th Scottish Rifles in 1911 and the social class of the man in the ranks was higher than that of any other regiment in Glasgow.'[25] Double VC winner Noel Chavasse, from Magdalen College School in Oxford and then Liverpool College, similarly joined the Liverpool Scottish Regiment, full of the professional and business classes.

London, however, saw the biggest growth in well-to-do Territorial battalions. The London Regiment's battalions included the London Scottish, the Queen's Westminster Rifles, and the London Rifle Brigade (LRB), all of whom charged entrance fees to join. This contrasted with the rather less smart Finsbury Rifles, known from the location of their drill hall as the 'Pentonville Pissers'.[26] The LRB had its own drill hall, billiard room and even boxing ring; officers and other ranks shot at Bisley, and enjoyed social functions together. It was typical of the smart type of Territorial regiment which attracted public schoolboys who enjoyed sport, the feel of military life, and the social atmosphere that went with both. One pre-war officer was Ralph Husey, who left Marlborough in 1899 and became a prosperous stockbroker in the City. He rose to the rank of Brigadier-General, won the DSO and bar, and an MC, and was killed in May 1918.[27]

The London Scottish were the first Territorials to see action, rushed to the front in London buses and arriving on 30 October to stop the advancing German armies, a task which they fulfilled gallantly, sustaining over 400 casualties. Public schoolboys among them were to be found in all ranks; so eager were they to join up quickly, they were willing to serve in the battalion even if not commissioned.

44

The next Territorial regiment in action was the London Rifle Brigade (LRB), fresh from training at Crowborough Camp in East Sussex. Among them was Wilfred Willett (St Paul's). His prescient fears were expressed over his last night in bed with his weeping wife, Eileen: 'Should I ever sleep with her again? Or should I be limbless or faceless next time? I would meet her in heaven but in what state?'[28]

The LRB's story sheds light on the experience of many. They struck camp during the evening of 3 November, caught a train to Southampton to the accompaniment of the band from the Post Office Rifles, and embarked on SS *Chyebassa* on the evening of 4 November. After a calm crossing, they disembarked at Le Havre the next day. On 6 November their 848 men, 68 horses, 22 vehicles and 2 machine guns were entrained for Saint Omer, arriving the following day. Long days marching followed, as the entire battalion made their way northwards toward the Ypres Salient, arriving at Ploegsteert Wood just south of the medieval town on 22 November. The men were cold and depressed by the loss of one of their transport horses, the Pride of Hammersmith, and by their first casualty, Rifleman J. Dunnett, only eighteen, killed by a stray shell while eating breakfast still some way from the front line. Once in the line, they found the trenches two feet deep in icy water and had no chance of getting clean or even dry. On 13 December the edge of the wood was recaptured, as were some of the houses that the Germans were using for sniping. On 13 December Willett was supervising repair work on the trenches when one of the men in his company called out that Sergeant Moore had been hit in No-Man's-Land. He promptly snatched up the special medical kit he always had near him and crept into No-Man's-Land, utilising the medical knowledge from his incomplete training at London Hospital to tend to Moore's shattered leg. While dressing the wound and before summoning the stretcher bearers, he was hit in the side of his head by a bullet. Now the company had to bring in two men, Moore who would clearly survive, and Willett, blood and brain matter pouring from the side of his head, who all assumed would not. Willett's story was dramatized in a novel and television production, *Wilfred and Eileen*, by Jonathan Smith (1975). Henry Williamson served alongside him and they became close friends.

Sportsmen were among the early Territorial casualties, including rugby players ready to fulfil their military obligations. In the last pre-war rugby international England beat Scotland by a single point at Inverleith. Frederick Turner (Sedbergh) played at wing forward. His career at school was rich in athletic achievement, and he went on to captain Scotland. He joined the Liverpool Scottish, landing in France in early November. In the line near Kemmel in Belgium he was

45

killed on 10 January 1915 by a sniper's bullet. His fellow officer and friend, Noel Chavasse, the battalion's medical officer, helped bring in his body.

Turner played in that last international against Ronald Poulton-Palmer (Rugby), who captained Oxford against Cambridge in 1910 and 1911, played for the Harlequins and finally England, which he captained in 1914. Poulton-Palmer was a three-quarter and a sinuous runner, who still holds the scoring record of five tries in a Varsity Match (in 1909). Despite his wealth – he was heir to the Huntley and Palmers biscuit fortune – he had a profound social conscience, was a committed Christian and active in Rugby School's mission to Notting Hill. Poulton-Palmer joined the Royal Berkshires, in which he served until 5 May 1915, when he was killed by a sniper near Ploegsteert Wood while supervising a working party in No-Man's-Land. His colonel recorded: 'When I went around his old company as they stood to at dawn, almost every man was crying.'[29] Like so many young officers, he was well remembered as a hero at his school. The Rugby magazine recalled that, 'He was a sportsman in the only sense worth mentioning ... he played the game for the sake of the game ... any trick or mean advantage would not only have been distasteful but simply unthinkable ... God send us more of his type'.[30] A fellow rugby international, Percy Kendall (Tonbridge), was killed a short while earlier by a sniper while serving with the London Scottish. Of him a Tonbridge contemporary wrote: 'We knew he would face death like a hero and take it like a man ...The thing was that he played the game'.[31] Whatever was written by people at home in early 1915, it had already dawned on those at the front that war was emphatically not a game.

The first TF officer to win the VC was Second Lieutenant Geoffrey Woolley (St John's Leatherhead), serving with the Queen Victoria's Rifles, who held off repeated German counterattacks in the desperately fierce fighting on 'Hill 60' on 20 April 1915. Only 14 of his company of 150 were still in action when relieved the following morning. Woolley, the son of a clergyman, was ordained after the war, taught at Rugby, and later became Chaplain of Harrow.

One regular officer to be killed that spring was Julian Grenfell (Eton), who went on from school to a glittering career at Balliol, Oxford as a scholar and athlete. Commissioned into the 1st (Royal) Dragoons in 1910, he arrived on the Western Front in October 1914, quickly establishing a reputation 'famous through all the army in France for light-hearted courage!'[32] On 13 May 1915 he was wounded in the head near Ypres, and died on 26 May at a hospital in Boulogne. The day his death was announced, his poem *Into Battle* appeared in *The Times* and was later selected by Robert Bridges, the Poet Laureate, for his anthology *The Spirit of Man* (1916). Grenfell personifies the academic brilliance and gilded youth of that fated generation. His older brother was killed in action two months later, his younger brother in a motor accident in 1926.

Gallipoli

Gallipoli is often seen as a campaign fought principally by Australian and New Zealand forces, the Anzacs, although the British numbers and casualties were in fact much higher. The magnificent Anzac contribution is discussed in the next chapter. The plan hatched in London in the early weeks of 1915, devised mainly by First Lord of the Admiralty Winston Churchill, originated in the desire to break the deadlock on the Western Front, until Kitchener's 'New Army' was ready to fight.[33] The plan was for the Royal Navy to force a passage through the Dardanelles, the long narrow channel lying between the European edge of Turkey and the great landmass of Anatolia, through which shipping had to pass for Constantinople and the Black Sea beyond. The intention was to force Turkey out of the war and open up a supply route to Russia, but the naval assault failed. Politicians and military planners therefore decided that a landing should be made on the Aegean side of the peninsula to neutralize the Turkish guns facing the Straits and make safe the passage for Allied shipping. General Sir Ian Hamilton was appointed to command the expedition. As a boy he had been taught stoicism by the fierce Master of Wellington, E. W. Benson, and was the bravest of soldiers with experience of Afghanistan, the Nile campaign of 1898 and the Boer War. Although he made mistakes at Gallipoli, the objectives of the mission were impossible to achieve.

The British believed that the Turks would be unable to resist simultaneous landings along the peninsula, but they had completely underestimated the huge difficulties of mounting an amphibious operation so far from home, the almost impossibly mountainous terrain and Turkish military preparedness. The first day, 25 April, did not go according to Allied plans, and the troops made little progress inland, either around Cape Helles or at Anzac Cove. Six public school VCs were won on the beaches around Cape Helles, by, among others, Major Cuthbert Bromley (St Paul's) and Captain Richard Willis (Harrow), regular officers in the Lancashire Fusiliers, which won 'six VCs before breakfast' as they struggled ashore through heavy Turkish fire and uncut wire on to the heavily defended 'W' Beach.

Captain Guy Geddes (Rugby) described how his Munster battalion disembarked from the *River Clyde* on to a beach raked with enemy fire:

'We got it like anything, man after man was shot down but they never wavered. Lieutenant Watts who was wounded in five places and lying on the gangway cheered the men on with cries of "Follow the Captain." Captain French of the Dublin's told me afterwards he counted the first forty-eight men to follow me and they all fell.' Geddes reflected on what he had seen: 'I think no finer episode could be found of the men's bravery and discipline than this – of leaving the safety of the *River Clyde* to go to what was practically certain death.'[34]

The Royal Naval Division, so key in the Gallipoli campaign, had been formed from surplus Royal Marines and sailors who had volunteered – without sufficient ships to accommodate them, they were made into an army-style unit under naval command. The Hood and Hawke Battalions of the RND included several celebrated figures in society, including the musician Denis Browne (Rugby), Olympic gold medal rower Frederick Kelly (Sydney Grammar School and Eton) and *Punch* columnist and humorist, A. P. Herbert (Winchester).

The best known of the division's officers had died just two days before the first landings. Rupert Brooke (Rugby) was the son of a housemaster at the school he loved: 'I had been happier at Rugby than I can find words to say ... I seem to see every hour golden and radiant and always increasing in beauty'.[35] From Rugby he won a scholarship to King's College, Cambridge. An athlete as well as a scholar, his understated biography in *Wisden Cricketers' Almanac* reads: 'Rupert Brooke, who died at Gallipoli in April 1915, was in the Rugby School first eleven of 1906, coming third in the bowling averages. He also gained a reputation as a poet.'[36] He had sailed with the Mediterranean Expeditionary Force on 28 February, but developed blood poisoning from an infected mosquito bite. His close school friend Denis Browne wrote: 'I sat with Rupert. At four o'clock he became weaker and at 4.46 he died with the sun shining all round his cabin and the cool sea-breeze blowing through the door. No one could have wished for a quieter or calmer end than in that lovely bay, shielded by the mountains and fragrant with sage and thyme.' He was buried at 11.00 p.m. that evening in an olive grove on the island of Skyros, where his grave is much visited today. His brother Alfred (Rugby) was devastated by the news, and joined his London Regiment battalion in France exactly a month later on 25 May. Within three weeks, on 14 June, he was killed in action, aged just twenty-four. Browne, who was a composer and music critic of some renown, and a Cambridge contemporary of Ralph Vaughan Williams, was himself killed at Gallipoli on 4 June. His body was never found. Though badly wounded, he had managed before his death to hand to a petty officer his wallet containing a note written to

Edward Marsh, private secretary to Churchill and a mentor to Brooke and many other glittering talents. 'I've gone now too; not too badly I hope', Browne wrote. 'I am luckier than Rupert because I fought. But there's no one to bury me as I buried him, so perhaps he's better off in the long run.'[37]

So heavy were the casualties that support from the Territorials was needed. The 42nd Division (East Lancashire) had been the first Territorial division to be sent overseas, arriving in Egypt in September 1914 to defend the Suez Canal against possible Turkish attack. It was therefore well placed to be called on, arriving at Gallipoli in late May 1915 and going straight into the third Battle of Krithia, suffering heavy losses. The public schools of Lancashire provided many of their officers, Bury Grammar School prominent among them. The school had a particularly close relationship with 1/5 Lancashire Fusiliers whose headquarters was in the centre of Bury town, and nine of its thirty-six officers were old boys, including the commanding officer, Lieutenant Colonel F. A. Woodcock, a Bury solicitor. Over 300 men from the Bury district died on Gallipoli, including several Grammar School old boys. One, Private Richard Wild, had emigrated to New Zealand and was proudly serving with the New Zealand Expeditionary Force when he was killed.[38]

The 52nd (Lowland) was the next Territorial division to reach Gallipoli, arriving direct from Scotland in early June, by which time the campaign had ceased to have any clear military purpose. The Scottish Rifles, one of its battalions, had been very popular with the professional classes in Glasgow. Eleven of its thirty officers came from Glasgow Academy, with another three from Fettes. On 28 June the battalion engaged the Turks at Fir Tree Spur, where machine guns ripped them to pieces. Twenty-five officers and 446 men became casualties. Glasgow Academy suffered particularly grievously: the school still has a photograph of eleven old boys in the Scottish Rifles proudly posing for the camera before they left for Gallipoli in December 1914. Eight of them were to be killed on 28 June.[39]

In the entire Gallipoli campaign no fewer than 196 pairs of brothers were killed, but of that total of 392 men, only 13 have marked graves.[40] Two such, both commemorated on the Helles Memorial, are Captain Austen Belcher and Lieutenant Humphrey Belcher, both Wykehamists serving in 5th Wiltshires and killed within three days of each other in August 1915. Their father was Rector of Chaldon, a beautiful Norman church in Surrey, where a memorial service for the brothers was held in October 1915, one of so many held in churches and school chapels across the country. The Bishop of Southwark, who had taught them at

Winchester, preached at the service, during which the brothers' swords lay unsheathed in the chancel, surrounded by harvest produce from the villagers.[41]

Much is made of the artists and athletes who died in the war, but less of the scientists. Few losses were greater than that of Henry Moseley (Eton), killed in a Turkish attack on 10 August. Born of brilliant parents, his father a professor of anatomy at Oxford and his mother a championship chess player, he was a King's Scholar at Eton, a science scholar at Trinity, Oxford, and went on to become one of the most brilliant physicists of his generation. Working first at Manchester University with Ernest Rutherford of atomic fame, he returned to Oxford and established the atomic numbers of key elements. Before Rutherford could stop him he joined up, and was killed at Gallipoli on 10 August, serving as a signals officer; it was a tragic waste of the intellectual talents of a man who many believed might well have been a future Nobel Prize winner. At the science school at Eton a memorial commemorates him thus: 'This tablet is placed here to remind Etonians that H. G. J. Moseley (KS 1901–6) began his study of Physics in this laboratory. In his short life he gave to science the discovery of the atomic numbers of the elements. "The rays whose path here first he saw/Were his to range in ordered law/A nobler law made straight the way/That leads him 'neath a nobler ray".'[42]

By late summer, even diehards in London had to accept the campaign was going nowhere. Hamilton was dismissed in October and replaced by General Charles Monro (Sherborne), who recommended closing the operation promptly and evacuating the entire peninsula. Hamilton had estimated that withdrawing without first defeating the Turks could mean incurring casualties of fifty per cent of the Allied forces. Monro achieved the evacuation of troops without a single loss of life to enemy action. In total, 44,000 British, Australian and New Zealand troops had been killed, and 97,000 wounded.

The 'New Army' and the Western Front in later 1915

The Battle of Neuve Chapelle in March 1915 had failed to break through the German lines. The subsequent loss of men in the Second Battle of Ypres (April–May) led to demands for changes at the top, after the politicians were unfairly blamed for the failure to provide sufficient shells to support the attack. The Liberal government fell and was succeeded by a coalition. Asquith remained Prime Minister but David Lloyd George was appointed to the key post of Minister of Munitions, responsible for resolving the shell crisis. Sir John French, the Commander-in-Chief of the British Expeditionary Force, replaced Smith-Dorrien as commander of the Second Army with Herbert Plumer, leaving Douglas Haig in command of the First Army.[43]

On Kitchener's appointment as Secretary of State for War in August 1914, he predicted that the war would not be over by Christmas 1914, but would be long and drawn out. Some two million men volunteered for his 'New Army' (NA) before the long queues dwindled and conscription had to be introduced in March 1916. The vast majority of officers were recruits just out of university and school OTCs, high on enthusiasm but low on skill. Guy Chapman (Westminster) realized how limited his OTC experience had been: 'We were in fact amateurs, and though we should stoutly have denied it, in our hearts amateurs we knew ourselves to be, pathetically anxious to achieve the status of the professional.'[44] Charles Sorley wrote to the Master of Marlborough in August 1915: 'I hear that a very select group of public schools will by this time be enjoying Camp somewhere in England. May they not take it too seriously! Seeing as how the training is washed out as you turn that narrow street corner in Boulogne.'[45] Second Lieutenant T. H. Barnes (Eton) realized his limitations when asked to take church parade for his platoon of Sherwood Foresters: 'To my utter consternation, the three leading files, instead of marking time when they reached the fence at the edge of the field, just climbed over and were marching away across the next field into the blue!'[46]

It soon became apparent that the pell-mell expansion of NA battalions had created a desperate need for experienced senior officers. Many who thought their days in khaki were long past found themselves summoned back into service. Arthur Addison (Haileybury) had retired with the rank of major in 1906. He was recalled aged forty-eight, to find himself in command of 9 York and Lancasters, a battalion of South Yorkshire miners he trained and took out to France in August 1915.

An optimistic report on the state of readiness of the NA was sent to French in May 1915, claiming that the quality of the recruits 'is undoubtedly of a higher standard than that of the average men we have usually recruited in the old army.'[47] The first NA division to reach France was the 9th (Scottish) Division on 9 May, followed shortly after by the 14th (Light) Division. This contained 41 Brigade, made up of battalions from the prestigious rifle regiments, its officers recruited almost exclusively from Oxford and Cambridge University OTCs and the more famous public schools. In 7th Battalion, The Rifle Brigade (7RB) served Donald Hankey (Rugby) as a private soldier, also Lieutenant Gilbert Talbot (Winchester), son of the Bishop of Winchester and President of the Oxford Union in 1913. The latter's politics were described in the Winchester Memorial Book as 'conservative by instinct, yet he felt convinced of the need of a constructive policy of social reform'.[48]

Marlborough masters Keith Rae and Ronald Gurner served in 8RB alongside their former pupils Sidney Woodroffe and Albert Hooker, as did two Eton masters, Edward Foss Prior and A. C. Sheepshanks. Many public school teachers who were also experienced OTC officers were at the Front by mid-1915. Gurner survived the war, winning an MC and becoming headmaster of Whitgift School between the wars. Rae had joined the Marlborough staff in 1912; though not a public schoolboy himself, he had become friendly at Balliol College, Oxford with Ronnie Poulton-Palmer, with whom he shared a Christian commitment, and together they worked at the boys' club in Saint Ebbe's in Oxford. Sidney Woodroffe was pleased to serve in the battalion alongside his brother Leslie, who taught at Shrewsbury School (their third brother, Kenneth, had been killed in May). Another was Billy Grenfell (Eton), brother of the poet Julian Grenfell. Billy had boxed for Oxford, won the coveted Craven Scholarship at Balliol and was intent on acquiring an All Souls fellowship when war broke out.

But intellectual talent was no protection against enemy fire, as 41 Brigade found when it went into the line near Hooge in the Ypres Salient in July. 'I can't help feeling anxious at their being put into such vile a place as Hooge', wrote Major Billy Congreve (Eton) in his diary; he was to win a posthumous VC the following year on the Somme. At Hooge the Germans threw them two surprises, a large underground mine which exploded early in the morning on 30 July to herald their attack, followed by another new weapon, the flame thrower, which spread 'liquid fire' thirty yards and more into British trenches, causing disarray before the infantry attacked. Among those lost that day was Keith Rae, whose family erected a memorial after the war at Sanctuary Wood to the east of Ypres, bearing the words 'Christ's faithful soldier and servant until his life's end.'[49]

Worse was to come when at midday the following day 41 Brigade was ordered to counterattack to recover the ground lost. Short on artillery support, the counter-attack proved a disaster. Billy Grenfell exhorted his frightened men to 'remember you are Englishmen – do nothing to dishonour the name'.[50] Grenfell then led the charge, only to be shot dead, whilst Sidney Woodroffe, already wounded, was hit three more times before dying as he tried to find a way through the German wire, for which action he was awarded his posthumous VC. Neville Talbot (Haileybury), Senior Chaplain of 6th Division, found the bodies of his brother Gilbert and Sidney Woodroffe the following day. A tribute to Gilbert Talbot, printed in *The Times*, recounted how 'Gilbert's platoon had to lead the attack ... The whistles blew. Gilbert rose at once crying, "Come along lads, now's your time." But only twelve men could be found to follow him. He ran forward and was hit in the neck by a bullet. He fell, gave a smile to his servant and rolled forward on his face ... His brother Neville could not endure to let his body lie unhonoured or unblessed, so crawled through the grass, in spite of shells and snipers, touched young Woodroffe's body, and knew that he was close to what he sought. Two yards further he found it'.[51] Along with the Revd Tubby Clayton (St Paul's), Neville Talbot went on to found Toc H, 'Toc' signifying the letter 'T' in the Signals alphabet used by the British Army during the war. Talbot House, founded in December 1915 at Poperinghe, to the west of Ypres, took its name from Gilbert Talbot and became a place of rest and prayer for soldiers of all ranks.

'Our losses have been great', wrote the Brigade Commander, Oliver Nugent, on 30 July. 'Officers of a class we shall never be able to replace, the pick of British public school or Varsity life ... They led their men with the most sublime courage knowing, as I'm certain they did, that they were going to almost certain death'.[52] 8RB lost 19 officers and 469 men over those two disastrous days. The Old Etonian writer Maurice Baring, from the Baring banking family, wrote of the Grenfell brothers, both now dead: 'Like Castor and Pollux, they are together, shining in some other place.'[53]

Too many families had to endure the double (and more) suffering of the Grenfells and Woodroffes. The commanding officer of 8 Rifle Brigade, Lieutenant Colonel R. B. Maclochlen, an Etonian, wrote to the Woodroffes' father on 2 August 1915: 'You will have heard of the tragedy which occurred from a bald War Office telegram. Your youngest son was killed in action at Hooge on the 30th at 2.45 pm and your eldest son was badly wounded, almost at the same time ... Your younger boy was simply one of the bravest of the brave and the work he did that day will stand out as a record hard to beat ... He was killed out at front, in the open, cutting the wire to enable the attack to be continued. He risked his life for others right through the day and finally gave it for the sake of his men. He was a splendid type of young officer, bold as a lion, confident and sure of himself too'.[54] So moved was Frank Fletcher, who had known the Woodroffe boys from when he had been Master of Marlborough, that he kept a copy of the letter in his scrap-book, which is still held in the archives at Charterhouse, where he went as headmaster in 1911.

The first NA experiences of battle had been shattering, but worse was to come as more battalions reached France. In September and October

1915 they saw action at the Battle of Loos, timed to coincide with the Champagne offensive by the French armies. The battlefield lies to the south of Ypres and Neuve Chapelle, and to the north of Vimy Ridge and the Somme. The German lines there were heavily defended and, with shells still in short supply, Sir John French decided to employ gas, its first use by the British. An early breakthrough of the German lines failed to be exploited because of the poor quality of shells and difficulties in communication, and the Germans were able to regain a tactical advantage from their elevated position on the slagheaps close behind their lines. The town of Loos fell to the British, but the Germans counter-attacked and within three days had recovered the lost ground. French was not to survive the failure of the battle, and was replaced as Commander-in-Chief by Douglas Haig.

Loos became a byword for military incompetence. Harold Macmillan, wounded on his first day in action, wrote that he learned here what was meant by the phrase 'the fog of war'; he described the whole battle as 'frightfully mismanaged'.[55] His young Eton contemporary, John Scudamore, was killed instantly well in front of his men when 'he had all but cut his way through the German wire', the manner of his death showing the forlornness of the task.[56] It was perhaps not surprising that nearly fifty years later another Etonian, Alan Clark, would characterize the soldiers of Loos as 'lions led by donkeys' and in the process help shape the popular British stereotype of the war and its generals.[57]

For many public schools the first day of Loos, 25 September, was second only to the first day of the Somme in men lost. Rugby, for instance, had fifteen old boys killed that day. Among the 60,000 British casualties, over three weeks of fighting, were countless individual stories of loss. One who fell on that first day was Douglas Gillespie (Winchester). His letter the day before the battle has survived: 'My Dear Daddy ... Before long I think we shall be in the thick of it, for, if we do attack, my company will be one of those in front, and I am likely to lead it. I have no forebodings for I feel that so many of my friends will charge by my side ... you remember Wordsworth's *Happy Warrior* ... it will please you to know that I am very happy, and, whatever happens, you will remember that'.[58] Major General Sir Thompson Capper (Haileybury) was Commander of 7th Division. Contrary to the canard that the top brass kept themselves safe behind the lines and away from danger, Capper was shot in the front line on 27 September. A memorial window created in his memory can be found in the chapel at Haileybury. A fellow staff officer commented of his death that, 'the ambition of his life was to be killed in action, which is some consolation. A braver man and better General never walked.'[59]

Another who met his end at Loos was John Kipling (Wellington), the youngest child and only son of author Rudyard Kipling. Helped by his father's connections, John, known to his family as 'Jack', secured a commission in the Irish Guards, despite severe short-sightedness. On his eighteenth birthday he was posted to France, and within six weeks was in action at Loos. Eyewitnesses reported seeing him fall with a wound to the neck, but his body was never found. His distraught parents used every possible contact to obtain news of him, hoping against hope that he might be a prisoner of war. Kipling wrote his poem *My Boy Jack*, which he included as a prelude to his book *Sea Warfare* about the 1916 Battle of Jutland. The first verse reads, '"Have you news of my Jack?"/*Not this tide*/"When d'you think that he'll come back?"/ *Not with this wind blowing, and this tide.*' Not until 1919 was his death finally accepted by his parents. In 1992 the Commonwealth War Graves Commission announced that the grave of an unknown Irish Guards lieutenant was that of Jack, though this has been strongly disputed. In 2007 the Imperial War Museum in London mounted an exhibition about him, and a book by veteran tour guides and authors Tonie and Valmai Holt was turned into a play for British television, with Daniel Radcliffe playing Jack.[60] Loos saw a great loss to literature with the death of Charles Sorley (Marlborough), son of a Cambridge professor. In one of his final letters, written to the Master of Marlborough, he enclosed a short poem in memory of Sidney Woodroffe, wistfully longing 'for a pair of shorts and my long loose coloured jersey – gules and argent. My love to Marlborough'.[61]

Jack Kipling's name is recorded on the Dud Corner Memorial at Loos, along with the name of Captain Sandy Morrison, school captain and later teacher and OTC founder at George Watson's School in Edinburgh, and one of thirteen Old Watsonians to be found on the memorial. Scottish schools and regiments suffered particularly heavily at Loos, paying the price for their military prowess in leading so many attacks. St Dunstan's College in South London was another whose old boys suffered grievously in the battle, with several serving together in the same company of the 1/20 London Regiment (Blackheath and Woolwich). One to die on 25 September was Private John Heap. His platoon sergeant wrote to his parents to say he had the opportunity of returning to his own section, but, 'it was plain to me that he wanted to be with his old school friends and share the dangers of the battle with them. It was the gallant action of a very brave man'.[62] He was mown down along with nine other Dunstonians by heavy German machine gun fire.

Captain Francis Townend had been at school at Dulwich, two miles to the north of St Dunstan's, just after P. G. Wodehouse (a friend of his brother). In an action of extraordinary courage, Townend, both legs blown off by a shell and balancing himself on his stumps, told his rescuer to tend to the men first and said that he would be all right, though he might have to give up rugby next year. He then died.[63] The fighting spirit of young officers was caught by James Hay Beith (Fettes), whose book about the early days of the war, *The First Hundred Thousand* (1915), became a best seller. The New Army was able to cope, he said, thanks to the public school OTCs. 'Very few of these young officers are alive now; but they saved the British Empire for the simple reason that they were ready and willing at a time when all were willing and few were ready.'[64]

The Somme

The last weeks of 1915 and the first months of 1916 were compara-tively quiet for British forces on the Western Front. Roland Leighton (Uppingham) was granted leave over Christmas in 1915 and had planned to meet his fiancée, Vera Brittain, at the Grand Hotel in Brighton. In his place she received a telegram saying he had been killed on 23 December, shot by a German sniper through the stomach while inspecting wire in front of his trenches. He is buried at the military cemetery at Louvencourt on the Somme. In mid-January 1916, after Vera went to see Roland's mother and sister Clare and found them opening a parcel of Roland's effects, she gave her brother Edward a glimpse of what grieving families had to experience: 'These were his clothes – the clothes in which he came home from the front last time. Everything was damp and worn and simply caked with mud ... The smell of those clothes was the smell of graveyards and the dead ... We discovered that the bullet was an expanding one. The hole where it went in in front – well below where the belt would have been, just below the right hand bottom pocket of the tunic – was almost microscopic, but at the back, almost exactly where the backbone would have been, there was quite a large rent'.[65]

More than any other battle of the Great War, the Somme, lasting from 1 July to 18/19 November 1916, made a deep impact on the public schools. For those who survived, and for the schools from which they came, life was never to be the same again. The extent of the casualties, and the failure to achieve the battle's objectives, mark it out as the greatest tragedy in British military history. Conceived as a joint Anglo-French assault at the point on the Western Front where the British and French lines met at the River Somme in Picardy, the plan went awry before the battle had even begun. The German attack at Verdun that February had drawn away so much of the intended French fighting contribution that the battle became much more a British than a joint operation.

Some 150,000 British troops participated in the first day of the battle on 1 July, with 19,000 killed and 39,000 wounded or missing. Nine of the sixteen British divisions committed on the first day were from the 'New Army', with up to ninety per cent of the officers, and a substantial minority of the men in the ranks, coming from every public school in Britain. Many were going into battle for the first time. The artillery barrage that lasted several days before the fighting commenced was clearly audible in public schools along the south coast like St Lawrence, Ramsgate and Brighton College. Some fifteen per cent of all public school Great War casualties occurred during the Somme. Some schools saw a considerably higher figure, such as Royal Belfast Academical Institution, twenty-five per cent of whose total dead fell in the battle, mostly in the 36th (Ulster) Division.[66]

Most of the 6,851 officers killed during the battle, including the 1,000 on the first day, were junior officers who had recently left school.[67] Thirty brigade and battalion commanders were also killed on that first day, showing again the physical danger faced by many senior officers. The most senior to die was Brigadier-General Charles Prowse (Marlborough), who had won a DSO as a company commander in 1914, at 'Prowse Point' near Ploegsteert Wood. Frustrated by his brigade's slow progress on the Redan Ridge between Beaumont Hamel and Serre, he went forward to revive the attack. There he fell, killed by a shell, along with three out of his four battalion commanders. One of them, Lawrence Palk (Wellington), commanded 1st Battalion, the Hampshire Regiment. A Boer War veteran and winner of a DSO in 1914, it was said that he donned his best uniform with white gloves and led his men across No-Man's-Land carrying a walking stick. All twenty-six officers under his command were killed or became casualties. Arthur Addison (Haileybury) was another lieutenant colonel to die, along with nearly 200 of his men, near Ovillers. Like so many, his body lay unrecovered in No-Man's-Land until it was found in September, together with a short diary which revealed that he had lived on for two or three days before succumbing.[68] One of the rare private memorials standing today on the Somme is to Lieutenant Val Braithwaite (Winchester), killed near Serre aged twenty. His body was never found, and after the war his father, General Sir Walter Braithwaite, bought the land where his son had fallen, erecting a wooden cross inscribed, 'God buried him and no man knoweth his sepulchre.'[69]

Not all old boys were Tories or Liberals; under the influence of Christianity in the main, some became Socialists, which explained also why some wanted to serve in the ranks. One such was R. H. Tawney (Rugby), a devout Christian and a distinguished economic historian. Before the war, he had lived with his social reformer friend William Beveridge (Charterhouse) at Toynbee Hall in East London, a cradle of radical thinking and the home of the Workers' Educational Association. Declining a commission, Tawney enlisted in the Manchester Pals and was wounded in the attack on Mametz near where Siegfried Sassoon (Marlborough) was fighting. He recalled the moment as like being 'hit by a tremendous iron hammer and then twisted with a sickening sort of wrench so that my back banged on the ground and my feet struggled as though they did not belong to me'.[70] Tawney had been shot through the chest and abdomen and lay in No-Man's-Land for thirty hours before being brought back in. Once in a field hospital, he was visited by a senior officer who warned the sister in charge of the ward that she was looking after a national treasure. Shocked, she rushed to Tawney and asked why he had not told her that he was 'a gentleman'.[71] He survived without further mishap, was elected a fellow of Balliol College, Oxford in 1918, where he wrote *Religion and the Rise of Capitalism* (1926), his classic work, then went on to become professor of economic history in 1931 at the London School of Economics.

Frederick Keeling (Winchester) was of a similar political persuasion. When at Cambridge, he had established a branch of the Fabian Society, went on to marry a suffragette, and became associate editor of the *New Statesman*, authoring a book on child labour published on the eve of war.[72] He promptly enlisted as a private in 6th Duke of Cornwall's Light Infantry, sending back regular articles and letters to the *New Statesman* and relishing the classless comradeship of the ranks. Promoted to sergeant, he refused to let his name be put forward for a commission despite his obvious merits; wounded in 1915, he was killed on the Somme near Delville Wood on 18 August 1916. Keeling thought deeply about the war, and the bravery of his conduct is enhanced by his doubts about the cause for which he fought. In a letter to Sir Robert Ensor, journalist and historian, in December 1915, he predicted a wave of pacifism after the war, led by soldiers who had fought. He was happy to fight against what he believed to be German militarism, but said, 'I will not hate Germans to the order of any bloody politician, and the first thing I will do after I am free will be to go to Germany and create all the ties I can with German life.'[73]

Another to reject a commission was H. H. Munro (Bedford), better known by his pen name 'Saki', who wrote a series of witty and often macabre stories satirizing contemporary society and culture. In his novel *When William Came*, published shortly before the war, he imagined a future in which the German forces had occupied London: 'sky-blue Saxon uniform' in Hyde Park, and the serving of 'lagerbeer, coffee, lemonade and syrups'. The prophecy, Charles Moore noted, was to come true even without the invasion.[74] Munro was in his forties when war broke out but enlisted and rose to the rank of Lance Sergeant in the Royal Fusiliers. He was to be killed at Beaumont Hamel while sheltering in an exposed shell crater on 13 November 1916; his last words were, according to several sources, 'put that bloody cigarette out'.

Left and right wing, sportsmen and aesthetes, the fearful and fearless; the Somme claimed them all. Among the sportsmen was Captain Billy Neville (Dover). A hero at school, he had been head boy and captain of hockey and cricket. Commissioned into the 8th Battalion East Surrey Regiment, he wrote home four days before the Somme opened in almost a parody of blasé unconcern: 'As I write the shells are fairly haring over; you know one gets sort of bemused after a few million. Still, it'll be a great experience to tell one's children about. So long, old thing, don't worry if you don't hear for a bit. I'm as happy as ever.'[75] In the same spirit, he had purchased four footballs, one for each of his platoons, to be kicked as they crossed No-Man's-Land. His aim was to make his men, who he knew would be afraid, more comfortable. Second Lieutenant Jocelyn Buxton (Marlborough) could have done with such jocularity as he tensed himself for the coming battle. Writing home on 26 June, he said, 'It is all going to be very huge and hideous ... It is best I feel sure just to keep hold of the faithfulness of God.'[76] Both men were to die on 1 July, Neville at Carnoy, yards in front of the German wire. Two of his footballs were later found nearby. R. C. Sheriff (Kingston GS), author of *Journey's End*, might have had both men in mind when he wrote: 'These public schoolboy officers were not soldiers in the ordinary meaning of the word. Very few of them would have wanted to stay on in the army when the war was done. They only wanted to get the thing over.'[77]

Public school officers played a prominent part in the 'Pals Battalions', made up of volunteers joining together in numbers from the earliest weeks of the war, fired by the civic pride of Britain's provincial cities and by the prospect of serving alongside friends or work colleagues. The Accrington Pals, properly 11th (Service) Battalion, East Lancashire Regiment, were amongst the best known. They had reached their full strength of some 1,000 men within the first ten days of recruiting opening in the Lancashire town. In command of one of their platoons was Lieutenant James Hitchon (Sedbergh), who had left school in 1910 to train as an architect. On 1 July he went over the top alongside his men in the third wave, only to die with a bullet in his stomach.[78] Of the 720 Accrington Pals 235 were killed and a further 350 wounded in the first half hour.

The Leeds Pals fought alongside them at Serre that day. This battalion was formed in September 1914 and landed in France in March 1916. Lieutenant Morris Bickersteth (Rugby) was a company commander. We have this diary account of 1 July: 'It was a lovely day and the sun was brilliant. Morris had been walking up and down his front line, encouraging his men ... They knew well enough what they were going out to, but no one wavered and at last the time came for Morris to go out. "Come on, lads", he cried, "Here's to a short life and a gay one." After going ten yards he looked round to see if there was any support from the trenches behind, and at that moment a shrapnel bullet struck him in the back of the head. He just rolled over without a word, killed instantly'.[79] Only a few of his men reached the German barbed wire.

Second Lieutenant Thomas Willey (Harrow) was another of the Leeds Pals to fall almost at once. Private Arthur Hollings wrote to his father, a Leeds solicitor, of how 'he never seemed so noble and courageous as he did at 7.30 a.m. last Saturday. On that fateful morning we all stayed in the front line trench for several hours subjected to a very heavy bombardment. At about 7.15 Mr Willey passed down the order. We then filed out, up the scaling ladder, through the gap in our own wire and through to our place as the first wave (the post of honour) in advance of our wire ... At 7.30 a.m. young Willey jumped up and, waving his revolver, shouted, "Come on 13 Platoon, give them hell".' A shell took off both his legs: his body was never found.[80] Fifteen officers and 233 other ranks died, most in the first few minutes after 0730 hrs. Private A. V. Pearson of the Leeds Pals famously recalled: 'The name of Serre and the date of 1 July is engraved deep in our hearts, along with the faces of our "pals", a grand crowd of chaps. We were two years in the making and ten minutes in the destroying.'[81]

One wonders what sense of foreboding the distant sound of gunfire evoked in those hearing it in the schools. For some headmasters, the impact of the war came home to them in the most tangible of ways. George Heslop, headmaster of Sevenoaks School, lost his beloved twenty-one-year-old son, also called George, a company commander in the Public Schools Battalion, in those opening hours. Little trace of his feelings is evident in a letter to a parent written that September: 'My boy was killed on 1 July in the first ten minutes of the great push. There is nothing to say. He had a duty to do and it was done.'[82] Robert Cary Gilson, headmaster of King Edward's School, Birmingham, suffered similarly. His son, Second Lieutenant Rob Gilson of 11th Battalion, Suffolk Regiment, commonly called the Cambridgeshire Battalion, was killed on 1 July by a shell near La Boisselle. When the news came through, his father was preparing to give away the prizes at the school sports day. He wrote later to J. R. R. Tolkien, a close friend of his son and a fellow old boy: 'Heaven grant that enough of you may be left to carry on the national life.'[83]

Of all the qualities associated with the public school ethos, courage was perhaps the one most needed in the ordeal by fire on 1 July, the courage which forced young officers, whistle in one hand, revolver in the other, over the parapet at the head of their platoons, knowing the likely fate in store. But the sense of duty learned at school was also strong. One young subaltern, Second Lieutenant Percy Boswell, of Alleyn's School and 8th Battalion King's Own Yorkshire Light Infantry, just twenty-two years old, wrote to his father on the eve of battle: 'I am just writing you a short note which you will receive only if anything has happened to me over the next few days. The Hun is going to get consummate hell just in this quarter ... I am absolutely sure that I shall get through all right, but, in case the unexpected does happen, I shall rest content with the knowledge that I have done my duty – and you can't ask more'.[84]

We could not establish with absolute precision exactly how many public school boys were killed or wounded during the Somme. Nor can anyone estimate accurately the extent of the loss to the country and beyond of their gifts. Many did not need to enlist, because their specialist skills could have been put to better use for the war effort in other fields, while many others were hopelessly unsuited to serve. One such was Second Lieutenant Stephen Hewett, whose strong Catholic faith compelled him to enlist even though, as the *Oxford Magazine* recorded, 'it was a greater wrench for him than for most to join the army. He had strong ties at home and was mistrustful of his own courage'.[85] At Downside School he had been a talented chorister, actor, cricketer and scholar, and head boy for nearly two years. He won a classical scholarship to Balliol College, and at Oxford won the Craven, the Hertford and the Ireland scholarships, as well as a hockey blue, and also authored some promising poems. This very gentle and cultured man had written earlier in the year to his mother: 'I am sure my sisters must think they are dreaming when they hear of their warlike brother crawling about in wet mud, with a pistol in one hand, a club studded with nails in the other and a mask over his face.'[86] Hewett was to be killed on 22 July.

As the battle ground on week after week, with pushes followed by lulls, the death toll rose steadily. On 15 September came the biggest attack since 1 July, especially near Guillemont, where the Guards Brigade was in action. For Eton it was a particularly tragic day, with over thirty officers killed, while the 2nd Battalion, Grenadier Guards had nine officers killed and nine wounded. One of those dead Grenadiers, perhaps the most celebrated of all those who fell in the entire Somme battle, was Raymond Asquith (Winchester), son of the Prime Minister and widely regarded as the brightest star of his generation. He won a scholarship to Balliol in 1896, and while at Oxford won many scholarships including the Craven, was elected a fellow of All Souls in 1902 and was called to the Bar in 1904. A brilliant career in law and politics awaited him, but he joined up in 1914, transferring to the Grenadier Guards in August 1915. After a spell on the staff, he requested to be placed on active duty with his battalion before the Battle of the Somme. He fell on 15 September leading his men in an attack at Flers. Shot in the chest, he died before he could reach a casualty clearing station. The news reached the Prime Minister the following day. As Margot Asquith later recalled, 'Henry opened the door and we stood facing each other. He saw my thin, wet face, and while he put his arm round me, I said: "Terrible, terrible news." At this he stopped and said: "I know ... I've known it ... Raymond is dead." He put his hands over his face and we walked into an empty room and sat down in silence'.[87]

On the headstone of his grave in the Guillemont Road Cemetery is carved a quotation from Shakespeare's *Henry V*, chosen because it describes a warrior king who himself had died in his thirties after campaigns in France: 'Small time but in that small most greatly lived/ This star of England.' Tall, handsome and effortlessly charming, he numbered many of the great figures of the Edwardian era amongst his friends. One was Winston Churchill, who wrote to his widow Katharine: 'I grieve myself for the loss of my brilliant hero-friend ... These gallant, charming figures that flash and gleam amid the carnage – always so superior to it, masters of their souls, disdainful of death and suffering – are an inspiration and example to all. And he was one of the very best. He did everything easily – I never remember anyone who seemed so independent of worldly or physical things'.[88]

His fellow Grenadier, the Etonian Oliver Lyttelton, later Lord Chandos and a minister in Churchill's wartime cabinet, won an immediate DSO in the same attack on 15 September. He wrote of his friend Raymond Asquith that, 'in him England lost one of its rarest men. Even a stranger could have seen that his good looks and noble profile disclosed a man of the finest character and powers ... but with all this brilliance he was simple and unselfish enough to take his chance and make the sacrifice with men who were not his equals'.[89]

September saw many fall whose death wrenched at the heart of their parents no less intensely for their not being famous. One such who also fell on 15 September was Eric Townsend (City of London). 'We shall live as those who by their sacrifice won the Great War,' he said in a farewell letter he penned to his parents to be sent in the event of his death. 'Our spirits and memories shall endure in the proud position Britain shall hold in the future ... thanks to all you have both done. I have crowded into twenty years enough pleasures, sensations and experiences for an ordinary lifetime.'[90] Edward Tennant (Winchester) wrote a similarly remarkable valedictory letter to his mother: 'Tonight we go up to the trenches and tomorrow we go over the top ... I feel rather like saying "If it be possible let this cup pass from me", but the triumphant finish "nevertheless not what I will but Thou willest", steels my heart and sends me into this battle with a heart of triple bronze. Your love for me and my love for you have made my whole life one of the happiest there has ever been ... God bless you and give you peace'.[91] He was killed in action two days later, on 22 September.

October saw no let up in the slaughter. One of those killed was Donald Hankey (Rugby), youngest brother of Maurice Hankey, who served Asquith as Secretary to the War Council and then Lloyd George as Cabinet Secretary (a position he held from 1916 to 1938). Donald wrote a series of articles in *The Spectator* under the nom de plume, 'A Student at Arms', published in many editions after his death. Shortly before his final action on 12 October, near Morval, one of his men recorded, 'The student knelt down for a few seconds with his men and he told them briefly what was before them: if wounded, "Blighty", If killed, the Resurrection.'[92] Arthur Addenbrooke (Warwick School) was another man devoted to serving others who lost his life that month. His school said of him that, 'a man of such character and personality may well be mentioned among the choicest products of public school life who have laid down their lives in the war ... no one will more surely abide in affectionate and grateful memory more than this singularly modest, accomplished and gallant gentleman'.[93]

The relationship between young public school officers and their men was tested and deepened by the Somme. About the nineteen-year-old Cecil Daly (Downside), killed at Guillemont on 18 August, his much older platoon sergeant wrote: 'He was an officer we would willingly have followed anywhere. By the fearless and brave example he set, he had a way of making us feel confident in our safety.'[94] Sidney Rogerson

(Worksop) described how Lieutenant Skett went out to find one of his men lying wounded in No-Man's-Land after a night patrol, but first turned to his servant and said, 'Here are the wages I owe you. You'd better take them while you can get them'; without more ado he then scrambled out of the trench. Hardly had he put a foot in No-Man's-Land than he fell back dead, his head split open by a random bullet.[95]

One of the last to die before the fighting petered out was Frederick Kelly (Sydney Grammar School and Eton), Rupert Brooke's pall-bearer and a man of formidable all-round talents, who fell at Beaucourt when rushing a German machine gun post. He had won a gold medal for rowing in the 1908 Olympic Games in London and was also one of the most promising musicians to be killed in the war. His memorial concert at the Wigmore Hall in London in May 1919 included his composition *Elegy for String Orchestra*, written at Gallipoli in memory of Rupert Brooke.

By the end of 1916 it began to seem as if the war would drag on forever. No prospect of one side gaining an advantage over the other seemed possible, and the bleeding dry of the soldiers seemed to provide the only prospect for termination. In 1917 the Russian Revolution led to the winding up of the war on the Eastern Front, and the death or exile of many aristocrats. In the west it seemed as if the upper classes would meet their fate in open battle. When Dick Levett (Eton) was killed that year, a rifleman in his platoon wrote to his parents: 'No one will ever be able to say that the upper classes have not given their all in this just cause.' In words that echoed the feelings of many ordinary soldiers towards the young officers who led them, he continued, 'Mr Richard was so unselfish – always thinking of the comforts of his men and was admired and respected by them. They would have followed him anywhere and if possible given their lives to save him.'[96]

Dick Levett's letters from the Western Front were published in a book by his grief-stricken parents. It mirrors similar volumes by the parents of Douglas Gillespie, Charles Sorley, Stephen Hewett, Rupert Brooke and many others killed in 1915 and 1916. They reflect not just the literary talents of their sons, the intellectual cream of the Edwardian public schools, but also the sense of shock and the desperate inability to comprehend the fate of so many members of that generation, unlikely soldiers, for whom war was not a profession but an abomination. The Somme brought to completion the loss of innocence, begun in 1914 as the volunteers began their training, speeded up by the experience of battle in 1915 on Gallipoli and the Western Front and its final destruction at Serre, Delville Wood, Guillemont and so many other places on the Somme. If there were any illusions left about the nature of the war by the end of 1916, either among public schoolboys at the front, or back home in their schools, they would be completely destroyed by the two long years of endurance and suffering to come. The war was not now about idealism but a fight to the finish in which victory was the only aim and the sole justification for all those deaths.

Chapter 3

Ireland and the Dominions

Across the world, above all in the Dominions, educational benefactors sought to model their schools on what was considered the very acme of educational excellence, the British public school. The United States after 1776 spawned several on the model, which still rank amongst its greatest schools today: Phillips Exeter, founded in 1781, Deerfield in 1797 and Lawrenceville in 1810. South Africa, Australia, New Zealand, Canada and India set up similar schools, with boarding houses, a sporting and physical ethos, a strong commitment to the classics, and respect for militarism and tradition. These notably British schools also drew personnel from the original public schools, particularly in the shape of British headmasters, as some still do.

When the call to arms came in 1914, these schools proved stalwart in support. The headmaster of one, Upper Canada College (UCC) in Toronto, made clear to his pupils in 1914 that, 'Our duty is plain today ... If we win, and under providence we shall win, it will be in the main the gentlemen of the Empire who will have done it. Look in England at the public schools ... The war lays heavy responsibility on the directing classes. *Noblesse oblige.* High position carries with it the obligation of service to mankind.'[1] That obligation was to be fulfilled by overseas public schools just as heroically as by their kin in the motherland.

Ireland

Ireland had been a constituent part of the United Kingdom since 1801, so Britain's declaration of war against Germany bound the country to fight. But attempts by Asquith's government in 1912 to introduce 'Home Rule' had divided Ireland down the middle and by 1914 had brought it to the brink of civil war. Protestants in Ulster resisted Home Rule at all costs, fearful of subjugation to the nationalist majority based in Dublin; they armed themselves as the Ulster Volunteer Force (UVF) to resist any moves to weaken ties with Britain. Elsewhere in Ireland, nationalists created their own armed units. The Home Rule Bill passed

Parliament in London weeks after the declaration of war, but was suspended until peace came. The UVF found it easier than the rest of Ireland to respond to the coming of war. In loyalty to the Crown, it volunteered, virtually to a man, to join Kitchener's New Army, mostly in the 36th (Ulster) Division. Irish nationalists in the south were encouraged by their leader, John Redmond, to join the Irish regiments in the British Army, since he wished to show support for a British government that was going to grant Home Rule once the fighting had finished. But more militant nationalists wanted nothing to do with what they regarded as a purely British affair against Germany, demanding instead immediate and total independence rather than the more limited form of self government offered by Home Rule.

Given the deteriorating position within Ireland, London never felt able to bring in conscription; nevertheless, some 200,000 Irishmen had volunteered for war service by the end of the war, of whom 30,000 were to be killed. Irish public schools figured prominently, above all amongst the officers. Although HMC listed only one Irish member in 1914, Campbell College in Belfast, several others had been HMC members, including St Columba's (1872), Bangor GS (1875) and Royal Belfast Academical Institution (1909), but had given up their membership.

Blackrock College in Dublin was still referred to in 1914 as the 'French College' and had 282 students in the Christmas term of 1914. The French priests who served as the teachers were said to be tolerant, 'admiring even', of the republican sympathies of current and former pupils. Many boys felt it their duty to go off to fight, inspired by Redmond's vision of Home Rule. The school is unsure exactly how many old boys fought in the British forces, but it is known that at least fifty-one, mostly officers, lost their lives. Those serving and the fallen were prayed for at evening prayers by staff and students each night, a practice that continued for many years after the war. But such were the ambiguities of the school's position that there was no memorial set up for those who died, and the sympathies of current pupils turned increasingly republican as the war went on. Building progress on the new concert hall slowed during the war, and the boys took to using the foundations as trenches, fighting mock battles against the Germans. After the Easter 1916 uprising, 'It was noted that the boys playing at war in the trenches were now fighting the British instead of the Germans.' Two old boys working in Germany before the war were interned as enemy aliens, but were recruited by Roger Casement for the rebellion he was planning against the British in early 1916. While several old boys were indeed to be prominent in the uprising, three being sentenced to death, another old boy, William Connelly, was the British officer who received the surrender of one of the rebels, Sean Heuston. Notes jotted in exercise books and on the flyleaves of textbooks, now residing in the school's archive, reveal that many boys were thrilled with the idea of the British taking a beating, while others show relief that the insurgents had finally surrendered. A minority were merely excited at being so close to major events – like 'the Dardanelles!' wrote one.[2]

Other Dublin schools had different affiliations. St Columba's had been founded in 1843 by the Revd William Sewell, four years before he founded Radley in Oxfordshire. Affiliated to the Church of Ireland, it boasted eighty boarders in 1914. Clongowes Wood, a Jesuit school just outside the city, had been founded in 1814 and numbered James Joyce amongst its alumni. It educated the children of middle-class Catholic professional families and had 268 boarders in 1914.[3] Tom Kettle, an old boy, epitomized the moral predicament of the Irish. A leading figure in the nationalist movement and an MP at Westminster, he had joined the Irish Volunteers in 1913 in anger at unionist opposition to Home Rule, and found himself in Europe buying arms for the nationalist cause when war broke out. He sped back to Dublin, volunteering to fight and being commissioned in the Royal Dublin Fusiliers.[4] Like many who had attended Clongowes, St Columba's or Blackrock, he believed he was fighting above all for his country Ireland against a common enemy.[5] The Easter Rising in 1916 provoked further conflicts of loyalty. Michael O'Rahilly (Clongowes), who always called himself 'The O'Rahilly', spoke out against the Rising, describing it as 'madness, but glorious madness'; he fought with his fellow republicans at the General Post Office in Dublin, and was killed while trying to evacuate the survivors. A proposed war memorial to Old Clongownians killed in the Great War proved too controversial to build, while the *Clongownian Magazine* in 1966 completely ignored the fiftieth anniversary of the Easter Rising.[6]

Life was much less complex for the Protestant schools of the north. Campbell College in Belfast had been founded only in 1894. The school had 155 pupils in 1914, mostly boarders, an OTC since 1909 and strong links to Ulster's commercial communities. RBAI, founded in 1810, and Methodist College Belfast, 1865, also served the professional and business classes of the city.[7]

These schools were not immune from the mounting turbulence. Minutes of RBAI's alumni association reveal poor attendance, blamed on old boys choosing to attend UVF training sessions. One of them, James Davidson, an old boy of both RBAI and Campbell, enrolled in the UVF in 1913, and in September 1914 was commissioned into the 13th Battalion, Royal Irish Rifles, part of the 36th (Ulster) Division.[8] Captain W. E. Wylie, an old boy of another Ulster public school,

Coleraine Academical Institution, and a King's Counsel, fought with British soldiers in Dublin against the republicans, arrested many republican leaders, including John McBride and Thomas MacDonagh, and then acted as Crown Prosecutor in the controversial courts martial that followed.[9]

The longer the war went on, the more deeply it polarized opinion in north and south. The bitterness can be heard in the speech of RBAI's chair of governors at prize day in November 1916, heavily critical as he was of republican resistance to conscription: 'That Ireland persisted in declining to join in taking her full share with the Irishmen who had volunteered and with her fellow citizens in England, Scotland and Wales was indeed a dark black spot that would tarnish her history ... In future it would tend to divide more bitterly than ever the people of Ireland'.[10] These words were spoken as the Somme was ending.

The losses that Ulster was to suffer there, at a time when some fellow countrymen were seen to be distracting British forces by rebelling in the south, caused enduring bitterness. The 36th (Ulster) Division launched its attack on 1 July from Thiepval Wood towards the Schwaben Redoubt, a known German strongpoint. While initial waves penetrated the German front line, succeeding attacks suffered from flanking machine guns and heavy German artillery barrages. By dusk on 2 July the division had suffered over 5,000 casualties. The news plunged the whole of Ulster into mourning. RBAI alone lost fifteen old boys. 'The great Somme offensive has brought Ulster and our people much honour and glory, but alas! Unspeakable sadness', wrote the editor of the *RBAI School News*, 'and as a school we have had since that date to mourn the loss of many a gallant boy.'[11]

Among the fallen were two pairs of brothers, the Hewitts and Hollywoods. 'Your little lad Willy led his platoon over the parapet, and the last I saw of him was his happy smile as I wished him luck', wrote Willy Hewitt's commanding officer to his father. 'They got across to the German trenches in front of which they came under an appalling machine gun fire. Your lad was hit and Sergeant Lally, who is now in hospital wounded, was with him when he passed over.'[12] James Davidson (Campbell College) was one of the officers who led his men up to the third German line on 1 July, where he established a defensive emplacement. By mid-morning, though wounded in the leg, he was still holding out with a Lewis gun and a few bombs. A message was sent back to the British lines to say, 'being pressed on all sides and ammunition almost finished'. Realizing the position was hopeless, Davidson tried to lead his men back to their own lines, across the German trenches so recently captured. Almost home, he was shot in the head in No-Man's-Land.[13]

Public schoolboys from the south also fought on the Somme, many of them in the 16th (Irish) Division, which arrived in the region only in late July. They were to see fighting principally in the areas around Ginchy and Guillemont in the first half of September, when 224 officers and over 4,000 men were killed. Lieutenant John Holland (Clongowes) had been seriously wounded at Ypres in June 1915, but returned to the front in July 1916 as bombing officer of 7th Battalion, The Leinster Regiment. He fought with extreme bravery on 3 September, successfully leading his bombers through the enemy barrage to clear out the German trenches, for which he was awarded the VC. One of his men later wrote to congratulate him: 'I was glad to read it in *The Times*. I remember your words that memorable day, 3 September 1916: "Boys – a Victoria Cross is to be won".'[14] He started that day with twenty-six men, and at the end of it just five were left alive.

Let us return to Tom Kettle, the old Clongownian and constitutional (as opposed to militant) nationalist. His first spell in the trenches in late 1915 resulted in the breakdown of his already fragile health, so he found himself in Dublin for the fateful days of Easter 1916. The militancy of the nationalists was heartbreaking to him: 'He used to say bitterly that they had spoiled it all – spoiled his dream of a free united Ireland in a free Europe.' But he was equally revolted by the British treatment of the rebels: 'What really seared his heart was the fearful retribution that fell on the leaders of the rebellion.'[15] He had seen enough, and though his physique was barely equal to the task, he insisted on going back to the front, and to the Somme. Assigned to take part in the battle for Ginchy, he was to be one of the many casualties that day, killed on 9 September while leading his men over the top. In a last letter to his brother he wrote: 'The bombardment, destruction and bloodshed are beyond all imagination, nor did I ever think the valour of simple men could be quite as beautiful as that of my Dublin Fusiliers. I have had two chances of leaving them – one on sick leave and one to take a staff job. I have chosen to stay with my comrades. I am calm and happy but desperately anxious to live. The big guns are coughing and smacking their shells, which sound for all the world like overhead express trains ... Somewhere the Choosers of the Slain are touching, as in our Norse story they used to touch, with invisible wands those who are to die.'[16]

On Kettle's memorial bust in Saint Stephen's Green, Dublin, are lines he wrote to his baby daughter Betty before leaving for France that last time: 'So here, while the mad guns curse overhead,/And tired men sigh, with mud for couch and floor,/Know that we fools, now with the foolish

70

dead,/Died not for the flag, nor King, nor Emperor,/But for a dream, born in a herdsman's shed,/And for the secret Scripture of the poor.'[17]

Willie Redmond was another moderate Irish nationalist who had volunteered to fight. Like Kettle, he had been educated at Clongowes Wood and had been a Westminster MP since the 1880s. He volunteered in 1914, even though he was in his fifties, in the hope that this would further the implementation of Home Rule. He served with the 6th Battalion, Royal Irish Regiment at the front from 1915, and, even after the Easter Rising had shattered his hopes of peaceful constitutional change, he could still write to his friend Sir Arthur Conan Doyle in December 1916 about Ireland: 'It would be a fine memorial to the men who have died so splendidly if we could, over their graves, build up a bridge between the North and South.'[18] In his last parliamentary speech in March 1917 he appealed to the government to implement Home Rule, concluding: 'We here who are about to die, perhaps, ask you ... to make our country happy and contented, to enable us, when we meet the Canadians and Australians and New Zealanders side by side in the common cause to say to them: "our country, just as yours, has self-government within the Empire".'[19] The speech summarized all that he had tried to achieve in his life and what he hoped might be helped by his death. On 9 June 1917, taking part in the great assault on Messines by the 16th Irish Division, he was wounded in the arm and leg and died in the casualty clearing station. With him and Thomas Kettle died also the hopes of moderate Irish nationalism.

Australia and New Zealand

When war was declared in August 1914, Andrew Fisher, Australia's Labour Prime Minister, declared that, 'Australia will stand behind the mother country to help defend her to our last man.' After the initial flood of volunteering enthusiasm slackened, the government tried to introduce conscription, but it was rejected twice in national referenda amidst fierce political opposition. Nevertheless, the country sent 330,000 volunteers to fight, of whom 58,000 were to be killed. New Zealand entered the war with equal alacrity, benefiting from compulsory military service for home defence. The country was vigorous in support of the war, and even when compulsory military service was extended to fighting overseas, there was little political opposition. This small country contributed 128,000 servicemen who fought overseas, of whom 17,000 were killed. The joint contributions of Australia and New Zealand were to prove vital. A Geelong Grammar School old boy wrote from England in 1916: 'It must often be asked how it is that England has been able to find amateur officers for an army of a million. I think the public schools and universities are responsible for training them. Here a man is inspired by the spirit that fits him for leadership. He falls into his place as naturally on the battlefield as he does on the football ground.'[20]

Australia's oldest public schools date back to the nineteenth century. King's School Parramatta near Sydney was founded in 1831 by an old boy of King's School, Canterbury, to provide an Anglican education for future leaders of New South Wales. Its aim, according to a prospectus on the eve of the Great War, was 'to develop the nature of the boys on every side, mentally, physically and in the weightier matters of manliness, public spirit and character'.[21] It was followed by similar schools in the other Australian states, reflecting the different ecclesiastical backgrounds of their founders. In Melbourne, Scotch College (1851), Melbourne Church of England Grammar School (1858) and Wesley College (1866) were founded to educate the elite of Victoria. With others like Geelong Grammar School (1855) and Sydney Grammar School (1854), this public school sector grew rapidly – Sydney GS had 571 boys by 1914, large in comparison with many British public schools of the time.[22]

Most of the officers in the Australian Imperial Force (AIF) did have a public school background, it being taken for granted that schools like these would provide the bulk of the leadership.[23] One old boy of Sydney Church of England Grammar School, usually known as Shore, wrote from France in 1917: 'Battalion commanders in seeking new officers have recognized the value of the boys the GPS (Great Public Schools) turn out ... The boy who has learned, as he must learn at Shore, that he who gives most gets most, who has learned to be responsible for others, who will think of his men's safety and comfort first and his own last, is going to make the good officer'.[24]

In Melbourne many public school volunteers found themselves in the Public Schools Company of the Fifth Infantry Battalion, where, according to one, 'there were no lines drawn between the different schools – they were all F Company men and proud to be so'.[25] The eager young volunteers from Australia and New Zealand imagined, when they left their shores in late autumn of 1914, that they were bound for the Western Front. But the entry of Turkey into the war in 1915 and the consequent need to defend the Suez Canal saw them diverted to Egypt, where they were brought together as the Australia and New Zealand Army Corps (Anzacs).

In New Zealand, Christ's College was the epitome of the English-style public school. Founded in 1850 for early settler children, with a

72

chapel built in 1867, it had a strong house system, rugby, a cadet corps (founded in 1881), and by 1914 had grown to 302 boys.[26] The school eagerly participated in a scheme of compulsory military training in 1909, with the result that some 300 old boys joined up early on. A photograph in Christ College's *Register* for December 1914 shows forty-one old boys who were serving in the New Zealand Expeditionary Force (NZEF), nineteen of whom were to be killed.[27]

The date of 25 April 1915 is forever engraved into the national psyches of Australia and New Zealand. Early that morning, their troops began landing at Anzac Cove; put ashore by the Royal Navy not at the planned locations, these raw troops had to claw their way up steep cliffs in the face of fierce Turkish fire. They eventually dug themselves in along a tortured landscape with names to become famous, such as Lone Pine, the Nek and Courtney's Post, named after an Old Melburnian, Lieutenant Colonel Richard Courtney, whose battalion took it on 27 April.[28] In that first week the Anzacs suffered over 8,000 casualties, including 2,300 dead. Yet they clung on to the small foothold they had gained, under constant shelling, sniping and machine gun fire, in the savage heat of the sun, amidst the stench of decaying corpses and the relentless assault of flies. Lieutenant Muir Smith (Shore, Sydney) was one of those killed on that opening day. One of his friends wrote to Smith's father: 'In the morning we got a great bag of Turks; during the afternoon we made two bayonet charges. [Your son] was one of the finest chaps I have ever met and a great pal of mine; he was hit in the leg but still hung on, but when leading a party to capture a machine gun, he was shot just behind me.'[29]

The long sea journey from Australia, and the time they spent together in Egypt, had brought together the young men from the various schools and forged strong friendships. Geoffrey Hall, from Scotch College in Melbourne, wrote to tell his parents about the help he had received in battle from old boys of Melbourne Grammar and Geelong after he had been wounded. Hall's father was so moved that he wrote to the head-master of Melbourne Grammar: 'It shows that our public schoolboys, though keen to fight each other in their battles on the football field, yet in the common cause of fighting for liberty are capable of showing that humanity and heroism are prominent features all over the British Empire of public schoolboy life.'[30]

'Nulla' Roberts was one of the more remarkable of the Anzac soldiers. Nearly fifty, and one of the oldest King's Parramatta men to fight, he had faithfully attended every school function since he left the school. Allocated the job of camp orderly, he had protested to the colonel that, 'If there was a scrap, he wanted to be in it.' He had his way, and was allowed into the front line. 'Nulla was having a sniping duel with a Turk at about 40 yards', an old boy of the school wrote, 'when he was struck in the head by a bullet from an angle ... What an example his life was to fellows at the school'.[31]

Private George Grimwade (Melbourne Grammar) was studying to become a doctor. Whilst serving in a field ambulance, he was killed by a shell on 23 September. A letter home to his parents described how, 'your son was brought in on a stretcher and died within two minutes. We buried him the same evening. Grammar boys dug his grave, for they would not allow anyone else to do so. He lies in Shrapnel Valley.'[32] The beautiful cemetery in which his body lies stands on the Lone Pine Plateau overlooking the sea. His grave attracts visitors today because leaning against the back of his gravestone is a darker piece of masonry inscribed with the words, 'This stone from the home of George R. Grimwade, Melbourne, Australia, was brought and placed here by his parents, April 1922.'[33] The emotions involved in such a long journey of pilgrimage so soon after the war can only be guessed at.

The losses of old boys from Christ's College were particularly severe. *The Times* carried these words from one, Noel Ross, wounded at Gallipoli: 'Twelve thousand miles away in New Zealand there is a slate-roofed, ivy-covered College Chapel where almost a year ago every seat in chancel or nave was occupied by past and present boys ... These men were on the eve of departure, volunteers going without question to succour a land most of them had never seen. Not a year has elapsed, and many of those present that evening are lying in nameless graves among the dwarf oaks of Gallipoli'.[34] A letter in the school's *Register* from J. D. Boys, written while recuperating in hospital, recorded: 'Every now and again you get a good clear shot at the Turk – when you promptly pot him if you're lucky. I think I can safely say I bowled over twelve at least, and I think several others, so I kept up the average.'[35] This depersonalization of the adversary, and the comparison of war to hunting, was more in tune with the hardier, fearless, even reckless mentality of the Anzacs than their British counterparts.

Few did more to build up the hardened 'digger' image of the Anzac soldier than Charles Bean, who had attended Clifton in Bristol before moving back to Australia to teach at Sydney Grammar School. In September 1914 he was appointed an official correspondent to the Australian forces, and after the war became Australia's official war historian. He wrote, 'The big thing in the war for Australia was the discovery of the character of Australian men. It was character which rushed the hills of Gallipoli and held on there.'[36] Of the role of the public schools in the Great War he later wrote: 'It is not unnatural that leaders, looking to the morale of their cherished units, should choose, as officers, boys from the schools that fostered the Arnold tradition in Australia.'[37]

Gallipoli remains the iconic campaign for both Australia and New Zealand, yet it accounted for only some twenty per cent of their casualties. The bulk of the rest came on the Western Front, to which the Anzacs began to be transferred after their withdrawal from Gallipoli at the end of 1915. One was Lieutenant Alec Raws, from Prince Alfred College in Adelaide, who came to the terrible fighting round Pozieres on the Somme in late July 1916. On 28 July his brother was killed nearby, and in a letter home on 4 August Raws wrote: 'One feels that on a battlefield such as this that one can never survive. For the horror one sees and the never-ending shock of the shells is more than can be borne. The Gallipoli veterans say that the peninsula was a picnic to this push. My battalion has been in it for eight days and one-third of it is left – all shattered at that ... My tunic is rotten with other men's blood and partly spattered with a comrade's brains'.[38] Raws was killed by a shell two weeks later.

Three Australian headmasters volunteered to fight in 1916. The Revd P. S. Waddy of King's Parramatta asked his council for leave of absence as an army chaplain. The governors refused, and he resigned his post. In September 1916 one of his old boys wrote: 'Who should come down into my dugout yesterday but Padre Waddy looking as fit as a fiddle and with a lot to tell me about the old School. We still follow the old School's doing out here, and it is fine when we can get hold of the school magazine.'[39] Harold Sloman was headmaster of Sydney Grammar, and he announced his decision to go at a Big School assembly in June 1916, telling his boys that he 'hoped he would not be away for long'. As the school magazine recorded, 'All present felt the deep solemnity of this unique occasion.'[40] Awarded an MC, but wounded in August 1917 in the early stage of Third Ypres, he spent three months recovering in hospital. On his return to the school in 1919 to a great welcome, he declared: 'The ultimate war memorial was not going to be put on the walls, it was going to be the continued sending-out of generations of Grammar boys of the same stamp and imbued with the same spirit as the Old Boys who had served.'[41]

The Revd William McClemans was founder headmaster of one of Australia's newest public schools, Christ Church in Perth (1910). Only twenty Christ Church boys were old enough to fight in the war. McClemans believed it was his duty to join up, and duly enlisted as a military chaplain. The six months he spent on the Western Front, in hospitals and casualty clearing stations, took their toll.[42] The carnage

75

confronted him with 'some of the most painful scenes of the battlefield', as he wrote back to the school, and on some days he had to bury as many as 200 young men.[43] By 1917 it had all but destroyed him, physically and spiritually. After his return he remained haunted by his experiences. He turned to alcohol, as many did, and in 1922 he was obliged to resign as headmaster, a broken man.

News of the deaths of old boys arrived regularly at Christ's College in New Zealand. *The Register* recorded the procedure when news arrived: 'During the morning service in Chapel, the name of the Old Boy is read out. After the service the school files out to a position facing the Big School. The Head Prefect hoists the flag to the masthead, while the School stands to attention and the bugler sounds the Last Post.'[44] Chaplain at Christ's College when war broke out was Guy Bryan-Brown (Tonbridge and former teacher at Glenalmond). He increasingly felt the need to be at the front, eventually securing release from the school and landing in May 1917 as Chaplain to the NZEF. His bravery and compassion rapidly made a big impression on the troops, but his sojourn in the trenches was not to last long. A fellow officer described how Bryan-Brown found himself caught in the open, near Passchendaele, while tending to the wounded: 'He was unafraid through a fierce bombardment and devoted to the fellows outside, for whom there was no floor space in the aid post. Three shells came in quick succession and I saw him fall ... I do not need to tell you he was simply idolized by the men'. A stained glass window was created in his memory in the chapel at Christ's College.[45]

The Australian and New Zealand public schools suffered heavily during the war. Among those surveyed, the highest casualty rate was at Geelong Grammar, where twenty-one per cent of the 444 boys who enlisted were killed. At Christ's College 132 of the 661 enlisted were killed, some twenty per cent. Total Australian battle casualties at fourteen per cent of those who fought are higher than the British figure of twelve per cent. Commanding the ANZACs in the latter stages of the war was Lieutenant General Sir John Monash (Scotch College), later described by Field Marshal Montgomery as 'the best General on the Western Front'.[46] The Australia and New Zealand to which his troops returned after the war were never to be the same again, nor were the schools from which the men hailed.

Canada
'We stand shoulder to shoulder with Britain and the other British dominions in this quarrel', said Canadian Prime Minister Sir Robert Borden on the outbreak of war. Despite a pre-war army of only 3,000

men, a formidable effort went at once into creating the Canadian Expeditionary Force (CEF), resulting in over 400,000 men going overseas to Europe. The vast majority were volunteers, though Borden's government did manage, despite political divisions, to introduce conscription in 1917, too late to make much impact. The main fighting force within the CEF was the 'Canadian Corps', comprising four divisions by 1917. Like the Anzacs, the Canadians were 'hailed as natural soldiers ... instinctively aggressive, hardened by the wilderness and inspired with democratic spirit'.[47] In total, 51,000 Canadians were to die in the war. Newfoundland, a separate colony of the British Empire until it became part of Canada in 1949, contributed 12,000 men, of whom 1,000 were killed.[48]

The coming of war was greeted with enthusiastic expectation in the Canadian public schools. At Upper Canada College (UCC), founded in Toronto in 1829 and modelled on Eton, the magazine's Christmas editorial was one which could have appeared in countless school magazines across Britain: 'Canada our country is at war. What does that mean to Upper Canada College, and what are we, who pride ourselves justly on being the premier school of Canada, doing in the matter? ... Those old boys [who] have gone to the Front because they realized their King and country needed them, and because they had determined to give their life blood'.[49] UCC, though small by English or Australian standards, with only 180 boys in its upper school in 1914, saw 1,089 old boys enlist, of whom 176 were to be killed. Trinity College School (TCS) in Port Hope, Ontario, founded in 1865, was a similar institution, with 86 boys in 1914, almost all boarders. Both schools had cadet corps founded in the 1860s, and they had similar military traditions. TCS saw 596 of its old boys volunteer for service, an incredible ninety per cent of all those who left in the twenty years before 1915, of whom 123 were to be killed.[50] Lakefield College School (LCS) was founded in 1879, and had forty boarders in 1914. The school was spartan, with regular hiking trips into the wilderness and time spent in very basic huts. The principal accommodation had no indoor plumbing, and boys took cold baths each morning in tin tubs. Of the 122 of its boys who served in the war, 20 were to be killed. All these Canadian schools thus had casualty rates very similar to their British counterparts, and considerably in excess of the overall ratio of Canadian deaths in the war.[51] Ridley College, also in Ontario, was founded in 1889. Some 400 old boys fought in the war, of whom 61 were to be killed.[52] Old boys from Ridley were among the pilots training for the front. They antagonized the head but delighted the current boys when they swooped low over Ridley's campus, narrowly missing the roofs. A line was drawn, however, when oil from a plane flown by an old boy splashed a baby in a pram in school grounds.[53]

Old boys of UCC flocked to join up from across the world. From Herschel Island came a Royal Northwest Mounted Policeman, and from even further north the explorer J. R. Cox responded to the call to arms, having heard about the war only a year after it started. One of the earliest to reach the Western Front was Gordon Grahame, a master at Lakefield College, who wrote to the headmaster, Alick Mackenzie, in April 1915: 'We had a most impressive Easter service in a field today . . . I hope that by the next big church day, Christmas, I shall be back home in my own Canada again. All my dreams are of Canada and Lakefield. I long for my canoe, the boys and the school.'[54] Fred Anderson and Vince Crombie similarly wrote to Mackenzie, in February 1916, to confess that although they had not been the best of old boys, they 'have never forgotten those happy days we each had in our turn under your supervision'. They were both to die later in the war, Crombie just two weeks before the Armistice.[55]

The first day of July brought particular tragedy to the small colony of Newfoundland. Young men had joined from across the rugged north-eastern territory, proud to be fighting in their own Newfoundland Battalion. Assigned to attack in the second wave at Beaumont Hamel, they became mired in the confusion and mayhem of the early minutes of the battle. Because of congestion in the communication trenches linking their own positions to their front line, they clambered out on top to position themselves for their assault, not realizing they had become visible to German machine gunners. Many were mown down before they even reached the British front line. 'The only visible sign that the men knew they were under this terrific fire was that they all instinctively tucked their chins into an advanced shoulder as if in a Newfoundland blizzard,' wrote one observer of the catastrophe unfolding before his eyes.[56] Of the 780 Newfoundlanders who went into battle that day, only 68 answered the roll call that evening: 255 were killed, the rest were casualties. Four of the officers killed came from the same well known Newfoundland Ayre family – two brothers, Eric and Bernard, who had been educated at Methodist College, St John's, before being sent to The Leys in Cambridge, and their cousins Wilfred (The Leys) and Gerald (Rossall). One British soldier later recalled the horror of the scene: 'On came the Newfoundlanders, but the fire intensified and they were wiped out in front of my eyes.'[57]

Newfoundland was never to recover fully from the shock of that day. As the Somme ground on, the casualty toll began to rise across Canada. Frederick Daw from TCS, who had survived Gallipoli, and whose brother Herbert had been killed in the Ypres Salient six months before, was killed in October. The shock of the casualty lists in the newspapers in Montreal, Toronto, Winnipeg, Vancouver and across the entire country brought the same dawning realization of the scale of loss as in Britain. Alick Mackenzie received a letter from another Lakefield master during the Somme, saying: 'The school is holding its end up. The more I see of this life, the more I wish all officers were of our Canadian boarding school type.'[58]

The Canadian Corps enjoyed its greatest success in the assault on Vimy Ridge on 9 April 1917, which transformed Canada's identity as a nation in a similar way that Gallipoli did for Australia and New Zealand. Vimy Ridge, familiar to all who travel on the *autoroute* from the Channel ports to Paris and beyond, is a high piece of ground just to the north of Arras. The Germans had held the ridge since 1915, when some 150,000 men were killed fighting for its high ground. The British took over the line overlooked by the ridge in 1916.

Haig insisted that the ridge be captured in early 1917, the task being given to the Canadians. General Sir Julian Byng (Eton) took over command of the Canadian Corps in May 1916. A thinker, he leant heavily on the analysis of Arthur Currie, Commander of the 1st Canadian Division, who had studied carefully the experience of the French army during the Battle of Verdun. They also determined that this attack had to learn from the failed British offensives of 1915 and 1916. Twelve tunnels were dug deep into the ground, from well behind the Allied lines and out of German sight, running right up to the front line. These allowed the safe transport forward of troops, ammunition and stores, and included large shelters for up to 24,000 men, who were able to wait in safety close to the German front line. A small hospital capable of full-scale surgery was built, as were prefabricated light railways to assist the speedy movement of supplies. Mines were then dug under the German trenches along the front of the ridge, ready to be detonated at the moment of attack. The planning process included a replica of the entire area, with soldiers being shown the lie of the land and rehearsing their exact roles. The artillery plan was refined to ensure that a 'creeping barrage' of falling shells would continue just ahead of the advancing troops, who were trained in what became known as the 'Vimy glide', a rate of advance with a particular walking gait that ensured a predictable movement of 100 yards every three minutes. The Royal Flying Corps was also to be deployed with great effect, denying the Germans control of the air for reconnaissance. The Allies' preliminary bombardment lasted a week, over 150,000 shells being fired each day, concentrated on carefully designated specific targets.

When the Canadians began their attack that Easter Monday, all this preparation meant that it took just two hours for most of the ridge to fall into their hands. The final objective, the highest point on the ridge itself, fell on 12 April.[59] Of the force of 100,000 soldiers who took part in the assault, under 10,000 became casualties. The cost to the schools was nevertheless considerable. Walter Curry (UCC) had been immensely proud to go overseas in October 1914. He had survived severe fighting in the Ypres Salient in 1915, but was one of the many casualties on that first day. Even in the face of so much death, the spirit of the Canadians remained high. One man who had both his legs shot off was seen trying to lever himself forward with his rifle, as if 'he was sitting in a canoe trying to paddle with his gun'.[60] Today, young Canadian students, some from Ridley and other public schools, proud of their heritage, come over each year to staff the national park at Vimy Ridge and explain the battle to visitors.

Canadian troops remained to the end in the most intense of the fighting, and their public school officers increasingly fraternized with their opposite numbers from Britain, with mixed results. 'I am completely surrounded by young men from Eton, Harrow and Rugby, most of whom are having their first taste of the army and almost drive me to distraction', wrote Captain Lampman (Lakefield). 'There are about ten Canadians here and we are looked on as some kind of curios, generally referred to as "Canada" or "Here come the dominions".'[61] Their pride in their schools remained undiminished. The Revd C. H. Brent wrote to his former headmaster in September 1918: 'My mind has gone out to Trinity College School tonight with undying loyalty and affection ... Tell your boys that an old boy sends them greetings from the battlefield of France. All that is best in me came from the influence of the school which, next to my dear mother, was the strongest factor in my early life'.[62]

South Africa

South Africa had been the location of the Boer War (1899–1902), in which old boys from British public schools had fought, many never to return. Dominion status was achieved as the 'Union of South Africa' in 1910. Though wounds were still raw from the Boer War, and the government was led by former Boer general Louis Botha, the country nevertheless declared war alongside Britain. The recent history made conscription for overseas service politically impossible, and troop numbers who went off to fight in Europe were smaller than from Canada and Australia. Many South Africans fought, however, in the campaigns in Africa and the Middle East, which accounted for the deaths of 3,000 South Africans, compared to the 4,000 men who died in France.

Public schools grew up in several South African provinces, most bound together by a common Anglican thread. Among the first was Diocesan College in Cape Town, founded in 1849 by the first Anglican Bishop, and commonly known as 'Bishop's'. Henry White, the first headmaster, had been a boy at Winchester, and he planted Latin and Greek at the heart of the curriculum. It acted as a university until 1910, when the University of Cape Town split off from it. Bishop's' model of boarding houses, cadet corps and sports was followed by many other schools, notably St Andrew's, Grahamstown (1855), in the Eastern Cape, and Hilton (1872) and Michaelhouse (1896) in Natal. The last was not atypical in lacking electricity before the war broke out; boys went to bed with candles, and the sanitary arrangements were primitive for all. When Anthony Brown was appointed headmaster in 1910 from Uppingham, he applauded the 'active manliness' of the boys, but 'felt these qualities were not compatible with scholarly habits'.[63]

Hilton was not unusual in being split down the middle by the Boer War: as the school history records, 'Boys left Hilton to join the forces, both British and Boer, and Hiltonians died on both sides.'[64] Those leaving to fight for the Boers were reportedly given as rousing a send-off as those who left to fight for the British. Three Hiltonians served in the British forces until the relief of Ladysmith in 1900, and were allowed to wear their medal ribbons on cadet parade on their return to school. By contrast, Louis Esselen, who had been at Bishop's, served as an ADC to the Boers' Commander-in-Chief, Louis Botha. St John's College in Johannesburg, founded in 1898, was forced to close the next year because of its vulnerable position in the heart of the Boer republic of Transvaal; it re-opened after the war and came under the care of the Anglo-Catholic Community of the Resurrection.

Sentiments expressed in school magazines and speeches on the outbreak of war eerily echoed the words uttered in Britain 5,000 miles to the north. 'We are all convinced that war was Britain's only course and that sooner or later our gallant army or navy must win', declared the school magazine at Bishop's.[65] The editor of the *Michaelhouse Chronicle* called on old boys to 'give their manhood in their country's behalf, without bluster, without flag-wagging, but with cool heads, quiet tongues and nerves of steel'.[66]

The existence of a German colony, South West Africa, on South Africa's borders brought an immediate threat. Prime Minister Botha, now a Bishop's parent and helped by Louis Esselen as his adjutant, conducted a swift and successful operation against German SW Africa and also crushed a more local Boer insurrection, known as the Maritz Rebellion, against involvement in Britain's war. The headmaster of Hilton took the salute of many of his old boys in the ranks of the Natal Carbineers, as they departed for the SW Africa campaign: 'As man after man broke from the ranks and rode up to say goodbye, it was a proud moment because I knew they were saluting their school.'[67] This was followed by a much longer campaign against German East Africa, which cost many British and South African lives, often from disease. Twenty St Andrew's boys died in East Africa, compared with eighty on the Western Front.

Public schools had also been established in the new colony of Rhodesia. St George's, founded by Jesuit Father Marc Barthelemy in 1896, was very much in the mould of Bishop's and St Andrew's. The school roll was 130 in 1914, but 190 old boys were to fight in the war, of whom 26 were to die. They fought in the gruelling campaigns in South West and German East Africa and on the Western Front as part of the South African Brigade. Lieutenant Hugh Baird, an old boy, wrote in 1918: 'The old school have done wonderfully well for the Empire. I often wish God had spared Fr Barthelemy to see how well its boys have answered the call.'[68]

It was only after South West Africa was subdued that Botha felt able to commit forces to the European campaigns. The South African Brigade duly reached Europe by sea in early 1916, commanded by Brigadier Tim Lukin, who had been at Merchant Taylors' School in the 1870s before serving in the 1879 Zulu War and many subsequent African campaigns. Though they were to see action in many theatres over the subsequent two and a half years, the South African story is much associated with a tiny area on the Somme battlefield, to become as symbolically important to South Africans as Gallipoli was to the Anzacs. The South African Brigade formed part of the 9th (Scottish) Division, which had successfully stormed the German second line on Longueval Ridge on 14 July. The South African troops were held back in reserve until the following day, when they were given orders to take and hold Delville Wood, as part of a larger offensive intended to secure the right flank on the Somme. The raw South African soldiers were sent into combat in what the military historian Liddell Hart described as 'the bloodiest battle hell of 1916'.[69]

The north-west corner of the wood was strongly held by German troops. Confusion reigned for much of the battle, with attack and counterattack, and South African troops suffered from sustained German artillery fire. On the third day of fighting, 18 July, an estimated 20,000 shells were fired on them in an area of less than one square mile, at a rate of up to seven explosions every second. Delville Wood became an inferno, the trees catching fire and burning fiercely despite a drenching rain storm. Units in battle were normally considered incapable of combat if casualties reached thirty per cent; they were then withdrawn. The South African Brigade suffered losses of up to eighty per cent, yet they managed to hold the wood until relieved on the afternoon of 20 July. When the brigade paraded before Lukin some days later, just three officers and 145 other ranks were present. One of his soldiers recalled that, 'When he took the salute, General Lukin uncovered his head and tears were running down his cheeks.'[70]

'The ghastly sights one saw were beyond description ... It was like a horrible nightmare', wrote H. M. Veale (Bishop's).[71] Private Egerton Bissett of St John's wrote to his mother, 'I don't know how it is that I am still alive. Out of my five messmates, I am the only one left. Poor Billy P was shot right through the heart ... He did not suffer, tell his poor mother'.[72] Victor Pattison (St Andrew's) took part in the attacks on 15 July and was found by his brother Charles, shot dead on the edge of a German trench. Charles' papers recorded his reactions: 'People talk of hell. "Well", said one lad, "if I had to take my pick, give me hell every time: they haven't got artillery there"'.[73]

One of the heroes of Delville Wood was Father Eustace Hill, a boy at Lancing College in the 1880s, a military chaplain in the Boer War and a master at St John's since 1905. Father Hill became a legend of gallantry in Delville Wood in those terrible July days, waving his surplice as a flag of truce to tend the wounded and the dead. In graphic letters back to his school he revealed 'the effect on flesh and blood of five hours' concentrated artillery ... St John's has given her bit. I buried Vernon Adams at Longueval; he died in an arm chair I collared. I carried him with a friend to a vast shell-hole in the garden ... We have a biggish list of men we don't know about, and until we clear the wood and get at our dead we shall not know'.[74] Twelve St John's boys went into Delville Wood on 15 July and only two came out unscathed; five were killed and five wounded.

Hill himself was wounded in November 1916 and lost his right arm. He returned to St John's and became its headmaster. Inside the War Memorial Chapel, finished in 1931, is a smaller side-chapel, the Delville Wood Memorial Chapel, where can be found Eustace Hill's MC, set into a crucifix he had made. Here too is one of only five Delville Wood crosses made from the wood of the original ravaged trees.

Ten St Andrew's boys were also to die in those five hellish days in Delville Wood, and four from Bishop's. The latter school was the fortunate beneficiary of scholarships endowed by Cecil Rhodes; of the scholars selected to attend Oxford between 1907 and 1914 four were to die in the war. One was Lieutenant Geoffrey Noaks, who died of wounds that August on the Somme. Another was Captain Reg Hands, son of the mayor of Cape Town, South African test cricketer and an England rugby international during his time at Oxford. In April 1918, while he was quartered in what he believed to be a secure position in a house safely behind his own lines, a chance gas shell exploded nearby. He died a few hours later in agony from the fumes.

Anthony Brown, headmaster of Michaelhouse, who had joined the school from Uppingham in 1910, worked hard to build up numbers to ninety-two by the outbreak of war. In a dilemma about whether to continue this work or go off to fight, he appealed to the Bishop of Natal for guidance. In August 1915 he was granted leave of absence. Commissioned into the Rifle Brigade, he was sitting on the parapet of a trench near Guillemont on the Somme in August 1916, directing improvements to the defences, when he was shot dead by a long-range sniper. He is the only known serving public school headmaster to be killed in the war. It fell to the Bishop, in England at the time, to cable the news to the school. Eight years later, when the school prepared its Stone of Memory, Brown's name was inscribed at its head.[75] Brown's selfless sacrifice was mirrored by many South African public schoolboys, whose casualty rates were considerably higher than their country's average, and equal to that of the public schools of Britain. At both St John's and Michaelhouse more than one in five of those who served were killed, and the proportion in the others was not very different.[76]

The 'manly ideal' was particularly strong throughout South Africa and its public schools, motivating both old boys and teachers to fight. One of the four Bishop's masters to enlist was the Revd Charles 'Oxo' Bull, described as 'priest, Cadet Corps Commander, mountaineer, a man amongst men'.[77] The numbers of teachers who joined up from the public schools meant that few were left behind to look after the young. Thirteen staff from St Andrew's went off to fight, two of whom were killed. In their place, former teachers were hauled out of retirement. Replacements had of course to be male. As one later headmaster at St Andrew's wrote, 'To have asked the ordinary South African school-boy to take kindly to the thought of being taught by a woman would have been to ask the impossible of his patriotism and nascent sense of manhood.'[78] It is to this subject, how the public schools in Britain managed to keep themselves running during the war, that we turn in the next chapter.

Chapter 4

School Life during the War

The war, with its casualties and deprivations, had impressed itself on school life from the moment hostilities began in August 1914. But the Somme's impact was transformative, and felt immediately from the summer term of 1916. It made the war far more real and serious for every schoolboy. Until then, if a boy did not have a father or brother at the front, it was possible for him to block the war out of his mind. But as a boy at Fettes recalled, 'In the first few days of this battle, nine recent members of the school were killed and, from then onwards, as a matter of course, the morning papers were opened first on the casualty lists.'[1] At Rossall in Lancashire another boy recalled how the atmosphere changed that summer: 'A hilarious party in the house to say farewell to a monitor, whose death we mourned within a week, and which took place within twenty-four hours of his setting foot in France.'[2]

Into the front line
In earlier British wars, schools across the country had not been in physical danger, bar the remote risk of foreign invasion. The First World War was different. Schools near coastal ports, like St Lawrence, Ramsgate, were at risk from shelling by enemy warships. Rossall boys could hear explosions out in the Irish Sea – German submarines attacking merchant shipping.[3] King William's School on the Isle of Man saw danger from those same submarines to boys and staff travelling to and from the mainland.[4]

Bombs falling from the sky, a new kind of warfare, posed the greater threat. Initially, this came from Zeppelins, then bombers, once aeroplane technology improved. Tragedy struck Trinity School in Croydon in October 1915 when a Zeppelin dropped its load on Croydon, killing fifty-nine people, including three brothers called Currie who were pupils at the school, and whose house suffered a direct hit.[5] Gresham's in Norfolk was flown over by Zeppelins at least thirty times, and a raid in January 1915 killed civilians in the town of Holt. In the absence of shelters at the school, a master suggested that in the event of further raids the boys should go out into the grounds and 'scatter'.[6] The proximity of the Rosyth dockyards in Edinburgh posed particular problems for the city's schools. In a raid on 2 April 1916 a Fettes boy recalled how, 'About twelve o'clock that night, we were roused with the warning that Zeppelins had crossed the coast. Looking out we could see searchlights crossing the sky and heard the rattle of naval anti-aircraft guns.'[7] Fettes escaped that night, but George Watson's was hit. At Lancing, the lights in its dramatically prominent chapel were switched off to deny a landmark to Zeppelins seeking out Portsmouth harbour further along the south coast.[8] London schools were under particular threat, especially those on the approach to the docks. Dulwich was hit by Gotha bombers in 1917. One City of London boy recalls taking shelter in a school cellar during a raid that December and singing to keep up spirits, with a bomb dropping just as the boys were singing the chorus of 'Clementine'.[9] High excitement was recorded by the boys at St Peter's York when searchlights picked out a Zeppelin which was subsequently hit by ground fire, the pupils surging out of their dormitories in their night clothes to watch the spectacle.[10] A similar destruction of a Zeppelin over Haileybury on 1 October 1916 provoked one young man to hyperbole: 'Those who saw the Zeppelin brought down in flaming ruin will never again need a reminder of the presence of the God of War. It was an emblem, that great red circle in the sky, of the star of Germany that shall soon lose its place in the heavens like Lucifer.'[11] Total war had arrived, and public schools were in the front line.

Death at school

Death at school was much more common a hundred years ago: school registers record losses in most academic years, from accident or illness. R. F. Bourne (Haileybury) fell into the former category when in the summer of 1915 he died after a blow from a cricket ball in 'house nets'. Just a month later, his brother was to die at the Dardanelles.[12] One of the worst outbreaks of disease during the war was at St John's Leatherhead, where a measles epidemic left six boys dead. 'The loss affected the school more, I think,' wrote one boy, 'than the ever growing list of casualties in the fighting.'[13] The influenza epidemic of 1918–19 hit many public schools. At Malvern a boy and two masters died, despite the War Office sending an RAMC doctor down to the school.[14] At Ardingly in Sussex a master and a maid died from it, but no boys,[15] while at Harrow a fourteen-year-old died just ten days before the Armistice.[16] Wellington was badly affected, with 450 pupils suffering and all the dormitories turned into sick bays. The nearby village of Crowthorne rallied round, and volunteers came up to the school to help. The Master himself was very ill, and though no boys died, a nurse and a maid were not so fortunate.[17]

In the early months of the war funerals of dead soldiers were held at schools, before the order in 1915 that no more bodies were to be repatriated to Britain. One such funeral was that of Lieutenant Vernon Austin (of the car family, and a former scholar at King's Canterbury), killed at La Bassée in January 1915; it was held at Canterbury in the presence of the headmaster and almost the entire school community, with the OTC providing a guard of honour.[18] Full military ceremonial could even be extended to cadets. Wellington School in Somerset held a military burial on the instructions of the headmaster, George Corner, when a thirteen-year-old member of the OTC died in 1915. His coffin was draped with the school flag and carried by his friends to the cemetery, where the school rifles fired a salute and the Last Post was played.[19]

Boys reacted in different ways to the regular news of death from the front. Younger boys seem to have been less directly affected, and older ones responded to the relentless bad news in a whole variety of ways. The popular novelist Nevil Shute (Shrewsbury) said in his auto-biography that he had no expectation of the future except to go into the army and probably get killed. He wrote about his reaction to hearing about old boys killed in battle: 'We knelt praying for their souls in chapel, knowing ... in a year or so, the little boys in our houses would be kneeling for us'.[20] George Lowndes, a boy at Marlborough, recalled that, 'It was uncanny to look across chapel during the Sunday evening service to the back row opposite and realize that within six months, half the boys would be dead.'[21] At Eton a list of the dead was kept in a glass case on the outside wall of College Chapel. 'We watched the list grow', recalled one Etonian, 'and wondered, not morbidly nor yet enthusiastically – just in a detached way – whether ours would be there one day and whether it would have a little Victoria Cross printed beside.'[22] At Cranleigh in Surrey photographs of the fallen were hung in the chapel corridor, and the Last Post was sounded every evening. Each death was presented to Cranleighians 'as an inspiring example of the public school ideal reaching its apotheosis'.[23]

Some boys were blasé, or recalled that they were blasé, making out that they were indifferent to the war and its losses. A boy at the City of London School said, 'English boys do not talk of death, and we never discussed the names which were read out each week from the platform in Hall.'[24] Rupert Croft-Cooke, a fourteen-year-old at Tonbridge, wrote, 'I cannot pretend the war had much meaning for me.'[25] When Second Lieutenant Albert Harris of Chigwell School in Essex was killed on the Somme, his younger brother, who was still at the school, wrote in his diary: 'Rice pudding today, but Bert was killed.'[26] Many boys coped by filling their minds with present activities and concerns, and tried to dismiss worries and grief to the perimeter of their minds. A historian of Winchester believed that the war did not affect most schoolboys 'at least until one was within a year of leaving school', when the inevitability of their own participation became inescapable.[27] Schoolboy Geoffrey Diggle at Gresham's expressed a truth no doubt widespread in most schools: 'The course of the war was seldom a topic of conversation among us. War news consisted of one copy of *The Times* placed on the house table for thirty boys to fight over once the housemaster had finished with it.'[28]

Those whose fathers or brothers had been killed would often wear black armbands. The news was broken to them individually by their housemaster or headmaster. Many dreaded what a summons to the office foretold. Stiff upper lips were the order of the day, not through unkindness, but from the prevailing belief that activity rather than introspection was the best cure for bereavement. Idolization of or even regular reference to a fallen brother or father could magnify pain. For Christopher Isherwood, whose father was killed in 1915, it became too much at Repton: 'I did so hate being everlastingly reminded of him when I was young. Everyone kept saying how perfect he was, such a hero and so good at everything ... I used to simply loathe him'.[29]

Headmasters carried a heavy burden, passing on bad news and setting the tone across the whole community. Many chose chapel as the appropriate place to communicate the latest losses of old boys, or in day schools without chapels used the formal assembly in the school hall. At Culford in Suffolk the boys remembered that their headmaster, a staunch Methodist, always had a catch in his throat as he read out the casualty list.[30] At Ruthin the headmaster would wear his OTC uniform on days he had a death to announce, delivering homilies on those killed and their school records.[31] At Christ's Hospital the headmaster would process to the chancel, turn to face the congregation, and read out the names; then a bugler in the quadrangle outside would play the Last Post.[32] At Rugby, as the list grew longer, the headmaster abandoned the practice of naming casualties in 1916 after the Somme began, because of the depressing effect it was having on the community.[33] For some headmasters, the solemnity of the occasion provided opportunities for display of their rhetorical skills. One of the more gifted was Gordon Selwyn, Warden of Radley, who preached on All Saints' Day in 1917 as follows: 'He is not the God of the dead, but the God of the living ... There are perhaps two of whom we think especially, only because we knew them so well, both of them quite lately Senior Prefects, the one succeeding the other ... Anyone who knew Geoffrey Adams or Alick Blyth knew how they hated war: yet, without a murmur, they went and they died ... So let us leave them, safe and at peace now in God's keeping'.[34] Both men were just twenty when they were killed, Adams on the Somme and Blyth at Ypres.

Schools and the Home Front

Even those boys at schools out of earshot of shellfire from Belgium and France saw with their own eyes the daily reality of war. Military camps sprang up all over the country, while schools near ports saw constant evidence of the military. 'Day and night we have lived in the presence of military sights and sounds', wrote Montague Rendall, headmaster of Winchester. 'College Street has been crowded with men in khaki ... Old Wykehamists en route to the front have spent their last few hours among old friends in the School, before embarking the same night at Southampton.'[35] Several schools found their buildings requisitioned for military usage. At The Leys in Cambridge the Royal Army Medical Corps (RAMC) demanded space for a hospital for 100 wounded in school dormitories, while many others lost playing fields to the army, since they were ideal spaces for troops to learn to dig trenches. Dauntsey's on Salisbury Plain provided billets for Canadian troops in the first winter of the war.

Schools found themselves swept up into the furnace of munitions manufacture, with school workshops adapted to their production. At Bedford School the Ministry of Munitions praised the quality of the submarine valves and 13lb shells produced as 'first rate'; boys, masters, wives and local residents all joined in the work.[36] At Bradfield a new headmaster, eager for his school to be 'doing its bit', persuaded Vickers to grant the school a contract to make shell cases. Work went on in holidays as well as term, and involved over 100 boys in the manufacture; the headmaster described it as 'serving a good purpose in giving boys, too young or physically unfit to take commissions, the chance of taking their part in the war'.[37] Emanuel School in South London made bullet pouches for nearby Woolwich Arsenal, a task which saw boys and staff working late into the night keeping pace with demand.[38] Glasgow Academy, inspired by an entrepreneurial English master, Walter Barradell-Smith, established a niche in making thick gloves for naval crew. Concerts and other events were organized in aid of the school's 'gloves fund', and production reached 5,000 pairs per year.[39]

The Public Schools National Service Scheme, established to utilize the pupils' labour 'in the national interest', saw Manchester Grammar School turn over its traditional summer scout camps to the cause. Sixty boys thus set off to Worcestershire to pick plums in the summer of 1915. Two years later, the school set up its own National Service Committee to find productive work for every boy, including digging potatoes, emptying railway trucks and delivering parcels. The *Daily Telegraph* was duly impressed, appraising the scheme as 'a golden page in the school record'.[40] Bedford School was one of many to see their games fields turned over to the growing of vegetables; ensuring nothing went to waste, more than one tonne of chestnuts, for use in munitions, was also collected from school grounds.[41] At St Peter's York the 'vegetable committee' decided that the fives court should become a cold frame, and that lettuces should be grown on the roof.[42] Several turned their skills towards tree felling: Glasgow Academy boys spent five weeks in 1916 at a timber camp in Largie, felling seven thousand trees to provide pit props and other timber for the Ministry of Agriculture.[43]

The OTCs, important to schools in peacetime, became of vital national interest as soon as war had been declared. When General Sir William Robertson, Chief of the Imperial General Staff, visited Bradfield in November 1916, his speech, widely reported in the press, stated boldly that, 'the army knows what it owes to the public schools'.[44] OTCs continued to be the most fruitful single source of fresh officers through-out the war, even after officers began to be promoted increasingly from the ranks.

Membership of the OTC became compulsory in virtually all schools and the time given to OTC activities in the school day dramatically increased. Attention focused on those about to leave school, with Sedbergh setting up a 'class of military instruction' to teach seventeen-year-olds the specialist skills they would need at the front.[45] OTC training now included bayonet drill; Sidney Savage, at Oundle School, recalled charging straw-filled sacks representing Germans and the difficulties of withdrawing the bayonet – 'we had to hold the "German" with our left boot as we withdrew the blade'.[46] School OTCs were given important military duties, with Wellington College boys patrolling local power works and railway lines,[47] and boys from King William's in the Isle of Man guarding German prisoner-of-war camps.[48]

Such activity was not to every boy's taste. At Harrow four parades a week had been instituted by Christmas 1914, with a long 'route march' every Thursday. One house refused to obey their OTC cadet officer, an act described by the Head of School as 'flagrant indiscipline verging on mutiny'. The ringleaders were given a 'monitors' whopping'.[49] Alec Waugh said of the Sherborne OTC that 'everyone was fed up to the teeth and took no pains to disguise the fact'.[50]

Wartime deprivations and the extra OTC activity saw a curtailment of games. Away matches became difficult to arrange, and many club sides and old boys' associations could no longer muster teams. Some staff took to grumbling about the standard of school teams because of the lack of senior boys. War sometimes had a more serious impact on school sport, including 'the choking fumes of nitrogen peroxide from the munitions factory at Craigleith', which affected Fettes boys during house rugby,[51] while at St Edward's, Oxford, bumping races on the river were cancelled in 1917 because of complaints, at a time of rationing, that 'consumption of food always goes up in the rowing weeks'.[52]

The Headmasters' Conference (HMC) spent much time considering how it should best respond to the war. Its annual conference in December 1914 in London debated the German invasion of Belgium. Edward Lyttelton (Eton) seconded the vote of sympathy to Belgian schools and universities, reporting that Eton had given hospitality to twenty Belgian boys. The heads stopped short, however, of supporting Henry Cradock-Watson (Merchant Taylors', Crosby), who argued for HMC funds to help repair the ruined library at Louvain instead opting to vote money from HMC funds to 'general war relief causes'.[53] In April 1915 HMC agreed that its schools would maintain a hospital in London for officers, which was superseded the following June by a scheme, at the request of the Red Cross, to pay for the upkeep of fifty-three beds at the Base Hospital in Rouen, together with the upkeep of two huts for other ranks. Its beds in Rouen, HMC was keen to stress, should treat officers regardless of whether they had attended public schools. The £10,000 per annum required was to be raised by the individual schools: at HMC's pre-Christmas meeting at Rugby in 1916 the minutes recorded that, 'some of the less wealthy schools had been among the most generous donors'.[54]

Sympathy for Belgium ran high. Kingswood in Bath offered its school sanatorium as a hospital for wounded Belgian soldiers. The patients arrived at the school to be greeted by intertwined British and Belgian flags, and were serenaded each day with a concert, at which any unable to sing *La Marseillaise* were free to sing *Tipperary*.[55] Many other schools welcomed refugees from war-torn countries. Sherborne took in four

Belgians, a Serb and a French boy, who later presented a school prize for French, while St Edward's Oxford took Belgians and Serbians. 'Very good fellows', a boy called the latter. 'I cannot say the same for the Belgians.'[56] Few were more accommodating than George Heriot's in Edinburgh, which took twenty-six Serbian boys. At the end of the war the refugees presented the school with a plaque which read: 'In as much as ye have done it unto one of the least of my brethren, ye have done it unto me.' The school link with Serbia continues to the present day.[57]

Girls' schools were not able to be members of HMC, but they too were heavily involved on the home front, few more so than Cheltenham Ladies' College (CLC). Founded in 1853, it had grown to 725 girls in 1914. Records show that over 2,000 of its old girls participated in war work – nursing, land work, looking after refugees, and clerical work in Whitehall. Six old girls died during the war, mostly from illness contracted in military hospitals.[58] In March 1915 the school set up a Voluntary Aid Detachment (VAD) hospital in one of its boarding houses, overseen by teachers and pupils past and present and taking in the wounded direct from France. Its fund raising extended to the provision of a mobile X-ray unit, presented to the War Office for use on the Western Front. During the war, school workshops produced over 55,000 separate items, including bandages and swabs, and iodine ampoules from the science laboratories. CLC's Headmistress Lillian Faithfull later reflected that the war had allowed her girls to develop their characters and learn much that they would not have done to the same extent in peacetime – self-sacrifice, resourcefulness and independence in action.[59]

One effect of the war on St Paul's School for Girls can be seen in the Roll of Honour published in each edition of *The Paulina* – fathers and brothers killed at the front. As at CLC, former pupils performed many different roles unheard of before the war, including teaching in boys' schools, breaking in horses for the army, and ambulance driving. Joan Bateson wrote to the school: 'I have taken a chauffeur's post in place of a man who has enlisted. The gentleman I drive for is the rector of a small country parish between Bath and Gloucester.'[60] The war played a crucial part in building the self confidence of young women for the enhanced role that they were to play in the post-war world.

The long reach of the war made the public schools forsake many of their academic aims. The diary of Walter Raeburn, who was a boy at Charterhouse and whose son David Raeburn was headmaster of Whitgift School from 1970 to 1991, shows the extent to which senior boys were mainly groomed for commissions in the army. Sport and

OTC took precedence over academic work, and 'the immediate issue was what lay ahead at the front rather than looking ahead to continued education'.[61] A sense of stasis filled many schools. A boy at King's Canterbury commented that, 'the Michaelmas term is a hollow mockery ... All the best people have gone to war. The monitors and "bloods" ... were merely awaiting their commissions. One by one they departed'.[62] The headmaster of Haileybury sought to help his pupils by offering lessons on 'European history since 1815', to allow them to understand better 'the context of the war'.[63] The prospect of going to university had disappeared: not a single Wykehamist went to Oxford in the 1915 academic year, while Oxford and Cambridge colleges were filled with officer cadets in training rather than undergraduates.

Most schools suffered from the loss of young masters to the war and the consequent problem of finding teachers to stimulate the young and to keep order. Sedbergh had sixteen teaching staff when war was declared; seven of them, as well as the Bursar, had gone by Christmas 1914.[64] Boys were not impressed by the replacements. Robert Bennett, a fifteen-year-old at Marlborough, recalled that, 'all the young masters not in Holy Orders had disappeared and their places were filled by a lot of "dugouts". Some I fear found the going a bit hard'.[65] A St Edward's boy complained that, 'wartime conditions made it necessary for the Warden to scrape the bottom of the Gabbitas and Thring barrel'.[66] Ardingly fared no better: 'It was the discipline in lessons which suffered ... The masters who arrived were a queer lot indeed and did not stay long'.[67] Boys at Winchester were delighted by a temporary teacher who had been a Belgian High Court judge; when giving private tuition in his home, he would offer cigarettes to his students.[68]

Anti-German sentiment ran high. One teacher at St Edward's 'had the terrible handicap of Teutonic contours, countenance and intonation. His lessons were pandemonium'.[69] Loretto's German master, Herr Krahnen, had to be interned. At Ipswich School the German teacher of several years' standing, despite commanding the OTC, was subjected to accusations of providing intelligence to the enemy ahead of a Zeppelin raid; the governors were asked to retire him and to replace German with Spanish in the curriculum.[70] St Dunstan's was situated near to a large colony of German families in Forest Hill whose sons attended the school; many chose to anglicize their own and even local street names: thus 'Berlin Road' became 'Canadian Avenue'. A governor tried and failed to get German removed from the syllabus.[71] Anti-German agitation by parents led to the sacking of Dr Tischbrock, the German master at Bedford Modern, while at Tonbridge William Arnold Hoffman, who had taught at the school since 1902, changed his name to plain

'William Arnold' in 1915, but still suffered from boys calling him 'Hoffy Arnold'.[72]

Not all schools succumbed. Chigwell stood out against the popular and press tide: it mourned the loss of its German teacher, Herr Sommermeier, killed in action fighting for Germany, who was described as 'friend, enemy and patriot', with a consoling line of Euripides.[73] Equally, Manchester Grammar School listed in its Book of Remembrance the name of former German teacher Dr Bernhard Neuendorff, killed fighting for the Germans against the Russians in September 1915.[74] Patriotism and good taste suggested that schools ease back on their traditional high days and holidays. Eton suspended its Fourth of June celebrations and Founder's Day feast, the money saved going to charity. Wellington cancelled much of its long-planned celebration of the centenary of the Battle of Waterloo in June 1915: France was now an ally after all. The Master of Wellington, William Vaughan, reported to the governors that a more subdued commemoration 'will gain in seriousness and reconciling power by the thought that the conquerors and conquered of 1815 are standing in a common peril as resolute allies in 1915'.[75]

Dissent in the ranks

What was the reaction in the schools to the sheer scale of the horror, the vast numbers cut down at such young ages, and the contrast between the idealism of those who left for the front and their return, broken in body or spirit? Was there a similar epiphany to that of the poets, from eager compliance in 1914 to the battle-worn and angry words of Siegfried Sassoon (Marlborough)? Our research reveals plenty of low-level grumbling, but precious little open dissent or even articulate questioning of the prosecution and objectives of the war. Boys saw much less reason to work hard when their destiny, at least in the short term, was military. Behaviour deteriorated after experienced staff left to fight and the age of prefects dropped below eighteen. At Malvern the Prefects' Minute Book throughout the war years is bursting with reports of bullying, indiscipline and an 'unhealthy moral atmosphere', which would have included homosexuality.[76]

Bullying had always been an ingrained feature of public school life. Teachers, when not themselves responsible for it, generally turned a blind eye, regarding it as part of the natural order of boys' character development. The long hours at school for boarders, and the cramped conditions, were fertile ground for the incubation of bullying. Boys at day schools faced different problems in the war. Home life changed utterly for most, with fathers away at the front and mothers struggling to run the family in their absence, with a constant eye open for the arrival of a telegram. At Manchester Grammar School a drive to make the boys work hard ran into problems, and truancy increased, with boys staying at home to help out domestically or running family businesses.[77]

The schools were full of highly intelligent young people and enquiring minds, which found expression in articles and school debates. As early as the autumn of 1914, Charterhouse debated whether newspapers should be allowed to self-censor during the war (the motion was defeated easily).[78] In February 1916 King's Canterbury debated compulsory military service, which it rejected, while Repton discussed whether, 'Events during the war justify the claims of women to the vote' (carried in the 'Upper House' but defeated easily in the 'Lower House').[79] Malvern held regular debates on subjects ranging from the morality of submarine warfare to compulsory war work in the holidays.[80]

Magazines were heavily censored by pupil editors and supervising masters, so it is hard to conclude how widespread disillusion and anti-war sentiment might have become in the schools by 1918, particularly among older pupils who faced the imminent prospect of the call up. Shrewsbury provided a rare example of dissent in *The Salopian* of October 1918, a piece entitled 'A Plea for Pacifism'. The editors prefaced it with the claim that they were not responsible for the opinions of contributors, but the article still seems as brave as it is unexpected. Although it was published in late October 1918, it was by no means clear at this point that the war was to end so quickly. It is based on an imaginary conversation about pacifism between a small number of men, one of whom is known as 'the pacifist', a much decorated soldier who has turned against war. It is clear that his views are those of the writer: 'Do you mean to say that after four years of this, you still think you're fighting for Empire? Why, man, Empire over the whole world would not compensate for the last four years.'[81]

An altogether more serious row broke out at Repton in Derbyshire, involving a head-on clash between two men who were to be among the most prominent moral figures of the mid-twentieth century. One was the school's head, Geoffrey Fisher, educated at Marlborough and at Oxford, where he took a brilliant first, returning to Marlborough as a teacher and being ordained just before the war. In 1914, at the very young age of twenty-seven and on the recommendation of Frank Fletcher, headmaster of Charterhouse and Fisher's former head at Marlborough, he was promoted to Repton, succeeding William Temple, whom he was later to succeed as Archbishop of Canterbury. Fisher occupied the see from 1945 to 1961, presiding over the coronation of Queen Elizabeth, supporting nuclear weapons, and serving as Grand Chaplain to the Freemasons. One of his children, Frank Fisher, became Master of Wellington College (1966–79).

His antagonist was Victor Gollancz, born to Jewish parents and educated at St Paul's and Oxford. Commissioned into the Northumberland Fusiliers in October 1915, Gollancz was transferred to Repton School to teach and help with the OTC in March 1916. After the fracas at Repton, he went into publishing, forming his own company in 1927 specializing in pacifist and socialist literature, and subsequently becoming a co-founder of the Left Book Club. He became a Christian socialist, and published a number of religious and topical books. One of the compilations he produced was *A Year of Grace* (1950), which draws on a wide range of spiritual and mystical texts across all religions and none. One extract, whose reference is given merely as 'from memory', so was presumably something he had heard, epitomizes his vision of life and explains perhaps what he was doing at Repton: 'The Grand Rabbi of Lyons was a Jewish chaplain to the French forces. One day a wounded man staggered into a trench and told the Rabbi that a Roman Catholic was on the point of death in No-Man's-Land, and was begging that his padre should come to him with a crucifix. The padre could not quickly be found. The Jew rapidly improvised a cross, ran out with it into No-Man's-Land, and was seen to hold it before the dying man's eyes. He was almost immediately shot by a sniper; the bodies of the Catholic and the Jew were found together.'[82]

The trouble at Repton began in 1916, when Gollancz started running a current affairs class with fellow teacher David Somervell, motivated by the belief that, if boys were going to be putting their lives at risk, they needed to have a fuller view of the issues at stake and the political systems that had brought the countries into conflict. In his unpublished memoirs Somervell captured Gollancz's brilliance and inspiration of the young, though he noted, 'One of the problems with Victor was that he never made any dividing line between boys and masters. Many schoolmasters draw it too sharply: Victor did not draw it at all.'[83] At twenty-four, Gollancz was the younger and more headstrong figure of the pair; Somervell was more mature, but utterly captivated by his younger colleague. Many Reptonians lapped up what these two unusual teachers offered them, but not all approved, and the atmosphere at school became highly charged. Boys in the Army Class took a strong objection to these radical teachers, and threw one pupil with left-wing views into the river. Peter Parker in *The Old Lie* quotes one traditionalist master announcing, 'It is our solemn duty to instil into the boys such a hatred of the Hun that for the rest of their lives they will never speak to one again.'[84]

Conservatives on the teaching staff were particularly incensed by a pupil publication emanating from these subversive lessons. *A Public School Looks at the World* (known colloquially as 'The Pubber') was first published in June 1917, and led to the outbreak of a minor civil war, with some masters writing vituperative letters about it to *The Reptonian*; this provoked counter-letters, further fanning the flames. The Debating Society became another forum for expression of strong views: at one meeting an Old Reptonian master announced that, 'The giants of Repton of thirty years ago would have thrown into the Steinyard [the local river] anyone who held such views.'[85] Little in his life hitherto had prepared Fisher for managing this Class A crisis. His response was to summon the whole community to a meeting in the school hall, where he told them that the arguments between left and right had to stop. For a while it seemed as if the issue had gone away, and Fisher heaved a sigh of relief.

Gollancz and his pupil editors then decided to push their luck, and placed the magazine on sale at a radical bookshop in London already under surveillance by the War Office.[86] The March 1918 edition of 'The Pubber' was thus advertised as 'Published by the Repton School Bookshop Limited and Henderson and Sons, 44 Charing Cross Road.' Even though 'published by' merely meant that the magazine could be purchased at the shop, the association with an outlet known as 'the bomb shop' was too much for the authorities to ignore. Disgruntled members of staff began feeding materials through to the War Office in London where, according to Somervell, 'a bulky Repton file began to build itself up ... The general drift of the documents was that a pacifist and disloyal movement was being fostered at Repton by two of its assistant masters'.[87] In July the War Office wrote to Fisher: 'I am commanded by the Army Council to inform you that it has been brought to their notice that during the last two terms at Repton School a certain amount of political controversy has been conducted, through the activities of a master, an officer of the Officer Training Corps, that a paper dealing largely with political matters was produced in the school and that it was placed on sale at a certain place in London.'[88]

Fisher was forced to act. Initially tolerant of the activities, he felt threatened, as any headmaster would be, by his school coming under the critical attention of the most senior echelons in Whitehall. He decided that the only way to exorcize the problem would be to get rid of Gollancz, who was sacked from the beginning of the summer term. The troubles still did not go away, and, after a further communication from the War Office, Fisher presented Somervell with an ultimatum, 'not to indulge in any further discussion of controversial political questions with any member of the school for the duration of the war'. Somervell felt he could not accept this and decided to leave. He went on to a successful career as a teacher, housemaster and historian of Tonbridge School.

Somervell was fairly caustic about Fisher, describing him as 'primarily an administrator and disciplinarian, cautious and rather cold-blooded ... I doubt if he either liked or disliked anyone in Repton. We were just pawns on the chessboard of his job and his object was to make a success of that job, as a stepping-stone to a bigger job'.[89] The old guard in the common room approved of Fisher, however, and breathed a sigh of relief after Somervell left. 'Well, we've had a long fight', one of them said to his Army Class, 'but we've won. We've got rid of the last of the traitors.'[90] At least one pupil at Repton, Amyas Ross, the editor of 'The Pubber', was a casualty of the affair, and left the school, presumably prematurely, at the end of the summer term along with Somervell. Life and fiction are full of stories of intelligent and impressionable school students captivated by charismatic members of staff, as was Ross. In an article entitled 'State Your Terms', Ross had echoed Siegfried Sassoon's call for a negotiated peace with Germany. His piece provoked fury at Repton in predictable quarters. Ross was unusual in being independent and such a free thinker: he argued fiercely at a special prefects' meeting in the summer term about 'political activity' against Fisher, who insisted that it should cease forthwith.[91] Whether the public schools were full of figures like Amyas Ross is not known, but it seems unlikely. Many young men at school must have shared his thoughts, but lacked mentors like Somervell and Gollancz to give them voice. Siegfried Sassoon's protest against the war in 1917 certainly does not seem to have inspired any rebellions at schools, and his protest went unrecorded even in the magazine of his old school, *The Marlburian*.

Best known of all the public schoolboy dissenters was Alec Waugh, older brother of the novelist Evelyn. They were sons of the independent-minded Arthur Waugh, a literary critic, author and publisher, and they mixed in literary and free-thinking circles from a young age. Alec found Sherborne a repressive experience, had nearly been expelled for homosexuality[92] and set out to justify his position and vent his frustration in a semi-autobiographical novel, *The Loom of Youth*, written soon after he left the school in July 1915, but published in 1917, by which time he had been commissioned into the Dorset Regiment.[93] The book, which Waugh later described as 'a love letter to Sherborne', runs to over 300 pages and describes the schooldays of Gordon Caruthers at 'Fernhurst'. Waugh was incensed by the tone of the large number of public school stories which were avidly read by so many, from *Tom Brown's School Days*, which popularized Rugby, to H. A. Vachell's *The Hill*, which glorified Harrow. Such books, he believed, 'invested public school education with an almost unearthly and elysian light'.[94] In contrast, a number of books critical of the public school system had been published in the years before the war, notably Arnold Lunn's *The Harrovians*, published in 1913 and very much the inspiration for Waugh's own book.

Waugh saw himself as telling the truth about public schools, showing that much of their widely admired ethos was a sham. He denounced cribbing in exams, widespread bullying, the obsessive cult of games, the insincerity of much religion, and the replacement of high-minded ideals by ritual. To Waugh himself, one of the book's chief virtues was its honesty about the extent of homosexuality in public schools, with the implication of hypocrisy on the part of staff who knew it was going on but did so little to stop it. Throwing together in monastic seclusion thirteen-year-old children and eighteen-year-old men, he believed, would have inevitable consequences. The writing might be turgid, but *Loom of Youth* was the work of a young man of seventeen, and as such, it represented a considerable feat of determination and indeed courage.

The furore the book provoked, unprecedented during the war, owed less to its whistleblowing about homosexuality and so forth, of which Waugh was so proud, and much more to its publication at a delicate moment of wartime, with its direct assault on the very public school ethos widely regarded as such an important contribution to the war effort. Further fuel was poured on the fire by the publisher, Grant Richards, mischievously choosing Thomas Seccombe, a professor of history at Sandhurst, to write a preface in which he said the public school system 'has fairly helped, you may say, to get us out of the mess of August 1914. Yes, but it heavily contributed to get us into it'.[95]

The storm provoked was out of all proportion to the literary or revelatory merits of the work. Angry letters and denunciations appeared in the national press. Headmaster Nowell Smith was furious and embarrassed, and, with Alec Waugh at the front, much of the blame was laid on his father, who he believed revised and improved the drafts (he perhaps did even more to the text);[96] he also blamed an English teacher, Stuart Mais, who became a prolific author after he left the school prematurely.[97] In his confidential annual report to governors, Nowell Smith criticised Waugh: 'A passion for self-advertisement, which had made the author a difficult boy at school, flattered by paternal and professorial adulation, induced the boy to publish what is in fact a gross libel on his own school and a cruel caricature of certain masters and boys.'[98] The word 'traitor' was never far from the thoughts of critics, and both father and son were forced to resign from the Old Shirburnian Society. Less well known is the fact that both were reinstated in 1933, and Waugh presented the manuscript of the book to the school in 1965. By then Alec Waugh had made a reputation as a popular novelist, bon viveur and socialite, if always eclipsed as a writer by his brother Evelyn – hardly the life that one might have expected for the student revolutionary.

A footnote to the affair was its impact on Evelyn's schooling, and thus on his subsequent writing. In the summer of 1916 Arthur Waugh, aware that *The Loom of Youth*'s imminent publication might have repercussions for the family, requested an interview with headmaster Nowell Smith to inquire whether Evelyn would still be welcome as a pupil at Sherborne. The school was 'a governing passion in Arthur's life', and he wanted Evelyn to follow the family tradition and, like Alec, board in School House. Arthur described the meeting, over lunch in a London club, as 'an amicable exchange of views', but it was clearly awkward for both sides.[99] If the book received any press coverage, it was unlikely to enhance the reputation of the school and would certainly infuriate those associated with Sherborne. Evelyn's position would be impossible in a school where anyone of the Waugh name was soon likely to become *persona non grata*, and it was agreed that he should go elsewhere. A last minute search saw him go off to Lancing, a decision about which he clearly still felt bitter years later. He considered Lancing an inferior and bleak establishment in wartime, too isolated on the south coast for his taste. He saw the choice as a 'stop-gap result', which he blamed on his brother's actions and his father's indecision.[100]

Whistleblowers commonly provoke fury, as well as allegations that their accusations are not representative and that they are mere attention seekers. The truth in the Waugh case is hard to ascertain. Another pupil, W. Hayman, left unpublished accounts of Sherborne in the school archives which portray a very different picture: 'The book tells the lives of a small set of boys in School House, their motives and their actions, but had members of other houses written their own stories, the pictures presented would have been very different ... Boys in those houses faced their own problems, rejoiced in their own success, but those problems and successes were not necessarily those of Alec Waugh'.[101] Our guess is that Waugh was sensationalising but still giving a broadly accurate portrait. It is easy to be dismissive of him as a difficult pupil, but he did ask questions of the public school system which might also have been asked by those in authority, especially headmasters. Curiously, the book does nothing to explain why Thomas Seccombe, in his preface, should have accused the public schools of contributing 'to get us into the mess of August 1914'. Nor does Waugh have anything significant to say about the major criticism of the public school system, then as now, a century later, that it polarizes the country and restricts social mobility. The greatest flaw of his case, though, is that the products of the public schools did not behave at the front as he alleged they acted at school.

Hard years: 1916–18

'The greatness of a public school education has never been so conclusively proved as in the manner in which the schools and universities have risen to the call of their country', said the Dean of King's Canterbury in November 1916, as he spoke about those old boys who had given their life in battle. 'It was conclusive proof that whatever else might be taught in the schools of England, at all events we taught the highest principles of character and duty.'[102] He spoke as the Somme was ending; the qualities he praised were to be even more urgently required in the harsh two years that followed. A pupil at Westminster in 1917 wrote in the magazine *The Elizabethan*: 'War has emphasised the true meaning of friendship, and added a fresh significance to the act of parting; in peacetime we might wish them a careless *au revoir*, now with heart and soul we bid them fervently *adieu*.'[103] At Campbell College, old boys by 1917 were turning their hands to clearing the grounds to grow potatoes, and the school announced, 'Last term we cut off voluntarily some of the luxuries to which we have become accustomed.'[104] At Lancing, beer for boys was a luxury to go in the general drive to conserve cereals and sugar, and by January 1918 local Sussex butchers could only provide half the already depleted quantity of meat.

Meatless days indeed were to become common in public schools.[105] One boy at Ardingly recalled that, 'Food gradually became worse as shortages and restrictions increased. The bread became well-nigh inedible. Our staple diet for breakfast was bread, margarine and tea, and dinner was an ordeal.'[106] Loretto operated a system of voluntary rationing from 1916, with two meatless days per week and sugar totally forbidden on porridge.[107] At Eton boys often went hungry in 1917 and 1918, a state not much alleviated by 'Miss Marten's pudding', made by a redoubtable school cook from all the scraps of bacon fat, cold sausage and suet that she could assemble.[108] At Harrow the head boy told fellow pupils that they were honour-bound to spend as little on food as possible,[109] while at Rossall a desperate boy resorted to killing a wounded seagull found on the beach and cooking it for soup.[110]

Hardship was experienced the length and breadth of the country. At Malvern the headmaster noted that, 'the cheek bones of the adolescent boy were unpleasantly prominent'.[111] At Lancing the cross-country course was shortened because of the boys' physical condition,[112] while Tonbridge schoolboy Walter Oakeshott, later headmaster of St Paul's and Winchester, noted: 'We must have been hungrier than any generation at school ever was. We ate ravenously whatever we could; we cadged food shamelessly from the fortunate; we robbed orchards.'[113]

German submarines were the principal reason for the added hardships of those final two years. By the end of 1916 U-boats were sinking 300,000 tonnes of Allied shipping per month, and in February 1917 alone, 230 separate ships bringing food and other supplies to Britain, mainly from North America, slipped beneath the waves. Schools coped as best they could. At Gresham's cold rice was substituted for potatoes, and boys were put 'on their honour' not to consume more than four and a half slices of bread per day; supper was a cup of cocoa and one slice of bread, each slice containing an average of 'three currants'. While rationing from early 1918 brought some order, no noticeable increase in food supplies followed. Lack of fuel for heating meant cold baths, and poor lighting created problems for boys reading in the evenings. Schools became even dimmer, colder and greyer places in the final months of the war. Morale often sank low.[114] Life on the front line was unimaginably harder, but the character virtues that the public schools had long been instilling in their young were put to a different kind of test for those still at school.

'Until the winter of 1917–1918 we could continue much as before with few apparent difficulties', said a pupil at Winchester. 'But the last year passed into a graver phase ... The food shortage was becoming really acute ... An epidemic of influenza in 1917, a foretaste of the scourge of 1918, forced us to go home for a few weeks'. Winchester housemasters, as their opposite numbers everywhere, were having a terrible time. The emotional distress of losing so many old boys from their houses was compounded by the difficulties of keeping the houses running, with staff and food shortages, while rising prices made it increasingly hard to meet their budgets. One boy at Winchester recalled, 'School Shop closed down and when Mrs Dean managed to get in a supply of jam now and again, a great queue would form down Kingsgate Street.'[115] School magazines had been for the most part defiantly patriotic throughout the war, but they reached new heights of jingoism in 1918. At the normally restrained Westminster the school magazine was reporting in early 1918: 'Every fibre, every muscle must be strained towards one object – Victory, absolute and smashing, with a lasting peace ... the British Empire is at death-grips with the German Empire and we fight for her with every ounce of energy we have'.[116]

Chapter 5

Headmasters and Teachers: the Toll of War

Headship is always a solitary experience, in any school at any time. That toll has never been more severe than during the Great War. To the constant pressures of running a school were added the emotional and physical strains of the war. Heads lacked the larger network of support by 'senior management teams' that they began to develop around them in the last decades of the century. They were trying to keep their schools full, as well as managing housemasters and running the curriculum largely on their own. Several buckled under the pressure.

Wartime worries

'Of the more repulsive solutions, two main ones appear', Aldous Huxley wrote to his brother about his need to find a job in the war. '(a) To disseminate mendacity in our Great Modern Press; (b) To disseminate the mendacity in our Great Modern Public Schools.'[1] Huxley chose the latter, opting for stints at Repton and Eton. A rum lot indeed became teachers during the war. A headmaster from Constantinople, the chaplain of a Cambridge College and the Vice Chancellor of a minor university all became teachers at Wellington, which saw more staff than many join up.[2] The 'most vigorous teachers were precisely those who went off to fight', Montagu Rendall of Winchester explained to his governors in his report in the first December of the war.[3] The obvious solution, women teachers, was considered neither practical nor viable. Not until the 1980s and 1990s did many of the traditional public schools begin to see women joining their ranks in any number. Dean Close in Cheltenham bucked the trend, with the headmaster's daughter, Miss Joyce Flecker, teaching some chemistry: her name appeared on the prospectus as plain 'J. Flecker'.[4] The headmaster of Sevenoaks equally fell back on family, engaging his two daughters in teaching.[5] The advance in the position of women in late Victorian and Edwardian Britain, which the Great War accelerated, had yet to make any meaningful impact on the public schools. Staffing problems were less acute in the girls' schools, as their all-female staffs were not going off to fight, though mistresses in many schools enlisted as VADs and in other war service. Girls' schools, if the experience of Cheltenham Ladies' College was typical, were also better at retaining their support staff. Lillian Faithfull, the headmistress, boasted that, 'Even the most wildly patriotic found themselves satisfied by continuing their familiar daily work, and adding to it the unfamiliar direct war service in the work-shop or hospital.'[6]

One logistical nightmare that heads were spared, in contrast to the Second World War, was evacuation of the entire school to a safer location. Only two schools, Dover College and St Lawrence Ramsgate, appear to have been evacuated because of the threat of naval bombard-ment and bombing: in 1916 the older St Lawrence boys went up to Chester and the junior school to Carmarthen.[7]

A press stunt, as unwelcome as it was unexpected, was the attempt to publish lists of school casualties and decorations in some kind of league table. Appearing from early 1915, this provided an uncanny foretaste of the response of public schools to academic league tables eighty years later. Many schools reacted negatively to what they considered an intrusive development and an unhealthy competition: 'It has been suggested from time to time that Rugby should follow the example of many other public schools and send statistics to the press', declared an editorial in its magazine in February 1915. 'We have not done so; and it is not a piece of self-exultation to say that we would never do so.'[8] That October, Frank Fletcher, in his capacity as chairman of HMC, wrote a letter to the *Morning Post* to complain about lists which the paper was intending to publish of the number of old boys and masters from each school serving, the numbers killed, and awards given. The Achilles' heel of the press in such compilations was their reliance upon the schools themselves to volunteer the information. Many thought it the epitome of poor taste. 'Lists of this kind', Fletcher wrote, 'seemed to suggest competition and comparisons inappropriate to a matter in which all schools are loyally doing their utmost.' He intimated clearly that public school headmasters would be refusing to supply the information that the press required.[9]

The war effort brought the spotlight on an area where public schools had not been strong: science teaching. Wartime Britain needed scientists in many different roles, and leading scientists expressed disappointment at the lack of progress in its teaching in schools. Frederick Sanderson of

Oundle had stood out as a rare champion of science in the curriculum. Many heads remained dyed-in-the-wool traditionalists, including Rendall at Winchester, whose reports to governors made frequent references of his strong desire to keep 'Winchester *par excellence* the classical school'.[10] In December 1916 the annual HMC conference placed the curriculum high on the topics it debated at its meeting at Rugby, the agenda including compulsory Greek, science education, war memorials and war economies.[11]

Oxford and Cambridge, despite lacking a single head of college with a science degree and hence no paragons themselves, tried insisting on a compulsory science paper for university admission. Heads were not happy at all, and were vocal in protest at the December 1916 HMC annual conference. By an overwhelming majority they passed this resolution: 'This conference deprecates the present proposals of the Oxford Council for making the past single examination in science an essential qualification of an Oxford degree.'[12] They did concede, however, the importance of 'the improving of the teaching of science and making it a reality in all public schools', the clear inference being that science teaching was deficient. The debate reads as if the heads have been smoked out and were joining forces to ensure none of their pupils suffered until they had put their houses in order.

The schools had taken financial stability for granted for many years. Haileybury's fees did not change between 1900 and 1913 – £70 per year for sons of clergy and £81 for others.[13] King's Canterbury was almost reckless in increasing their fees to £84 in 1913 from the £81 they had charged since 1900.[14] Suddenly, war hit the schools in a perfect storm, with parents finding it difficult to meet fees at the very moment when school costs escalated severely. Worse, schools were unable to raise their fees during the war, though HMC at its annual conference in 1916 voted for it in principle. Wealthier schools like Winchester, with endowments and land, found life a little easier: in 1917, the school was able to boost its salary budget out of its 'educational fund', a luxury unavailable to smaller public schools.[15] While some fathers' businesses did well, especially those supplying the war effort, many parents saw their incomes slump, and requests for financial help from schools multiplied greatly, notably from families who lost their breadwinner. In 1916 the Harrow headmaster was approached by a widow asking if her son could be admitted on reduced fees; such requests became common.[16] The distress caused to grieving widows who suddenly found it impossible to pay school bills is a plea heard regularly in the contemporary documents. Some schools began remitting as much as seventy-five per cent of their fees for families in dire need,[17] while the

Harrow headmaster was empowered to collect money privately to boost the income of the bursary fund.[18]

Headmasters traditionally are inclined to respond generously to parental pleas for financial help; bursars and governors, meaner folk, less so. But the ability of schools to be generous was restricted, because housemasters themselves commonly charged parents for boarding, and they lacked much of a buffer to enable them to be generous. Worse, heads had to pay salaries to staff absent on military service, on top of finding money for current teachers. Then inflation bit, above all of food prices, which the arrival of rationing in 1918 did little to relieve. Ardingly was one of many particularly badly hit. By 1917 governors were having to adjust to 'the tremendous rise in prices of foodstuffs', which was to have 'a disastrous effect on the school's finances'. The response of many was to cut back on meals and also fuel, reductions which are believed to have exacerbated the influenza outbreak in 1918.[19] A boon for most schools was an increase in numbers: Trent College thus doubled from 144 in 1914 to 295 in 1918, while Rossall expanded from 295 to 444.[20] Larger schools expanded, but proportionately less – St Paul's from 546 to 676 and Marlborough from 590 to 707 – during the war years.[21]

Economies became both inescapable and patriotic. At the London HMC conference in 1915, sacrifices schools should be making were discussed. A motion was proposed by William Vaughan (Wellington) to ask conference 'to consider the best means of reducing the expenses of school life ... and to seize this opportunity of making simplicity of living and industry a more marked feature in English public schools'.[22] Spending on new buildings, and wasted food, were two areas he mentioned. Money spent on games he particularly deplored, with certain types of staff clearly in his sights: 'We all know men who take it as if it was the most serious thing for boys to practise on a bumpy wicket.'[23] HMC headmasters, who had risen to the heights by dint of their scholarship rather than sporting prowess, might have been expected to applaud. But many were passionate advocates of games, so derogatory comments about sport were often not well received. The annual conference opted to set up an economies committee, which reported in 1916. Abolition of evening dress suits, the trading of second-hand books within schools, margarine being served instead of butter, and the cutting back of long-distance sports' fixtures, were among its suggestions.[24]

The sexual behaviour of boys had long been a concern of headmasters, principally homosexuality and masturbation. The risk of sexual relations with girls was far less pressing, given their scarcity in the monastic environments of boys' schools. In 1905 the annual conference of HMC had discussed pornographic literature being sold on station bookstalls; after 1914, worries that opportunities for sexual intercourse would be greater in wartime led to fresh concerns among heads. HMC was duly represented at a conference to consider the report of the Royal Commission on Venereal Diseases, set up in 1916. An outcome was that schools were asked to give every leaver 'a general warning against impurity, but also such instructions about the facts of the situation as to enable him to face it with the right attitude,' as the HMC minutes faithfully recorded.[25] How many lectures on 'impurity', were given, and whether learning about the 'facts of the situation' resulted in changes of behaviour, remains unclear. Henry Cradock-Watson, headmaster of Merchant Taylors' Crosby, was one of the many heads deeply concerned by the 'demoralising effect of the war on the young of both sexes'. He argued strongly in favour of 'more careful instruction' at schools about the need for morality in sexual relations, believing that too much emphasis was being placed merely on the physical risks of 'immoral conduct'.[26] Music halls with their louche acts had come to the attention of headmasters, along with the free availability of unsuitable (i.e. sexual) magazines. Annual conference debated whether a letter should be sent to all public school parents, warning them of the dangers to their sons.

Homosexuality had long been rife in public schools, operating under a curious moral code. Amongst the fraternity of boys it was deemed acceptable if older boys formed homoerotic friendships with younger boys or indulged in sexually frustrated same-sex encounters with boys of the same age, for in such cloistered surroundings there was no other outlet for romance or sexual passion. However, predatory or exploitative relationships between older and younger boys, or relationships in which the participants were thought to be clearly homosexual, were condemned by both boys and adults. Many heads appeared content to turn a blind eye to the former, which seems from the literature of the time to have been fairly widespread, but they usually acted firmly when instances of the latter came to light. The evidence for the frequency of such incidents is hard to establish, but Robert Graves recalled 'five or six big rows' during his time at Charterhouse.[27] The publication of *The Loom of Youth* in 1917 led to a near moral panic in public schools about homosexuality. But there was little schools could in fact do to reduce it. Some heads fell back on hoping that chapel and Christian teaching would ward off the danger. Heads knew they were powerless, and prayed no incident would come to light on their watch. Luck deserted the headmaster of Winchester, whose summer

108

1916 report to governors admitted that he had had to expel two boys for 'immorality'.[28] At Epsom, the Revd Walter Barton had detected the presence of such 'immorality' shortly after his arrival in 1914. Two years later, a major incident at the school, we are told in the documents, led to 'public floggings and expulsions'. Communal sanctions were imposed, and remedies to stem immoral behaviour included the installation of electric light in all dormitories (to be quickly lit in the event of any alert and to reveal the culprits), and the institution of 'a regime of cold showers' and an 'exhausting timetable' of compulsory games.[29] Alec Waugh made much in *The Loom of Youth* about his revealing of the hypocrisy over homosexuality in public schools. In reality, the presence of homosexuality and the clumsy efforts to deal with the issue are not unexpected.

Even while the war was being fought, attitudes to the social stratification the public schools helped perpetuate were changing dramatically. In the temporary graveyards that were to spring up along the Western Front, the son of a butcher was afforded equal status with the son of an aristocrat, an equality that was enshrined in perpetuity when the Imperial War Graves Commission was granted its Royal Charter in May 1917. Headmasters of Victorian public schools had taken class distinctions as part of the natural order of life. Their job was to run schools effectively for gentlemen and to turn out the leaders that the empire and the country needed. The war called into question all these beliefs. Whitehall was forced into considering the status of the public schools when preparing legislation about the future of state schools, deliberations which bore fruit in the 1918 Education Act. Lewis Selby-Bigge, a leading civil servant at the Board of Education and educated himself at Winchester, argued that public schools must accept state inspection if they wished to share in the benefits of the post-war national education system, such as access to pensions. The HMC annual conference in 1917 debated the status of the public schools in the post-war world, their worry being that discussions which bore fruit in the 1918 Superannuation Act and the 1919 Burnham Committee on teacher pay would make teaching in state schools more attractive. They were concerned that they might lose some of their best teachers, and hence voted to participate in the new national teachers' pension scheme.[30] They were also to respond, as soon as their funds permitted it after 1918, by raising the average annual salaries of teachers, which in the state schools went up from £225 in 1914 to £451 in 1922.[31] In 1919 a delegation from HMC approached the Board of Education to suggest that well-endowed public schools might take a certain percentage of elementary schoolboys along the same lines as state-aided schools.[32]

But the offer, which might have had a major impact on the relationship between state and independent sectors and on social mobility, was rejected.

Public school heads after the war, for a whole host of reasons, wanted to open up their doors to pupils from state schools, but in the absence of state funding they found it hard to raise the money to do so. Writing to *The Times* in 1935, Frank Fletcher argued that public schools had been willing since 1918 to open themselves up to bright state school-boys, but their eagerness had run into two obstacles: who would pay, and suspicions from the state schools about their top pupils being 'creamed off'.[33]

Headmasters were thus kept busy during the war years. Concerns over the escalation of costs, pornography and moral behaviour, league tables, social mobility and attracting top quality staff were high amongst their worries. Little has changed in a hundred years.

Teachers at the Front

The death rate of public school teachers was very high in the war. Some twenty-six per cent of teachers on active service, excluding those who stayed behind to man the OTCs, were killed, a figure which is twice the national rate. For teachers joining up from public schools in Australia, New Zealand and South Africa the figure is as high as twenty-eight per cent, considerably greater than the casualty rate for officers at large and, indeed, above the death rate for public schoolboys, which averaged twenty per cent.[34] Shrewsbury suffered particularly grievously, with five of its ten staff on active service killed, on top of two former teachers and a school governor. Merchant Taylors' in London had thirteen teachers on active service, five of whom were killed, while at Clifton, seven out of sixteen died.[35] The reason for this is hard to judge, but the longer you spent at the front, the more chance you had of being killed, and most young public school teachers, with their OTC experience, volunteered in the first year of the war, generally in the infantry with its higher casualty rate, and reached the front in 1914 or 1915.

The first master believed to have been killed was Lieutenant Alexander Williamson (Highgate School) on 14 September 1914. A boy at the school, he returned to teach at his alma mater in 1912. Proud of his commission in the Special Reserve, and leaving for France in mid-August, he wrote to his brother: 'I think I have realized to the full the possibilities of my position and am quite ready for any service to which God may call me.'[36] He was to be killed shortly after by a shell on the River Aisne.

His enthusiasm to join up, mirrored by that of countless public school teachers up and down the country, put headmasters in a dilemma. They wanted to support the war effort to the hilt, and to be seen to be doing so; equally, they had to run their schools with proper teachers. Frank Fletcher, Chairman of HMC, was the doyen of public school headmasters. We know much about him thanks to a beautifully crafted biography by a subsequent headmaster of Charterhouse, John Witheridge. In August 1914 Fletcher was summoned to the War Office to talk to Kitchener about the public school contribution to the war effort. The meeting appeared to go well, and Fletcher left believing Kitchener had given him assurances that the minimum age for a commission would remain at eighteen, and that indiscriminate enlistment by school-masters would be discouraged.[37] Fletcher himself had come under pressure at Charterhouse from one of his own masters, George Mallory, who felt he was being prevented from exercising his duty to enlist. Following the death of his friend Rupert Brooke, Mallory wrote in April 1915: 'There is something indecent, when so many friends have been enduring such horrors, in just going on with one's job, quite happy and prosperous.'[38] Not until late 1915 did Mallory have his way. He survived, but his life was to be claimed in 1924 when, together with climbing partner 'Sandy' Irvine, he perished near the summit of Everest.

Fletcher wrote to Prime Minister Asquith in December 1914 to seek further clarification of the government's views on military service for public schoolmasters. 'If the need for officers and soldiers outweighs the need of the schools of the country,' he wrote, 'we are ready to spare them, and they are ready, more than ready, to go.'[39] A reply came, not from Downing Street but from Kitchener himself, just five days later. Permission to join up should be, the War Secretary said, 'for those, and those only, who can be spared without impairing the work of the schools and the training of the OTC, for at the present moment both are equally important.'[40] Fletcher was pleased with this, and promptly passed it on to his fellow heads.

Fresh pressure on schools came with conscription, enshrined in the Military Service Acts of January and May 1916, specifying that all men between eighteen and forty-one should be called up for military service. Most able-bodied masters of the specified ages had already joined up by 1916, but HMC were exercised and divided over whether staff running school OTCs merited exemption from war service. The issue came out in the open at the annual conference at City of London School in September 1917. Sedbergh headmaster William Weech argued that it was very hard to justify to local tribunals, let alone public opinion, the retention of OTC officers, and he cited the case of one

111

school which he said had five men under the age of thirty-one helping run the OTC. Powerful support came from a headmaster, unnamed in the minutes, who argued, 'It is extremely difficult for any head, who has seen men of forty, with seven small children, called up, to allow young men of twenty-six to remain in schools.'[41]

C. H. Greene, headmaster of Berkhamsted and father of novelist Graham, retorted strongly, 'I have only thirteen of my pre-war staff left out of thirty, and two of the OTC officers happen to be specialists who cannot be replaced. I have tried to get substitutes for them but they cannot be found.' Others agreed that to lose those commanding the OTC risked damaging the military as well as the academic side of their schools irreparably. Others argued that it was vital to retain OTC staff to train up new cohorts of young officers to go straight from school to army. The motion to back OTC officers being called up was carried, with a proviso for headmasters to be able to retain men if they could not be 'adequately' replaced.[42]

Another difficult area for headmasters was the continuing pay and status of those who went off to fight. Larger schools could often afford to keep their jobs open for them on full or nearly full pay. The Winchester headmaster thus reported to his governors in December 1914: 'I have paid masters on military service their full salaries, after deducting £90 per term to supply a substitute.'[43] Rugby equally continued to pay full salaries to those on war service, less £30.[44] At Manchester Grammar governors resolved they should be paid the difference between their army pay and their teacher's salary.[45] Most schools agreed to hold positions open until after hostilities were over. Only if a master was killed, would his replacement be granted the permanent position.

The delicate matter of teachers 'missing in action' raised further uncertainties. Lionel Ford of Harrow thus wrote to one temporary teacher, Fred Leaf, in May 1916: 'I think we must assume that both Werner and Lagden are dead, and therefore I need not any longer delay to confirm your appointment here as a master.'[46] But what of the dependants of teachers killed? While some schools remitted fees for sons of fallen parents and old boys, it is less easy to discover the provision made for the children of deceased teachers, or what happened to widows living in houses owned by the school. No universal pension scheme was in existence, and one can only imagine the difficulties faced by widows.

School 'servants' who helped to run schools posed additional problems of status. Charterhouse decided they merited inclusion in the school magazine, *The Carthusian*, if they were killed in action. The February

1915 issue thus listed the names of 'fifteen school servants serving in His Majesty's forces, one of whom, Private Smith, had already been killed'.[47] Haileybury's response was to place a framed list of the 'Subordinate Staff serving in the Great War' outside the dining hall: in mid-1915 it contained twenty-two names, two of whom had already been killed and a further two wounded.'[48] Tonbridge School made a distinction between 'OTC, Games and Gym Staff', and more lowly 'school servants'. Among the latter, Sergeant Boag, shop manager, was killed in September 1914, and Private Mills, a school porter, was wounded four times in France and won the Military Medal in June 1917.[49]

Bloxham in Oxfordshire was more enlightened than most. When Harry Ayres, an eighteen-year-old school servant, died in hospital from wounds, the magazine reported: 'We should be lacking generosity if we failed to express our sympathy to Mr and Mrs Solomon Ayres and their family in their present bereavement.' His body was brought to Bloxham for burial in the village churchyard, with the school proud 'to furnish the firing party and buglers to pay the last military honours'. Ayres' name was placed on the village war memorial though not on the school war memorial. Bloxham has now tracked down his great-niece, who is still living in the village, and plans to place his name at last on the school memorial.[50]

George Fletcher epitomized the cavalier spirit of the young teacher who went off to fight. A scholar and Captain of School at Eton before he left in 1906, he spent three years teaching at Shrewsbury before returning to Eton. So desperate was he to join up in August 1914 that he served as a motorcycle dispatch rider during the retreat from Mons, before taking a commission in 2nd Royal Welch Fusiliers. Apparently fearless, his brave actions included lying perfectly still just in front of the German wire, utilizing his expertise in German to pick up snatches of conversations. Another feat saw him crawling through the German wire into their front line and rescuing a captured trench flag which had been hanging there provocatively. Fletcher sent the flag back to Eton, where it was put on display in School Hall and now hangs in College Chapel. In February 1915 he wrote to Malcolm White, a colleague from his time teaching at Shrewsbury, 'Death; one becomes a fatalist on this subject and looks forward resignedly to the prospect of extinction: "That moving Finger writes and, having writ, moves on".'[51] The following month, Fletcher's luck ran out and he was shot clean through the head by a sniper on 20 March. Something of his spirit was captured by a fellow officer who wrote: 'He will be a great loss, not only for his gallantry, but for his personality and his conversation at mess. To return off a cold and sticky digging-party and to find him sitting up with a decanter of rum with Wynne-Edwards, and chanting in Greek a chorus from Aristophanes ... or to watch him blowing smoke-rings while he parried the CO's chaff about "university education" was an essential part of the mixtures of those days'.[52] A whole page in March 1915 of the *Eton Chronicle*, bordered in black, was devoted to his death, and he was described as 'an Eton master killed fighting for his country and for us; such a thing has never happened before'.[53]

Charles Werner was of similar intellectual brilliance, having achieved a first in classics at King's College, Cambridge, and was one of the seven Harrow masters already joined up by October 1914. He rapidly made his mark as an officer of real courage, and was last seen alive leading an attack on Aubers Ridge on 9 May 1915. 'No man ever enjoyed any kind of fight more than Charles Werner; he had never in his life known what fear meant', reported the *Harrovian*. 'It is difficult to be sorry for the manner of his death since it is above all things what he would have desired.'[54] George O'Hanlon taught at Sherborne and was lucky enough to survive. Educated at Rugby, he had been taking his Sherborne cricket team on a tour to Plymouth when war broke out. His passionate ambition was to join up as quickly as possible, writing in his diary on 18 September, 'Took VIth Form again in afternoon – for the last and final time.' He won the MC and returned to Sherborne to teach in 1919 before becoming a housemaster; Alan Turing, the future Bletchley Park code breaker during the Second World War, was a boy in his house.[55]

Age and seniority were no guarantee of teacher survival. Few public school masters had more military experience than Alan Haig-Brown, the Cambridge soccer blue and sometime footballer with Tottenham Hotspur, who had commanded the Lancing OTC for nine years and written a book, *The OTC and the Great War*, in 1915.[56] He won the DSO, but was killed in action leading his battalion in the opening days of the German spring offensive in March 1918. Lieutenant Colonel Thomas Boardman had been OTC Commanding Officer of another Sussex school, Christ's Hospital. In 1916 he took command of a battalion of the Royal Inniskillings. Hit by a shell in the Ypres Salient in August 1917 when he went outside the dugout to check if his men were all right, he was badly wounded and brought back under cover to be tended, while he died, by one of his former house monitors, Lieutenant Robbins.[57]

At least five public schoolmasters won the Victoria Cross during the war. 'Conspicuous bravery and fine leadership' during the hazardous crossing of the Canal du Nord on 29 September 1918 was the citation for Lieutenant Colonel Bernard Vann, Chaplain of Wellingborough before joining up as a combat officer in the infantry. Vann served almost to the end, only to be killed leading an attack in the final month of the war.[58] Lieutenant William Forshaw of North Manchester School, a feeder for Manchester Grammar, was awarded his VC at Gallipoli. His citation read: 'When holding the north-west corner of "The Vineyard" against heavy attacks by the Turks, Lieutenant Forshaw not only directed his men but personally threw bombs continuously for over forty hours. When his detachment was relieved, he volunteered to continue directing the defence. Later, when the Turks captured a portion of the trench, he shot three of them and recaptured it. It was due to his fine example and magnificent courage that this very important position was held'.[59] Later, Forshaw was to comment that, 'it was like a big game. I knew it was risky, of course, but in the excitement one loses all sense of personal danger.'[60]

Heads love celebrated alumni coming back to their school to inspire current pupils. In October 1915 Forshaw was asked to visit Manchester Grammar School, and this entailed a two-mile procession from the railway station in open brougham with band and pipers, to be greeted on arrival by every senior and junior schoolboy. The school magazine recorded: 'Lieutenant Forshaw, as he passed the cheering multitudes, acknowledged their enthusiasm ... The High Master then, in stirring phrases, compared our hero to stubborn Ajax holding the Trojans at bay'.[61] He was presented with a silver tea service and an illuminated address by a grateful school, and the boys listened in rapt attention to details of his exploits defending his position for over forty hours against repeated Turkish attacks, his main weapon being bombs lit from cigarettes. After the war, he founded two prep schools, both of which fell into difficulties, and he died in 1943.

Teachers who had had a 'good war' often received promotion within their schools; whether this was due to inherent qualities of character or a recognition of war service is open to dispute. Over twenty headmasters listed in HMC lists in the 1930s held either the DSO or the MC, and four held both: the Revd E. C. Crosse of Ardingly, W. D. Gibbon of Campbell College, N. P. Birley of King's Canterbury and F. R. Dale of City of London.[62] In the 1930s such men must have viewed the future with great sadness and foreboding as the world, and their pupils, drifted towards another world war.

Headmasters at the Front

Active service was denied most headmasters because of their age and the need to stay in charge of their schools. Anthony Brown of Michaelhouse, South Africa, is the only serving public school head known to have been killed in action, on the Somme in 1916. Three Australian heads were granted leave of absence by their governing bodies to serve, one of whom, Harold Sloman of Sydney Grammar School, won the MC. There is no record of a serving British public school head enlisting, but some former heads served. Richard Ashmore was headmaster of Bangor Grammar School in Ireland before running a school in British Columbia. He returned to Europe with the Canadian Expeditionary Force, and was killed in May 1917 near Vimy Ridge while working as a stretcher bearer.[63]

No tale of a head was more tragic than that of the Revd Harold Ryley (Emanuel School 1905–11). He established and commanded the OTC and had been conspicuously successful in raising numbers to 562 at the South London school. But in 1911 he suddenly resigned from the job he was doing so well because of 'private troubles and ill health'.[64] Financial impropriety and his behaviour towards two schoolmistresses in the preparatory school seem to have been the problems.[65] Ryley's health was breaking down from nervous exhaustion and from the strain of his wife being confined in a mental institution throughout his time at Emanuel. In January 1914 he decided to sail to a new life in the USA, and no further action was taken by his governors.

Ryley's two sons, who had both attended Emanuel, remained behind, and both were commissioned in 1914. The younger was killed on the Somme at Delville Wood on 5 September 1916. On hearing the news, Ryley immediately returned to England, determined to fight himself, and was duly commissioned into the Suffolk Regiment. Just three months later, his elder son was reported killed in February 1917. Ryley at once demanded to be moved out of garrison duty in Harwich to active service. Sent to Palestine, he was killed in action in December 1917. Whatever his misdemeanours, the school forgave everything. 'The sad news has reached us that Rev. H. Buchanan Ryley has laid down his life, treading the path of honour and glory over which, only a few months previously, his two sons had walked', declared the school magazine.[66] By his name on the Emanuel war memorial were engraved the words, 'A man greatly beloved'. You can still read his name there, together with that of his two sons, and of the many Emanuel boys he had inspired in the OTC to join up.

Reginald Owen was one head who did not fight, and who was the object of opprobrium for not doing so. Appointed headmaster of Uppingham in November 1915 aged only twenty-eight, he succeeded the staunchly patriotic Revd Harry McKenzie, who had presided over Roland Leighton's final speech day on the eve of war. Taking over from a strong head is never easy, especially if one is only twenty-eight and coming to the job straight from a fellowship at Oxford, lacking experience of either schools or leadership. Academic ability was not the only thing, however, going for Owen: he was also an athlete, with a rowing blue from Oxford, and a strong character. Questions increasingly began to be asked, however, sharpened by some unpopular actions he took in his first year, about why he did not join up. His wife recorded that a bad bout of pneumonia, which Owen had suffered a few years previously, prevented him from being passed fit for overseas service, although his OTC record held in the Ministry of Defence contains no evidence of this. Neither did he use this excuse himself to staff or boys. The gossip around school was increasingly that Owen was a shirker, or worse. His predecessor's public pronouncement, that one was 'better dead' than refusing to fight, resounded in the ears of many. The anger rumbled on for two years, and deepened when, in the summer of 1917, he was ordained at a time when some bishops were refusing to accept for ordination young men of an age to fight. Dissent erupted in the form of demonstrations by old boys at their first post-war reunion in June 1919, and again at their London dinner in January 1920. The unpleasantness did not prevent Owen continuing as headmaster until 1934. He returned to academic life at university before becoming Archbishop in New Zealand from 1952 until his death in 1961. In the 1980s, when the history of the school was being written, its author received many letters from old boys criticising Owen's failure to fight.[67]

The conscience of heads

Edward Lyttelton of Eton was another headmaster in trouble during the war. A sportsman-scholar, and a nephew of the great Liberal Prime Minister W. E. Gladstone, he had played cricket for Middlesex and had been headmaster of Haileybury before being appointed to Eton in 1905. Lyttelton's love of cricket was such that he confessed later in life that, 'I never go into a Church without visualising the spin of the ball up the nave'.[68] But as it transpired, he was to be far from the establishment figure many had expected, nor was he a leader amongst public school heads in the mould of a Frank Fletcher or a Frederick Sanderson, the pioneer of science education at Oundle. Early in his tenure at Eton Lyttelton had created a stir by inviting a deputation of unemployed men to address the boys.[69] He became known as a maverick, in part for being a teetotal vegetarian. Nothing prepared the school, or indeed the country, for the furore that was to be unleashed by his sermon at St Margaret's, Westminster on 26 March 1915, an occasion which he thought was private. Whenever the headmaster of Eton pronounces, it is apt to become front-page news, even if it is, as it was here, an apparently unexceptional Christian message, urging caution before condemning the entire German population, and asking Britain to be prepared to act compassionately in any final peace settlement.[70] But the press, especially those titles owned by Viscount Northcliffe, had been attacking the Church of England for being 'feeble' in its lack of leadership in failing to condemn Germany in the most extreme terms. Lyttelton then poured petrol on the flames by a letter to *The Times* which decried 'empty bombast about "pulverising" a great nation'.[71]

Goaded by the press, the national mood towards Germany had hardened markedly over the preceding months. The school had been affected badly by the costly failure of Neuve Chapelle that spring, in which several Old Etonians were killed, and this made many furious with his stance. The press seized mercilessly on Lyttelton as pro-German. 'Dr Lyttelton's Sermon Circulated by Germany', blared the *Morning Post*.[72] *The Times* maliciously claimed at the foot of its letters page that the school had closed a day early for the holidays because of an outbreak of 'German measles'.[73] Editorials appeared in the *Daily Telegraph, The Times, Evening Standard* and *Daily Mail*, criticising him. The press was in tune with the national mood, which was solidly behind winning the war regardless of niceties, and any extension of the Christian message to the German nation was deemed ill-timed and inappropriate. Author Peter Parker cites a letter from an unnamed 'Winchester master', which distils the case against Lyttelton: 'He has sinned both against his country and his school ... against his school because he has broken the unwritten law that headmasters should put the good of their school before their own personal feeling ... I write as one who has been an Englishman for more than seventy years and a public-school master for more than forty'. The elderly correspondent was incensed that the headmaster of such a distinguished school could not be relied on to play the game, and condemned any 'expression of opinion on matters of public policy which shock the parents of their boys or diminish the confidence with which their masters and the school should feel towards them'.[74]

Lyttelton was in deep trouble, and a special meeting of the Fellows (i.e. governors) was convened on 22 April to consider his future. The hapless Lyttelton apologized fully. The Fellows listened to him and then, in his absence, debated what to do. There were insufficient grounds, they decided, to dismiss him, and they settled instead for a rebuke: 'The Provost [i.e. chairman] and Fellows cannot but regard the headmaster's recent speech and letters as detrimental to his authority and the welfare of the school. They feel bound to add that their confidence in him as headmaster of Eton has been seriously impaired.'[75] Many heads would not have wanted to remain after such a humiliation, and would have promptly resigned.

On 17 August 1915 the Earl of Rosebery, the former Prime Minister and now a Fellow of Eton, received an anonymous letter: 'My Lord, Are not the Governing Body of Eton going to remove that pestilent lunatic Edward Lyttelton from the position which he now disgraces. It is a humiliation and exasperating thought to hundreds of Old Etonians that a man so unbalanced in mind and with so unbridled a lust for publicity should be permitted to remain in such an office.'[76] Rosebery suggested that a 'resignation at Christmas would not be at all premature or unwelcome'.[77] Lyttelton clung on, but the next few months were difficult: other Fellows made it known that they thought he should have gone, and even his German maid was faced with a trumped-up charge of spying.[78] Lord Stamfordham, King George V's private secretary, also let Lord Rosebery know of the King's concern about Lyttelton's comments on internationalizing Gibraltar as a conciliatory gesture, a matter of particular sensitivity given the presence of Prince Henry of Gloucester as a boy in the school at the time.[79] It all proved too much for him and, in the summer of 1916 he left to become Curate at St Martin's in the Fields in London. He went on to become an Honorary Canon at Norwich Cathedral and then at Lincoln until his death in 1942, but there was to be no archiepiscopal throne, not even a mere bishopric, for this good man whose interpretation of the Christian gospel was more faithful than that of most clerics.

The point of this story is that Lyttelton, at the apex of the public schools, was a brave and rare voice articulating the nation's Christian faith and its core tenet of 'love your neighbour'. His advice, not to humiliate Germany in any peace settlement, was to prove remarkably prescient. Yet he was condemned for his beliefs, not by public school heads, but by the press, the church (notably Bishop of London), and by the court of public opinion. Rather than being ridiculed for his unworldly beliefs, and his character attacked for being attention-seeking, he could have been revered, then or now, for being a brave leader of boys, and a conscience to the nation, showing there was another way to the monotone story trumpeted by the establishment.

Lyttelton's Christian compassion towards the Germans found an echo in the ideas of Dr Cecil Reddie, founder, in 1889, and headmaster of Abbotsholme School in Staffordshire, a progressive school of just twenty-two boys in 1914. An educational visionary, Reddie favoured openness and friendship across national borders. Parents chose the school because they liked his preference for internationalism over nationalism, and a modern curriculum, which linked science to farm work on the estate and offered German and French rather than Latin and Greek. Peter Parker suggested that parents withdrew their children from the school in protest at Reddie's pro-German views,[80] but the school strongly contests this, arguing that he was not 'pro-German', although they concede that Reddie 'liked a handful of traits in the German character, especially their organisational ability'.[81] Commemorated on the school's war memorial, listing thirty old boys who died, are two Russians, one French soldier and two Germans.

The war posed particular problems for heads of Quaker schools. The Society of Friends, the body that oversees Quakers, did not rule out men joining up, but said it was a matter of personal conscience. While some Quakers believed that it was a just war, others were ardently pacifist. The issue came into stark relief only when conscription was introduced in 1916. While the Act allowed for conscientious objectors to be exempted, it committed them to alternative civilian tasks or non-combatant work in the army. Some 16,000 people in Britain registered as 'conscientious objectors', many of them Quakers. While some 10,000 agreed to work in non-combatant areas such as stretcher-bearing, 6,000 refused any form of service, and this usually resulted in imprisonment with hard labour. Two of the better known 'absolutists' who went to prison were Stephen Hobhouse, an Etonian, and the fiery socialist pacifist Fenner Brockway, who had been at Eltham College; the two men collaborated after the war on a campaign for prison reform. The issue could split families: Tom Attlee was a conscientious objector, while his brother Clement, a Haileyburian like himself and the future Labour Prime Minister, served gallantly on Gallipoli and in Mesopotamia. Military tribunals treated objectors as shirkers who were benefitting from the sacrifice of others. Questions that those registering for exemption had to answer included: 'How can you reconcile enjoying the privileges of British citizenship with this refusal to undertake any kind of work of national importance?'[82]

Arthur Rowntree (from the famous confectionery family) was the headmaster at Bootham School in York, the only Quaker school in HMC. Rowntree was adamant that his boys follow their conscience, and he ensured that first-aid training was available as an option for those not comfortable with combat. Some fifty boys opted for it in 1915, working towards a first-aid certificate to qualify them to work in the Friends' Ambulance Units when they were old enough.[83] Some 130 old boys went off to work in the Friends' Ambulance Units, and a further 289 served in the army or navy, leaving fifteen who, as the Bootham magazine proudly recorded, 'served in prison'.[84] The memorial in the library records that fifty-six old boys died fighting for their country.

Leighton Park in Reading was another prominent Quaker school, albeit not in HMC. Charles Evans was the headmaster, and a pronounced pacifist. But he worked hard to ensure that the community was afforded freedom of conscience to respond to the war as they thought fit: 'We desire that the school should stand for all that is best in Quakerism, with its firm testimony against war ... but never has there been a time when the call to arms has found so great a response amongst the lovers of peace. Many Leightonians are now in khaki, including several who little thought ever to find themselves serving as soldiers'.[85] His former pupils' responses covered the full gamut. One, E. P. Southall, wrote to him, 'If one lacked faith and strength of purpose, solitary confinement would be a nightmare.' The letter was written in Wormwood Scrubs prison. A long-serving member of staff, F. J. Edminson, was sentenced to hard farm labour, a task which apparently he grew to like.[86] Basil Bunting, a boy at Leighton Park in the earlier part of the war, was arrested in 1918 for refusing any kind of national service. He argued that if he was to engage in any non-combatant work, it would release another man to go off and be a killer. The popular press was vitriolic about conscientious objectors, and damned Bunting in the *Illustrated Chronicle* with the accusation that he was a 'conchy' who would sooner see the 'Huns overrunning the country than kill a man'. He spent most of the rest of the year in prison, during which he went on hunger strike. After his release, he became a modernist poet of some note.[87] Leighton Park alumni, however, equally encompassed Private Raymond Ashby, whose award of the Distinguished Service Medal (DCM) was celebrated in the school magazine *The Leightonian*: his death two months later at Flers on the Somme was reported with great sadness, the magazine reporting 'how much he was loved by his men'.[88]

The strain on headmasters and housemasters

The most harrowing task any teacher might ever be called upon to fulfil is breaking the news to a child of the death of a parent or sibling. Headmasters, if they had been in office in the period before the war, would have personally known all their old boys from the years which saw the highest incidence of casualties. Many heads suffered grievously during the war. Frank Fletcher, Master of Marlborough 1903–11 and now at Charterhouse, kept a scrapbook full of photos of young men he knew, official letters and black-edged letters from parents; one item dated May 1915 was from an Edward Hunter, who said: 'I have often thought of the schoolmasters during this war and think that their sorrows must be next to the parents, as they know the boys so well.' Fletcher also mourned a Charterhouse master, Lieutenant Colonel Harry Kemble, with a letter in the scrapbook from a former Marlborough pupil and one of Kemble's subalterns, saying how much the battalion owed to him and how 'you will miss him too. He always spoke with affection of you all'.[89]

Several heads buckled under the strain during the war years. McKenzie of Uppingham was one of the first, his breakdown in health forcing him to resign aged sixty-four. His departure made way for the inexperienced Reginald Owen to succeed. McKenzie's collapse was attributed to the stress of the war, the constant news of old boys being killed in action and anxiety about the safety of his own son, who joined up from Uppingham in 1915.[90]

Headmasters of some of the grandest schools, many already of advanced years, suffered particularly. James Gow had been head-master of Westminster since 1901. His health was not strong and his eyesight had been deteriorating. The shock of the death of his youngest son at Jutland in 1916 hit him grievously, and was believed to have exacerbated problems which led ultimately to his blindness. Gow felt it his duty to continue until the war was over, resigning in 1919. He died just four years later, in February 1923.[91] Charles Lowry, headmaster of Tonbridge and a former chairman of HMC, saw his health collapse in the middle of the 1917 summer term, and he was ordered by doctors to take a complete rest. He did not return until after Christmas. The school history records: 'He was one of those on whom the deaths in battle of his own pupils … placed an almost unbearable strain'. In February 1922 his health broke down again, this time irretrievably, and he died later that year.[92] Vaughan of Wellington, described as 'a big man in every sense of the word',[93] also found the strain increasingly difficult to handle in the first three years of the war, and in March 1918 was ordered to take two months off work entirely. His health collapsed in November and his condition was described as being 'rather worse' than in the spring.[94] Vaughan, however, recovered once the war was over, and went on to head Rugby School, retiring in 1931.

Frederick Sanderson at Oundle (1892–1922) was another of the big figures to suffer. His son Roy, a former head boy and captain of the rugby 1st XV, went off to the front recently married. Roy was constantly in his father's mind. In April 1918 the news came that he had been killed at the age of twenty-nine. On the following Sunday his distraught father preached a heart-rending sermon in chapel on the text, 'I will not leave you desolate. I will come unto you.'[95] The writer H. G. Wells sent his sons to Oundle, and Sanderson was the inspiration for the progressive headmaster in his novel *Joan and Peter* (1918). Wells subsequently became his biographer in 1924, the only biography Wells wrote. Just days before the Armistice, with Sanderson's health already under considerable stress, he received another blow in the death of a friend and master at the school to whom he was particularly close, Lieutenant Colonel G. A. Tryon. Sanderson soldiered on after the war but died in 1922 when delivering a lecture in London. H. G. Wells was one of those in the audience. Horace Pyne, headmaster of Warwick, learned his son had been drowned in the Mediterranean in May 1917, torpedoed on the way to the Salonika front. In his memory, his grieving father paid for an extension to the chapel, with a plaque and stained glass window.[96] George Smith, Master of Dulwich College, was another to lose his son, also called George, who had left Rugby at Easter 1915, where he had been head of his house and captained the 1st XV in his final term. He won the MC in November 1916, but was killed by a shell at St Eloi six weeks before the Armistice. 'He was one of the bravest and most conscientious men I have ever known', said his Colonel, while his Major wrote, 'he was a true gentleman in the highest sense of the word!'[97] Dulwich College was one of several schools to suffer heavily through loss of teachers. When one member of staff, T. G. Treadgold, retired in the 1920s, he reflected on the war years that, 'My room was full of shadows by the end.'[98] George Corner, head of Wellington School in Somerset, would have agreed. When old boys gave him a retirement gift in November 1939, he told them: 'We pray that you may be ... spared some at least of the horrors of 1914–18. Life at school was then a continual nightmare'.[99]

A nightmare is certainly an accurate description of the war experience of George Howson of Gresham's, perhaps the best known example of a headmaster broken by it. Headmaster since 1903, he knew individually almost all the old boys who were wounded and killed, and it left a terrible mark on him. The last photograph of him was taken in July 1918, and it was said, 'the once stocky figure was much reduced'.[100] Though clearly unwell, he insisted on continuing with his work. In early January 1919 he went down to London for the Gresham's War Memorial Committee and the HMC annual conference, but the effort proved too much for him, and he died on 7 January. The Duchess of Hamilton, who knew him well, and had given out prizes on speech day in 1915, was clear about the cause: 'The war killed him as "straightly" and surely as if he had fallen at the front.'[101]

Many retired heads also suffered loss. The correspondence of Warden John Millington Sing, who had only retired from St Edward's, Oxford, in 1913, is full of letters from boys at the Front he had known, and, more sadly, from the parents of those killed. The mother of William Dore, who had only left school in 1914 and was killed the following year wrote: 'You must feel pretty badly with this ever increasing roll of your young men who have been cut off in their prime.'[102] More personally, the roll of the dead included many sons of retired heads, including those of Loretto, Clifton and Bedford. Thomas Belcher, headmaster of Brighton College from 1881 to 1893, lost three of his four sons – one in 1915 and two in 1917. The surviving son became headmaster of Brighton himself in the 1920s.[103]

Heads of girls' boarding schools faced similar challenges. Most girls had older brothers, fathers or uncles fighting, and it often fell to the head to pass on the bad news. At Cheltenham Ladies' College a prayer room was set aside for the girls, and in it a book was kept listing the names of brothers and fathers at the front. The room was in daily use, and girls were encouraged to bring in postcards from brothers away fighting, with their photographs and those of their comrades. The headmistress, Lilian Faithfull, described in her memoirs how one day she heard that a brother had been killed in action: 'Realising what it would mean to the sister, I was so much of a coward that I feared to send for her.' An hour later, she passed the girl in the school hall and called out her name. 'She turned round, her face alight and smiling and all she said was, "I am far too proud to be sad".'[104]

We might have assumed 'stiff upper lips' were in evidence mainly on boys, but clearly girls resorted to the same tactic. The masking of inner turmoil with outward bravado was a helpful mechanism at the time, but in the longer term it stored up problems which might only come to the surface many years later. For housemasters in the public schools, and housemistresses in the girls' schools, the emotional cost was great, because they were the figures who best knew the pupils. They learned about casualties from lists in the newspapers, from personal letters or telephone calls from relatives. One housemaster wrote a letter to a grieving mother using words that would have been often written to parents: 'I recognised your writing this morning with a feeling of dread. I cannot tell you how grieved I am at the news your letter contained.'[105]

Retired or current housemasters often accepted the task of keeping records of the war dead, publishing them periodically in the school magazine or other journals. In some schools the names were collated and published after the war. At Fettes John Mackay-Thompson over-came his disappointment at being declared unfit for military service by meticulously recording the Fettes Roll of Honour. His original printed ledger in the school's archives shows the updates he made in his precise hand throughout the war, with military decorations in red ink and the names of the fallen underlined, together with small details about the dead and how they had been killed.[106] At Tonbridge the housemaster taking on the task was Henry Stokoe, who meticulously recorded in a series of small notebooks the service details of all old boys, the first list being published in the *The Tonbridgian* in 1914. As a labour of love he edited and produced *Tonbridge School and the Great War*, one of the several exceptional memorial books produced by the public schools. Inside it are the names of over forty dead who had once been with him in his own boarding house. One of the entries, for an officer killed in 1915 by a British rifle grenade prematurely exploding against a trench parapet, was that of Bertram Stokoe, his own son.[107]

Chapter 6

The Eternal Bond

The public schools refined and deepened character traits and convictions already implanted by family and shaped by 'prep' schools. Those four or five years in the senior school, with their codes of honour, duty and loyalty, and imperatives of courage, became an all-important part of the psyche of every public schoolboy for the rest of his life. The bond which continued to tie so many of them to their school had always been present in an understated way in civilian life, but it became far more real with the onset of war. To the many often frightened men who found themselves in the terrifying environment of war, the memories of the certainties of school, the comradeship of school friends, and the care of benign adults, above all their housemasters, assumed an almost mystical significance, especially for those only just out of school.

Mementoes and names

Jack Girling took pride in being both an athlete and a scholar at Wellington College. He played rugby for the 1st XV, wrote poetry, and won a scholarship to Corpus Christi, Oxford. He was also proud of being commissioned as a second lieutenant in the Hampshire Regiment and arriving smartly on the Somme battlefields on leaving school, aged eighteen, in 1916. One cannot imagine how such a young and sensitive man managed to acclimatize himself to a world so utterly alien. He took with him to France his rugby colours scarf and pinned it above his bed, as it reminded him of happier and more secure times. Its image prompted him to write a short poem, *School Colours*, while in his dugout near Lesboeufs, waiting to go over the top. It is easy to ridicule it as jejune and sentimental, but the truth of what he felt shines through the lines: 'It hangs before me on a nail/For when I gaze on you above/I see dear Wellington again;/And in the mud and drifting rain/In fancy play the game I love.'[1]

We do not know what Girling felt as he prepared for battle, but like many in the trenches he must certainly have been aware of the heavy losses in the first weeks of the battle. He led his platoon over the top, in an attack on 23 October whose mission was unclear, and was shot clean through the chest. His grieving father consoled himself by collecting his poems and publishing them for private circulation, writing in the preface that, 'His friends will pardon any immaturity for the sake of the boy that they knew and loved'.[2]

Scarves were poignant mementoes, denoting an attachment to a school or a house, and connoting status too, as scarves were awarded for particular distinctions at school. A French officer, who, for reasons that are lost, was familiar with the Charterhouse colours, wrote to the school to say that he had been passing through a village on the River Aisne which had been hotly disputed the year before, when he came across a grave marked by a wooden cross: 'There was no name on the cross, but round it was tied an Old Carthusian scarf.' Moved by the sight, he decided that he would 'mark it well with stones, and tied the scarf securely to the cross'.[3]

The principal vehicles for keeping old boys in touch with their school were the old boys' associations – the 'shock troops' of the public school system, helping their members stay close to the alma mater and to each other. Their publications, sports teams and social events bound old boys together in thriving social networks, which extended to wherever they might be across the world, meeting on special school occasions such as Founder's Day, to sing the school song and swap stories of the old days. Only 'good men' belonged to these old boys' associations, and there was a natural presumption that those who did so were to be trusted. One potent facet of this trust was the 'old boy network' – older alumni appointing younger ones to their firms and practices. The custom even extended to Prime Ministers when forming their administrations, and it was not just Etonian Prime Ministers who liked to pepper their teams with chums and old boys from school. In 1923 Stanley Baldwin, who had recently become Prime Minister, addressed the Old Harrovian Association: 'When the call came for me to form a government, one of my first thoughts was that it should be a government of which Harrow should not be ashamed. I remembered how in previous governments there had been four, or perhaps five Harrovians, and I was determined to have six.'[4] During the war itself, battalion and regimental commanders would pull strings to get into their command young subalterns who shared their alma mater. In war, as in peace, the old school tie really did matter.

The old boys' association at King's School Ely had encouraged A. M. Coate, who was training to be a gunnery officer, to visit his old school. The school magazine recorded how he showed the current boys that 'he had not lost his old skills in fives'. So smart a trainee did Coate prove that he was sent to the front earlier than expected. 'The school wishes him the best of luck',[5] recorded the magazine. That luck eluded him when in September 1918 he was killed in action. The *Eton Chronicle*, March 1915, recorded with pleasure how many Old Etonians would return to the school before they went off to fight, 'to play their games once more, to walk in the playing fields or on Sundays to sit again in Chapel'. What the visits signified, the magazine stated, was 'that Etonians neither forget their duty to their country, nor their debt to their school'.[6]

Familiar names became enormously significant to those who were fighting far from home. Trench systems were named after the streets and places familiar to those who fought. An Old Carthusian arrived at billets named 'Tay Farm' by the Scottish Division which had been stationed there. During the night he painted out 'Tay Farm' and replaced it with 'Charterhouse Farm'. He wrote back to his school boasting of his clever calligraphy, 'in the hope that some other Old Carthusian may read them and, if he should pass this way, some happy chord in his memory be struck. For to Old Carthusians out here, in the shadow of Death, Charterhouse is a great and living reality'.[7] In Laventie in France, an Old Wykehamist junior staff officer, J. C. Charles, noted how someone in 1915 had renamed battalion HQ as 'Winchester House', and that someone else had written on a board by it the Winchester College motto: 'Manners Makyth Man'. An invitation was given for any Wykehamist passing by to inscribe his name on it; eighteen names were thus written, and later on in the war the boards were crated up and sent back to the school, where they can still be found.[8]

School magazines
Schoolboys wrote avidly back to their old school magazine throughout the war. Originating in the nineteenth century, and boosted by the formation of old boys' associations, the magazines in the years before the war appear pretty turgid to outsiders, little more than a compilation or chronicle outlining in unremarkable prose the various events that made up the school calendar. The war, ironically perhaps, was the making of the school magazine, for the duration at least. The appetite to hear news about school and how old boys had fared grew stronger. Not that the news was often reassuring, because within the main body of the magazine, or as a separate supplement, schools published sobering 'war lists'. The information was gathered from the *London Gazette* and other press outlets, as well as from family and friends, and gave details

of old boys promoted, decorated, mentioned in dispatches, missing, wounded or killed. *The Harrovian* war supplement of June 1917 ran to thirty-two pages, and included regiments in which Harrovians were serving.[9] Ambivalent though heads were about newspapers publishing 'league tables' of schools' dead and decorated, such information was a source of great pride to individual schools.

Published letters from old boys suggest how widely the magazines were read. A former pupil of Christ's Brecon in Wales wrote: 'I spent the whole of last month at Divisional Training School ... While there, I had last term's *Breconian* and spent hours with my head buried deep in its pages'.[10] Post to soldiers fighting on fronts across the war theatres worked astonishingly well. 'Yesterday I saw the old grey "Rag" lying on my table and I said to myself I must write and tell the fellows what our chaps are doing here', said a King's Canterbury old boy writing back from Mesopotamia. 'This morning a chap brought certain papers for me to sign. His name was Lee-Warner. I said "Are you a brother of the great George Lee-Warner of KSC?" "Yes," he said. And so we bucked considerable and all had to stand around and wait until we had eased off some of the reminiscences of that great hero.'[11]

Old boys, then as now, were keen to ensure that their old school magazines mentioned what they had been doing, and did so accurately. From the Western Front a Melbourne Grammar School boy wrote back to say: 'I notice in your last issue of *The Melburnian* that W. H. McInery and Edgar Anderson claim to be the first OMs at the Flanders front. As a matter of fact I was in France on August 13th and was at Mons on 22nd; also Fred Steel, who has been killed, came out shortly afterwards, so we were the first OMs at the front. Would you kindly correct this?'[12] A humbler note was sounded by a Catholic military chaplain from Stonyhurst: 'I must send you a word of thanks for the *Stonyhurst Magazine*, which was most welcome. I am passing it on to one or two O.S.'s about here. The last number too was tremendously appreciated in the officers' mess ...'[13]

Letters

If headmasters could act like a grandfather, an uncle or even a chaplain to the boys in their care, then housemasters could be akin to their parents. The bond is always potentially there, especially in boarding schools, but became far more intense under the special circumstances of war, particularly when so many of the writers had only just left school. Housemasters, along with favoured teachers, could become the recipients of extraordinary outpourings of emotion from their protégés.

'Dear Sir, I am going to the Front tomorrow and I want to write to you on the eve of my departure and thank you for what ... you have done for me', wrote a self-effacing leaver from Wellington College to his headmaster, Vaughan. 'You perhaps won't remember me. I was not an athlete or a scholar but I owe a great deal to Wellington. It made me into a man and a gentleman. I just wanted to write and tell you that I am happy to think that I have the honour of being an OW.'[14]

Another officer who wrote on the eve of his departure was Lieutenant E. J. Porter: 'I need scarcely say, on the eve of going to France, how much I treasure all my memories of the three years spent at Manchester Grammar School. My best wishes for the continued prosperity and renown of the great school ... All I dare pray for is the courage to do my duty'.[15] He died of wounds in September 1916. At Wellington School in Somerset headmaster George Corner put up letters from old boys so all could read them. Second Lieutenant C. J. Malet-Veale wrote thus: 'On some of the most weary bloodthirsty days in France I used to sit and imagine what was going on at "home". On Saturdays I imagined the football or cricket ...'[16] Corner appears to have been closer to his pupils than many headmasters. His letters to old boys collectively at the front were later published in the magazine. One read, 'My dear Old Boys serving in the forces ... we have now heard of the loss of J. M. Kidner, who died of wounds in the Dardanelles, the first OTC boy to lay down his life for his country's honour ... May you be spared to return and gladden the homes left at such a sacrifice. This is the prayer of your old friend and Master, G. C.'[17] A different note was sounded by T. G. Houston, headmaster of Coleraine Academical Institution in Northern Ireland and an ardent Unionist, who wrote at Christmas to his old boys: 'I know of 231 old boys (including 4 of my colleagues) who have given that proof of their manhood ... My great regret is I cannot join you in what is the proper work of every true Briton'.[18]

Retired headmasters were also tenacious correspondents, especially if of the type who formed close emotional bonds with their boys. One such was John Millington Sing, who had retired from St Edward's, Oxford, in 1913. He had from Harry Cresswell of the RAMC the kind of letter that heads are wont to receive: 'I always look backwards with sincere regret that I left Teddies a year too soon and I often wondered if you would have made me a prefect had I remained ...' Some letters made no effort to spare details of the horrors of war: 'Twice I was buried alive and once knocked down by a shell into a 7 foot hole', wrote one old boy. 'My servant was hit by my side, his leg being simply shattered by a shell and he has now lost it.' The archives at St Edward's are full of letters of condolence Millington Sing wrote to the families of old boys who had been killed. The mother of one, Charles Ranson, wrote back to him in September 1917: 'We have none but happy memories of him. He never caused us an hour's anxiety. To you and the other masters at St Edward's he owed much of what he was.'[19]

Correspondence with housemasters and tutors displays a more intimate language, as the personal relationships that were formed over the years were often much deeper. One house tutor at Shrewsbury, Everard Kitchin, was a notable correspondent; his command of the OTC prevented him joining up and serving alongside his beloved boys. The gossipy content and the stoicism are typical of such letters. To one recently departed Salopian he wrote: 'My dear old James, Please forgive me for not having written. I'm awfully sorry to hear about your Hun measles ... I saw Bobby Hanmer in hospital about a month ago; he's getting on slowly – he got the MC. Dick Higgins is here and staying with Prior – he got a bullet through the lower jaw but the disfigurement is much less than I expected. Inspection is over and it was such a success the General asked for a whole holiday ... Best of luck, yours ever, Kitch'.[20]

The depth of the house bond is revealed fully in this letter sent in January 1917 to Eton housemaster Hugh Macnaghten: 'The past week or two has not been exciting ... but tonight we are really going to get busy ... It will be the first time I have had much responsibility in a real fight. I hope I shall do alright. I must hurry as orders have just come. Well, I hope to come through safely, but, if I don't, goodbye and God bless you ... I think my last thoughts in this world, whenever I die, will be of Mother, Eton and you. Such a Mother and such a friend are more than most people can hope for'. The letter was never finished. It was found in the writer's pocket after his death, and sent to the housemaster he so admired.[21]

A. C. Rayner-Wood was an Eton housemaster, and regular correspondent, who devised a novel way of sending the same text to all his old boys from the house. A message would appear on the house notice board: 'War Work for All. Forty Scribes wanted. A letter to the Old Boys will be dictated in Pupil Room from 7.00 pm to 8.00 pm tonight (Sunday). Volunteers bring pens!' The scribes frequently added their own personal messages, one being, 'To Nigel Anson, I fagged for you last summer half. Good luck. Signed Logan.'[22]

None has expressed the strength of the bond between housemaster and former pupil better than a retired Eton housemaster, Henry Luxmoore, who wrote most movingly in a letter to a friend in December 1917: 'My losses in the war are heart-rending: it would seem as if the very pick and the best of all are marked for death, and the blows come so steadily ... How the nation is to recover in the next generation I can't see at all, since the fittest do not survive'.[23]

Some letters from the front are breezy and full of bravado: 'A sniper had the cheek to hit our best frying pan this morning. Suppose that was a couple of feet off me. I got a large quantity of French mud down my neck', wrote Darrell Vowler back to Sherborne from France in January 1915. 'The trenches were 4 feet deep in water', he continued. 'Things are much better now, but one can still sink in mud over the knees in places.'[24] T. C. Burrows from Kingswood School in Bath laughed off his injury from his hospital bed in Cardiff, writing back to a former teacher about his 'ill-judged, if successful, attempt to interfere with a shell-splinter which was exceeding the speed of light ... I believe that the extraordinary thickness of my skull caused you much exasperation when, in the old days, you used to take the upper fifth in mathematics, but its possession today is to me a source of congratulation'.[25] Sport was never far from the minds of the young men: it brought relief, happiness and familiarity to the strain of their daily lives. 'When our brigade was in reserve, we played cricket under shellfire', wrote H. S. Tindall to Haileybury in July 1917, 'but we had to adopt an impromptu rule that, if a shell was in the air at the time, the ball was to be counted as a "no ball". Certainly one shell which fell about 50 yards off, put me off a catch while I was fielding in the deep.' The Third Battle of Ypres was raging that month. Tindall's letter made it into *The Haileyburian*, but the editor added his regret, at the end of it, that the author was killed nine days after he penned the words.[26]

Other letters displayed no hint of jocularity and would have left recipients in no doubt about the state of mind of their writer. 'The keenest vigilance has to be maintained every second owing to the extreme proximity of the Turkish trenches', wrote an old boy back to his alma mater, Sydney Grammar School. 'At one point under my command the two lines of trenches are separated by less than ten yards. This means that if the enemy choose to make a rush, they could breach us in about three seconds. Just over our parapet are over 200 dead bodies.'[27] Another was clearly struggling when he wrote to John Lyon School in north-west London: 'I have kept in touch with the old school and its events by means of the little blue-covered magazine, but latterly the news has been only too sad. The world will never seem the same again, especially when one gets thinking of Eric Stearns, Tommy Lyon ...'[28] To Trant Bramston, compiler of the 'War Roll' at Winchester, an old boy wrote: 'One man in my company was stuck in the mud for three days and three nights under intense shellfire: when we got him out, he died of exhaustion ... The trenches are "hell with the lid off", as one of my men called it ... I think my heart and spirit have been broken by the difficulties. A month with you now, Trant, in a peaceful winter is the highest conception of heaven for me at the minute. God must be dead, Trant, to let this go on – man was not made to stand it.'[29]

For sheer poignancy it is hard to beat the letters from Second Lieutenant Douglas Gillespie, another Old Wykehamist, whose brother Tom, an Olympic rower, had been killed in October 1914. So moving were they that they were published in 1916, entitled *Letters from Flanders*. He wrote of a German 33-pounder bomb, 'like a big turnip with a long handle', tumbling in the air as it came over a row of trees towards the British trenches: 'I felt like a small boy at Winchester waiting for high catches in the deep field, for the sausage seemed to hang in the air above your head ... and you wondered when the thing was going to come down'.[30] He remembers hearing a nightingale sing at school, and thinking about all those who had heard it sing but were now dead, like his brother Tom. He compared them to 'Hector and Achilles, and all the heroes of long ago who were once so strong and active and now are quiet.'[31] Rudyard Kipling said of one of Gillespie's missives that it was the finest letter known to him. Montagu Rendall, the Winchester headmaster, to whom the letter was sent, was so moved by it that he wrote to the editor of *The Wykehamist*, asking for it to be included as 'a beautiful revelation from a rare personality'.[32] Gillespie was thinking in it about the end of the war, and proposed as a suitable European war memorial a tree-shaded *via sacra* (sacred road) to run between the trench lines from Switzerland to the English Channel. Of this imaginary 450-mile memorial he wrote, 'I would like to send every man, woman and child in Western Europe on pilgrimage along that *via sacra*, so that they might think and learn about what war means from the silent witnesses on either side.'[33] Gillespie did not live to discover whether his proposal was to come to fruition: he was killed in action at the Battle of Loos on 25 September 1915.

Meetings and dinners at the Front

The sight of a familiar face, even if its owner was not known well or even particularly liked, could be a great source of comfort at the front. Encounters between old boys of the same school were surprisingly common, above all from the larger public schools. Those who had gone on to university also established new networks of friends who shared common backgrounds. The likelihood of meeting contemporaries from the same school were heightened because of the custom of regiments maintaining a connection with a particular school. Etonians thus were likely to be found in the Guards' Regiments, Wykehamists in the Rifle Brigade, and alumni from Scottish public schools in regiments such as the Royal Scots or the Highland Light Infantry. The columns and letters pages of school magazines are full of stories of such encounters.

Lionel Sotheby, a recent Eton leaver, was thrilled, once out in France, to discover 'heaps of Etonians arriving ... Among the 60th Rifles I met Fowler, awfully nice fellow whom I knew at Eton. He was at Wells'. There was also Sherlock of Somerville's and Hordein of Churchill's. Hordein I knew very well. We went through the school together and I like him immensely'.[34] Sotheby was in the 1st Battalion, The Black Watch, and had come out to France in February 1915, taking part in the Battles of Neuve Chapelle and Aubers Ridge. A platoon commander, he wrote, has a duty 'to encourage his men and expose himself more than anyone. For an attack he has to be in the front and first in everything'.[35] On 4 June, following an Old Etonian dinner at Bethune, he wrote: 'To die for one's school is an honour ... to die for one's country is an honour. But to die for right and fidelity is greater honour than these ... Be thankful that such an opportunity was given to me ... *Floreat Etona'*.[36] Sotheby was to die at the Battle of Loos that autumn, aged twenty.

Meetings of old boys occurred in the most surprising and precarious of circumstances. An officer from King's Canterbury wrote to the school from Mesopotamia, 'I met R. E. Gordon actually under enemy fire at Akway on 12 April 1915.'[37] Another wrote from India, 'I met ... R. E. Gordon in the Taj Mahal [Hotel] Bombay, who didn't at all like to be reminded that the last time I'd seen him was "readjusting his impressions" after eight of the best from Townend.'[38] Chance encounters of old boys could release tension at times of great danger: 'Our objective was a wood and we got to it ... bristling with machine guns and snipers but we won through,' wrote an officer back to Christ's Brecon. 'I was ordered to reinforce the Welch, and joined a body of them commanded by Jack Brooker. We recognised one another at once and even reminisced about the time he bowled A. P. James the first ball after tea in 1907 ... I have heard he came through alright'.[39] Captain Freddie Llewelyn Hughes of Christ's Hospital met one school friend in a shell-hole on the Passchendaele battlefield, and the first thing they said to each other was 'Compris Housey?'[40] to which both answered 'Oui, tres bon'.[41]

Paul Jones (Dulwich) had been 1st XV captain and won a scholarship to Balliol, before joining the army in April 1915. In April 1917, now an officer in the Tank Corps, he wrote to his brother, his pride in his school shining through: 'The more I see of life the more convinced I am of the greatness of the old school. Wherever you meet a Dulwich man out here, you'll find he bears a reputation for gallantry, for character, for hard work, and for what may be termed the "public school spirit" in its best form. Our Roll of Honour and the simply amazing list of decorations bear this out. Of my own old colleagues, there is not one who has not either been hit (alas! killed in many cases) or received some decoration or both; and that, mark you, though we are not what is known as an "army school" like Eton, Cheltenham or Wellington.'[42] Three months later, he was killed on the first day of the Third Battle of Ypres. Corporal Jenkins, the NCO in his tank, wrote: 'Your son was shot by a sniper. The bullet passed through the port-hole and entered your son's brain. Death was almost instantaneous.'[43]

Meetings with old teachers could be a source of awkwardness, but also of great comfort. When Gilbert Talbot met a Winchester master, Harry Altham,[44] in Ypres in May 1915 just after the Second Battle of Ypres, his mentor offered to show him around the town which had rapidly become such a powerful emblem of British resistance. The heart of Ypres, then as now, was the Cloth Hall and Cathedral, suggesting the economic might of this small Flanders town. 'Nothing has brought the war home to me as has this town', Talbot was to write subsequently to his parents. 'Harry and I remembered that the last expedition we made together was to Oxford. I tried to think of the peace and loveliness of Magdalen and Christ Church on that May evening and to contrast it with the blackened ruins we were now seeing.'[45]

An encounter between five Old Blues of Christ's Hospital was made famous because the poet Edmund Blunden, who had left in 1915, wrote so enthusiastically about it. Under the title 'The Feast of Five' Blunden had this letter published in the school magazine *The Blue* in June 1917: 'Gentle and Benevolent Editor, – recent statistics having proved beyond all possible shade of doubt that there were five Old Blues in this battalion, it was decided to have a mass meeting, *non sine Baccho* [i.e. with alcohol], at the earliest chance. A timely return to the civilised area having now allowed of this, I beg to send you a photo.'[46] The bibulous reunion took place in the spring of 1917. Blunden had another letter published four months later, during the Third Battle of Ypres, under the title 'A Tribute from the Field': 'You were good enough to print in your July number a letter written in happier days ... I should be grateful if you would put on record a rough tribute to two of the very best men and officers that any battalion ever had. We took part in the Flanders offensive and our brigade was responsible for taking St Julien and some country to the north of it. Vidler and Amon took their companies over ... and we all three met on the final objective. Did ever three Old Blues meet in a stranger situation – cold, grey morning, lacerated ground littered with ruins, the tanks wallowing forward ... It was then that I first heard Collyer had been killed in no man's land and Tice very seriously wounded ... now we are back in the quiet, the news has come that Tice has died of his wounds – I wonder if people in England realise the price we are paying for victory? Sometimes the war seems like a quicksand to me, playing shipwreck with everyone and everything that was worthwhile ...'[47]

A postscript concerns Blunden's friend Vidler, who suffered so grievously from emotional strains in the war that he took his life in 1924. Blunden, deeply distressed, paid tribute to him in his poem *A.G.A.V.*, which he quotes in his memoir *Undertones of War*: '... if one cause I had for pride, it is to have been your friend,/To have lain in shell holes by your side, with you to have seen impend/The meteors of the hour of fire, to have talked where speech was love ...'[48]

Old boys' dinners were often hard-drinking events in peacetime, so it is unsurprising that dinners organized at the front, which public schoolboys bent every rule to attend, were high on alcohol consumption. 'We had an old Shirburnian dinner (of a sort)', wrote Harold May in 1915, who was a teacher at, as well as an old boy of the school. 'It was a merry party and the gathering increased as the evening wore on – Repton, Clifton and Marlborough had their representatives and we talked of things of yore.' Within a month of writing the letter May had died of wounds sustained at the front.[49]

Schools from the Dominions were particularly successful at holding impromptu old boy dinners. The archives at Christ's College, New Zealand, contain a signed menu of a dinner at Heliopolis, Egypt, in January 1915. Of the sixty-six signatures on the menu card which can be deciphered, nineteen were killed within a few months at Gallipoli, eighteen were to be wounded, and six were subsequently killed in France; only eighteen of the signatories survived the war unscathed.[50] Melbourne Grammar's archives similarly contain letters from old boys about dinners at the front: 'Sometime ago we had a dinner at St Omer and I'm sending you a menu with signatures of the participants', wrote an old boy on 28 August 1917. 'Everywhere one goes one sees OMs and it makes one feel more than proud to belong to the old school. We are determined to see this business through, no matter how greatly we long to be back among you. Little nights like these take you back many thousands of miles.'[51]

Winchester staged one of the odder old boys' dinners in November 1917 at the Salon Godbert in Amiens, safely behind the British lines on the Somme. In peacetime it is not uncommon for heads to travel abroad for old boys' dinners; but in wartime, as Montagu Rendall, the headmaster, did on this occasion, it was most unusual. The proposal for a Winchester war memorial was the reason given for Rendall's attendance. Seventy Wykehamists obtained leave of absence from their regiments to participate in the Salon Godbert's fare – quite a remarkable occasion, with the Third Battle of Ypres reaching a climax at Passchendaele, and the Battle of Cambrai beginning. Seven generals and twelve colonels graced the dinner, as well as three young subalterns whose names would appear on the war memorial they discussed that night.[52]

Etonians can be relied upon to take traditions seriously, none more so than the Fourth of June celebrations (marking the birthday of King George III). In 1916 the *Eton Chronicle* reported that the headmaster had received telegrams about dinners taking place in Sinai, East Africa and Mesopotamia, as well as in diverse locations in Belgium and France. The *Chronicle* recorded: 'The Fourth of June was spent quietly at Eton this year, but neither supper nor fireworks were forgotten by our representatives at the Front, where the celebration seems to have been held in a manner thoroughly worthy of the occasion.'[53]

One dinner at the front has been remembered by their school today. In January 1917 sixty-eight Old Marlburians attended a dinner at Bailleul, a town near the Belgian border and ten miles south of Ypres. A regimental band was arranged to serenade the diners, there was raucous singing of old school songs and several speeches. The menu survives to tell us that the guests, who included four major generals, enjoyed *soles frites, filets de boeuf, poulet sur canapé, anges à cheval,* coffee and liqueurs, washed down by Heidsieck and Veuve Clicquot champagne, then Sauternes dessert wine and port. In 2012 a party of Old Marlburians, including several descendants of those who attended the original dinner, held a ninety-fifth anniversary celebration in Bailleul: they enjoyed exactly the same menu.[54]

The death of friends
The death of soldiers in the Great War affected their immediate family above all. But it had a marked, and cumulative, impact on the friends who had grown up with them over the key adolescent years of their lives at school. With burials from 1915 taking place in the battle zones, and no further repatriation of bodies, memorial services became the focal point for grieving families and friends at home. Schools held such memorial services for their old boys throughout the war, attended by

those school friends able to come, by teachers and former teachers. Memorial plaques, windows and other memorials began to appear, in schools and chapels across the country. In June 1918, for example, a stained glass window to Captain Charles Henderson MC, killed on the Somme, was unveiled on the north side of the Radley chapel.[55]

Since boys from the same school often fought in the same battalions, they inevitably found themselves witnessing the deaths of friends. Second Lieutenant F. M. Wookey (Campbell College) was immensely proud to serve in the Royal Irish Regiment, especially under a school friend as adjutant of his battalion. Wookey was killed in the spring of 1915, leading an advance along a road near Saint Eloi just to the south of Ypres. The adjutant wrote to his parents to tell them what happened: 'I went back later to the dressing station to see him; the doctors feared the shock of his wounds would prove fatal, but hoped for the best. That was the last I saw of your son ... I am proud to be able to say I was a school fellow of your son (we were in the same form at Campbell College). If it be God's will that I die in this war, I pray that I die as gallant a death as your brave and only son'.[56]

School friendships also extended to taking responsibility for burying the bodies of the fallen. On 24 May 1915, Private Thomas Flook (Christ's Hospital) was killed at Festubert in northern France, when serving in the Civil Service Rifles. He had left school in 1910 and had been eager to volunteer once war was declared. A battlefield burial was impossible in the midst of the fighting, but in a lull two officers from the same house as Flook quietly insisted that it was for Old Blues to conduct the committal.[57] Carthusians felt the same when Second Lieutenant Righton Burrow was killed in October 1915, with his fellow old boys ensuring that a proper funeral took place. One who served in the same battalion, Captain Oliver Wreford Brown (himself to be killed on the Somme the following summer), wrote to Burrows' father, who was Bishop of Sheffield: 'Righton died for his country, going to aid of a wounded soldier ... I had always held such a high opinion of Righton ever since I came across him at Charterhouse. He was a man to follow. There were not many dry eyes when we carried Righton out'.[58]

Schoolmasters serving at the front could feel a sense of responsibility for apprehensive young men straight out of school, particularly from their own schools but also from others. We can see this avuncular feeling in the tenderness shown to the young subaltern Raleigh in *Journey's End* by Osborne, the older officer and public school master. One such was Lieutenant Charles Eyre, who had been head boy of Harrow in 1901, as well as captain of cricket and football, and who returned to teach there five years later. Once at the front, the school and

138

its old boys were constantly in his thoughts. With mounting horror at what he was witnessing, he wrote in March 1915: 'As long as no one in England talks about peace until we have won – really won – all is well. The next generation must be spared the horrors of modern war.' In his last letter, written on 19 September 1915 on the eve of the Battle of Loos, his thoughts returned to his old school as he knew the new academic year would be starting: 'I shall be thinking of you all rallying on the Old Hill this week. I have tried to do my best for it according to my lights . . . It is grand to think of the great response it has made to the war's appeal. And I shall be proud to be amongst the Old Harrovians who fell in the Great War'.[59] He was indeed to fall, on the opening day of the battle, 25 September 1915.

The story of Evelyn Southwell and Malcolm White epitomizes the friendship that can exist between two colleagues teaching in the same school. They were two of a talented group of schoolmasters that Cyril Alington recruited to Shrewsbury in the years before the war; head-masters like to boast of the quality of the teachers they recruit, and he was no stranger to that curious vanity. He wrote of them, 'They loved the life and work of the schoolmaster as only born schoolmasters can.'[60] Southwell, a classicist and rowing blue, arrived at Shrewsbury from Oxford in 1910, and White, a classicist and musician, arrived from Cambridge the same year. They rapidly discovered a close bond, accelerated by living in accommodation, the 'New House', specially built by Alington for his bachelor masters. Boys thronged to it as the place to go to for lively debate, for concerts and for planning walks into the nearby hills.

Much as they loved the school, they felt compelled to join up. White wrote: 'I never pretend that I want the trenches, but one part of myself says to the other – "This war is an ordeal which I dare you to face; I don't believe you can" – and the other part replies – "Lord, then I suppose I must try." '[61] Southwell went out to France in October 1915, followed by White in February 1916. While waiting to go in the front line, Southwell wrote to his mother about taking Communion at a village school behind the lines: 'Today was Sunday and there was Celebration in the school here, and we knelt in the familiar desks in the room all hung with maps, and I saw the blackboard and remembered that I was a schoolmaster too.'[62] Despite serving in separate Rifle Brigade battalions, the two kept in close touch by letter with each other and former colleagues. On hearing of the death of one of their colleagues, White wrote to Alington: 'He was so very much part of the place and still is. Do you think that we all continue to have our part in the place after death, even when not remembered?'[63] White's unit was chosen to be part of the first wave on the Somme. On 27 June 1916 he wrote to Southwell: 'Oh Man, I can't write now, I am too like a coach before the bumping races or Challenge Oars. So Man, good luck. Our New House and Shrewsbury are immortal.'[64] He was killed by a shell on the Redan Ridge that morning of 1 July. Southwell, too, saw action on the Somme. On 13 September he wrote to his Shrewsbury colleague, Hugh Howson, with similar thoughts about the reassuring beginning of the new school year: 'Shrewsbury will, I suppose, be beginning again soon after you get this, and among a list of good things there will be autumn mists, and new faces, and new books, and the sound of early football.'[65] Two days after writing the letter he was killed by a sniper in Delville Wood. Howson brought together his and White's letters into a memoir, *Two Men*, published in 1919. 'Those of us who knew Malcolm White and Evelyn Southwell are left with a strange yearning', said the review in *The Salopian*, 'an almost overwhelming sense of the debt we owe them, and a strengthening of our belief in the Public Schools, especially Shrewsbury.'[66]

Anglican and Catholic chaplains

'I have seen many terrible sights', wrote the Revd Julian Bickersteth, 'but nothing more sad than a young public school officer, handsome, blue-eyed, nineteen years old perhaps, straight from the battle, who reached our aid-post only a few hundred yards behind the firing line. He was in terrible agony, one arm blown off, the other seriously injured, and could not live. I shall never forget his piteous moan and then eager voice, "Padre, is that you? Is there a God?" My quick answer and assurance of the never-failing love of the All-Merciful brought out the words, "Yes, yes. You must be right, but it's hard, isn't it, to understand." '[67]

Julian Bickersteth had been a boy at Rugby, and then chaplain at Melbourne Grammar School from 1912 until 1915, when he came home to serve, just one of many school chaplains who volunteered. The public school officer mentioned above was no older than some of the boys he had been teaching just eighteen months before. The role school chaplains left behind was, and still is, an important one in the life of a school, both spiritually and pastorally. Chapel was an essential ingredient of the routine of every public schoolboy, the spiritual heart of the school as well as the place where the deepest meanings of the public school ethos were imparted and absorbed, including the ideals of service, compassion and ultimately of sacrifice. The ritual of the school meeting together in chapel was something boys remembered, even those lukewarm in faith, and in wartime they came back to their schools in uniform just for the comfort chapel could provide. The mother of Gilbert Talbot (Winchester), killed in July 1915, later wrote: 'We spent his last Saturday in England at Winchester, with the charm and beauty of the place at their highest. The last service before going to the front in the Chapel of so many loved associations could not fail to be very moving.'[68] Chapel was where the whole school assembled, where hymns were sung whose tunes carried great emotional resonance, and it was where boys listened to their headmasters, the majority of whom were in holy orders. In Catholic schools, such as Stonyhurst and Downside, chapel could be even more important, and the headmaster even more central, in his capacity as head of the community. All teachers in these schools were likely to be priests or monks, as were the housemasters, who had not only a pastoral but a spiritual role in the lives of the boys in their care.

The public schools, the Church of England and the military had long had close associations. About ten per cent of regular officers before the war had fathers who were clergymen: Bernard Montgomery (St Paul's), the son of a bishop and the future field marshal, was one of them. Shot in the lung and knee in October 1914, he recovered to serve as a general staff officer during the battles of 1917 and 1918. Many public schoolboys went on to take holy orders: Marlborough was known as a school for 'sons of clergy' and saw many leavers go into the church. The army needed chaplains for ministering to the soldiers' spiritual needs, providing support alongside stretcher-bearers and doctors, counselling the ill and despairing, and overseeing the details of deaths. At the start of the war there were only 117 who were 'Chaplains to the Forces' – that number was to rise to 3,475 by 1918, 60 per cent of whom were Anglican, 25 per cent Catholic and 15 per cent other denominations and faiths.[69]

One of the hardest tasks chaplains had to endure was to attend those soldiers sentenced to be shot. During the war just over 300 British soldiers were executed, mainly for cowardice or desertion. Julian Bickersteth was particularly distressed by one such case in December 1917, of a young soldier condemned for desertion, which he described in his diary: 'Once again it has been my duty to spend the last hours on earth with a condemned prisoner. I have, I hope, learnt much from the simple heroism of this mere lad of nineteen, who has been out at the front since 1914, when he was only fifteen and a half, and in spite of two wound stripes on his arm and all that service behind him, has met his end. It was my privilege to comfort and help him all I could ... and to stand by his side until the very end ... There are few deaths I have witnessed which have so wrung my heart-strings as this one ... As they bound him, I held his arm tight to reassure him and then he turned his blindfolded face to mine and said in a voice which wrung my heart, "Kiss me, sir, kiss me", and with my kiss on his lips, and "God has you in his keeping" whispered in his ear, he passed on into the Great Unseen'.[70]

Life at the front tested faith in a way that would not have occurred in peacetime. Death was all around, and soldiers were asked to go into battle with, they knew, a possibility of being wounded or killed. 'Did God exist?' 'If they died, would they go to a better place?' 'Was it preordained if they were to live or to die?' Many such questions went through men's minds. Captain Eric Whitworth (Radley), later head-master of Bradfield and Tonbridge, captured a central ambivalence: 'In billets there was a voluntary service on Sunday and thirty-four of my company went, but very few altogether. This is very curious as the men's letters are full of expressions of trust in the Almighty both through themselves and their relatives.'[71]

Anthony Eden, who left Eton in 1915, was not a particularly religious man, according to his biographer, D. R. Thorpe. In February 1913 he had written about Eton chapel in his diary, 'Usual dull service', but he had a spiritual side which came out with the experience of war. In a later reflection he wrote this about himself: 'We each had our form of weakness. Some might try to strike a bargain ... if Almighty God you do this for me, I will obey the Commandments scrupulously ... For me the prayer was always at heart the same: please God if I am to be hit, let me be slightly wounded or killed, but not mutilated'.[72] Such confidence in the spirit if not the practice of religion was by no means uncommon in public school Anglicans.

The Revd Ernest Crosse, an assistant chaplain at Marlborough who became a regimental chaplain, complained that, 'The officers as a whole have very little time for religion.' When he first went out to the front he asked his commanding officer for a chapel to use in his ministry. 'The suggestion seemed to him simply ludicrous', Crosse recalled in anger. The problems experienced by the overwhelmingly public school and middle-class clergy in communicating with the rank and file soldiers was another source of dismay to him: 'The whole setting of men's lives was so totally different ... To speak to them in terms which had any real meaning was like learning a whole new language'.[73]

Bickersteth, like Crosse, was disappointed by the lack of enthusiasm among officers to take Christianity more seriously, as well as by the Church of England's failure to reach out to men in the ranks who had 'never been brought into contact with sacramental teaching of any

142

Preparations for War

Charterhouse OTC Parade, *Greyfriar Magazine* drawing, 1912. *(Charterhouse archives)*

Cheltenham Ladies' College Red Cross practice, 1911. *(CLC archives)*

Wellington College Cadets: inspection of Wellington College lines, Tidworth OTC Camp, 1910. (*Wellington archives*)

St Paul's School shooting team at Bisley, 1908. Sergeant Wilfred Willett is seated second from right. (*St Paul's archives*)

Dr Cyril Alington (second left), Headmaster, watching cricket at Shrewsbury School, summer 1915. On his right Philip Bainbrigge (with spectacles) and Malcolm White, Shrewsbury schoolmasters, killed in action 18 September 1918 and 1 July 1916 respectively. (*Shrewsbury archives*)

George Howson, Headmaster of Gresham's, with his prefects in 1918. Howson died in January 1919 – 'the war killed him as surely as if he had fallen at the front'. (*Gresham's archives*)

The King's School OTC forms part of the funeral cortège of Lieutenant Vernon Austin in Canterbury, February 1915. His was one of the last bodies to be returned from the battlefield. (*King's School Canterbury archives*)

Public School VC Winners

Public School VC winner: Sidney Woodroffe (Marlborough) (seated centre left, with back to sandbags) in the trenches with other Rifle Brigade officers, summer 1915. (*Marlborough archives*)

Albert Ball (Trent and Nottingham HS) – fighter ace.

Noel Chavasse (Magdalen College School and Liverpool) – the only man to win two VCs in the war.

OTC Cadets entrenching on Hango Hill, King William's College, Isle of Man, 1915. (*King William's College archives*)

Christ's College, New Zealand: (*Top*) Christ's College Old Boys in the NZEF in August 1914. Of the forty-one men photographed, nineteen were killed. (*Left*) Guy Bryan-Brown – Chaplain, killed at Ypres 4 October 1917, while serving with NZEF. (*Right*) Ernest Crosse – Marlborough and Devonshire Regiment Chaplain, later Headmaster of Christ's and Ardingly. (*Christ's archives*)

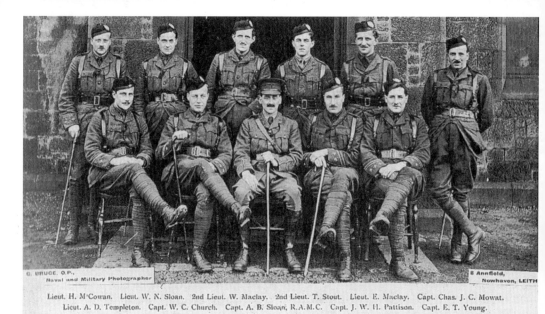

Lieut. H. M'Cowan. Lieut. W. N. Sloan. 2nd Lieut. W. Maclay. 2nd Lieut. T. Stout. Lieut. E. Maclay. Capt. Chas. J. C. Mowat.
Lieut. A. D. Templeton. Capt. W. C. Church. Capt. A. B. Sloan, R.A.M.C. Capt. J. W. H. Pattison. Capt. E. T. Young.

Eleven Glasgow Academy officers serving in the 8th Cameronians (Scottish Rifles) in 1914. Eight of them were killed at Gallipoli on 28 June 1915. (*Glasgow Academy archives*)

House hockey team at Marlborough 1913 – Harold Roseveare, the captain, was killed in September 1914, six weeks after leaving school. Thomasset, Blech, Gould and Empson were also killed. (*Marlborough archives*)

R. H. W. M. EMPSON.   L. J. WOODHOUSE.   M. P. ROSEVEARE.   W. JOYCE.

G. T. THOMASSET.   E. L. BLECH.   H. W. ROSEVEARE   J. C. T. LEIGH.   W. J. GOULD.
(Capt.)

P. C. COLLYNS.   A. G. CUTHBERT-SMITH.

Killed on the Somme

Anthony Brown (Michaelhouse), the only serving head to be killed in action. (*Michaelhouse archives*)

Evelyn Southwell, Shrewsbury teacher, whose letters to and from Malcolm White are so poignant. (*Shrewsbury archives*)

Raymond Asquith (Winchester) – 'this star of England'.

George Butterworth (Eton, and Radley teacher), 'the greatest loss to music'.

Patients and Staff of St Martin's Hospital, 1916. St Martin's was a Cheltenham Ladies' College boarding house which became a hospital, staffed by former pupils and current staff. (*CLC archives*)

Lilian Faithfull (Principal of Cheltenham Ladies' College), at the wheel of her car outside St Martin's Hospital, 1916. (*CLC archives*)

Sportsmen

Ronnie Poulton-Palmer (Rugby), Captain of England rugby XV 1914, killed in action 4 May 1915. (*Rugby School archives*)

Rex Sherwell (Tonbridge), Public School cricketer at Lord's 1914, killed in action 3 July 1916. (*Tonbridge archives*)

Sherborne Cricket XI 1915. Alec Waugh, author of *The Loom of Youth*, is seated left. (*Sherborne archives*)

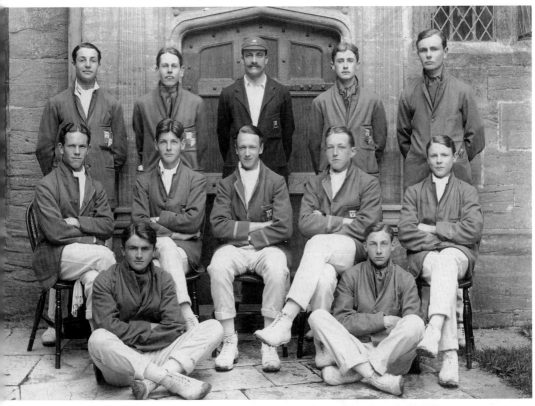

Writers

Siegfried Sassoon (Marlborough).

Rupert Brooke. (*Rugby archives*)

Douglas Gillespie. (*Winchester archives*)

Private R. C. Sherriff (Kingston GS), about 1916. (*Kingston Grammar School and the Surrey History Centre*)

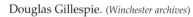

General the Earl of Cavan addresses the school during the visit of Old Etonian Generals in 1919. (*Reproduced by permission of the Provost and Fellows of Eton College*)

Unveiling of Fettes War Memorial by Major General Sir William Macpherson, 15 October 1920. (*Fettes archives*)

Dedication of Memorial Cloister and Bronze Group, Geelong Grammar School, 24 June 1927.
(*Geelong GS archives*)

Major General Sir Edmund Ironside inspects the Tonbridge OTC at dedication of the war memorial,
October 1925. (*Tonbridge archives*)

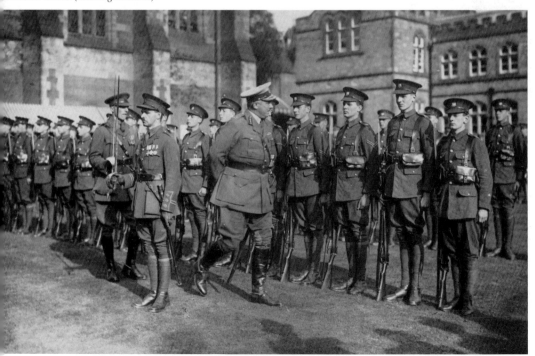

Winchester College War Cloister, re-dedication to the dead of 1939–45. Field Marshal Earl Wavell in front of the microphone. (Winchester archives)

kind'.[74] He applauded the care officers displayed in looking after their men: 'However young he may be, he has to act as their father and guide ... he has a fine sense of duty and faces the danger – "going over the sandbag" as he calls it – in a half jocular, half serious way'. But he bemoaned the fact that, 'the average public school officer disregards entirely, with one or two exceptions, his spiritual responsibility to his men'.[75] Bickersteth was awarded the MC in January 1918, becoming headmaster of St Peter's, Adelaide in 1919, and subsequently of Felsted in Essex.

The Revd Victor Tanner of Weymouth College, which was to close in 1940, was a chaplain who refused to be downhearted in his efforts to bring Christianity to his men. During the Third Battle of Ypres he was attached to a battalion of the Worcesters caught up in the thick of the fighting in September. At one point he left his pillbox to comfort some soldiers under shellfire nearby: 'After another shell fell close, I said "Now lads, I am going to ask you to do something which perhaps you have not done yet. I am going to ask you to close your eyes and pray that God will protect and keep the boys in the front line and that He will extend the protection to us" ... and God heard those prayers'.[76] Tanner survived Ypres and in December 1917 went back on leave to Weymouth College: 'Instead of school prep at 8.00 pm, I went into the big school room and gave the boys an account of the Battle for Passchendaele Ridge.' Tanner, too, was awarded an MC, returned to Weymouth after the war, and subsequently went to his old school, Dean Close. His diaries give no hint that war in any way diminished his faith.[77]

Ministering to so many men under great duress took its toll. Chaplains themselves lacked anyone with whom they could share their burdens. Some came to question their whole calling. The Revd Geoffrey Studdert-Kennedy (Leeds GS), known as 'Woodbine Willie', was an Anglican priest with a gift for mingling with ordinary soldiers and renowned for his liberal handing out to them of cigarettes. But as the historian Richard Holmes recorded, the work plumbed the depths of his despair: 'What the bloody hell is the church doing here? An amateur stretcher-bearer or amateur undertaker? Was that all a Christian priest could do in this ruin of a rotten civilisation?'[78]

The Revd Monty Guilford (St Lawrence, Ramsgate) was another who, because of his experience of war, questioned not just his role but his faith. Arriving in France in 1916, he endured the Somme and the battles of 1917, and then in December 1917 had to accompany to his execution Private Joseph Bateman, sentenced to death for desertion. These experiences left him, by the end of the war, a deeply scarred man who had temporarily lost his faith. He only regained it by working at St Martin-in-the-Fields church in London with the Revd Dick Sheppard, a Marlburian, whose own war experiences as a military chaplain had converted him to pacifism; Sheppard was to found the Peace Pledge Union in 1935.[79]

By contrast, P. B. 'Tubby' Clayton (St Paul's) was an Anglican chaplain whose faith deepened in the war. He was responsible, with the Revd Neville Talbot (Haileybury), for setting up Toc H in Poperinghe, a social centre and chapel for officers and men, in memory of Gilbert Talbot. A notice greeted new arrivals, 'All rank abandon, ye who enter here', and by his welcoming open-door policy Clayton broke down social barriers and provided spiritual support for men taking short breaks from the front. To visit now the original room in Poperinghe is to gain an overpowering sense of the thousands of soldiers who passed through and prayed that their cup might pass.

Ernest Crosse has given us a vivid account of the work of an army chaplain. At the Somme, on the morning of 1 July 1916, Crosse was positioned above Mansel Copse, from where the Devonshires were to launch an attack on the village of Mametz. As the clock edged towards 0730 hours, Crosse was watching anxiously the unfolding scene from the reserve trench, alongside the doctor and the stretcher-bearers. 'At 1530 hrs, Doc and myself walked down the road to Mansel Copse', he later wrote in his diary. 'The road was strewn with dead ... In every shell hole all across the valley and up to the German saps were badly wounded. I bandaged up a few as best I could and then returned with stretcher bearers'. On 3 July he began the harrowing task of collecting the dead, and received permission from senior officers to bury them. 'Altogether we collected 163 Devons and covered them up in Mansel Copse. I buried all I could in our front line trench ... At 0600 hrs, in the presence of the General and about sixty men, I read out the funeral service'. When the trench had been filled in, Crosse asked the pioneer sergeant to paint a board with red lead to mark the cemetery. He put up the board with the words 'Cemetery of 163 Devons Killed July 1st 1916' and then placed twelve crosses in two rows and wired in the area. To many visitors to the battlefields, the Devonshire cemetery ranks amongst the most moving of all the sites on the Western Front. Crosse's original board and message has now been replaced with a stone marker and the hauntingly simple words, 'The Devonshires held this trench, the Devonshires hold it still.' Crosse went on to win the DSO and the MC, returning to Marlborough briefly before going out to New Zealand in 1921 as headmaster of Christ's College, and subsequently returning to become head of Ardingly in Sussex. In the tranquillity of the inter-war years, he reflected on his time at the front and on the significance of his pastoral care for officers and men: 'From a religious point of view it showed to the men, far better than any preaching, God's care for them. If the padre's presence was appreciated in the trenches at normal times, it was doubly so in those awful periods in the small hours of the morning waiting for the moment of the attack.'[80]

Another Anglican chaplain to respond sympathetically to the challenge of war was the Revd Theodore Bayley Hardy (City of London School), who had once been chaplain at Nottingham High School, before taking a country living. The calling to minister to the needs of the soldiers was something he felt very powerfully, and at the age of fifty-three in 1916 he went across to France. In July 1918 he was to win the VC for rescuing wounded men from No-Man's-Land under heavy fire, and for digging out men buried by the mud from shellfire. He was looking forward to continuing his ministry in peacetime, but on 18 October, just three weeks from the end of the war, he died at Rouen from wounds received in action while tending to wounded soldiers. Hardy had already won the DSO and MC and is usually regarded as the most highly decorated army chaplain of all time.

For public schoolboys lucky enough to possess deep faith, it could be a source of great strength, imparting a sense of purpose to an alien world that for so many seemed stripped of all meaning. Second Lieutenant Jack Engall (St Paul's) was one of many who were committed Christians. On 30 June 1916, on the eve of going over the top, he wrote to his parents: 'I took my Communion yesterday with dozens of others who are going over tomorrow and never have I attended such an impressive service. I placed my soul and body in God's keeping ... I have a strong feeling that I shall come through safely, but should it be God's holy will to call me away, I am quite prepared to go ... and you, dear Mother and Dad, will know that I died doing my duty to my God, my Country and my King'.[81] Engall, aged just twenty, was one of the 19,000 British soldiers who were to be killed on 1 July. One Bible scholar who did not aspire to a commission was Lance Corporal John Pinkerton (Daniel Stewart's, Edinburgh). He had gained a first at Cambridge, after degrees at Edinburgh and Heidelberg, and enlisted when engaged in scholarly work on the Syriac New Testament. He was killed on the Salonika front in October 1916, when carrying a wounded comrade to the dressing station, leaving in his will all his academic research to the British and Foreign Bible Society.

Catholic chaplains at the front had a different responsibility, less overtly pastoral and morale-boosting, and more expressly religious and focused on the saving of souls. In those diaries and letters of

Catholic chaplains which have survived there are fewer discussions of the purpose of war, or reports of the talk in the officers' mess, and more about the spiritual needs of soldiers. The requirement for Catholic chaplains to administer extreme unction to the dying led them to spend more time in or near the front line. Guy Chapman (Westminster) was no doubt being unfair to Anglican chaplains when he wrote in his book *A Passionate Prodigality* (1933): 'These Catholic chaplains impressed me … The Church of Rome sent a man into battle mentally and spiritually cleaned. The Church of England could only offer you a cigarette. The Church of Rome sent its priests into the line. The Church of England forbade theirs forward of Brigade headquarters'.[82] As Chapman himself acknowledged, it was not fair to blame the Anglican chaplains, who were under strict instructions to avoid the front line – an instruction that many chose to ignore.

Catholicism was certainly more demanding of its flock than Anglicanism, whose priests would look wistfully at the ease with which their Catholic counterparts garnered large numbers of their flock for services. 'At 0700 hrs we had Mass for the battalion in a wood on two bully beef boxes, and everybody went to Holy Communion', wrote Lieutenant Gethin (Stonyhurst). 'It was a wonderful sight to see everyone kneeling in the slush and soaked to the skin, praying and hearing Mass – some for the last time.'[83] For Gethin it was to be his last mass. He died in battle two days later.

The Jesuit Father Willie Doyle was unusual for a Catholic chaplain in having a public school background. A boy at Ratcliffe College, he taught at Clongowes in Dublin before being appointed Catholic chaplain to the 16th (Irish) Division in 1916. Doyle made his mark quickly and won an MC for bravery and dedication on the Somme. We are fortunate in that he left a particularly vivid diary. In June 1917 he took part in the Battle of Messines, the precursor to the Third Battle of Ypres, and wrote about standing on the top of the trench and giving his men Absolution as they went over the top. 'I climbed out of the trench and ran across the open, as abject a coward as ever walked on two legs' he wrote, 'till I reached the three dying men and then the perfect trust came back to me and I felt no fear. A few seconds sufficed to absolve and anoint my poor boys …'[84] German mustard gas attacks, diving into shell holes full of water and human body parts, and ranging widely over the battlefields looking for wounded men and dead to bury, were all part of his day's work.

'Sitting a little way off I saw a hideous bleeding object', he recorded at one point in his diary. 'A man with a face smashed by a shell, with one if not both eyes torn out. He raised his head as I spoke. "Is that the priest? Thank God, I am all right now." I took his blood-covered hands in mine as I searched his face for some whole spot on which to anoint him.'[85] Doyle's luck ran out on 16 August 1917: when ministering to a wounded soldier, on the Passchendaele Ridge, he was killed outright by a shell. In the archives at Clongowes is a letter Major General Hickie, General Officer Commanding 16th Division, wrote to Doyle's father: '[He] was one of the best Priests I have ever met and one of the bravest of men ... He did his duty (and more than his duty) most nobly and has left a memory and a name behind him that will never be forgotten'.[86]

Doctors at the Front

The work of doctors at the front was similar in intensity to that of chaplains. James Ross (Fettes) was a medical officer in the Royal Naval Division who believed that chaplains were in fact more useful at the front than members of his own profession: 'A few words whispered in a severely wounded man's ear by his priest are almost magical in effect. He thinks no more of his wounds, death has now no terrors for him and he passes into the great hereafter content and uncomplaining.' That thought did not prevent Ross taking into battle a full arsenal of medical equipment: 'Hypodermic syringe, a bottle of morphia solution, two water bottles – one full of brandy, the other of water – shell dressings, tourniquets, a few instruments and an abundant supply of cigarettes.'[87]

Public schoolboys provided the vast bulk of medical officers during the Great War, because the profession was open only to those who attended schools offering a science education which equipped them for university and medical schools. State grammar schools, however, increasingly offered science and prepared their young men for medical careers. Some public schools had established traditions of promoting science in the curriculum and producing doctors. Epsom, which became 'Epsom College with a Royal Medical Foundation' in 1911, provided the highest proportion of doctors of all English schools, offering foundation scholarships to children of impoverished doctors and further scholarships to medical schools. Nearly half the boys who left Epsom in each year group before 1914 became doctors.[88] Scottish public schools were also well represented in the medical services, with fifty old boys from Fettes serving as medical officers in the war out of just over 1,000 who joined up.[89] In contrast, only 2 out of 103 who entered Radley between 1900 and 1901 entered the medical profession, and only 3 Tonbridgians out of 179 in the same years.[90] It should be noted in passing that in a war where horses played a major part, so movingly dramatized by Michael Morpurgo (King's Canterbury) in *War Horse*, the role of the

Army Veterinary Service was crucial, commanded by another alumnus of King's Canterbury, Major General Sir Layton Blenkinsop.

The Royal Army Medical Corps (RAMC), with just 1,500 medical officers at the outbreak of war, had grossly inadequate numbers for the task ahead. By 1918 their number had grown eightfold to over 12,000.[91] Expansion came from recruiting civilian doctors into the armed forces, and by accelerating recruitment of trainee doctors in medical schools. Many temporary RAMC officers had no military training beyond what they might have picked up in their public school OTC, but relished the challenges ahead. Geoffrey Keynes (Rugby), younger brother of the economist John Maynard Keynes, was an enthusiastic recruit: 'War did not suggest unnamed horrors, but to a young surgeon meant ... rewarding work, gaining extraordinary surgical experience from thousands of operations of all types, from minor injuries and fractures to abdominal, thoracic, cranial and even cardiac emergencies ... while doing his ... duty for his country'.[92] Keynes became a medical pioneer, whose portable blood transfusion device saved thousands of soldiers' lives. A versatile man, he was also a close Cambridge friend of Rupert Brooke, and was appointed his literary executor in 1915.[93] The excitement of setting out to the front and 'doing one's bit' proved too strong an impulse for some trainee doctors who, fearful it might all be over before they qualified, abandoned their training to join up. One such was Wilfred Willett (St Paul's and Cambridge), who quit his training at the London Hospital to rush out to the front. The head wound he suffered at Ploegsteert Wood in December 1914 meant he was never to study medicine again.

The RAMC broadly divided into two: younger doctors who became regimental medical officers (RMO) and who were attached to frontline battalions, and more senior doctors and consultants who carried out surgery in the Casualty Clearing Stations (CCS) behind the front lines and at base hospitals as at Etaples in France or in hospitals in Britain. RMOs had the more dangerous task of establishing Regimental Aid Posts (RAPs) close to (or even in) the front line, where they would make quick assessments of each man's wounds, patch them up as best they could, and give him pain relief. Many who came to them, especially with head or stomach wounds, would not survive. Casualties were taken back down the line by stretcher-bearers, along the winding communication trenches, which in battle could easily become clogged. They would be taken to Advanced Dressing Stations or onwards to the CCS, often near a railhead and with facilities for more complex surgical procedures. Here doctors and surgeons, often exhausted, would face terrible dilemmas over which patients to treat. Howard Somervell

(Rugby), later a member of George Mallory's Everest expeditions, worked in CCSs in the Amiens and Albert areas during the Somme. 'The wounded had to lie not merely in our tents and shelters but in the whole area of the camp, a field of five or six acres, which was completely covered in stretchers,' he later recalled. 'It was a terrible business ... to select from the thousands of patients the few fortunate ones whose lives or limbs we had time to save ... Even now I am haunted by the touching look of the young, bright anxious eyes, as we passed along the rows of sufferers. Hardly ever did any of them say a word, except ask for water or relief from pain ... There all around us, lying maimed and dying, was the flower of Britain's youth'.[94]

The doctor who did most to improve the treatment of the seriously wounded in the war was Sir Anthony Bowlby (Durham School), who had worked as a volunteer surgeon in the Boer War, and who had joined the Territorials along with many fellow surgeons and doctors at St Bartholomew's Hospital in London. The son of Thomas Bowlby, who was killed during the Opium Wars when serving as a war correspondent, he was also the father of John Bowlby, the pioneering British psychiatrist who developed 'attachment theory'. In 1916 Bowlby became 'Consultant Surgeon, British Armies in France', with responsibility for coordinating surgical work along the whole Western Front. He realized that men were needlessly dying because of the time it took them to get to the CCSs, so he had the CCSs moved nearer the front line and ensured that they were better staffed. He realized that during times of the greatest battle stress, the need was for mobile surgical teams consisting of a surgeon, anaesthetist, sister and orderlies, and he duly instituted these units. When touring base hospitals in 1917 after the Battles of Arras and Messines, he learned that these changes were resulting in lower mortality rates, especially among those suffering from infection or liable to gas gangrene. They even improved the prospects of those with abdominal wounds. At the Somme in 1916, the statistics, admittedly not fully reliable, suggested only eighteen per cent of those with abdominal wounds recovered; but by the end of the Third Battle of Ypres in 1917 this proportion had risen to forty-nine per cent.[95]

W. H. R. Rivers (Tonbridge) was a figure who made a comparable impact on psychological illnesses. With a research interest in neurology and psychology, he became a fellow of St John's, Cambridge in 1902, and founded the *British Journal of Psychology* in 1904. At Craiglockhart Hospital in Edinburgh officers came before him suffering from a wide range of mental and emotional illnesses. His pioneering and compassionate approach is familiar today because two of his patients were

Siegfried Sassoon and Wilfred Owen, a story made famous by their own writing and in the novels of Pat Barker and others. Rivers was no soft touch, however. As Sassoon records in his memoirs, Rivers persuaded him that 'going back to the war as soon as possible was my only chance of peace'.[96]

One of Rivers' students was Charles Myers (City of London School). After Cambridge, he trained at St Bartholomew's Hospital and in 1911 joined Rivers as joint editor of the *British Journal of Psychology*. In 1915, he was the first to coin the term 'shell-shock' in the medical journal *The Lancet*,[97] and the following year was appointed to the post of 'Consultant Psychologist to the British Armies in France', based at Le Touquet. He fought a running battle with many traditionalists in the military and in the medical profession, the former being worried about the impact on morale should stress become recognized as a legitimate illness and thus a medically-endorsed reason to leave the front line. As officers and men with outstanding records of courage began to break down during the war, the understanding grew of an involuntary component to their problems, and that they were neither cowards nor 'shirkers'. By the end of the war it was estimated that the number suffering from shell shock or 'war neurosis' amounted to 80,000 men.

Charles Wilson (Pocklington) was another doctor to study the psychological impact of war on soldiers. A passionate rugby player, in 1902 he was dissuaded by his parents from a literary career and went instead to St Mary's medical school, London. When war broke out he joined the RAMC and was attached to the Royal Fusiliers, winning the MC on the Somme in 1916 and ending the war in Boulogne Base Hospital. He became fascinated by what caused some men to break down, while others carried on. The careful notes he made at the time bore fruit in lectures in the 1930s which formed the basis of his book *The Anatomy of Courage* (1945). His conclusions on the nature of courage are summarized thus: 'Courage is will-power, whereof no man has an unlimited stock; and when in war it is used up he is finished. A man's courage is his capital and he is always spending. The call on the bank may be only the daily drain of the front line or it may be a sudden draft which threatens to close the account. His will is perhaps almost destroyed by intensive shelling, by heavy bombing, or by a bloody battle, or it is gradually used up by monotony, by exposure, by the loss of support of stauncher spirits on whom he has come to depend.'[98] Wilson became best known as Churchill's personal physician throughout the Second World War and until his death in 1965. Created Lord Moran in 1943, in 1966 he published *Winston Churchill: the Struggle for Survival* , which, in its detailed portrait of Churchill's medical condition, was felt to have breached the code of confidentiality between doctor and patient, and led to deep anger in the Churchill family.

The qualities of selfless service, courage and dedication, which lay at the heart of the public school ideal at its best, were never realized more fully than in the actions of innumerable doctors across all the theatres in the Great War. Hugh Shields (Loretto) went on to the Middlesex Hospital after Cambridge, qualifying in 1912 with a commission in the RAMC. One of the first out to France in August with the Irish Guards, he rapidly made a name for himself looking after the wounded under heavy fire. 'I make a point of entirely disregarding fire when it comes to the point of seeing to a wounded man', he wrote in a letter home. 'After all, I always think that if one is killed doing one's duty, one can't help it, and that is the best way of coming to an end.' Shot dead by a sniper during the First Battle of Ypres in October 1914, he was described by one of those in his care as 'the bravest man I ever saw'.[99]

Glyn Hughes (Epsom) was one of those school heroes who managed to be both head prefect and captain of the 1st XV. As RMO to battalions of the Wiltshire Regiment and the Grenadier Guards, he served during the Battle of the Somme, during which at least 400 RAMC officers were to become casualties, but survived, winning the DSO and Bar, the MC and *Croix De Guerre*. His DSO citation from 1916 recorded, 'He went out in broad daylight, under heavy fire, and bandaged seven wounded men in the open, lying out in an exposed spot for one and a half hours. At nightfall he led a party through a heavy barrage and brought the seven men back.'[100] Harold Ackroyd (Shrewsbury) was another to survive the Somme, winning the MC during fierce fighting around Delville Wood. A man of exceptional courage, he knew that the Third Battle of Ypres was going to be testing. His battalion went into action at the opening on 31 July 1917, and he was beside the men as they fought from waterlogged shell hole to shell hole, being fired on from a succession of German pillboxes around Glencorse Wood. For his work for 'many hours up and down, and in front of the line, tending to the wounded ... moving across the open under heavy machine-gun, rifle and shell fire' he was awarded the Victoria Cross. Ten days later, he was killed in action, one of the 300,000 British casualties in the futile Third Battle of Ypres. 'The hottest shellfire never stopped him going to a wounded man,' wrote a fellow officer to his widow. 'The men used to simply stare in wonderment at his bravery.'[101]

Of all the extraordinarily heroic and self-sacrificing doctors in the RAMC, perhaps none can compare with the legendary Captain Noel Chavasse. One of four sons of the Bishop of Liverpool, he began his education at Magdalen College School, Oxford, before his family went north and he moved to Liverpool College. After gaining a first class honours degree at Oxford, and blues in two sports, he represented England in the 400 metres at the 1908 Olympics. Commissioned in 1913 into the RAMC as RMO to the Liverpool Scottish, he won the MC in 1915. During the Somme, he was judged to have exhibited exceptional bravery at Guillemont in August 1916 when tending the wounded in the open all day under heavy fire and in full view of the enemy, and the next day when bringing back a wounded man over a distance of 500 yards, despite himself being hit by a shell splinter in his side. That night, he went out to rescue a further three wounded men from a shell hole just 25 yards from the German lines. One of his stretcher-bearers wrote: 'The Captain took no more notice of the enemy's fire than he would of a few raindrops, and even when bullets were whistling all around he didn't get in the least bit flustered in his work.'[102] It is estimated that his actions saved the lives of twenty badly wounded men, for which he was awarded the VC.

The Liverpool Scottish were in the Ypres Salient for the opening stages of the Third Battle of Ypres. Chavasse set up a temporary RAP in a former German dugout, which afforded greater protection from British fire than German. A splinter from a German shell wounded him in the head. He was encouraged to retire briefly to have the wound dressed, but returned to the RAP, where he worked for two days and two nights without sleep and with very little food, attending all the time to the stream of casualties being brought in. Despite the constant German shelling, he went out at night with his torch to scour the ground for survivors. Despite being hit again by splinters of shell casing he continued relentlessly until the early morning of 2 July, when the RAP suffered a devastating direct hit from a shell, which killed or seriously wounded all those inside. Chavasse himself sustained terrible injuries, including a gaping abdominal wound. He died two days later in the CCS. News of his death caused considerable shock waves, and the battalion turned out in force for his burial. The award of his second VC, unique in the Great War, was gazetted in September 1917. In a sermon in 1935, his twin brother Christopher, who became Bishop of Rochester, quoted a comment that Noel had made to their father: 'The fact is, I can't bear to think of my boys lying out there needing me.'[103]

After Chavasse's first VC had been awarded, the proud headmaster of Liverpool College wrote to congratulate him. Chavasse replied: 'I think one values one's letter from one's old headmaster more perhaps than from anyone else. We still feel like schoolboys before him and long to please him more than anyone. And, I can assure you, sir, that I shall do my best to be worthy of you and the old school.'[104]

Chapter 7

To the End on Land, Sea and Air 1917–1918

'That indefinable something was what was instilled into a boy at public school', wrote R. C. Sheriff on the fiftieth anniversary of the war's ending. 'Very few public schoolboys came from the landed gentry or distinguished families ... Very few of them would have wanted to stay on in the army when the war was done. They only wanted to get the thing over and return to the jobs they had planned to do'.[1] The last two years of the war were to test the public school character to the very breaking point. While the French and German armies were turning to mutiny, the British army kept plugging away – right up until 11 November 1918. Public school alumni were at the heart of driving the war forward to the very end.

The battles of 1917 – Arras and Vimy Ridge

As the Somme was drawing to a close, R. H. Tawney (Rugby) was one of a growing number who became critical of the high command, believing the battle was being continued long after it became clear that the strategy was not working, and that the price in loss of life and broken bodies was not worth paying. While recuperating from wounds he received on 1 July, he wrote 'Some Reflections of a Soldier', published in *Nation* that October: 'You assume that we shall speak lightly, of things, emotions, states of mind, human relationships and affairs which are to us solemn and terrible. You seem ashamed, as if they were a kind of weakness, of the ideas which have sent us to France, and for which thousands of sons and lovers have died. You calculate the profit to be derived from "war after war", as though the unspeakable agonies of the Somme were an item in a commercial proposition.'[2]

The Somme had changed everything. Gone forever was the innocence and optimism of Kitchener's army, destroyed in just a few hours on that eighteen-mile front in northern France. 'I am certainly not the same as I was a year ago', wrote an unnamed officer of his experiences in 1917. 'I can no longer write home to you, as I once did, of victory. We just live for the day and think of little else but our job, the next show and our billets and rations. I may be a better soldier and know my job better than I did, but I dare not think of anything beyond that.'[3]

Young officers nevertheless were confident in the ultimate victory and prepared for, or resigned to, the sacrifices which would be needed. Stephen Hewett (Downside), who was not to survive the Somme, had expressed this in a letter of July 1916: 'There were times when the issue of this war seemed doubtful ... Now it is certain: and, if we have to suffer the heaviest losses, and even have a hard time for the rest of our lives, we should consider ourselves not unlucky ... Poor old Crux is killed – one of my best friends – and Dux is a wounded prisoner in Germany. These are items in the price we have to pay. But we are going to win – win this year, and in any case we have proved equal in heroism and romance to any age in history'.[4] Another, Lieutenant Leslie Sanders (St Olave's School, London), made clear in February 1917 what he felt the country would have to go through to win: 'If English people want to win this war, they must be prepared for things scarcely dreamed of as yet – for starvation rations, for unremitting labour of man, woman and child, for death in every home in the land. These things may not come, but unless they are faced and accepted in spirit, we cannot truly win.'[5] Sanders did not survive long enough to see if his predictions came true; he was killed in March 1917.

Young officers were becoming concerned about and, indeed, critical of the conduct of the war on different levels. The Etonian subaltern Christopher Lighton, interviewed in 1992, said of the Somme and subsequent battles: 'Even then we wondered who was running the show and what kind of brains they had.'[6] Guy Chapman (Westminster), serving temporarily as a staff officer, witnessed the despair of a fellow officer ordered by a superior to make an impossible attack during the Battle of Arras in April 1917: 'One major, a plump little man, whose eyes belied his fierce moustache, stammered through trembling lips, "Look here, you don't expect us to do this? You know we hardly have an officer left. Two battalions are commanded by junior officers, and the men, what there are left, are badly shaken". There was a moment's pause. My companion viewed the pleader coldly. "Those are your orders," he said. "Obey them." '[7]

What is striking, and can seem either pusillanimous or admirable, is that the public schoolboys repressed their reservations: obedience to senior commanders won out almost every time. Siegfried Sassoon

(Marlborough) was the most celebrated of all the public school officers openly to rebel, when he declined to return to the front line in 1917, encouraged by his pacifist friends Bertrand Russell and Lady Ottoline Morrell. His letter of explanation to his commanding officer was read out in Parliament: 'I believe that the war on which I entered as a war of defence and liberation has now become a war of conquest.'[8] He threw the ribbon of his Military Cross into the River Mersey. The War Office decided not to court-martial him but sent him to Craiglockhart Hospital instead, from where, under Rivers' counsel, he returned to the front line.

Sassoon was not the only one to express a growing disillusion. Even before the Somme Raymond Asquith had written to his wife, Katherine, in March 1916: 'I have been reading some letters from Indian troops this afternoon: one man says "I never think about the chance of being killed, nor do I feel any particular satisfaction at the idea of going on living." This is a mood one recognises.'[9] Explicit doubts or disillusion about the direction of the war are hard to find, which suggests that public schoolboys were conditioned to doing what they were told or, possibly, that there was some wider educational deficit on the part of those who ran schools in not doing more to educate their boys about the meaning of war and its likely nature. Growing war weariness and fatalism are more in evidence, although mixed with a commitment to seeing the business through, even from men who were the most unlikely soldiers. The gentle Winchester and Balliol scholar, Arthur Adam, could write home during the Somme battle, in which he was killed: 'That show [the Somme], as you may guess has not gone quite right ... None the less one may still hope that Germany will crack before the winter. Then maybe I shall come home, and the true business of life will begin'.[10]

The Battle of Arras, which lasted from 9 April to 16 May 1917, opened with the Canadian attack on Vimy Ridge and a wider British attack to the east of Arras itself. Although the attack on Vimy Ridge succeeded, the Arras offensive as a whole achieved no breakthrough, advancing only an insignificant distance before being negated by the failure of Nivelle's offensive further south on the Chemin des Dames near Rheims. The latter precipitated serious mutinies in the French Army and meant Britain had to take the leading role on the Western Front.

Arras destroyed several literary figures of prominence. Captain Tommy Nelson (Edinburgh Academy) had been a Scottish rugby international and was head of the Nelson publishing house. A man of considerable social conscience and compassion for those he employed in his business and on his estates, he revelled in the company of literary folk, among them John Buchan, a friend from Oxford. Aged thirty-eight at the outbreak of war, Nelson's one thought was to serve his country, and he did so by joining the Lothian and Border Horse, working as a staff officer overseeing observation posts, before becoming an intelligence officer in the new Tank Corps. On 9 April, on the first day of the battle, he was killed by a shell.[11] 'He crowded his days with honourable activities and made his world immeasurably the better for his presence', wrote Buchan about him. 'We mourned especially the loss of talent for living worthily and for helping others to do likewise.'[12]

Nelson's firm published *In Pursuit of Spring*, the last volume to appear before the war written by Edward Thomas (St Paul's), one of the greatest of the literary losses of the Great War. He was to die on the same day as Nelson. Thomas was a restless soul, who was emerging as an increasingly sophisticated poet, perhaps best remembered for his poem 'Adlestrop', written on the eve of war, about a quintessentially English moment when an express train stops unwontedly at a tiny station in the Cotswolds. His later writing combined his love of nature with themes of war, rarely caught better than in the poem 'In Memoriam' from Easter 1915: 'The flowers left thick at nightfall in the wood/This Eastertide call into mind the men,/Now far from home, with their sweethearts who should/Have gathered them and will never do again.'[13] The melancholy Thomas had a remarkable gift for friendship, notably with the poet Eleanor Farjeon, the Welsh tramp-writer W. H. Davies and above all the American poet, Robert Frost, whose poem 'The Road Not Taken', discussing the element of chance in decision-making, could have been mocking Thomas' agonised indecisiveness about enlisting.

Thomas had married Helen while still at Oxford, and as a mature married man with children could have avoided enlisting; but in 1915 he decided to do so and in November 1916 was commissioned into the Royal Garrison Artillery. In the early months of 1917 he returned on leave to see Helen and the children. The agony that girlfriends and wives went through when bidding farewell to their loved ones leaving for the front, and the long days spent waiting for news, are mostly lost in time. But a vivid portrayal of the emotions experienced, shared by hundreds of thousands of other women, has been left us by Helen Thomas. She describes his departure on their last morning together: ' "Helen, Helen, Helen", he said, "remember, that whatever happens, all is well between us for ever and ever." And hand in hand we went downstairs and out to the children who were playing in the snow. A thick mist hung everywhere and there was no sound except far away in the valley, a train shunting. I stood at the gate watching him go: he turned back to wave until the mist and hill hid him. I heard his old call coming up to me: "Coo-ee!" he called. "Coo-ee!" I answered … panic seized me and I ran through the mist and snow to the top of the hill and stood there a moment dumbly, with straining eyes and ears. There was nothing but the mist and the snow and the silence of death, then with leaden feet which stumbled in the sudden darkness which overwhelmed me I groped my way back to the empty house'.[14] On his return to the front, Thomas rapidly found himself swept up in plans for the big attack. On the opening day, 9 April, he was smoking his pipe in his observation post when a shell took his life. Helen went into a deep depression, and wrote her two-volume memoir *As it Was* and *World without End* in part as therapy. Thomas' gravestone can be found at the Agny cemetery in an unprepossessing location on the outskirts of Arras. Cherry trees, which blossom in late spring, greet visitors, recalling his poem: 'The cherry trees bend over and are shedding/On the old road where all that passed are dead,/Their petals, strewing the grass as for a wedding/This early May morn where there is none to wed.'[15]

Officers and men

Public school officers in the Royal Engineers (RE) performed vital service at Arras and elsewhere, although they rarely received the recognition awarded to others. Their work included construction of railway tracks, repair of trenches, and creation of dugouts and strong points, much of it done in or near the front line and therefore under fire. RE mining companies dug tunnels and planted explosives in hollowed-out chambers under enemy trenches, a world vividly recreated in Sebastian Faulks' *Birdsong*. Lieutenant John Glubb, who left Cheltenham in 1914, came from one of those public school military families so common in the regular army. When he was commissioned into the RE in April 1915, his father was already Major General and Chief Engineer, Second Army. Glubb's war diary gives a vivid account of the work and the dangers faced by an RE Field Company. On one occasion, just before the Arras offensive, he had been asked to excavate a large dugout on a long open hillside, to be used as a brigade headquarters in the coming attack, along with two splinter-proof dugouts for use as dressing stations. The work was done through the night, supervised by himself and another subaltern, Rowland Chaplin: 'Just as dawn was breaking, the sappers were putting the finishing touches to the dressing stations, and Chaplin was standing superintending. As often happened at dawn the Boche put down an artillery barrage and a shell fell right into the little group of them. It burst close to Chaplin's head and killed him instantly, together with eight sappers.'[16] Glubb himself was wounded three times by shellfire; the last time his jaw was shattered, keeping him in hospital for months. He later became 'Glubb Pasha', Commander of the Arab Legion in Jordan from 1939 to 1956, until he was dismissed by King Hussein, a show of independence by Arab rulers that was a precursor to Nasser's nationalization of the Suez Canal in July 1956.

By 1917 changes were taking place in the supply of officers. From 1914 to 1916 the officer corps had been all but monopolized by public school officers with OTC experience. But the casualty rates on the Somme, and the expansion of the army with the coming of conscription, led to serious shortages. The continuing flow of public school leavers with OTC experience was not nearly large enough to plug the gaps; the army had to look beyond this traditional constituency and start promoting men from the ranks – the ebullient Trotter in *Journey's End* being a sympathetic and not atypical example. Officer training also became more organized. From February 1916, aspirant officers were required to undergo basic training in the ranks and to attend a four-month course at an Officers Cadet Battalion (OCB), often located in an Oxbridge college. Those wanting a regular commission continued on to Sandhurst or Woolwich, where a public school background remained a distinct advantage.

Officers promoted from the ranks could face some unattractive reactions from their public school colleagues. OCB courses were, in effect, crash courses in the public school ethos, including basic leadership skills, social etiquette in the officers' mess, looking after men appropriately, and participation in team sports. This 'finishing school' did not totally dissipate the sense of 'them and us'. James Neville (Eton) revealed disdain for an officer who did not come from the 'right' school: 'He got on to the subject of Eton and started running down the traditions and dress ... which made my blood boil and I fear I was rather rude'.[17] R. T. Rees, a teacher at Dulwich before going off to the front, believed that the knowledge of how to look after men in your command was learnt as a prefect in boarding houses, and he doubted if those who had not been to public school would have had the same opportunity to develop it.[18] The extent to which such remarks were driven by rank snobbery or, as R. C. Sherriff put it, by being 'conscious of a personal superiority that placed on their shoulders an obligation towards those less privileged than themselves', is open to argument.[19]

Officers from a wealthier background knew how to share the better things of life, in or out of the trenches. In December 1914 Lionel Cohen (Eton) wrote home from the trenches to thank 'for the pheasants and clothes, and to mother for the butter', adding that 'the brandy has again arrived and I am looking forward to getting the weekly edition of *The Telegraph*'.[20] When Oliver Lyttelton, of Eton and the Grenadier Guards, sent a request home in March 1915, he insisted that three of everything be sent for himself and his two mess companions, including 'strong knives and forks, and some horn cups, very small for port etc ... sorts of things like tongue (tinned), tinned lamb and peas, pate or even a cold chicken are very popular. I shouldn't order a fixed show from Fortnum and Mason, but if you could send say once a week a selection of the above kind of things, together with a bottle of port (F and M No. 4) it would be splendid'.[21]

Such luxuries were particularly welcome in the primitive dugouts officers shared close to the front line. In 1917 and 1918 these still followed the basic design of one described by Stephen Hewett (Downside), who was on the Somme in 1916: 'In the ditch are little holes with deep flights of steps which lead down to cellars hacked out of the chalk. In one of them are three wooden frames strung with wire on which I and two other officers sleep. They are lit by candles guttering in bottle-necks and some of them are roughly furnished, as for example my company HQ where I am now writing and where seven officers eat, talk and read. They are all very draughty, we have nothing but our clothes and mackintoshes ... but a brazier of coke dispels some of the gloom'.[22] R. C. Sherriff gives a similar description of a dugout in March 1918 when scene-setting *Journey's End*: 'A few rough steps lead into the trench above, through a low doorway. A table occupies a good space of the dugout floor. A wooden frame covered with wire netting stands against the left wall and serves the double purpose of a bed and a seat for the table. Another wire-covered bed is fixed in the corner. Gloomy tunnels lead out of the dugout to left and right. There is no other furniture, save the bottles holding the candles, and a few tattered magazine pictures pinned to the wall of girls in flimsy costumes.'[23]

The requirement to look after your men first was of central importance in the conduct of officers and their relationship with those under their command. It was said of Lieutenant Colonel John Maxwell (Marlborough) DSO, MC that, 'he was the servant as well as the leader of his men: at all times and in all places they came first in his thoughts, and until they were made as comfortable as circumstances permitted, he gave no thought to himself'.[24] Captain Graham Greenwell (Winchester), given command of a company of 200 soldiers just before the Somme battle at the age of only twenty, was completely confident in his ability to lead them into battle, and care for their needs, because he had learned about discharging responsibility selflessly as a prefect at school. Lionel Cohen, during the Battle of Neuve Chapelle in 1915, promised his platoon sergeant, who had been badly wounded, 'to look after his wife and child if he were not to get better'.[25] Captain Eric Whitworth (Radley), later headmaster of Bradfield and Tonbridge, complained about the behaviour of two new platoon officers who, on each halt during a hot and tiring route march, fell out at once and stretched full-length on the ground: 'They paid no attention to the men, nor talked to them ... When we came in, I pointed out that it is the essence of leadership never to show oneself done in. I don't think it would ever have been necessary to tell a subaltern fresh from Rugby or Radley such a thing as this. He has learnt in leading his house or team and, in spite of the general criticism that public schools foster class feeling, he has learnt really to care for his men'.[26]

The regard felt for officers by their men is revealed strongly in the many letters written by other ranks to the relatives of dead officers. Courage is particularly highlighted and admired. When Lieutenant Glynne Yorath (Queen's Taunton) was killed at Passchendaele in November 1917, the Company Sergeant Major wrote to his father: 'Your son was perhaps the coolest and most courageous of those officers in our company, and as he walked up and down the line encouraging the men, one and all of us felt more than proud of him. Not once until he was killed did he cease to cheer and encourage his men on.'[27] The servant of Second Lieutenant Charles Vaughan (Harrow) wrote to his parents after Vaughan's death at Loos that, 'I never served a better officer ... We knew he was offered leave just before the attack came off, but he refused and said he would take it after we were relieved, and I can assure you his platoon were proud of him; as the Jocks say, "he was the best wee spud that ever wore a kilt"'.[28] Not all officers were viewed as heroes, as a British private recorded of one unnamed officer: 'We could see where the shells were dropping and we had an officer with us and I knew he was a windy devil ... he come to me and said, "What shall we do?" I said to him we should press on and get across. I told him that and we got across ... anyway I don't know what happened to him but I knew he was a windy bugger'.[29]

The battles of 1917 – the Third Battle of Ypres and Cambrai
The second half of 1917 was bad for the Allies on the Western Front. Russia was collapsing under two revolutions, while the French, mentally and physically exhausted after Verdun and the Chemin des Dames failure, were on the back foot. The United States joined the war in May but its troops did not arrive in force until mid-1918. David Lloyd George, Asquith's successor as Prime Minister from December 1916, did not enjoy a good relationship with Haig, but was unable to replace him, or to counter his proposal for a major offensive at Ypres. Haig wanted to break out of the salient and advance over the low-lying land towards the English Channel to capture the German U-boat bases at Ostend and Zeebrugge, which were creating havoc with Allied

160

shipping. The Third Battle of Ypres opened on 31 July, but was to prove as ineffective as the Battle of the Somme. It lasted till late November, and is commonly known by the name of the shallow ridge on which the battle finally petered out, Passchendaele.[30]

The bad fortune for the British forces was that the battle had to be fought during an unusually wet summer and autumn, compounding the tactical problems they faced in attacking up the slope towards fortified German positions and pill-boxes on higher ground. The offensive suffered also from a six-week lull between the ending of the successful British attack on Messines to the south of the salient and the launching of Third Ypres itself. Nearly 4,000 officers were to be killed and a further 14,000 wounded during the four months of fighting. Many wounded here and elsewhere were to be adversely affected for the rest of their lives, such as Jack Cohen (Cheltenham), who lost both of his legs above the knee on the opening day of the attack, 31 July. Cohen became a Conservative MP in Liverpool for thirteen years, a founder of the Royal British Legion and the 'Not Forgotten Association', a service charity for the wounded founded in 1920. Cohen was fortunate; many of the wounded were unable subsequently to lead such productive and fulfilling lives.[31]

The appalling conditions of the battlefield are described in the testimony of a wide number of participants. Arthur Ashford (Caterham) spoke of surviving an intense German bombardment: 'It is scarcely pleasant to be shelled, properly shelled, so the air is screaming and shrieking, the earth is trembling and shaking and rocking with all the explosions, smoke stings the eyes and dries the throat. One wonders when the shell will come which is going to burst right inside one's own particular traverse or dugout, an end to the suspense.'[32] Captain J. C. Dunn (Glasgow Academy) went up to the line at Passchendaele in November: 'Many scarcely recognisable dead lie around, a few of them German. Passchendaele is not quite levelled. Its fields are a shell-crater swamp ... mud flows through entrances ... an impassable sea of mud ... under this ordeal one of my officers lost his nerve and had to be sent away'.[33] Commanding the 1/4 Battalion King's Own Yorkshire Light Infantry, lower down the Passchendaele Ridge, was Lieutenant Colonel Harry Moorhouse, whose son Ronald was a company commander in his father's battalion. Both were educated at Silcoates School in Yorkshire. Ronald was mortally wounded during the opening phase of the attack, and as his desperate father crossed into No-Man's-Land to find him, he too was shot dead. Father and son died within an hour of each other.[34]

Barbara Adam, later Baroness Wootton of Abinger and a renowned sociologist and criminologist, was another whose life was changed forever by Passchendaele. In 1914, aged only seventeen and a pupil at Perse School for Girls, Barbara had met Jack Wootton, ex-head boy of Nottingham High School and a Cambridge friend of her brother Arthur, and they had fallen in love. Both Arthur and Jack went to France with New Army battalions in 1915. Left behind to ponder their fate, Barbara attended many memorial services that year in Cambridge college chapels for young men who had been killed. She was struck, and disconcerted, by the unashamed public grief of the fathers: 'The sight of distinguished professors and famous men, whom I had been brought up to regard with awe, openly crying in church, disturbed me profoundly.'[35]

Jack Wootton was wounded on 1 July 1916 and returned to help run the OTC at Cambridge, where Barbara, now at Girton College, saw much of him. Both were devastated by the news of the death of her brother Arthur on the Somme in September. She and Jack decided to get married in September 1917 and planned a fortnight's honeymoon. The day before the wedding, Jack, now fully recovered from his wound, received a telegram ordering him to the front within two days. The wedding still went ahead, they spent their wedding night in a farm-house near Cambridge and the last night before his departure at the Rubens Hotel in London, close by Victoria Station. A month later, while repairing wooden tracking through the Passchendaele mud, Jack was shot in the eye and died in an ambulance train two days later.

Like Vera Brittain, who lost her fiancé Roland Leighton, Barbara resolved to channel her energy into building a better post-war world. With thirteen per cent of all British men in their twenties killed in the war,[36] and with the death rate considerably higher amongst the upper and middle classes, it was not always easy for well-to-do widows and bereaved fiancées to find suitable new husbands. Both Barbara and Vera, however, subsequently married, Barbara preferring to keep her first husband's surname. In her memoirs published in 1966 she wrote: 'At forty-nine years distance the emotions connected with these happenings are, in the nature of things, wholly spent. But, to this day, if anyone suggests an appointment in the Rubens Hotel, I am disposed to think up an excuse for proposing an alternative meeting place.'[37] Wootton was ennobled by Harold Macmillan as one of the first women in the House of Lords in 1958, and came to terms perhaps better with the loss of her brother and husband than did Vera Brittain. When Vera died in 1970, aged seventy-six, she asked that her ashes be scattered on her brother Edward's grave in the British military cemetery on the Asiago Plateau in Italy. 'For nearly fifty years much of my heart has been in that Italian village cemetery,' she wrote. The request was honoured by her daughter, politician Shirley Williams, in September 1970.[38]

The year 1917 finished with the Battle of Cambrai in November, when the Royal Tank Corps attacked with over three hundred tanks, advancing to a depth of five miles. These gains could not be held against German counter-attacks, but the value of tanks had been proved. The main strategist of Cambrai, and a leading advocate of the value of tanks, was Colonel J. F. C. Fuller (Malvern), a staff officer in Tank Corps HQ. Captain Denis Monaghan (Uppingham), a rugby player at Rosslyn Park before the war and an engineering graduate of London University, commanded one of the tanks in the attack. Conditions inside any tank were desperately uncomfortable. The engine took up much of the interior, and into the rest of the cramped and noxious space were fitted eight men to work the guns and the controls. Vibration inside was intense and the heat and fumes of carbon monoxide close to overpowering, summer temperatures climbing to well in excess of 100° Fahrenheit. When bullets struck the outside of the tank, bits of metal would break off from the inner hull and ricochet around the interior, so the crew wore chain mail masks. Monaghan commanded a section of four tanks at Cambrai, but also had the role of reconnoitring the route forward for all the tanks. On 24 November he was out of his tank for this purpose near Bourlon Wood when a shell decapitated him.[39] Inside the tank was not necessarily safer; Lieutenant Paul Jones (Dulwich) was killed on 31 July 1917 when a bullet passed through the porthole of the tank and hit him in the head. By the second half of 1918 the British tanks had improved in both speed and tactics, and were playing an increasingly important role, in combination with infantry, artillery and air power; on 8 August Captain Henry Smeddle (Dulwich) led his troop of three tanks into a town well behind the German front line: 'The enemy were evidently quite unaware of the rapidity of our advance, for just as we were opposite Harbonnières we saw an ammunition train steaming into the station as if nothing was the matter. It was immediately shelled by all the 6-pounder guns of the approaching tanks and burst into one great sheet of flame.'[40]

The Royal Flying Corps

Flying was in its infancy when the Great War broke out in 1914: the English Channel had only been flown as recently as 1909 by Louis Blériot. The cost of learning to fly and gaining the coveted Royal Aero Club certificate, and the leisure time required to do so, put pre-war aviation beyond the reach of all but the wealthiest. It was therefore public schoolboys – officers from the army and navy, as well as gentlemen of means – who dominated the early days of flying.

The first two pilots to achieve the coveted Royal Aero Club (RAC) certificate in March 1910 came from Harrow and Eton. The first was John Moore-Brabazon (Harrow), who flew with the RFC on the Western Front and later became Minister of Aircraft Production in Churchill's Second World War government. The second was Charles Rolls (Eton), joint founder of the Rolls-Royce car company in 1904, who was also to make the record books for being the first Briton to die in a flying accident, when in July 1910 the tail broke off his Wright Flyer in an aviation display at Bournemouth. Over half of the 860 pilots who achieved their RAC certificate before war broke out were serving officers in the army or navy, among them Hugh Dowding (Winchester), an officer in the Royal Garrison Artillery who transferred to the pre-war RFC and went on to head Fighter Command during the Battle of Britain.[41]

Public school alumni were equally prominent in the design of aeroplanes. Geoffrey de Havilland (St Edwards, Oxford) disappointed his father by failing to enter the church; instead, he trained as an engineer, going on to build motorcycles and cars. In 1908 he borrowed £1,000 from his grandmother and designed a plane, which first flew in 1910. Shortly after, he began working for the army's aircraft factory at Farnborough, transferring to the RFC after its formation two years later to begin designing its new planes, including reconnaissance machines, fighters and bombers. In 1912 de Havilland flew a B.E. 2a, designed by himself, to an unheard of height of 10,000 feet, taking him eighty minutes to make the climb; his passenger that day, Major Frederick Sykes, later Chief of the Air Staff, wrote later that it was difficult 'to estimate the debt which British aviation owes to Captain Geoffrey de Havilland'.[42] Rival designers were the brothers Frank and Harold Barnwell (Fettes). Frank qualified as a pilot in the RFC in 1914 and conceived one of the war's outstanding planes – the Bristol fighter. His brother Harold was chief test pilot for Vickers, before being killed in 1917 testing a new prototype.[43]

Selection boards for the Royal Flying Corps (RFC), formed in 1912, were drawn almost exclusively from public school senior army officers, who tended to favour those of their own social background. Military aviation was thus born in the public school stable, with its slang, the closed world of the mess, drunken games and bravado, practical jokes and studied informality. As in the army, the urgent requirement for fresh recruits to fill officer spaces from 1916, along with the rapid expansion of the RFC, meant a widening of recruitment beyond the public school class, and the War Office sanctioned a major increase in the number of NCO pilots. Nevertheless, the public school background remained strong in the service through to the 1940 Battle of Britain and beyond.

The army resisted recognizing the independent value of military aviation, and insisted that the RFC initially consist of a Military Wing (alongside a smaller Naval Wing). On the outbreak of war in August 1914 the RFC consisted of 63 aircraft and 103 officers; by December 1916 the number had risen to 6,500 officers, and then tripled to 18,000 by the time it became the Royal Air Force (RAF) on 1 April 1918. This spectacular growth underlines how quickly the aeroplane came to be regarded as a major weapon over the course of the Great War.

Once hostilities began, aeroplanes quickly began to prove their worth on the Western Front. The first reconnaissance sortie across enemy lines is believed to have been carried out on 19 August 1914 by Lieutenant Gilbert Mapplebeck (King William's, Isle of Man) and Captain Philip Joubert de la Ferté (Harrow). Mapplebeck became the first to drop a bomb from a plane and, that September, the first to be wounded at the hands of an enemy pilot. The following March he was shot down behind enemy lines near Lille but managed to evade capture and return to England via Holland. Ironically, and indicating how perilous any kind of flying then was, he died in an air accident in Britain in August 1915.[44] The first RFC officers to be killed in action, indeed the first British officers to be killed in the war, were Second Lieutenant Vincent Waterfall (Brighton College), who had gained his RAC certificate in March 1913 aged twenty, and twenty-three-year-old Lieutenant Charles Gordon Bayly (St Paul's), great nephew of General Gordon, the Victorian hero of Khartoum. Bayly was a qualified pilot but on 22 August he was flying as Waterfall's observer in an Avro 504, tasked to confirm rumours of German troops marching through Belgium towards the BEF at Mons. They swooped low over the German columns near Enghien, but too low, for the slow speed of their plane made them an easy target for ground fire, which brought them down.[45]

The first VC awarded to an RFC officer went to Second Lieutenant William Rhodes-Moorhouse (Harrow), one of the early romantic figures of flying, who had flown his bride across the Channel for their honeymoon in 1912. On 26 April 1915 he was ordered to participate in a raid on the railway junction of Courtrai in northern France, in order to slow the flow of German troops to the front. The only one of four pilots on the mission to reach the target, he brought his plane down to 300 feet to bomb the target, and was badly wounded in doing so. Despite blood pouring from his stomach and thigh, he nursed his plane back to base, only to succumb to wounds the next day.[46] He left behind his young wife and a one-year-old son, whose whole dream became to follow his father's illustrious example. The son, William Henry, educated at Eton, had his way and joined the RAF, only to be killed in the Battle of Britain twenty-five years later; his ashes are buried with those of his father at Parnham House in Dorset.

In the early months of the war a mutual respect and sense of chivalry existed between pilots on both sides. An unnamed and certainly heroic Etonian, flying in a two-seater as an observer, had to climb over his dead pilot to bring his spinning plane under control and then land it safely behind German lines. 'On capture,' he wrote to his old school, 'I met two German officers, who knew several English people that I knew and they were most awfully kind to me. They gave me a very good dinner of champagne and oysters etc and I was treated like an honoured guest.'[47] Less gallantry was apparent when RFC pilots finally managed to shoot down one of the mighty German Zeppelins. The fear these machines inspired and the destruction they could cause from early 1915 was felt keenly, not least in schools. Unreliable though Zeppelins were as a military weapon, they flew so high in the darkness that attacking them was a difficult task, and not until September 1916 did Lieutenant William Leefe Robinson (St Bees') become the first pilot to shoot one down, an achievement which earned him the VC. Later that month, Lieutenant Fred Sowrey (KCS Wimbledon) achieved the same feat. He was a good example of a public schoolboy whose keenness for flying and proficiency in the air stemmed from his interest in science and technology at school. His approach to shooting down the Zeppelin, for which he won the DSO, was courageous and measured: 'At 12.45 am I noticed an enemy airship on an easterly direction and manoeuvred into position underneath it … I fired at it. The first two drums of ammunition apparently had no effect, but the third one caused the envelope to catch fire in several places. I watched the burning airship strike the ground'.[48]

The sense of romance about the early air war was partly a product of its relatively low casualties. In the first eight months until March 1915 only thirty RFC officers were killed. But as the numbers flying increased, and the deadly sophistication of anti-aircraft guns and aeroplane armaments developed, casualties mounted rapidly. Over 250 RFC officers were killed in the Battle of the Somme alone.[49] The higher death rate was also the result of deliberate policy. Brigadier-General Hugh Trenchard, commanding officer of the RFC in France from 1915 and later known as 'the father of the RAF', believed in relentless offensive action to support the army, including high-risk patrols across the lines to shoot down enemy reconnaissance planes and lure German fighters into dogfights.

To eighteen-year-old public schoolboys the attraction of flying can easily be understood, as was their keenness to show off to their former juniors. Tonbridge School displayed for many years the propeller of a plane flown by a former pupil who made a forced landing on the school playing fields, while a Haileyburian passed low over the College in 1917 and 'managed to get a wave out of some of the boys doing open order work in the Twenty Acre'.[50] Felsted School recorded a visit in 1916 by F. D. Holder and N. L. Knight: Knight 'fouled the Shrubbery with consequent damage both to the shrubbery and the machine', while Holder 'landed near the cricket nets, the boys soon wrapped round his machine'.[51] Not all aspirants were natural aviators: one Sherborne boy recorded a school friend who had been pulled off pilot training to become an observer, 'as the Staff think he will be pushing daisies before his time if he is a pilot'.[52]

The most evocative account of the air war came from Cecil Lewis, who joined the RFC straight from Oundle in 1915, aged only seventeen. He made light of the dangers, comparing his lot as an RFC officer favourably to that of soldiers: 'We were never under fire for more than six hours a day. When we returned to the aerodrome, our war was over. We had a bed, a bath, a mess with good food and peace until the next patrol ... we were never under any bodily fatigue, never filthy, verminous, or exposed to the long, disgusting drudgery of trench warfare'.[53] Lewis finished the war with an MC, went on to be a co-founder of the BBC in 1922 and to write the best known aviation memoir of the war, *Sagittarius Rising* (the inspiration, along with *Journey's End*, for the 1976 film *Aces High*).

As the air war intensified, so the casualty toll rose. Of the twenty-five RFC officers from Tonbridge killed in the war, only one died before July 1916. They were, typically, very young: twenty-two of the Tonbridge dead were under twenty-four, and eight were twenty or younger.[54] Downside's first RFC casualty did not come until April 1917, with seven more to follow during the war, all but one in their early twenties. Two of their eight were killed in accidents.[55] Accidents accounted for well over half of the casualties of the air war, the majority of them in training.[56] The future VC ace, Albert Ball (Nottingham High School and Trent College), while on a training course at Hendon, wrote to his father: 'I am very sorry to say that a great many of our men have been killed in the last few weeks. Yesterday a ripping boy had a smash ... he had a two-inch piece of wood right through his head and died this morning'.[57]

Death was an ever-present companion in air combat, the life expectancy of pilots during the Somme and in 1917 being estimated to be six weeks or less. Denied parachutes by War Office ineptitude or worse, pilots had little hope of escape from a falling plane, or of a quick and painless end. Flying deaths were often intensely painful. Engine and structural failures were common, offering the pilot little chance if either occurred. Training of new pilots was brief, and dangerous in itself because of poorly maintained planes and instructors who had in many cases been sent back from the front with their nerves shattered. The greatest fear was of the plane catching fire in the air, with flames from unprotected fuel lines condemning pilots to an appalling death. The ever-present prospect of that fate, and the regular disappearance of colleagues and friends, meant that life for men so young and inexperienced could be unbearably stressful. A pilot from John Lyon School wrote to his school magazine to record a meeting with a pilot friend, who 'has flown various types of machine ... but has now lost his nerve for fighting'.[58]

April and May 1917 were two months that saw the highest RFC casualties, the fateful lack of experience of young pilots being a key factor. Major Sholto Douglas (Tonbridge), later a senior RAF commander in the Second World War, subsequently wrote: 'The severity of our losses early in 1917 was not entirely due to the superiority of the German fighters ... The increasing demands of the RFC meant new pilots being sent to the front with far from enough training, or even sufficient hours of bare experience in the air'.[59] Inexperience may well have done for Second Lieutenant Pieter Johnson (Haileybury), who left school in February 1916, five months before his eighteenth birthday, and joined the RFC that August. He wrote back to his school in high spirits, in early January 1916, to say that he had met three other Haileyburians playing rugby against another squadron. He had had 'one scrap' so far in the air with 'three Boches firing at me at the same time, but they gave it up after hitting everything on the machine except the observer and myself'.[60] On 27 January 1917 he wrote to tell his mother excitedly that a fellow pilot had brought down a German plane in flames; his mother's reaction to this news is not recorded, but most mothers would have been unlikely to find the story reassuring. The day after writing, Johnson went missing on patrol. While flying above enemy lines, assisting British artillery batteries to find their targets, his plane was struck by an anti-aircraft shell. It spun to earth near Serre on the Somme. Johnson was aged eighteen and a half.[61]

One public school pilot at least was the subject of racial prejudice. Hardit Singh Malik joined Eastbourne College from India in 1910; in 1914 he played cricket for Sussex, won a scholarship to Balliol College,

Oxford, and a golf blue, an impressive record by any measure. Told there were no vacancies in the army for Indian students, he promptly joined the French army to drive ambulances. When he later applied for the French air force rather than the RFC, his Oxford tutor intervened, and Malik was commissioned into the RFC in 1917. In October 1917 he went out to France and, flying his Sopwith Camel, was shot up during a dogfight with four German planes. 'There was a smell of petrol and a sharp pain in my leg,' he later wrote. 'I crash-landed behind our lines and fainted. The plane had more than four hundred bullets in it. Doctors wanted to amputate my leg but I persuaded them not to. Bullets remained in my leg for the rest of my life.' He wore his flying helmet over his turban, and became known as the 'flying hobgoblin'. Prejudice persisted throughout the war, and he later recalled how one night a South African pilot complained about having Indians in the RFC: 'My observer, a Scot, lunged across the table at him and gripped his throat until he apologized.' After the war, Malik was instrumental in persuading the RFC to accept Indian cadets into Cranwell.[62]

British public schools and universities attracted several sons of Indian princes and other wealthy elites in the period before 1914. An issue arose when two young princes from Indore attended Bible classes at Rugby in 1914, causing concern in the political department of the Government of India that the Indian press would accuse the British of trying to convert them from Hinduism.[63] Malik himself, in later life, said of his time at Eastbourne: 'When I arrived some of the boys started ragging me. They wanted to see what was under my turban ... I said I would kill the first boy who touched it. I must have looked fierce because they all backed away and I was never troubled again. It was a lovely school. I escaped fagging because I got into the cricket eleven early. I went to chapel because it was not compulsory and I liked the hymns'.[64] India was of huge significance in Britain's war effort; its army, officered mainly by the products of public schools, was deployed first on the Western Front and then in the Middle East. The racism experienced by Malik in his clash with the South African pilot may have been endemic at this time in British colonial attitudes, so memorably and subtly portrayed in *A Passage to India* by E. M. Forster (Tonbridge), but the Indian Army, together with Indians serving as officers in British forces, made a magnificent contribution to the final outcome.

A pilot who made another gallant contribution was Major Robert Gregory, whose name would be commemorated in one of the more famous poems of the war. Gregory had narrowly missed selection for the Harrow cricket eleven, but took eight wickets in the only 'test' match he played, for Ireland against Scotland in 1912. He became better known as an artist of international renown, and devoted his time to managing the family estate at Coole Park in western Ireland, boasting a cricket ground played on by George Bernard Shaw, and where his mother, Lady Gregory, was the patron of the poet W. B. Yeats. Gregory joined the Connaught Rangers in 1914 before transferring to the RFC in 1916. He shot down nineteen German planes and won the MC in 1917 before being killed on the Italian front on 23 January 1918.[65] The day after his death a distraught Lady Gregory wrote to Yeats: 'Robert has been killed in action. It is very hard to bear. If you feel like it sometime, write something down that we may keep. You understood him better than many.' Two poems were written that summer by Yeats, *In Memory of Major Robert Gregory* and the better known *An Irish Airman Foresees His Death*, which has come to epitomize the Great War airman's romantic desire to live for the moment, when issues of life and death are in such precarious balance.[66]

Britain lacked an equivalent of Manfred von Richthofen, the 'Red Baron', the best known German pilot of the war and perhaps, indeed, the most celebrated fighter pilot in history. She did, however, have Captain Albert Ball, who won the VC, DSO and two Bars, and MC, and who shot down an estimated forty-four enemy aircraft. Cecil Lewis was in Ball's squadron, and in *Sagittarius Rising* recalls Ball returning from one particularly hazardous mission: 'When Ball taxied up to the sheds, we saw his elevators were flapping loose – controls had been completely shot away ... it was incredible he had not crashed ... he was so angry at being shot up like this, that he walked straight to the sheds, wiped the oil off with a rag, and ordered out his Nieuport and within two hours was back with another Hun to his credit'.[67] In early 1917 Ball wrote to his father to say that he had grown tired of always having to kill, and would be pleased when the war finished. On 7 May he was flying a patrol with Cecil Lewis, who flew into a cloud with him at 8,000 feet. When Lewis emerged into blue sky, he could no longer see Ball. He had been shot down behind enemy lines. The Germans honoured him with a full military funeral.

Of all the public school heroes in the Great War in all three services, none caught the popular imagination quite like Ball. An instinctive flyer, and a dead-eye shot, it was the example he set of sustained, even reckless, aggression and courageous leadership which brought him the Victoria Cross. As his photographs reveal, he was neither a flamboyant nor an arrogant figure, but diligent and extraordinarily focused. His commanding officer wrote that he was 'a striking example of what courage means',[68] and his death, aged just twenty, sparked a national wave of mourning.

The Royal Navy

The Royal Navy believed, along with the Jesuits, that you needed to catch boys early if they were to be moulded properly, which explains why the numbers joining the navy from the traditional public schools was so much lower than for the Army. For much of the nineteenth century, and long into the twentieth, it operated an 'early entry' system for cadets, with boys being sent to HMS *Britannia*, old wooden ships moored in the Dart, and subsequently to the land-based college at Dartmouth. At first the *Britannia* scheme took boys midway through their secondary school careers, and although often candidates were sent to specialized 'crammers', Portsmouth Grammar School made a special provision from the 1880s for naval entry, with its own 'navy class', specializing in subjects that boys would need for entry to the *Britannia* and which would help them in their naval careers.[69] Other boys with public school backgrounds entered the Royal Navy at eighteen as Engineering and Supply Officers.

In 1903 an even more exclusive system of officer entry began with entry for both seamen and engineers at twelve and three quarters, later raised to thirteen. The boys first went to the Royal Naval College, Osborne, on the Isle of Wight from where, after two years, they transferred to the Royal Naval College (RNC), Dartmouth. Both the RNCs at Osborne and Dartmouth were members of the HMC when war broke out, and their headmasters attended all HMC annual conferences. Their status as 'public schools' is a matter of debate among historians.

In 1913 the Admiralty Board decided to institute a significant change to recruitment, known as 'the public school special late entry scheme' for boys of seventeen and eighteen. That December, Sir Alfred Ewing, Director of Naval Education, was invited to address the HMC Annual Conference, in Reading, where he told headmasters: 'For the first time in British history, the navy says to the public schools "Send us your finished products." '[70] The minutes record that the assembled company welcomed the proposal; but, on further reflection, they expressed concerns about a compulsory paper in engineering. Schools that did not offer science at advanced level worried that their pupils would find it difficult to pass and they would be at a disadvantage. Nevertheless, in the first exam after the new scheme was introduced, sixty-four boys from public schools sat the exam and forty-one passed, the top mark going to a boy from St Paul's. The navy's plan was for the successful candidates to undergo an intensive eighteen months of specialist training, but the outbreak of war cut this to just eleven months. Other public schoolboys with nautical interests took advantage of the creation of the Royal Naval Volunteer Reserve, which was regarded with some suspicion by the Admiralty. In the event many of these officers fought ashore in the Royal Naval Division, where the Navy suffered most of its casualties.

Conventional public school boys formed only a relatively small proportion of those who served in the Royal Navy during the Great War. Out of 3,500 old boys from Charterhouse who served in the armed forces, just 120 served in the navy; at Dulwich, it was 173 out of 3,052, at Eton only 163 were in the navy out of 5,650. Analysing the Rolls of Honour of twenty-four leading public schools, which between them suffered nearly 6,000 deaths, the Royal Navy accounts for just one per cent of the casualties – and many of those dead were in the Royal Naval Division. Seven Marlborough boys died in the Navy out of total deaths of 733, Westminster 4 out of 220.[71] During the whole war, moreover, just five per cent of serving naval officers were killed, compared to fifteen per cent of army officers.[72]

Some schools had special connections with the sea services. The Royal Hospital School boasted a long history of association with the Royal and Merchant Navies. Founded in 1712 and overseen by the Admiralty, it was located until 1933 at the Greenwich hospital, from where it moved to Holbrook on the River Orwell in Suffolk. It ranks with Dartmouth and Osborne as a particular type of public school, fee-paying but limited to a very specific purpose. Entry was limited to the sons of sea-farers, and its boys were required to wear naval uniform and on leaving to join either the Royal or Merchant Navies, or the Royal Marines. Approximately 5,000 Royal Hospital old boys served in the Great War; at least 440 were killed in the Royal Navy, and many more in the Merchant Navy, which suffered grievously from losses to German submarines, notably in 1917 and 1918.[73] Several other schools had strong traditions of old boys joining the Royal Navy, above all those in or near naval towns. At Plymouth College, ten per cent of their dead were in the navy, while at Portsmouth Grammar School it was seventeen per cent.[74]

As for the new Special Public School Late Entries, four of the initial cohort of 41 were sent to join HMS *Inflexible* and took part in the Battle of the Falklands Islands, one of the first major naval battles of the war, in December 1914, in the South Atlantic. The German Asiatic Squadron, whose major units were the armoured cruisers *Scharnhorst* and *Gneisenau*, diverted from their attempt to return to Germany to attack the British base at Stanley in the Falklands; there it found the Royal Navy's more heavily armed battle-cruisers HMS *Invincible* and HMS *Inflexible* that had been sent south to deal with them. On board *Inflexible*, Midshipman L. D. Morse (Cheltenham College) sent his school magazine a dramatic account of the engagement: 'At 6:12 the *Gneisenau* sunk. Directly after she had sunk we in the other ships put out all boats to pick up the survivors. There were crowds of them in the water catching hold of wreckage ... the wails and cries of the poor creatures was awful'.[75] It was a significant British victory, with Admiral von Spee's German squadron, that had sunk two older British armoured cruisers in the Pacific, successfully neutralized.

Rugby was prominent amongst the schools that took advantage of the new late entry scheme, and more of its boys were to join the navy via this route than from any other public school, the strength of its science teaching no doubt being a key factor. The entry of June 1915 saw 63 successful candidates out of 116 applicants, including G. N. Oliver from Rugby, who became the first from this scheme to reach the rank of admiral. At the Battle of Jutland on 31 May 1916, the largest, if ultimately inconclusive, naval battle of the war, there were over ninety 'public school special late entry' midshipmen, from the three intakes so far, serving in the Grand Fleet. Jutland saw the largest loss of naval life in a single action, partly because of the loss of almost all hands on three British battle-cruisers: HMS *Queen Mary*, HMS *Invincible* and HMS *Indefatigable*. More than 3,000 sailors went down with them. Cuthbert Hill had left Gresham's School in 1915 at the age of seventeen, entered the Royal Navy via the special late entry scheme and was serving as a midshipman on *Invincible*. He was only just eighteen on the day of the battle, and must have died almost instantly as the ship blew up. One of his friends, who was still at school, wrote to Hill's grieving mother to provide a few words of comfort: 'The head preached tonight and spoke of Cuthie: it was rather moving, as he meant what he said and we knew what he said was true ... I do hope that Cuthie can know [what] he will always be to one of his friends; he *must* know'.[76]

John Esmond was a product of more conventional naval entry. He had entered Downside in 1910, leaving two years later for RNC Osborne, aged twelve. At the age of fifteen, he was sent to serve on *Invincible*, and was just seventeen when he went down with her at Jutland. A survivor wrote to his father: 'Your son was at his station in 'A' Turret, and died, as I am sure he would have wished to die, full of fight and enthusiasm ... there was a tremendous explosion aboard at 6.34; the ship broke in half and sank in 15 seconds. Death must have been instantaneous and painless'.[77] Anthony Eden (Eton) had been in France only a short while when he heard in June 1916 that his sixteen-year-old younger brother, Nicholas, had been killed in the *Indefatigable*; his older brother, John, had already been killed in Belgium in October 1914. Witnesses told one of Eden's early biographers that when he heard the news about

Nicholas: 'he leapt over the parapet and led a charge like a man demented, charging and fighting with the strength of ten men'.[78] One can only imagine how his parents might have reacted to the news had their third son been killed also. Anthony Eden went on to be awarded the Military Cross and finished the war at the age of twenty-one as the youngest brigade major in the British army. He was Prime Minister from 1955 to 1957.

Portsmouth Grammar School boys were conspicuous in action during the battle of Jutland: thirteen were mentioned in the dispatches of Admiral John Jellicoe, who was in command of the British Grand Fleet – a record unmatched by any other public school. Major Francis Harvey, Royal Marines, was one of them, a major in charge of 'Q' Turret on Beatty's flagship, the battle-cruiser HMS *Lion*. A direct hit on the turret killed most of those inside but Harvey, though mortally wounded, ordered the magazine doors closed and flooded to prevent the kind of explosion which had destroyed the other battle-cruisers; for this he was awarded the posthumous VC.[79]

Another Portsmouth GS product, Lieutenant Norman Holbrook, left at thirteen to go to Dartmouth, from where he joined the submarine service in 1910, attracted by its prospects for young officers to have early independent command. In the pre-war years, submarines were still in their infancy, with limited firepower, range, capability and safety. By December 1914, Holbrook was in command of *B II*, a submarine of primitive 1907 design, which he managed to navigate down to the Eastern Mediterranean, itself quite a feat. His orders were to patrol the Dardanelles, but he chose to dive under five rows of mines to attack and sink a threatening Turkish cruiser, before returning to the greater safety of the Mediterranean, having been submerged in Turkish waters for nine hours. For this he was awarded the VC, the first of the war for the Royal Navy, and became something of a hero, particularly in Australia, where a small town was named after him in New South Wales.[80]

The Royal Naval Division had been formed from RNVR volunteers, whom the Navy did not trust in ships. These included Rupert Brooke and a coterie of his friends. The Division fought as infantry under naval command at Antwerp in 1914, at Gallipoli the following year, and on the Western Front from 1916. It saw its fiercest action in the final stages of the Somme battle on 13 and 14 November 1916, around the village of Beaucourt. One of the many casualties was Frederick Kelly (Sydney Grammar School and Eton), one of Rupert Brooke's pallbearers, Olympic oarsman and professional musician. Another was Vere Harmsworth, son of the newspaper magnate Lord Rothermere and nephew of his brother Lord Northcliffe, who had gone to Dartmouth as a boy in preparation for a career in the Royal Navy. He wrote home from the Somme in October 1916 to describe 'the awful nightmare of seeing one's own men – that one has been with for so long – being struck down all around one will never move from one's mind'. He had refused a staff job, stating 'the greatest honour an officer can receive is to lead his men over the parapet'. When leading a dawn attack on 13 November he was hit twice before reaching the German third line, when a shell killed him outright. His 'Hawke' battalion went into action with 20 officers and 396 men: no officers came back unhurt and just twenty men. Shortly before the attack, he wrote to Lord Northcliffe: 'I feel I might have been born just to live my twenty-one years and then fade away ... if I fall, do not mourn, but be glad and proud it is not a life wasted but gloriously fulfilled'.[81]

The last great naval attack of the war was the raid on the port of Zeebrugge on 23 April 1918. The port was being used by German U-boats and light ships to create havoc with Allied shipping, especially in the Channel. The British plan was straightforward enough, to sink three old cruisers in the mouth of the port and thus block its use. But multiple mishaps meant the plan went awry, and nearly a third of the 1,700 British men involved in it became casualties. With the British Army on the back foot in the early stages of the German Spring Offensive, propaganda requirements demanded the raid be sold to the public as a victory. Eight VCs were to be awarded, six going to public schoolboys. One of these went to Lieutenant Commander Arthur Harrison, who would have been familiar with the port of departure from his schooldays at Dover College and who was the only winner of the VC to have played rugby for England. His task was to lead the naval assault parties attacking the German guns on the mole at Zeebrugge; during the early stages of the action a shell fragment broke his jaw, but he pressed on with the attack until he fell still leading his men, all but two of whom were to be either wounded or killed.[82] One of his contemporaries recorded that 'Harrison's charge down that narrow gangway of death was a worthy finale to the large number of charges which, as a forward of the first rank, he had led down many a rugby football ground. He had played the game to the end.'[83]

Seven boys from Dulwich College took part in the raid, five of whom were to die. Frank Brock was one: from the famous firework family, he joined the Royal Naval Air Service (RNAS) in 1914, as a pilot, and invented the 'Brock Bullet', an incendiary weapon particularly effective against Zeppelins. Officers in the RNAS were officially in the naval wing of the Royal Flying Corps, another way in which public school boys could don a dark blue uniform, albeit with different insignia. At Zeebrugge, Brock created the smokescreen to attempt to hide the attacking force, and, like a true inventor, he was killed searching for a German range-finder, which he wished to take back and examine.[84]

Credit for the Royal Navy's overall dominance should also go to code-breakers in the Admiralty's Room 40, whose successes included anticipating the German fleet sortie at Jutland and decrypting the Zimmerman Telegram, which helped bring the USA into the war. Many of these code-breakers were civilians, public-school educated Oxbridge dons like Dillwyn Knox (Eton), Francis Birch (Eton) and Walter Bruford (Manchester GS), all of whom went on to work at Bletchley Park in the Second World War. Here Knox, as Chief Cryptographer, played a key role in cracking the German Enigma ciphers. Public schoolboys may not have served in large numbers in the Royal Navy, but they made a significant contribution to its command of the seas.[85]

The battles of 1918 and the end of the war

The final year of the war saw the rapid movement of belligerent armies. The German generals Hindenburg and Ludendorff gazed at a bleak future that January, with unreliable allies in Turkey and Austria-Hungary, the Allied blockade starving Germany of resources and food, and domestic unrest growing. They gambled on a major offensive in the spring forcing the British to the peace table before American troops could make their presence felt on the Western Front. Russia's leaving the war allowed them to transfer fresh forces to the west, making success a possibility. The plan was to launch the attack where the French and British lines met to the south-east of the Somme region, and to drive the British back towards the Channel. The date chosen was 21 March.[86] Public school alumni were to be prominent in resisting the attack, and were to suffer heavy losses over the three months until its momentum was reversed.

This attack forms the background to *Journey's End*. Sherriff did not participate on 21 March as he was still recovering from wounds received in August 1917 during Third Ypres, but one company of his former battalion, the 9th East Surreys, did take part and was rapidly overrun by the German assault. The play describes one such company's plight. Sherriff's writing was coloured by his seeing battered survivors of the first wave of the attack at Ypres pointing in desperation to the German wire which had not been cut, the screaming in the dressing station, and the anguish of the stretcher-bearers trying to distinguish the living from the dead .[87] He remained critical for the rest of his life of the senior commanders who had ordered men to attack in such impossible conditions, characterized by the impervious colonel in *Journey's End* who orders the suicidal raid in which Osborne, the avuncular public school master, is killed.

The year 1918 is the least familiar to the British public of all the years of the Great War, but in terms of loss of life, including public school casualties, it was as devastating as the previous two. In only ten separate months throughout the war did the numbers of officer deaths exceed 1,100; five of those months fell in 1918, with August being the third worst month of the whole war for officer deaths. Analysis of the rolls of honour of twenty-six public schools shows that just over a quarter of all deaths came during 1918 (heavily weighted to the six and a half months following 21 March).[88] Ten per cent of Downside's total deaths came in just three months between 8 August and the Armistice in 1918.[89]

Oliver Lyttelton, Etonian and Grenadier, was one of many to become a casualty, and his experience gives us an insight into the debilitating effects of gas on the human body: 'On 22 April 1918 I was writing some orders at Brigade HQ in a woodman's cottage in the forest. We were being shelled by gas shells, and one of them hit the cottage. I had on my gas mask but I was spattered with liquid mustard and had a few superficial wounds, no more than scratches. The warmth of your body vaporizes the gas, and in an hour I was blind, and huge blisters began to appear in my groin and armpits. I was evacuated to the casualty clearing station, but I never saw it because I was completely blind by then and for the next three or four days ... My burns nearly reached the limit beyond which you die, and the journey in a bumpy train to Boulogne was agony. The most trying part of extensive gas burns is that you cannot sleep, and your resistance to pain becomes impaired'.[90] Lyttelton recovered, one of the fortunate ones, and later became a prominent politician and Colonial Secretary in Churchill's peacetime government.

The Germans made rapid advances on 21 March and subsequent days. At least twelve public school VCs were won in the first four days of the fighting, half of them posthumous. Lieutenant Colonel Wilfrith Elstob (Christ's Hospital, and a French teacher before the war at Merchiston Castle School), had risen from private soldier in 1914 to commanding a battalion of the Manchester Regiment by early 1918, winning a DSO and MC along the way. The Germans initially overran his position, known as 'Manchester Hill', but the second wave had the task of mopping up British strongpoints. Elstob organized the defence for a whole day, throwing bombs himself and constantly firing to repulse attack after attack. He was able to speak to Brigade HQ to assure them that he would fight to the last man. The Germans called out for him to surrender, but he shouted back from the hill, 'Never'. Realising the position was hopeless, he climbed out of the last trench to throw more bombs at the advancing Germans, before being shot dead.[91]

The pressures created by the British retreat are shown in the words of another commanding officer, Lieutenant Colonel Christopher Buckle (Marlborough), of 2nd Northants, to his mother when on leave in April 1918. He was an experienced and resolute professional soldier who had won the DSO and MC, and had been wounded five times in his three or more years of front line service. At Charing Cross, as he boarded the train, he turned to his mother: 'If I last through the summer, I shall give up the command ... Everyone's nerve is bound to fail after commanding a line regiment for three years and no Colonel of Infantry has a dog's chance in a retreat such as this'. At that moment Mrs Buckle knew that she would never see her son again. He was killed on the Aisne on 27 May, when his battalion was overrun and he was seen to fall at the entrance to his dugout, pistol in hand.[92]

A dominant arm throughout the war, on all fronts and with all armies, was the artillery. In 1918 the much increased accuracy and devastating firepower of the British artillery bombardments played a vital role both in slowing down the German advance and then in supporting the Allied counterattack. One British artillery officer to distinguish himself in 1918 was Captain Eric Dougall (Tonbridge), who had been commissioned into the Royal Field Artillery in 1916. At Messines in June 1917, when over two thousand guns fired three to four million shells over several hours to support the successful British attack, Dougall had won the MC when acting as forward observation officer, a vital role up in the front line with a telephone link back to his battery, ranging his guns on specific targets. Dougall was hard pressed, during and after the German attack on 21 March 1918, making difficult judgements about when to stand and bring his guns into action and when to use the horses to move them back away from possible capture. On 1 April he wrote to his cousin describing the challenge: 'We have been converting an old shell hole into an observation position. We have most exciting times trying to see our targets. We have to crawl along from shell hole to shell hole hoping that snipers will not see us and the German shells will miss.'[93]

On 10 April Dougall found himself having to fire his guns at the enemy infantry he could see advancing towards the British positions, using open sights. Artillery batteries were generally well to the rear of the infantry positions, but the immediate crisis and rapid movement meant that they now stood shoulder to shoulder in the same line:

'Captain Dougall rallied and organized the infantry and formed a line in front of his battery, harassing the advancing enemy with a rapid rate of fire. Although exposed to heavy fire he inspired the infantry with his assurance that "so long as you stick to your trenches, I will keep my guns here" '. So ran the citation for the VC which Dougall was awarded. Five days later he was dead. The chaplain of his brigade wrote to Dougall's parents that seldom had he met 'an officer who commanded such unbounded devotion from his men and unqualified admiration from his brother officers'.[94]

The German advance threatened, at points in May and June, to engulf the whole Allied line; but by July it had been contained and the Allies were ready to go on the offensive, under the unified command of Marshal Foch and against an enemy who was by now close to exhaustion. On 8 August, described by Ludendorff as the 'black day of the German Army', the counterattack began round Amiens and made immediate gains. Hammer blows by British, French and American forces at different points in the line sustained this advance through what came to be known as the 'Hundred Days', between 8 August and 11 November, one of the most successful campaigns fought by the British Army.

Credit for the success of the war-winning campaign has been handed variously to Haig (Clifton) and his five Army Commanders – Horne (Harrow), Plumer, Byng and Rawlinson (all Eton), and Birdwood (Clifton), as well as the Australian Monash (Scotch, Melbourne). Whatever view historians have taken of the callousness or competence of some of the high command's decisions, it is a calumny that British generals all stayed well out of danger in their chateaux behind the lines. Fifty-eight men of the rank of brigadier-general and above were killed during the war and some three hundred wounded. All those who died succumbed to shell or bullet, which says something about their proximity to the front.[95] Many of them were old enough to have their children fighting, and several lost sons, including General Allenby (Haileybury), whose son Michael, a Wellingtonian, was killed just after his father had left England to take command of the Egyptian Expeditionary Force.

One of General Allenby's tasks in 1917–18 was to support the role of the legendary Colonel T. E. Lawrence in leading the Arab Revolt against their common Turkish enemy. Lawrence had attended City of Oxford High School, a fee-paying HMC school in 1914, founded by a Balliol don in 1888, academically strong and with few of the social pretensions found elsewhere in the public school system. After a glittering academic career, he worked before the war as an archaeologist in the

Middle East, and was drawn into military intelligence in Cairo in 1914. His knowledge of the area, and friendship with Arab leaders like Emir Faisal, allowed him to lead the Arab Revolt and co-ordinate it with wider British strategy. He is perhaps the one soldier in the Great War who changed the course of history, leading an extraordinarily success-ful guerrilla campaign which helped Allenby to capture Damascus in October 1918 and drive the Turks out of their former empire.

These successes, and the publicity given him by the American journalist Lowell Thomas, brought Lawrence iconic status, and much of the exotic mystery surrounding him persists to this day, sustained by the film epic, *Lawrence of Arabia,* directed in 1962 by David Lean (Leighton Park). His post-war career was less happy. He failed to persuade the British government to honour their promise of independence to the Arabs, from which stemmed many of the problems of the Middle East today, and he then retreated from the public gaze, sustained mainly by his prolific writing and his many friends, until his death in a motorcycle accident in 1935. One of these friends, John Buchan, wrote that he could have 'followed Lawrence over the edge of the world. I loved him for himself, and also because there seemed to be re-born in him all the lost friends of my youth'.[96] This image of Lawrence as representative of the 'lost generation' echoes with another short memoir Buchan wrote of his brother Alastair and six of his friends killed in the war, including Raymond Asquith.[97] Lawrence had himself lost two of his brothers on the Western Front in 1915, and both he and Buchan must have seen themselves as part of that lost generation of survivors who failed to make the post-1918 world a better or safer place.

Not all those promoted to the rank of brigadier-general were pro-fessional soldiers from the pre-war army. One 'amateur soldier' was Roland Bradford (Epsom), who started as a second lieutenant, won the VC commanding a battalion of Durham Light Infantry on the Somme and was killed at Cambrai commanding a brigade in November 1917, aged just twenty-five. Another was George Gater (Winchester), who had been Director of Education for Nottingham before the war. He joined up in August 1914, was commanding a battalion by October 1916, with a DSO and Bar, and a brigade by October 1917, when he was only thirty-one. He led this brigade through the rest of the war before returning to the civil service, finally heading the Colonial Office in 1940.[98]

The most romantic figure among the 'amateur generals' was Arnold Strode-Jackson, Olympic athlete and much decorated soldier. A boy at Malvern, he did not take up serious running until Oxford. He won the mile against Cambridge and, on the strength of this, was selected for the 1912 Stockholm Olympics. Even by the standards of the time his training was casual, consisting of little more than golf and walking, and he interrupted a fishing holiday to run in Stockholm, where he won the gold medal in the 1,500 metres in a new Olympic record time, beating the American world record holder. When the war started he joined the King's Royal Rifle Corps. Wounded three times, he won the DSO and no fewer than three Bars, all in 1917–18, one of only seven officers to achieve this distinction, and was mentioned in dispatches six times. Promoted to brigadier-general as the war ended, he was in the British delegation at the Versailles Peace Conference before retiring from the army.[99] His record of gallantry was matched by Humphrey Gilkes, son of a former Master of Dulwich, where he himself was at school: Gilkes won four MCs in 1917–18, one of only three officers to achieve this distinction.[100] The records of Bradford, Gater, Strode-Jackson and Gilkes are testimony to the qualities of the public school 'temporary officers' of 1914, who proved themselves worthy of high military rank by exhibiting personal courage and qualities of leadership.

Officer battle casualties totalled 1,100 in the week ending 6 November 1918, and were still as high as 300 in the following week.[101] It is impossible to know how many public schoolboys from Britain and her Dominions died in those last days, but they continued to be at the heart of the war, its fighting and leadership, right through to the Armistice on 11 November. One of those tough South African soldiers who served the Empire well, Lieutenant Colonel Deneys Reitz (Grey College, Bloemfontein), commanding a battalion of Royal Scots Fusiliers, moved them forward at dawn on 11 November in preparation for an attack towards Mons. Reitz had fought for the Boers in 1899 and for the British in South-West Africa and on the Western Front. On this day he remembered that, 'by eleven o'clock we were in the battle zone, British and German guns were firing, and there came the crackle of rifles and machine guns ahead. Suddenly, far off, we heard the faint sound of cheering borne upon the wind, which gathered volume as it rolled towards us ... Then the brigade major handed me a dispatch which contained momentous news; "Hostilities will cease at 1100 hours today, 11 November" '.[102]

One who did not live to see this day was a younger version of those idealistic public schoolboys who had flocked to the colours in 1914. Geoffrey Lamont left Mill Hill only in the summer of 1917, after achieving many honours, including the positions of senior monitor and company sergeant major of the OTC. Commissioned from the OCB into the Grenadier Guards in 1918, he won the DSO for his leadership and gallantry on the battlefield, a rare award for a nineteen-year-old

181

subaltern. His colonel wrote of him that he was 'everything a Guards-man should be – a brave soldier, capable officer and a leader of men'.[103] 'How well I remember him,' wrote his servant of his last hours, 'the early morning we left to take the position, reading his little Testament which he made so much of.' Lamont was killed instantly in action on 6 November 1918, his death announced on the day of the Armistice. A Mill Hill pupil remembered the 'utter devastation when the head-master, Sir John Maclure, announced the news to the assembled school'.[104]

Chapter 8

Armistice and Commemoration: No End to Conflict

The fighting may have stopped at 11 a.m. on 11 November 1918; but this was no full stop marking a final end to the Great War. For hundreds of thousands of soldiers it denoted no significant ending at all, but just another day in their broken and shattered lives, as it was for their families. For some, even, it was the beginning of suffering and hardship that was to endure for many years. In Britain, the 'war to end all war' led to an expectation of better living conditions, including 'homes for heroes', which the government, least of all once the Depression set in, was in no position to provide.

Internationally, the Paris Peace Conference of 1919 produced not peace, but a pause before Europe again erupted into conflagration. Medically, the Spanish influenza epidemic, exacerbated by the conditions of warfare, ravaged Britain and the rest of the world, killing a minimum of 50 million people, more than all the deaths in the Great War, and taking the lives of many young men who had survived the fighting. Within the public schools, the arguments that were to ensue about how best to commemorate the war and the fallen were to eclipse in intensity any disagreements that occurred about the nature and prosecution of the war itself. The peace and better world for which so many had fought and died was to crumble even as people began to remember.

Life and death
Particular sadness clings to those killed in the last few days of fighting. One well known story is that of Wilfred Owen. With four children to educate, public school fees were beyond the Owen parents,[1] but Wilfred was commissioned in 1916 and became friendly with literary figures like Siegfried Sassoon and Robert Graves, and with the Eton scholar, Shrewsbury schoolmaster and poet, Philip Bainbrigge. Owen was killed

in action on 4 November, whilst crossing the Sambre Canal near Ors, where he is now buried. The bells were ringing euphorically the news of the Armistice at 11 a.m. on 11 November when the telegram announcing his death arrived at his parents' home. The story of Wilfred's brother Harold seeing his ghost in khaki in his cabin is well known, but in fact Harold Owen's experience was one of the clearest statements of what was a not uncommon experience: the appearance to loved ones of soldiers who had died, which many took to be the departed returning one final time as an act of reassurance that their death was not final.[2] Yet again, the Armistice was far from the definitive closure that it appears with historical hindsight to have been.

John Bennett (King's College School, Wimbledon) won a scholarship in mathematics to Oxford, but with the outbreak of war went instead to the Royal Military Academy at Woolwich and became a second lieutenant in the RE, with responsibility for signals and telegraphy. In March 1918, while working as a dispatch rider, he was blown from his motorcycle in France by an exploding shell. While in a coma for six days in a military hospital, he experienced the sensation of floating above his body and seeing himself lying in his hospital bed. He subsequently wrote in his autobiography: 'It was perfectly clear to me that being dead is quite unlike being very ill or very weak or helpless. So far as I was concerned, there was no fear at all. And yet I have never been a brave man and was certainly still afraid of heavy gunfire. I was cognisant of my complete indifference towards my own body.'[3] This 'out-of-body' experience convinced him of the existence of a human soul. Bennett was later to become celebrated as an industrial scientist, but also as a spiritual author, and in particular a champion of the mystical writers Gurdjieff and Ouspensky.

The ubiquity of death in the war led many grieving family members and friends to try to make contact with their loved ones. Interest in spiritualism and the occult peaked during the war and post-war years. As historian Jay Winter observes, 'The enduring appeal of spiritualism was related directly to the universality of bereavement in the Europe of the Great War and its aftermath.'[4] Arthur Conan Doyle (Stonyhurst), the creator of the ultra-rationalist Sherlock Holmes, is the best known figure to have become caught up in this quest. The possibility of communication with the dead had captivated him since the death of his wife Louisa in 1906, but it was the loss of his soldier son Kingsley (Eton), from influenza in October 1918, contracted while convalescing from wounds suffered at the Somme, that was the major catalyst for Conan Doyle. On the night Kingsley died, Conan Doyle was lecturing in Nottingham and wrote later: 'Had I not been a Spiritualist, I could not have spoken that night. As it was I was able to go straight on the platform and tell the meeting that I knew my son had survived the grave, and that there was no need to worry.'[5] He attended many séances, seeking desperately to prove scientifically the existence of supernatural phenomena, and his fame naturally attracted many others to the same quest. It mired him in controversy with scientists during the 1920s, until his death from a heart attack in 1930.[6]

More conventional believers held that the souls of the departed were still present, albeit imperceptibly, in the presence of their loved ones. The headmaster of Taunton School, at a commemoration service in late November 1918, said that while the dead could no longer answer their names which had just been read out, 'may we not believe that this afternoon, near to us, very near to us, hover the immortal forms of those whose sacrifice we commemorate?' He exhorted all present to emulate 'that glorious band of Taunton's hero sons, to be revered, honoured, loved and copied till time shall be no more'.[7]

The Armistice

The arrival of the Armistice on 11 November had not been predicted. 'The enemy are on the run', wrote Julian Bickersteth, the school and army chaplain, on 10 November. 'I had to stay behind to bury the dead, some thirty today ... Everyone thinks peace is certain to come within a day or two. Personally I am not so sanguine, though we must be near the end'.[8] One officer he may well have buried that day was a Marlburian, Edmund Giffard, one of those very unlucky ones who had served all through the war, with the Royal Field Artillery, only to be killed the day before it ended. Battlefield deaths were now being accompanied by a growing toll from the influenza epidemic sweeping across Europe. In November 1918 Brighton College lost one soldier in action, but three to pneumonia brought on by the 'flu.

For soldiers, the Armistice was as much a time of reflection and sadness as of joy. Charles Douie (Rugby) wrote that, whereas for civilians the Armistice was a day of noise and celebration, 'most soldiers will speak of the unwonted silence, for the first time unbroken by gun or rifle fire after four long years'.[9] Captain J. C. Dunn (Glasgow Academy) recalled the Armistice as an 'anti-climax', relieved by 'some spasmodic cheering when the news got about and by a general atmosphere of slacking off for the day'. He picked up one 'sound' that had not been heard in four years: 'The most uncanny feature of that day and night was the silence.'[10] Robert Graves (Charterhouse) was away from the front that November, at a camp in Wales. After the most harrowing years of his life, jubilation was very far from his thoughts: 'The news

185

sent me out walking along the dyke above the marshes, cursing and sobbing and thinking of the dead … Armistice-night hysteria did not touch our camp much'.[11] For the writer C. S. Lewis (Malvern), recovering in England from a wound, any celebration revealed a lack of judgement and humanity. He wrote to his father just after the Armistice: 'The man who can give way to mafficking at such a time is more than indecent … I remember five of us at Keble, and I am the only survivor. I think of Mr Sutton, a widower with five sons, all of whom have gone. One cannot help wondering why'.[12]

For boys still at school, the Armistice came as a mixed blessing: disappointment that they would not be able to prove their manliness at the front was tinged with relief, and more than relief, that they would survive to face neither the death nor mutilation suffered by so many who had gone through the school before them. Their feelings were often exuberantly expressed. Henry Luxmoore, a retired Eton house-master, wrote, in the jaundiced way that retired schoolmasters can: 'I feel more inclined to cry than to shout, thinking of all it has cost us. The boys are different, they paraded the town wrapped in flags and beating tom-toms and making those odious noises which nowadays are taken to express joy.'[13] The mayhem of Armistice Day was also felt at Marlborough: 'We all streamed down the town (against the rules) to hear the Mayor, one of our masters, announce the news … When we got back to school, the boys in Upper School began to throw anything, books, kishes,[14] ink-bottles, coal through the large windows. The waste-paper baskets were burned and I personally burned all the notices. There was an unholy mess'.[15] At Sherborne on 'that momentous Monday, the school bell began to ring. Within a minute the whole School (that is with the exception of one science class who with admirable stolidity carried on) was gathered in little groups in the courts … Mr Sainsbury made a gallant attempt at singing the National Anthem, and soon the whole School were following his example'.[16] Five years later, headmaster Nowell Smith recalled the waves of relief that over-powered him that day: 'The actual cessation of slaughter came like the incredible release from some hopeless nightmare.'[17]

What about girls' schools? St Paul's girls were mostly on a half-term break, but 'the few Paulinas who were at school went on to the roof', and when the flag was hoisted, it was greeted with 'cheers and the ringing of the school bell'. At the special thanksgiving service on the next day in the hall all the girls were present and were exhorted by their headmistress to 'dedicate their lives to the ideals for which the dead died – stern justice, but no malice or hatred towards the vanquished enemy'.[18]

186

Across the Dominions, too, the same whoops of joy were heard. At Sydney Grammar School the acting head convened a special assembly. When the assembled company were told about the Armistice, uproar broke out lasting several minutes: 'We will never forget the roar which followed Mr Lucas's announcement, and, as he pointed to the Honour Roll and said, "This has not been in vain".'[19] Celebrations were more muted, however, at St Andrew's in South Africa; two thirds of the school had been struck down by the influenza epidemic, which resulted in the death of one young pupil, whose brother, ironically, survived the war despite risking death daily flying with the RFC in France.[20]

Headmasters responded with a whole range of emotions. Fearful always of unbridled displays of student enthusiasm getting out of control, many were nervous about maintaining order. Headmaster Stephenson at Felsted was relieved to report to his governors: 'I was specially pleased with the boys on Armistice Day. They gave full vent to their spirits without annoyance to any or destruction.'[21] Dr Rouse, headmaster of The Perse, in contrast, was not minded to celebrate, believing that the British had given up fighting too early, should have pursued the Germans deep on to their own soil, and truly punished them for their wrongdoings. After noisy demonstrations by the boys in Hall, he was forced to concede a holiday, but made it only a half day.[22] Heads of smaller schools were especially aware of the scale of their loss. At Christ's, Brecon, the school magazine's editorial recorded that, 'we cannot lose sight of the fact that [Armistice Day] was accomplished by great sacrifice of life'. As if to underline the point, John Robinson, a maths teacher at the school and lieutenant in the Royal Navy, died from influenza on 13 November 'at the very hour of peace and victory'.[23] At Silcoates in Yorkshire the school magazine recorded: 'Our little school sent out 248, in itself a worthy proportion. Of our 248, there are 211 survivors. Silcoates fallen thus numbers one in seven. Is that not something worth telling to the future Silcoates boy, when he has to learn the price that England paid for freedom?'[24]

At Charterhouse, Gilbert Murray, Professor of Greek at Oxford and one of the leading advocates of a League of Nations, was staying with Frank Fletcher in the headmaster's house. Fletcher had asked Murray to talk to the boys about the post-war international settlement at 9:30 a.m. on 11 November. By the time the two men arrived back at the headmaster's house, the telephone was ringing with the news of the Armistice.[25] Fletcher rapidly convened a service at midday, for boys and staff, staff families, and the men and women who worked on the school estate. 'For more than four years, day after day', said Fletcher in a sermon later that month,' I had looked round the School Chapel, with the knowledge that of the 600 faces before me many would before long be looking on the sordid horrors of war, silently asking myself how many, before a year was passed, might be lying dead on some battle-field ... Suddenly, we knew that it had passed, and that that nightmare of anticipation was lifted'.[26] For Fletcher the nightmare might well have passed. But for the families and friends of those Carthusians who had suffered during the war, as for those from other schools, the nightmare was still in its infancy.

The origin of commemoration

In the course of their school days boys and masters had grown familiar with memorials to the fallen of the Crimean War, the Afghan Wars, the Boer War and other imperial engagements of the nineteenth century. At Cheltenham College a stone obelisk stands outside the school on the Bath Road as a memorial to the fifty of its old boys who died in the Boer War, while in the town of Tonbridge a memorial stands to the 'twenty-four townsmen of Tonbridge or Old Boys of Tonbridge School' who fell in South Africa. Eton suffered more Boer War casualties than any other school and commemorated them by building a Memorial Hall.

From the earliest news of casualties in 1914, schools began to ask themselves how most appropriately to commemorate their fallen. These questions had a national context. Discussions were profoundly affected by the War Office's decision in May 1915 not to allow the bodies of dead soldiers to be repatriated to Britain, but to bury them close to where they fell. In September 1914 a forty-five-year-old former teacher and journalist, Fabian Ware, arrived in France to command a Red Cross unit. He had come out to the Western Front with no known interest in the burial of war dead, but he became concerned about the haphazard recording of graves, and decided that his own unit would register, and tend as best they could, the British graves they found. By February 1915 Ware and his team had so impressed the authorities that they received official recognition from the War Office as the 'Graves Registration Commission', to be renamed in May 1917 'The Imperial War Graves Commission' (IWGC), and then in 1960 'The Commonwealth War Graves Commission'.

A key decision Ware lobbied to achieve was that all the dead should be treated equally, regardless of rank, wealth, religion or distinction in service: 'In ninety-nine cases out of a hundred', he wrote, 'the officers will tell you that, if they are killed, they would wish to be among their men.'[27] Individual families, mostly from the wealthier classes, had lobbied hard for their own lost ones to be afforded special status, and some had succeeded in bringing their bodies home, including the father

188

of Lieutenant Vernon Austin of King's Canterbury, killed in early 1915. The repatriation of the body of one particular soldier brought this issue to a head. This was Lieutenant William Gladstone (Eton), grandson of the former Prime Minister, killed in action in April 1915 near Laventie in France. His family oversaw his return to be buried on the Gladstone estate at Hawarden. A grand funeral was attended by hundreds. It subsequently became known that Gladstone's body had been disinterred by soldiers of his regiment near the front line while under fire, and this gave moral force to the belief that no lives should be endangered in repatriating those already dead.[28] The Adjutant General was concerned, too, about 'hygiene' grounds in reburial. Gladstone was officially the last British soldier to be repatriated.

However, the case continued to be made vehemently by families, with the IWGC receiving some ninety letters a week from relatives demanding the right of repatriation, or requesting the adoption of a different style of headstone to the standard rectangular stone with rounded top favoured by the Commission for all ranks. The IWGC held out, and its stance was confirmed at the Commission's first official meeting in Whitehall in November 1917: the brotherhood which had developed among all ranks at the front should be maintained in death, and all graves should thus have the common format of name, rank, regiment, regimental crest and a few chosen words.[29] In the words of the historian Adrian Gregory, 'a peculiar alliance of aesthetes, trade unionists and imperialists, in the name of a silent majority of the bereaved, overruled those who represented the vocal bereaved'.[30]

The notion of 'in perpetuity' was another key principle. In previous wars, officers were often buried individually, but other ranks anonymously in mass graves. Land was now sought in the form of plots from French farmers which the French government donated 'in perpetuity' to the care of the British and imperial governments. This was a radical departure since, as a Commission historian wrote, 'never before had ordinary men and women had any chance of being remembered'.[31] Churchill was prominent in arguing forcefully for equality of treatment and for permanence, notably in his closing speech in the Parliamentary debate held on 4 May 1920: 'The cemeteries ... will be supported and sustained by the wealth of this great nation and Empire ... and there is no reason at all why, in periods as remote from our own as we are from the Tudors, the graveyards in France of this Great War shall not remain an abiding and supreme memorial to the efforts and glory of the British Army and the sacrifices made in that great cause'.[32]

The inability of many families to travel to the cemeteries in Belgium and northern France, let alone further afield, posed the significant problem of providing focal points for national mourning. One response was to place the 'Tomb of the Unknown Soldier' in Westminster Abbey, an idea copied in many other countries. Another was the erection in London's Whitehall of the Cenotaph (whose literal meaning is 'empty tomb'), designed by Edwin Lutyens. Initially put up in wood and plaster for the victory parade in 1919, to which two million came, the government subsequently asked Lutyens to rebuild it in stone. It has become the focal point of the nation's remembrance ever since. Lutyens deliberately chose a design, to the upset of the Church of England, that was neither Christian nor expressly religious at all.

The two-minute silence became another means of remembrance. The ritual originated in South Africa, the first collective silence being held in Cape Town in November 1916. A member of the South African parliament, Percy Fitzpatrick, suggested formalizing the practice when his son Nugent, an alumnus of St Andrew's, was killed in action in 1917. He then wrote to the British Cabinet in 1919 suggesting that the three-minute silence, which had become the norm in South Africa, be adopted across the Empire. George V decreed that two minutes was ample time, one minute in remembrance of those who had died, and another in gratitude for those who survived. The practice began on 11 November 1919, and has been observed in Britain ever since.[33]

While the war was still being fought, the IWGC and the British government began to consider how to commemorate, on the battle-fields, the hundreds of thousands of British soldiers who had no known grave, to give their loved ones a visible sign of remembrance. The solution was a small number of major war memorials, inscribed with the names, which should be clearly legible from ground level, of the fallen who had no known grave. Ware invited the two leading architects of the day, Edwin Lutyens and Herbert Baker (Tonbridge), to go to the Western Front. Lutyens was profoundly depressed by what he saw, and wrote to his wife, 'what humanity can suffer is beyond belief'.[34] The two men disagreed strongly on the style, Baker favouring the use of symbolism and making the Christian cross central in commemoration, Lutyens preferring a more abstract representation. Their heads were banged together by Frederic Kenyon (Winchester), director of the British Museum, who worked with Ware to ensure that disagreements were kept private.[35]

The two biggest memorials resulting from the visit of Lutyens and Baker were at Ypres and Thiepval. The Menin Gate at Ypres, designed by Reginald Blomfield (Haileybury) and opened in 1927, contains the names of 54,896 soldiers who died in the Salient and have no known grave. The Thiepval Memorial to the Missing of the Somme, designed by Lutyens himself and opened in 1932, is, with 72,191 names, the largest British battle memorial in the world. As the first major memorial to be erected, the Menin Gate became the object of some pungent reactions. Siegfried Sassoon was particularly bitter in his poem 'On Passing the New Menin Gate', claiming the dead of the Salient would 'deride this sepulchre of crime'.[36] Stefan Zweig, who was one of the best known writers of the time, praised the Memorial's simplicity and lack of overt triumphalism, describing it as 'more impressive than any triumphal arch or monument to victory that I have ever seen.'[37] A further 35,000 names of those who died after 15 August 1917 in the Salient are inscribed on the back walls of the Tyne Cot cemetery on Passchendaele ridge, the work of Herbert Baker, who, with a background of designing major buildings in South Africa, was also responsible for the memorial to South African soldiers at Delville Wood on the Somme. Other Commonwealth countries have their own national memorials, the most visually impressive being the Vimy Ridge Canadian National Park and Memorial, where the young, some of them from Canadian public schools, still act as guides.

Lutyens, Baker and Blomfield were the three principal architects associated not just with the bigger memorials but also the IWGC cemeteries. All were well known, Lutyens as the architect of country houses for the wealthy Edwardian classes, Baker for many of the great public buildings in South Africa, and Blomfield for his churches, schools and private houses in Britain. They worked closely with Rudyard Kipling and Gertrude Jekyll, the garden designer, to shape the cemeteries and memorials, fusing together architecture and landscape into a uniform harmony of stone walls, iron gates, carefully planted trees, shrubs and flowers so reminiscent of an English country garden; their aim was to provide solace and something recognizable and reassuring to the many families and friends who travelled out to the Western Front to see the graves and memorials. All three architects had their reputations substantially enhanced by their work for the IWGC, and it is not surprising that schools sought to use them for memorials in Britain.

Memorials at the public schools
The commemoration of old boys killed in the war presented the public schools with several difficult questions: should any commemoration be an act of triumph, or a more sober memorial to the fallen, including even any old boys or staff who had fought for enemy nations?[38] Should the memorial be in the form of scholarships and bursaries to enable children of old boys who had died to attend the school; or should it be a physical structure? If the latter, should the money go to new buildings

or sports facilities of utilitarian value, or something of a purely aesthetic nature? What price should be put on commemoration, and how should the money be raised? How should control of the whole process be established as between school governors, heads, grieving parents and alumni young and old, from whom much of the money would be requested? Differences of opinion between alumni and teachers of different generations, and between governors and heads, raged for a considerable time, some schools resolving their differences more successfully than others. New and more ambitious heads saw this as an opportunity to advance their dreams of expanding or improving their school, while others viewed such ideas as merely naked ambition. The extent to which the commemoration of the dead became entwined with promoting the future development of the school was a moral issue which many heads and governors had to try to resolve.

Well before the war ended, heads were besieged with requests from parents for memorials to their fallen children. At Loretto in Edinburgh, even as early as 1915, families pressed the school to dedicate vacant panels in the chapel to their sons. As the requests increased, and the remaining space diminished, a form of selection had to be imposed, the largest panel being devoted to the three sons of Henry Almond, a former Loretto headmaster, and placed close to his own memorial.[39] Many other schools had held memorial services for dead pupils during the course of the war and accepted gifts from parents as memorials; at Radley in 1917 a stained-glass window was dedicated in Chapel to the memory of Second Lieutenants James Whittet and Gilbert Freeman.[40]

Montagu Rendall, headmaster of Winchester, was one of the first heads to conceive a collective memorial. As early as October 1915, in his report to the Warden and Fellows, he wrote: 'Our first war memorial will be the scheme for officers' sons, which has received your approbation ... But I should like to put on record my own feeling that no other scheme would be so suitable as that of a large school hall'.[41] One year on, he admitted in his report: 'I cannot say there has been much enthusiasm for the idea of a school hall',[42] but he spoke enthusiastically about his latest idea, a 'large central gate', flanked by two halls, providing space for a war museum, a new masters' common room, a new classroom, and a 'war cloister'. After much discussion, and trips by Rendall to see Old Wykehamists in France and elsewhere, it was this last idea which was to be sanctioned.

With no further human remains being repatriated to Britain, the school war memorial listing the names of the fallen became the primary focus of fund-raising and grieving. These were the places, as Jay Winter has written, 'where people grieved, both individually and collectively'.[43]

192

Parents, family and friends all came to the unveiling ceremonies of these war memorials, and would regularly return to gaze at, and indeed touch, the name of their loved one. Services on Armistice Day, and later Remembrance Sunday, would traditionally see headmasters read out the names of the fallen, and would be attended by families and friends of the deceased. These relatives have, of course, long since ceased to come, but the services in the public schools, the hymns and the readings, continue to this day.

What of the cause for which the war was fought? Schools, like the Church and indeed the nation, struggled to find meaning in all the loss. No simple answers being forthcoming, schools fell back on the memory and the example that the fallen gave to those who followed. J. R. Eccles, headmaster of Gresham's, spoke at the 1923 Armistice Service of 'Old Boys, whose honoured names are recorded for all time in our chapel'.[44] A booklet published in 1928 to accompany the memorial's unveiling at Bedford School said that, 'in such a home of youth and memory, a War Memorial, a familiar sight for boys and masters, revisited often by Old Boys, recalls the dead as they were in youth. Later generations will remember less their persons than their general example'.[45] At Tonbridge School the war memorial was known as the 'Gate of Remembrance', through which all boys would pass daily on their way to chapel.

A book published in 1927 entitled *British Public Schools War Memorials* collated the various acts of memorialization by the schools. Few exhibit any form of triumphalism, although defence of freedom did feature in many memorials. The bronze tablets at King Edward's Birmingham, for example, bear the inscription: 'These sons of the School, at their country's call, gave their lives in the cause of liberty and right.'[46] At KCS Wimbledon the memorial takes the form of a Greek athlete holding aloft a wreath of victory,[47] while at Denstone in Staffordshire the memorial is a statue of St George clad in full armour and holding a sword aloft by the blade in the form of a cross.[48] The Dominions were less restrained. At Geelong Grammar School the memorial suggests the triumph of youthful heroism over evil,[49] while at Brisbane Grammar School one of the memorials was a field gun captured in Palestine in September 1918. It was unveiled in August 1921 by Brigadier-General L. C. Wilson, who originally captured the gun, and he told the boys: 'This stands as an emblem of victory to remind you of the spirit in which Australia answered the call of the Mother Country.'[50]

In stark contrast, Leighton Park, the Quaker school in Reading, lists on its war memorial the twenty-eight names of the school's fallen. 'They died for great ideals', the memorial declares. There was no grand ceremony or public opening, but every year, on Armistice Day, the attention of pupils is drawn to their duty to prevent war in future.[51] In gentler vein also, several schools, including Bloxham, Nottingham High School and Alleyns, assembled, in addition to a physical memorial, books of photographs to commemorate the fallen.

If there was to be no general wallowing in glorification of the nation, or in the cause for which the war was fought, such as it was, celebration of the schools' role in the war was permitted. Services inaugurating the memorials provided ample opportunities for celebration, glorification indeed, of the public school ideal. Field Marshal Plumer declared at a memorial service at Charterhouse that he thought the war had proven 'a complete vindication of the English public school training in enabling inexperienced soldiers to take responsible posts success-fully'.[52] At Rossall, the Archbishop of York said: 'I shall always think that the spirit of our Public Schools rose to its highest power in the flame of sacrifice which lit up those fateful years.'[53] Admiral Lord Jellicoe summed up the mood in his foreword to *British Public School War Memorials*: 'The book is a record of magnificent service for the Empire and of splendid self-sacrifice. Our Public Schools have ever in the past given Leaders to the Nation, and it is the character training which plays so important a part in the Public School life which develops leadership both in peace and war.'[54]

Raising and spending money for remembrance

All parties in schools were signed up, from at least 1916, to an under-standing that an effort unprecedented in history would be required to acknowledge those former pupils and members of staff who had been killed. Jealousies and rancour soon floated to the surface, however, disagreements emerging over how much money could be raised, how best to raise it, and how most appropriately to spend it. The older generations of alumni, longer-serving headmasters and grieving families favoured war memorials with the main purpose of commemorating the past, whereas younger old boys and newer headmasters seemed to prefer to look forward, to benefit future generations. Control of the process could become an issue between the different parties.

Dulwich College debated hard over the most suitable memorial. By 1917 the governors had already decided that bursaries 'for boys good, bad or indifferent' would be a suitable memorial, but at the end of the war there was pressure from old boys for a new chapel or a memorial hall. The Alleynian Club met in 1919 to vote; the result was 277 for a chapel, 170 for a monument and just 45 for a hall. In the event, lack of sufficient funds for a new building ruled out a chapel, and the memorial that finally emerged was a Latin cross, dedicated in 1921, although old boys also raised further funds for scholarships and bursaries.[55]

Emotions often ran high about the most suitable form of commemoration. In December 1917 a young Carthusian officer in France wrote to the school magazine advocating scholarships, for 'no more worthy memorial could be devised than that of affording to the most deserving of succeeding generations access to the School ... such a memorial would be as visible and permanent as the most stately building. It is, after all, not bricks and mortar, but masters and boys, that make a school'.[56] Many younger veterans wanted to put the war behind them, a view characterized by R. F. Delderfield in his novel *To Serve Them All My Days*, based on his time as a boy at West Buckland School in Devon. The book's hero, David Powlett-Jones, who goes into teaching after being invalided out of the army with shell shock, argues with the OTC commander, who had not been at the Front, about whether a war memorial is needed at all. Many schools did include, within their memorial funds, provision for scholarships for the sons of old boys killed in the war. At Tonbridge the War Memorial Fund allocated £10,000 in January 1918 for this purpose; by June 1939 over £7,000 had been paid out. One of the beneficiaries was Deryck Boyd-Moss, whose father had been killed at Gallipoli, and who was to perish himself at El Alamein in 1942.[57]

Putting out the begging bowl has never ranked high amongst the most favoured jobs of headmasters, but, regardless of their personal feelings, they seem to have thrown themselves fully into the task. At Stonyhurst an appeal was made in 1917 to 'all boys past and present, their parents, relatives, guardians, and all friends of the college', to help raise £20,000. The school recognized the amount was large, but said it represented 'a debt of gratitude to their brave schoolfellows of days gone by'. The headmaster made it known he was happy to receive pledges spread over a number of years, and to accept subscriptions in War Stock, as well as hard cash.[58] Walter Barton, headmaster of Epsom College, wrote in May 1918 to an Old Epsomian, John Raymond Smith, an able seaman in the Royal Navy who had left school just the year before: 'Do your best to help us in this great endeavour. I know you can't have much to spare from your wages!! Still I suppose you have a modicum of pocket money, and it is well worth having a share in commemorating such fellows as you know here, to have done all they could. I don't discount the glory of it all: it is a golden thought; but oh! The hideous cost ... shall I write to your brother or will you write and ask your father for something on behalf of both?'[59] George Corner, headmaster of Wellington School in Somerset, wrote a letter on New

Year's Day 1919 to all his old boys, appealing for contributions: 'First and chiefest of duties, the setting up of a monument in which can be enshrined our reverential love of the spirit of our race and our hope of the gallant boys who fell. Can we not build a commemoration School Chapel? What help can my Old Boys give me? This I must know if I am to make an appeal to the sympathy of others.'[60]

Appeals could take many years to come to fruition. Whereas at Stonyhurst the memorial, consisting of Altar Shrine, marble Reredos and Crucifix, was unveiled in June 1922,[61] it was not until May 1931 that Wellington School dedicated its new chapel. Inevitably, many donors had died, sometimes from war wounds, before their gifts came to fruition. Occasionally, old boys donated funds during the war itself to war memorials on which their own names would appear: one such was Edward Brittain, brother of Vera, who sent five guineas to the Uppingham fund in 1918, a short while before he was killed in Italy.[62] Even schools as wealthy as Eton encountered problems raising money. Lord Rosebery wrote to the Provost, as early as 1916: 'I have received the papers with regard to an Eton memorial which is to cost the college £10,000 and Old Etonians £90,000 ... Have my colleagues any binding facts as to where this is to come? Remember the Old Etonian class is no longer a wealthy class. The only wealthy classes are the shipping and munitions people, who are rarely, I suppose, Old Etonians. The Old Etonians are chiefly landlords'.[63] Eton had in fact commemorated the Boer War with a building on a grandiose scale for 171 dead, so how to commemorate 1,157 dead posed problems of scale; in the event the much smaller scale memorials to the Great War remain decidedly moving.

Headmasters had to devote considerable time to fund-raising committees, meetings with alumni, staff, governors, relatives of those killed, and then to further meetings with lawyers, accountants, architects and builders. In the decade following the war, no single activity took up more time. The money raised often fell far short of the high hopes of the emotion-filled meetings of the early days. Wellington College had raised £15,000 for war exhibitions in 1917, which subsidized the fees of sons of Old Wellingtonians killed or totally incapacitated, and by 1919 there were fourteen such exhibitioners in the school. The War Memorial Committee which met in May 1919 hoped to raise a further £20,000 for a memorial reading room, but two years later had collected only a third of this sum. It was therefore decided to commission Edwin Lutyens to design a memorial in the chapel, which cost just over £4,000. This statue of St George slaying the dragon is on a striking base of black and white marble, the lack of Christian imagery on it unsurprising for anyone familiar with Lutyens' thought. The balance of what was left in the Wellington War Memorial fund, about £1,300, was 'to be applied to the War Exhibitions Fund, to supply any needs that the existing fund may be inadequate to meet'.[64] Wellington, like many other schools, was therefore generous in looking after its own, but some greater imagination by schools, perhaps with support from government funding, might have used the opportunity of post-war commemoration to offer scholarships to children of the fallen from a less socially exclusive background.

Physical memorials in schools were a mix of the purely commemorative or aesthetic, and the utilitarian. They always list the names of the Old Boys, sometimes also the teachers and other school employees, and are usually found in chapel, or for schools that lack one, in the main school hall. The honour boards are made of wood, bronze or parchment, and the names are sometimes recorded on stone obelisks or cenotaphs. Some schools have a cross of sacrifice, a gate of remembrance or a memorial arch. At Clifton College in Bristol, in June 1922, the memorial gateway was unveiled by the most famous Old Cliftonian, Earl Haig, who took the salute as the OTC paraded and was treated as a hero without stain. His statue now overlooks 'The Close', the cricket field of Newbolt's famous poem 'Vitaï Lampada'. Michaelhouse in South Africa, by contrast, has an avenue of trees called 'Warriors Walk'.[65] At Shrewsbury the names are inscribed on the base of a statue of a figure from another age, Sir Philip Sidney. Statues and sculptural memorials standing alone are less common: one such is at Fettes, a bronze figure of a mortally wounded and kilted young soldier, his hand raised to heaven urging others to follow him, with the words at the base: 'Carry on'.[66]

Memorial books listing the fallen exist in all schools. Some are single copies, beautifully illuminated and kept in chapel or in another special place; while other schools published their lists of fallen, often listing details of military service, and sold them to the whole school community, with proceeds going to the memorial fund. An outstanding example is the memorial book produced at Downside by Dom Lucius Graham, an Old Gregorian and member of the community, who lovingly describes the lives and service of the boys and staff known personally to him.[67] Another is the *War Book of Upper Canada College*, as fine a record of service as any produced by public schools in Britain.[68]

School buildings had often been neglected during the war years, when the attention of headmasters and governors had been elsewhere. As the war receded, heads became keen to use the monies raised to invest in repairing existing buildings and, indeed, erecting entirely new ones, not least to cope with numbers which had expanded during the war itself and after. School prospectuses began to feature increasingly the facilities on offer to prospective parents. Marlborough was one of some twenty-five schools to use funds raised to erect a memorial hall. The initial plan was estimated at £75,000, but after appeals failed to raise that sum, the scale was reduced. When it was nearing completion, the concrete raft over the water meadows on which it was being erected, began to sink, delaying the opening and increasing the cost.[69] At Scotch College, Melbourne, old boys raised £50,000 for their memorial hall. At its opening, the famous Australian general and old boy, John Monash, told pupils, 'we should look for leaders in the future, first in the boys of the great Public Schools. You should be proud to be inheritors of such a record'.[70] Bedales successfully acquired a new library, designed by Ernest Gimson, described by Nikolaus Pevsner as 'the greatest of the English architect designers'.[71] Completed in 1921, it is a Grade 1 listed building today.

Playing fields were acquired with memorial funds by, among others, Merchant Taylors', Loretto, and Shore in Sydney, while new sports pavilions were erected by Christ's Brecon, Cranleigh and Truro. Edinburgh Academy built a gymnasium, while St Albans and Pocklington used the funds to build new swimming pools. At King's Worcester the senior master drew a popular analogy: 'This Pavilion ... was erected in memory of those who, having learned in this place to play the game for their school, played it also for their country during the years 1914–1918'.[72]

Chapels, perhaps not surprisingly, proved a particularly popular form of memorial. Oundle's was designed by Arthur Blomfield (cousin of Reginald) and enhanced later with stained-glass windows by John Piper. On the rood beam across the chancel are engraved the words: 'In living memory of those who died.'[73] Rossall extended its chapel with a new altarpiece by Eric Gill, the new east window being donated as a memorial by Frank Fletcher's family, many of whom had been boys at Rossall.[74] New or extended chapels blossomed across the Dominions, with Hilton in South Africa, King's School, Parramatta (Australia), Lakefield College School in Canada and King's, Auckland in New Zealand all devoting substantial sums to this purpose. At Bishop's in Cape Town, the Reverend Harold Birt, appointed headmaster in 1919 from Radley, identified a new chapel as the cornerstone of his development plan. Although the school only had 320 boys at the time, the war memorial chapel was designed to seat 750, a pledge of confidence in the future fully justified by events. Some 4,000 people attended in June 1927 the consecration of the new chapel at Charterhouse, designed by Giles Gilbert Scott and built by the school's own works department. Inside, a congregation of 1,000, including the relatives of many of those killed, heard Fletcher remind everyone that for every ten boys then at Charterhouse, eleven names were recorded on the chapel memorial.[75]

But what of those three architects whose designs for the IWGC had brought them national fame? Richer public schools were able to give them commissions. Reginald Blomfield designed the cross of sacrifice at his old school, Haileybury, imitating his design in war cemeteries across the Western Front. He also designed the memorial cross at Highgate School. Nearby University College School across Hampstead Heath secured Edwin Lutyens to design their memorial, later destroyed by fire. Herbert Baker designed the War Memorial building at Harrow and the memorial at King's Canterbury, but his most celebrated design, and perhaps the most distinguished of all war memorials at public schools, is the War Cloister at Winchester College.

Montagu Rendall's odyssey of visits to his old boys succeeded in securing a pledge from the Winchester governors in late 1917, 'that the primary object should be to establish an outward and visible memorial within the precincts of the College of such a kind as to make the strongest possible appeal to the imagination of future generations of Wykehamists'.[76] Herbert Baker was given the commission that month and submitted his initial design in April 1918.[77] In 1921 a larger scheme, in which Baker envisaged the Cloister to be just a part of a grander design, was abandoned through lack of funds. All the time, Rendall had to contend with sniping from those who felt something of more practical value would be more fitting. Baker himself was caught up in the disagreements, writing to Rendall in April 1922: 'Smith, I understand, suggests a sundial and someone else a sarcophagus. The dial I would rule out ... because it would not express the essential sentiment of a school war shrine. A sarcophagus I would rule out because it would express a part only – and the more depressing part of that sentiment: death and not hope or victory after death'.[78]

The small, intimate and tranquil War Cloister is regarded by many as Baker's masterpiece. Its critics have argued that it expresses less the feelings of the young front-line officers than the wish fulfilment of their elders, 'who idealised them and their dread experience in terms necessary to their own comfort and faith'.[79] Such critics might well have had in mind Rendall himself, who in his final report as headmaster in 1924, the year the Cloister was dedicated, wrote: 'Mr Baker's genius has not only erected a worthy monument to the 500, but has translated into stone an idea which I have come to associate with Winchester: that Public Schools carry on as a direct inheritance, in peace or in war, the traditions of Christian Chivalry'.[80]

One way that some public schools expand their inheritance, a hundred years after the Great War, is by establishing branches overseas, such as in the Gulf and the Far East. A forerunner in founding schools abroad was Eton, whose old boys paid for a school in memory of the 340 Old Etonians who fell in the Ypres Salient, to educate the children of those working in Ypres town; it was known initially as the Eton Memorial School and subsequently as the British Memorial School. By the late 1930s it had 130 pupils, some coming in on buses supplied by the IWGC from neighbouring towns like Passchendaele. The education was very British, including the saluting of the flag on Empire Day and the playing of cricket. The school, which did not re-open after its closure in the Second World War, stands adjacent to St George's Church in Ypres. This was built to serve the large British community resident in the town and designed by Reginald Blomfield. Every single item in the church is a memorial to a regiment or a fallen soldier, from the pews to the stained-glass windows. In the last few years, public schools have started putting up brass plaques on the south and north walls to commemorate their old boys who fell in the Great War, or in both world wars. As the centenary of 1914 approaches, the number of these plaques is blossoming.

Family grief and private memorials
Not satisfied with either the national or school memorials, some families sought to perpetuate the memory of their lost sons in a personal and distinctive way. The wish to recall a loved one is readily understandable, and it is perhaps odd that there were not more such requests to schools. They came in all shapes and sizes, and began well before the end of the war. Harrow published a list of such gifts in 1919, some of them direct bequests from dead soldiers, others from relatives. They included the Oliver Sichel Prize for Singing, in memory of a young officer killed in October 1918, and £2,000 as a legacy from the estate of Lieutenant A. F. Blackwell MC.[81] At George Watson's in Edinburgh, the Eric Milroy Trophy was donated for the 'Place and Drop-Kick Competition', in memory of a player who had toured South Africa with the British rugby team in 1910 and was later killed at Delville Wood.[82]

Among more substantial donations, the family of C. R. Roth, who had left Loretto in 1916 and was killed in 1917, donated £5,000 in his memory to fund a new swimming pool, which was opened in 1920. At St Columba's in Dublin the Masterman Library commemorates Second Lieutenant F. M. Masterman, killed on the Somme. In memory of her son Allen Wedgewood, killed on Gallipoli, his mother bought for Marlborough a large acreage for playing fields. At Wellington College private bequests on behalf of two old boys killed in action, Lieutenants J. B. Capper and A. V. Stansfield, together with a further gift in memory of Lieutenant C. Allom, helped to transform the school's Old Hall from 'an ugly and faded schoolroom to a stately and dignified assembly hall'.[83]

The Mothers' Window at Denstone is a particularly moving memorial, a stained-glass window in the chapel paid for in 1916 by the mothers whose sons had been killed, as well as by others who wished to show solidarity with all grieving mothers.[84] A stained-glass window in the chapel at Brighton College is in memory of Captain Harold and Major Raymond Belcher, both of whom were killed in 1917. A third brother, Captain Gordon Belcher, had been killed two years before. All three were sons of Thomas Belcher, headmaster from 1882 to 1893.[85] In the chapel at Rugby a lectern records the names of the fallen, with the bronze figure on top designed to resemble Lieutenant W. E. Littleboy, killed near Gheluvelt in Belgium in October 1917, and bearing the inscription: 'God made trial of them and found them worthy of Himself, as gold in the furnace He proved them.'[86] Nearby is a memorial tablet to Rupert Brooke, close by the pews where he sat as a schoolboy, and where his father sat as a housemaster, engraved with the words of *The Soldier*.

Three private memorials stand out, not for their pathos, which is shared by all, but for the grandeur of their ambition. Edward Horner, brother-in-law of Raymond Asquith (Winchester), had been a boy at Eton and a rising star as a barrister. Twice wounded at Neuve Chapelle in 1915, and losing a kidney, he insisted on returning to the front, only to be killed at Cambrai on 21 November 1917. The Horner family had had their tombs since 1524 in St Andrew's Church, a beautiful building at Mells in Somerset. Edward's name is on the Roll of Honour alongside that of Raymond Asquith, his brother-in-law, and twelve others. Within the church is the Horner Chapel, consisting of a large equestrian statue sculpted by Alfred Munnings, on a plinth designed by Edwin Lutyens. The latter also designed the village war memorial in the churchyard, where Siegfried Sassoon was later buried in 1967. On the Munnings statue is placed the original wooden cross from Horner's grave in France, and words from another Etonian, the poet Shelley: 'He hath outsoared the shadow of our night'. With Edward's death, the male Horner line came to an end; while inspecting the churchyard before he designed the war memorial, Lutyens noted of the Horner family and other locals who accompanied him: 'All their young men are killed'.[87]

Close to Raymond Asquith's grave at Guillemont Road on the Somme lies another poignant memorial, to George Marsden-Smedley, who had left Harrow in the summer of 1915, having been captain of the 1st XI in both cricket and football. Just before his nineteenth birthday he joined the Rifle Brigade at the front in July 1916. Five weeks later he took part in an attack on 18 August between Trones Wood and Guillemont, where he was killed. His body was never recovered, and his name can be found on the Thiepval Memorial. The grieving Marsden-Smedley family travelled to the Somme in 1920 and purchased from a local farmer a plot of ground on the spot where they believed George had died. Here they erected a small cairn in his memory, with words echoing those written in the Book of Samuel about Saul and Jonathan: 'Lovely and pleasant in life, in death serene and unafraid, most blessed in remembrance'. At Harrow itself a memorial seat was placed by the family on the sports fields where he played, inscribed with his name and regiment and bearing the words: 'To love the game beyond the prize'.[88]

In the village of Burghclere, deep in the Hampshire countryside, stands another remarkable private memorial. Lieutenant Henry Willoughby Sandham, who had been a boy at Uppingham, died in 1919 as a result of malaria contracted in the Salonika campaign. His sister, Mary Behrend, commissioned a chapel to be built in his memory at Burghclere, designed by Lionel Pearson; inside it, the artist Stanley Spencer was commissioned to produce a cycle of nineteen paintings which depicted his own war in England and Macedonia, serving first as a medical orderly and then in the infantry. Spencer had remained haunted by his own experience of war long after it ended and was intent on representing the everyday life of the ordinary soldier. The paintings move from the poignant to the mundane – a convoy arriving with wounded soldiers, scraping frostbite off a soldier's feet on a hospital bed to the ordinary business of scrubbing floors. The narrative of his war climaxes in the stunning central composition, *The Resurrection of the Soldiers*. Spencer's masterpiece was not completed until 1932, and the building and paintings are now one of the National Trust's less well known treasures. Spencer himself became one of Britain's foremost artists of the twentieth century, knighted just before his death in 1959. In this memorial Spencer's vision of war, Mary Behrend's generosity and the memory of Henry Willoughby Sandham combine to give succeeding generations insight into the nature of the Great War and the private grief of those left behind.[89]

Moving though these monuments are from the Horner, Marsden-Smedley and Sandham families, we should not imagine that their grief was any greater than that of the families of the hundreds of thousands of the British soldiers killed who either could not afford, nor deemed it appropriate, to establish such individual memorials as a sign of personal remembrance. Equality in death remained the overriding principle to which the public schools as a whole, and the IWGC, adhered.

Visits to the Western Front

In any review of public school fiction before 1914, there must be a place for Billy Bunter, the 'Fat Owl of the Remove', created by Frank Richards. Bunter's adventures at Greyfriars School, supposedly a typical public school, were serialized in over 1500 issues of *The Magnet*, a weekly story paper for boys first published in 1908. The stories had an enormous circulation, disseminating public school life and ethos to all classes of the population. In one 1919 issue Bunter and a party from Greyfriars visit the battlefields, and the cover has a drawing of them standing in the ruins of Ypres. The story is written as a travelogue, by a writer who must have visited the area himself, recording that 'the whole countryside for mile after mile is made sad by the hundreds and hundreds of little wooden crosses that mark the resting-places of those brave fellows who gave their all for Britain and what she stands for'.[90]

The first actual school visits to the battlefields took place in the 1920s, though it is unclear exactly which school was the first out. Boys from Cranleigh seem to have visited in 1920, and in many subsequent years, while Fettes boys made a trip through the Ypres Salient in 1925 and were captivated by the rebuilding of the Cloth Hall and St Martin's Cathedral in the town, as well as by the domestic buildings, and astonished by the debris of war piled high around sites along the front, such as at Sanctuary Wood.[91] Six boys from Solihull School visited that same year, but this seems to have been part of a more general visit to Belgium, rather than a battlefield tour. On their last day they arrived at Ypres, taking a motor tour around the Salient; the vast quantity of 'unexploded ordnance' particularly caught the attention of the boys.

It is probable that many individual public schoolboys visited the mangled ground of the Western Front on personal pilgrimages with their families to find the graves of fathers and brothers. One such family pilgrimage occurred in 1922, when May Reid went in search of the grave of her brother Percy (Marlborough), killed near Arras in May 1917. Taking a train to the town of Arras, she continued her journey from the station by car through land which, four years on, was being cultivated again, but which was still full of rusty barbed wire, piles of meat tins, hand grenades, the remains of boots and tin hats, and even derelict tanks. In her personal memoir of the journey she described the cemeteries as being bare of grass and flowers, the graves marked by temporary crosses, with the massive task of reburial of bodies in the neat IWGC cemeteries still in progress. She described the landscape as, 'every square yard a shell-hole, the whole ground a tortured mass covered with yellow broom'.[92]

Kipling had been a regular visitor to France before the war, reporting for both the Automobile Association (AA) and the Royal Automobile Club (RAC) on hotels and roads. In 1915 the French General Nivelle gave him a personal tour of the front line, remarking, as Julian Barnes recounts in *Through the Window*, that, 'All these men know your books'.[93] Kipling's anguish at the loss of his son John at the Battle of Loos meant he threw himself into works of commemoration, including serving as a commissioner for the IWGC for the last eighteen years of his life from 1918 to 1936. Kipling was a regular traveller to the battle-fields after the war in his Rolls-Royce, visiting twenty-four British cemeteries in one three-day period alone in 1924, making meticulous notes and suggestions for improvements.

In 1933 the IWGC reported that some 800 British schoolchildren had visited the Menin Gate that Easter, and that parties of boys from major public schools were being conducted around the battlefields by a variety of organizations, including the 'Ypres League' and Toc H.[94] It is unknown quite how many school trips were made to see the Western Front during the interwar years, but schools as far away as Campbell College in Belfast visited Ypres and Poperinghe in 1936, under the encouragement of Toc H. Boys from Bury Grammar School visited the battlefields, including Vimy Ridge, in the summer holidays of 1939. 'The history of those years was made very vivid to us as we walked in the trenches', reported the school magazine, 'and gazed in reverent awe at the beautifully tended military cemeteries. It was indeed a strange irony that brought us face to face with another war but a few days after our return.'[95] The trips were encouraged by the Revd Tubby Clayton of Toc H, disturbed by the impact that a swathe of anti-war books was having on the understanding children had of the Great War and the significance of the war memorials.[96]

Trips by public schools in the forty or so years following 1945 appear to have been comparatively rare. The focus was then much more on the war that had recently ended, and the history syllabus in schools seldom touched the First World War. This all began to change in the 1980s, partly in response to the new GCSE syllabus embracing the war. A small group from a production of *Journey's End* at Whitgift School visited the Somme and Ypres in 1984, and the two authors first took a group from Tonbridge in 1988. By the 1990s most public schools were making annual visits, with new museums and visitor centres responding to the demand.

On many nights, especially in the summer term, the 'Last Post' ceremony at the Menin Gate is packed with school children waiting to lay wreaths. The bugles have played the 'Last Post' at 8 p.m. every night since 1928, with the exception of 1940–44, when the Germans occupied Ypres. Anzac Day (25 April) commands similar reverence and interest in Australia and New Zealand. On 25 April 1917 King's, Parramatta held a special service and parade, and Australian and New Zealand public schools continue to mark Anzac Day to the present. In recent years, too, several schools have organized trips to Gallipoli and the Western Front. The frequency of visits to the sites of the Great War easily eclipses interest in the longer and more diverse Second World War, but it remains to be seen whether that interest will outlast the centenary.

Chapter 9

The War Becomes History

Public school alumni dictated the way the war was fought, and suffered a disproportionately heavy toll in its prosecution. They have also played a dominant role in shaping the images, written and graphic, through which the war has been interpreted and portrayed. There is not one truth about the Great War but many. Each individual and each generation sees the war through their own eyes. But two interpretations stand out at polar opposites, and as historians, writers, poets, politicians and film-makers, public school alumni are at the heart of both. The first sees the war as inevitable and Britain's involvement justified, mostly well fought, and with ultimate victory vindicating the loss of life. The second sees the war as unnecessary, questions Britain's need to get involved, and criticises the conduct of it. Between these 'rationalist' and 'emotional' interpretations stand a myriad of others. The reaction against the Great War began even while it was still being fought.

The public schools as nurseries for the arts
If the biggest literary and artistic output from the war came from boys educated in public schools, then a brief understanding of the place of the arts in those schools is apposite. Schools differed widely in the way they treated the creative arts. Schools as diverse as King Edward's in Birmingham, The Leys in Cambridge and Shrewsbury all offered interesting opportunities for artistic expression, but for them, as for most schools, those opportunities largely existed outside the taught curriculum.[1] At Marlborough, the alma mater of so many artistic and literary figures of the last century, one old boy recalled: 'Music flourished in a vigorous if unpolished way, and Colonel Hughes had a few disciples in his small art room. Beyond that there was no space or stimulus for creative activity.'[2] Schools appear to have distrusted the spontaneity and sense of liberation that went with free expression across the creative arts.

One hundred years on, many public schools boast their own theatres, art schools, dance studios, concert halls and creative writing courses, embracing culture in its widest sense. It was a different world in 1914. 'Virgil and Wisden's [Cricket] Almanac blocked the door of his mind, letting little else through. He died without hearing of Marcel Proust', said an old boy of King's Canterbury dismissively about his former headmaster, Algernon Latter (1916–27).[3] Even allowing for hindsight, the comments of old boys must contain some truth: the artist Richard Nevinson had unhappy memories of Uppingham in 1903–7. In a letter to the *Daily Express* in 1931 he wrote: 'In theory the public school code embodies honest dealing, self-sacrifice and a certain culture of the mind, body and spirit. In actuality it expects privilege without talent and contempt for all the finer fruits of civilisation, culture and intellect'. His father subsequently wrote: 'Very likely the school was not in itself much worse than the average public school for a boy whose main interest lay in art. Indeed one can imagine no more fatal characteristic for ensuring the contempt of boys and ordinary masters alike.'[4]

Art, referred to usually as 'painting' or 'drawing', did not rank highly in school priorities. The belief was that it was not a subject to engage the serious interest of young men; however, several significant artists did pass through public schools. Max Beerbohm was at Charterhouse from 1885 to 1890, studying under long-serving 'drawing master' Struan Robinson, who did much to encourage cartoon drawing.[5] Henry Tonks, distinguished principal of the Slade, had been inspired at Bloxham, where painting was the strongest of the art forms.[6] Schoolboys interested in art could be regarded as 'freaks'. Percy Wyndham Lewis, a boy at Rugby at the end of the 1890s, recalled: 'Instead of poring over my school books, I would copy an oil painting of a dog. I remember a very big boy opening the door of the study, putting his big red astonished face inside, gazing at me for a while ... and then, laconic and contemptuous, remarking "you frightful artist" before closing the study door – and I could hear his big slouching steps going away to find some more normal company.'[7] But Rugby did not put him off art, and he went on to the Slade and to University College London. Neither did the artistic blindness of King's Canterbury headmaster Latter discourage the visual imaginations of two of Britain's greatest film directors of the mid-twentieth century, both of whom arrived at the school with him: Michael Powell and Carol Reed.[8]

Drama seems to have received little prominence either, puzzlingly in view of the scholarly recognition given to so many British playwrights. Shrewsbury staged a school play every summer, invariably Shakespeare. At King's Canterbury there appear to have been no school plays leading up to 1914, but short extracts from plays were performed in different languages on Speech Day; in 1913 this meant Aristophanes, Livy (a speech), Molière and Shakespeare. Eton discouraged drama, but short scenes and speeches were declaimed on the Fourth of June.

Literary discussion, by contrast, flourished in many schools. Rupert Brooke enjoyed Rugby's Literary Society, which put on a talk in his final term on 'Modern Poetry'.[9] At Marlborough the Literary Society is often referred to in the letters of Charles Sorley: 'With the longer evenings and shorter games, I have been getting through a lot of reading lately. At a meeting of the Literary Society on Wednesday, a paper was read on J. M. Synge and since then I have read three of his plays.'[10] Synge's best known play, *The Playboy of the Western World*, was a hot topic: the play had caused a sensation when first performed at the Abbey Theatre in Dublin in 1907. Some considered it an offence to public morals, and an insult to Ireland.

Music often fared better in the public schools. The Music Society at Eton put on concerts and invited professionals to perform for the boys, a significant number of whom took music lessons in their own time. The Leys was able to benefit from its proximity to King's College, Cambridge: its first musical director directed music in King's chapel also, and school organists could play its organ. However, the Music Master at King's Canterbury, with its strong choral tradition, complained in 1914 that OTC activity was eating into the time available for music, so that 'concerted work of any musical value is impossible'.[11] It has taken schools many more decades to find the right balance between artistic creativity, sport and cadet corps. Musicians whose compositions were to shape the understanding of the war passed through the pre-war public schools: Ralph Vaughan Williams, for instance, had been a boy at Charterhouse from 1887 to 1890, studying the violin and organizing a concert. His parents chose the school for its serious attitude to music, but regarded his passion as a harmless hobby.

This necessarily brief survey of the place of the arts in schools does not suggest hostility, or even indifference, to cultural and aesthetic values. There are many schools in which music, art and particularly literature, received plenty of encouragement, but the priority given to sport and OTC, and the narrowness of the taught curriculum, meant that opportunities were limited. Although peer pressure and pupil conformity could also make life difficult for the artistic individual, who perhaps succeeded in spite of the system rather than because of it, there are enough examples of cultured and talented individuals emerging from pre-1914 public schools to belie the notion that they were places as philistine as they are sometimes made out. One such individual was the novelist E. M. Forster, who left Tonbridge in 1897, a school he later caricatured in *The Longest Journey*. Forster was academically successful at Tonbridge, which instilled in him a love of the classics, but was unhappy in himself and developed a lasting aversion to authority and tradition, along with a strong respect for individualism. In the war, which he regarded as unjust, Forster showed his individualism by registering as a conscientious objector and undertaking Red Cross work in Egypt. This response was clearly at odds with the traditionally patriotic and militarist elements of the public school ethos, but shows that, in some individuals, the public school education had, before 1914, even if not by design, instilled rather different values.

Contemporary images of war 1914–18

No single vehicle had more impact in conveying the war to those at home than the *Battle of the Somme* documentary film, released on 21 August 1916. Chance decreed that the war broke out just when the cinema arrived, and it is unsurprising that governments on both sides alighted on the propaganda potential of the new medium. Although public schoolboys played no part in producing the film, the first senior officer to view parts of it, Brigadier-General John Charteris (Merchiston Castle), Douglas Haig's Chief of Intelligence, was quick to see its propaganda value and advised that it should be released to the public as soon as possible. It was seen by 20 million people in the first six weeks after its release, believed to be a higher proportion of the British public than any film since, and the government judged it a success in raising morale. At King's Canterbury the whole school was taken, on 20 October 1916, to St George's Cinema to see the Somme film, missing two morning lessons in the process.[12]

The two cameramen, Geoffrey Malins and John McDowell, arrived in the Somme sector on 23 June, the day before the army began its artillery bombardment of German positions. The 8,000 feet of film produced during the battle were edited down to just seventy-seven minutes, and contained a mixture of images shot behind the front lines and staged scenes of British soldiers going over the top. For all its imperfections, the film is regarded as a major historical document today. Essentially reportage, it does not steer the viewer towards any particular inter- pretation of the war. It has thus been seen in diverse ways at different times. It is often viewed today as illustrating the futility of war, but to many who saw it at the time, as historian Brian Bond has written, it 'strengthened [them] in their resolve to persevere to achieve victory'.[13]

Public schoolboys were to have more influence on the way the war was depicted in art, which was to become anything but objective. The artist and curator William Rothenstein (Bradford GS) was consulted by government early on about the use of art as propaganda, and was influential in the appointment of official war artists, many of whom were public school products. One was Eric Kennington (St Paul's), who was wounded on the Western Front. His portrait of infantrymen, *The Kensingtons at Laventie*, is still much admired for displaying the quiet heroism and endurance of the ordinary soldier. Perhaps the most iconic painting of the war was, however, by the American John Singer Sargent: *Gassed*, finished in 1919, depicts the victims of a mustard gas attack and now hangs in the Imperial War Museum.

Not all the artists proved dependable. Paul Nash (St Paul's) had served in the trenches as an officer until 1917, when he was invalided out. Posted as a war artist to the Ypres Salient in 1917, his paintings of the landscape around Passchendaele, including the *Menin Road*, *The Ypres Salient at Night* and the ironic *We Are Making a New World*, rank among the most distinguished war art of the century. In their critical power they are the equal of, if not superior to, the most bitter of war poems. Nash rapidly saw the missionary potential of his role, writing to his wife from Ypres: 'I am no longer an artist, interested and curious. I am a messenger who will bring back word from the men who are fighting to those who want the war to go on forever. Feeble, inarticulate will be my message, but it will have a bitter truth and may it burn their lousy souls.'[14] He hated the way that the government increasingly censored writers and artists: 'It is intolerable – I cannot read the papers – it is just humbug from end to end ... Out here men have been think-ing ... Hammering in their minds a hundred questions, festering in their hearts a thousand wrongs. The most insistent question is "Why am I here?"'[15] Disillusion bit deep. He told his wife that he and his men were 'sad and sick with longing for the end of this unending madness ... What is God about?'[16] John Nash (Wellington College), younger brother of Paul, painted in similar vein. His most celebrated image of the war is *Over the Top*, based on an episode in December 1917 in which he took part, when the Artists' Rifles attacked near Cambrai; he was one of twelve (out of eighty) men to come through unscathed.

Paul Nash was advised to become a war artist by Richard Nevinson, the unhappy schoolboy from Uppingham. At the outbreak of the war Nevinson had joined the Friends' Ambulance Unit, an experience he found disturbing, and subsequently volunteered for the RAMC, before being invalided out. Given his antipathy to the war, it appears surprising he was appointed an official war artist. His early painting in 1915, the futurist *La Mitrailleuse* depicting three stony-faced French machine-gunners, attracted considerable notice. His heavily ironic

210

Paths of Glory, painted in 1917 and depicting two soldiers lying dead in No-Man's-Land amidst barbed wire and battlefield debris, is among the most bitter painted in the war. Officially censored by a government beginning to wonder what forces it had unleashed, Nevinson exhibited it privately during the war. Percy Wyndham Lewis (Rugby), who had served as a Forward Observation Officer in the Third Battle of Ypres, was appointed an official war artist in December 1917. *A Battery Shelled* was his first celebrated war painting. Each artist in their own way depicted the depth of human suffering at the front. As with the poets, the suffering and the tortured landscape they beheld turned them against the war from as early as 1915–16. Paul Nash, indeed, writes like a poet, as in a letter quoted by art historian David Boyd Hancock: 'I have seen the most frightful nightmare of a country more conceived by Dante or Poe than by nature ... sunset and sunrise are blasphemous, they are mockeries to man ... the rain drives on, the stinking mud becomes more evilly yellow, the shell holes fill up with green-white water'.[17]

Poetry paints images in the mind as vivid as those of artists, and poems are among the most familiar records of the war. Every single public school had its war poets, and school magazines are full of examples of their work, most long forgotten even within the portals of the school. Many gems and poignant truths await rediscovery. During the war itself the patriotic poems of Rupert Brooke, whose father was a housemaster at Rugby, remained enormously popular, and through the 1920s, while the passionate indignation of Wilfred Owen's poetry struggled to achieve recognition until the 1931 edition came out with a memoir by Edmund Blunden (Christ's Hospital). *Into Battle* by Julian Grenfell (Eton), celebrating the exhilaration of battle and published in *The Times* on the same day as news of his death in 1915, became as popular as Brooke's poem *The Soldier*. Little poetry published during the war itself was overtly critical of the war's conduct; its focus was chiefly the exceptional circumstances of death, suffering, and the battlefield horrors, as well as the companionship of the trenches and the ubiquitous compassion with their fellow men on both sides.

The biting satire of Siegfried Sassoon (Marlborough), taking aim at the generals and the home front, is thus unusual from the public school poets: similar criticism is harder to find in the work of other well-known poets, such as Charles Sorley (Marlborough), Laurence Binyon (St Paul's) and Ivor Gurney (King's Gloucester). Edward Thomas (St Paul's), killed in 1917, was arguably the greatest poet of them all, but his poems, with 'their bleak and oblique rural ruminations' are far removed from those of Sassoon and Owen.[18] One of the most commonly anthologized poems is *Before Battle* by William Noel Hodgson (Durham), written on the eve of the Somme battle in which he was killed; it expresses the hopes, fears and faith of a man about to go into battle, but not the cynicism later associated with the genre. Poetry in the Second World War similarly was rarely cynical: poems conveying powerful anti-war fervour, especially in relation to nuclear weapons, belong rather more to the second half of the twentieth century, along with the rediscovery of Sassoon and Owen as support for that anti-war cause.

Composers worked in softer colours than the poets and artists, and their music was descriptive of feelings rather than judgemental. Ralph Vaughan Williams enlisted in the RAMC in September 1914 and was in France by June 1916, in time for the Somme, where his contemplative, pastoral symphony began to take shape in his mind. 'It's really wartime music – a great deal of it incubated when I used to go up, night after night with the ambulance wagon at Ecoivres, we went up a steep hill and there was a wonderful Corot-like landscape in the sunset', he later said. Today, a large military cemetery stands on the site of the field hospital that inspired his music.[19] A close friend of Vaughan Williams was Gustav Holst. Educated at Cheltenham Grammar School, Holst was director of music at St Paul's Girls' School when in August 1914 he wrote *Mars the Bringer of War*, part of his suite *The Planets*, composed between then and 1916. Holst had been repeatedly rejected for military service on the grounds of ill health, but no composer better captured the mechanized nature of the Great War.

The great majority of the composers associated with the Great War had attended public schools. One of the most promising, E. J. (Jack) Moeran, had been at Uppingham before enrolling at the Royal College of Music in 1913. But he never fully recovered from the head wound he sustained at the Battle of Arras in May 1917, and his health was to be erratic until his premature death in 1950. Arthur Bliss (Rugby), who also served on the Western Front, was to draw inspiration from the Great War. One of his best known works was *Morning Heroes (Spring Offensive)*, composed as a tribute to his brother Kennard, a promising painter and musician who had been killed on the Somme in July 1916, and to help exorcize the enduring horror of his war experiences. He later wrote: 'Although the war had been over for more than ten years, I was still troubled by frequent nightmares. They all took the same form. I was still there in the trenches with a few men: we knew the armistice had been signed, but we had been forgotten.'[20]

Cecil Coles (George Watson's) had been assistant conductor of the Stuttgart Royal Opera before the war. He was killed in April 1918 in the Somme sector, while bringing in wounded, when serving as band-master and stretcher-bearer in the Queen Victoria's Rifles. He had continued to compose while at the front, sending mud-bespattered and shrapnel-torn manuscripts back to his friend Gustav Holst. His *Behind the Lines*, composed at the front in 1918, has a particularly powerful and haunting last movement, 'Cortège'. It is said that his wife was so traumatized by his death that she refused to have music ever again played in her home.[21]

The composer whose death in action is often regarded as the greatest loss to music was George Butterworth, who had been a boy at Eton and teacher at Radley. He joined his friend Ralph Vaughan Williams to revive English folk music before the war, and the latter's *London Symphony* was to be dedicated to Butterworth on its publication in 1920. Butterworth's surviving work mostly comes from the period 1910–14. His rhapsody, under the title *A Shropshire Lad* and based on the poems of A. E. Housman (KES Birmingham and Bromsgrove), was given its premiere in Leeds in 1913, the same year that he wrote another very popular piece, *The Banks of Green Willow*. *A Shropshire Lad* had its London premiere in the 1917 season of Henry Wood Promenade Concerts, and the music critic of *The Times* wrote: 'This is not the sort of music to like or dislike immediately at a single hearing, and one hopes that the orchestra will ... give us another opportunity of realising what it is we have lost in the composer's early death, and of remembering in what cause it was lost'.[22]

Butterworth was commissioned in the Durham Light Infantry, won the MC in July 1916, and was then killed on 5 August 1916 near Pozières, aged thirty-one.[23] His brigadier was astonished to learn after his death that he was one of the most promising composers of his generation, but wrote to Butterworth's father: 'A brilliant musician in times of peace, and an equally brilliant soldier in times of stress.'[24] Some of Housman's words used by Butterworth were often found on the service sheets of memorial services for young public schoolboys at their school chapels and home churches up and down the land: 'They carry back bright to the coiner the mintage of man/The lads that will die in their glory and never be old.'[25]

Why the war was fought

Cecil Spring-Rice (Eton) wrote the poem *I Vow to Thee, My Country* in 1908. He served during the war as British Ambassador in Washington. Shortly before his death there in February 1918, he rewrote the first verse so it concentrated on the losses suffered by British soldiers in the Great War. Three years later, Gustav Holst, while still teaching at

St Paul's Girls' School, adapted *Jupiter* from *The Planets* as a setting for it, and it has become a much loved hymn, often used on Remembrance Sunday, at memorial services and other national occasions. The patriotism of the first verse was far more typical of the general mood of 1918 than the critical tone of the war poets and artists.

Which contemporary voices more closely capture the mood of the time – the stoicism and resolution of the early poets, artists, and composers, or the critical tones of those coming later? Few of the letters and memoirs published during and immediately after the war contain statements of disillusion, though expressions of war-weariness are ubiquitous. Many of these letters were written by men who did not survive, their writings gathered into published collections by grieving parents; they have an immediacy and innocence which tends to be absent from the more reflective memoirs published years after the war. The writers understate the horrors but are under no illusions about the suffering and sacrifice to be endured as the price of the victory, which they regarded as certain. The sensitive Douglas Gillespie (Winchester) wrote in 1915, just before he was killed at Loos, 'We must get the Germans driven out of France and Belgium before we begin to talk of peace, and we shall do it, though, of course, the cost will be very heavy.'[26] The same thinking was present in a letter from Stephen Hewett, the gentle Downside scholar killed on the Somme: 'There were times when the issue of this war seemed doubtful ... Now it is certain; and, if we have to suffer the heaviest losses, and even have a hard time for the rest of our lives, we should consider ourselves not unlucky'.[27]

The relentless nature of the war forced many to re-examine their original motives for enlisting. But even the harrowing Third Ypres, and the prolonged German offensive from 21 March 1918, did not break the spirit of the army. Many soldiers felt uplifted to the end by the sense that the struggle in which they were involved was worthwhile, and indeed principled; while the comradeship that they enjoyed in the trenches helped them to endure what seems, to the contemporary mind, unendurable. In his last letter before he was killed, Douglas Gillespie, anticipating the coming attack at Loos, was comforted by thoughts of present and dead comrades: 'I have no forebodings, for I feel that so many of my friends will charge by my side ... Tom himself will be here to help me, and give me courage and resource and that cool head which will be needed most of all to make the attack a success'.[28] The questioning and the disillusion mostly came long after the last gun had fallen silent, as the inter-war years ground on and it became evident that this had not been 'the war to end all wars'.

The first wave of dissent in public schools 1919–27

'A disgusting idea of artificial nonsense and sentimentality', wrote the sixteen-year-old Evelyn Waugh (Lancing College) in his diary at 11 a.m. on 11 November 1919 about the two-minute silence being widely observed across the country. In a message from Buckingham Palace only four days before, King George V had asked his subjects to observe it at 11 a.m. precisely. Waugh was not impressed: 'If people have lost sons and fathers, they should think of them whenever the grass is green or Shaftesbury Avenue is brightly lighted, not for two minutes on the anniversary of a disgraceful day of national hysteria. No one thought of the dead last year. Why should they now?'[29] Many in the schools thought differently. At Sherborne, the school Waugh yearned to attend until the antics of his brother ruled it out, the silence was observed by boys and staff in chapel, followed by a special service. In his diary that day, one Sherborne teacher wrote, 'Anniversary of Armistice. Silence at 11 am all over England. We had a very impressive service in Chapel.'[30]

A chasm was growing between the older generation in schools who believed passionately that the war had been worthwhile and fought for a set of values they held dear, such as patriotism and empire, and some of the most thoughtful among the young, who reacted in violent disagreement. J. R. Eccles, headmaster of Gresham's, epitomized the former when he preached on Armistice Day that, 'the war took a heavy toll of our best. The same was true throughout the Public Schools. They left it to you to carry the torch. For their sakes ought you not to dedicate yourself afresh to the service of the highest?'[31] The ideals of duty, loyalty and service were the ones they wanted the younger generations to follow, and they were saddened and uncomprehending when such ideals were reviled. Lord Rosebery had reportedly requested *The Eton Boating Song* be played to him on the gramophone as he lay dying in 1929; as a former Prime Minister, and an Eton governor, he symbolized the old world that was passing. Fellow Etonian George Orwell, who left in 1921, wrote about himself: 'He never was very successful at school – he did no work and won no prizes – but he managed to develop his brain along the lines which suited it. He read the books the headmaster denounced from the pulpit and developed unorthodox opinions about the C of E, patriotism and the Old Boys' tie.'[32] *The Old School Tie* was the name that Graham Greene gave to an anthology of reflections he produced in 1933. Among his authors was the poet W. H. Auden, who denounced his old school, Gresham's, and the poet William Plomer, who spoke of the drudgery he experienced at Rugby. In his introduction to the book, Greene, whose father had been headmaster of Berkhamsted throughout the war, commented that, 'this book will, I hope, be superficially more funny than tragic, for so odd a system of education does not demand a pompous memorial ... For there can be no doubt that the system which this book mainly represents is doomed'.[33]

By the early 1930s it became almost de rigueur for young intellectuals to be contemptuous of the establishment, in a similar way to the current of opinion that blossomed thirty years later with the founding of *Private Eye* (1961) and the satirical television programme *That Was the Week That Was* (1963). At Wellington College, the Romilly brothers Esmond and Giles, socialist sympathizers while also nephews of Winston Churchill, inserted pacifist leaflets into the school's hymn books at the page of *O Valiant Hearts*. They launched their own paper at school to 'champion the forces of progress against the forces of reaction, from compulsory military training to propagandist teaching'.[34] To the Romilly brothers, in the words of Noel Annan, the public schools were 'part of the organised hypocrisy of capitalism'.[35] After they left, they published a book about their experience, *Out of Bounds: the Education of Giles and Esmond Romilly* (1935).[36] Esmond moved to London and worked in a communist bookshop, founded a centre for boys who had 'escaped' the prison of their public schools, and was later renowned for marrying Jessica Mitford, one of the famous sisters, in 1937. He volunteered as a pilot in the Canadian Air Force and was shot down over the North Sea in 1941, at the age of twenty-three. Giles served as a war correspondent in the Spanish Civil War and in the Second World War, was captured by the Germans in 1940 at Narvik in Norway and later famously escaped, but died of a tranquillizer overdose in California in 1967, aged fifty.

While at Wellington, Esmond and Giles had refused to join the Officer Training Corps, fast becoming the focus of adolescent dissent at the time. At Kelvinside Academy the OTC had never recaptured the central position of kudos it had enjoyed in the school before the war. Membership became voluntary, forty per cent of boys opted not to join, and the OTC commander was forced to defend it against the charge that it was encouraging militarism.[37] Across the country, boys saw the OTC as a bore, and out of kilter with a world in which war was, as the League of Nations was proclaiming, a folly of the past. By the early 1930s, many schools which had after the war been given German field guns to display as trophies were seeing them as relics of a bygone era, and as insults to Germany. Debate flared at Dulwich College in mid-decade on the pages of *The Alleynian*, and the Dulwich guns were later to be melted down in 1940, perhaps for practical reasons.[38]

Harrow fought a staunch rearguard action to maintain its OTC at the heart of school life, with compulsory attendance by all boys aged over fifteen, and a minimum of two parades a week. Opposition to it surfaced from about 1928, with Terence Rattigan a key figure in the rebellion. He leaked to the press stories about opposition to excessive drill practices, and dark rumours that the boys were threatening not to turn up on parade. In the winter of 1929/30 heated correspondence took place in *The Harrovian*, with one boy correspondent arguing that the government was spending more on OTCs in schools and universities than it was contributing to the League of Nations. A petition was whipped up demanding reduction to only one parade a week, signed by, it was claimed, 400 Harrow boys. Public school headmasters of latter years tend to think that the media have been interested in salacious stories only during their tenures, but the avidity with which the newspapers seized on the activities of the Romilly brothers and the discontent at Harrow shows that the press has long had such an appetite. The Harrow School historian thinks that such protests were 'expressions of frustration at what seemed an unthinking and exaggerated obeisance to habit and control as much as of hostility to overt militarism',[39] and he may well be right. Below the surface, and far beyond the understanding of most headmasters and their staff, a deep cultural shift was taking place, and those who sought to perpetuate respect for the Great War and its perceived lessons of duty, control and order were finding their world increasingly undermined by social and economic forces over which they had no control.

Few intellectuals before 1914 had been disaffected, even in the universities. It is the lack of protest at the reasons for the war and its conduct which surprises us today, rather than the vehemence of the attacks on it. For a decade after the war the intellectual reaction was mostly subdued, not least due to exhaustion and the need to take stock after such cataclysmic events. By the late 1920s the reaction of intellectuals was beginning to crystallize. The new generation increasingly questioned the right to govern of the mostly elderly men who ran their institutions and wanted to cling onto 'time-honoured practices that were becoming obsolete in their fathers' time'.[40] The generation which grew up in the wake of the war, and dominated academic and cultural circles during the inter-war years and beyond, were described by the Oxford don, Maurice Bowra, as 'Our Age'.[41] A boy at Cheltenham College, which he had disliked, Bowra had served in the trenches in 1917–18, an experience which he had disliked even more; it had bequeathed to him a detestation of all things military. Many of his privileged ilk disdained to wear their old school tie or attend celebrations organized by Old Boys' associations, and regarded the Great War as one which could have been avoided, or halted earlier. Their blame fell on the older generation who ran the country, and whose ideas, or lack of them, had been responsible for the widespread slaughter. They recoiled too from the mores of the older generation, epitomized by their headmasters, with their denial of individual liberty and their repressive attitude to sex.

Anthony Blunt, the art historian unmasked as a Soviet spy in 1979, who was at Marlborough in the early 1920s, was one of the early figures to rebel. Blunt and a group of friends reacted against what they saw as the reinstitution of the games culture after the war, feeling themselves to be sufficiently numerous to be openly defiant. As he later reminisced in *The Marlburian*, 'On Saturday evenings we went upfield to where other boys were playing cricket and infuriated them by playing catch with a large brightly-covered ball right across their game.'[42] They founded a magazine, *The Heretick*, which in Blunt's words was designed 'to express our disapproval of the establishment generally, of the more outspoken and pedantic masters, of all forms of organised sport, of the OTC and all the other features we hated in school life'.[43] His near-contemporary at Marlborough, John Betjeman, made his own point by bowling a hoop through the courtyard with a green feather behind his ear.

Novels began to appear portraying the public school world in a jaundiced light. Ernest Raymond's *Tell England*, published in 1922 and subtitled *A Study in a Generation*, had romanticized the sacrifice of that generation. Reprinted fourteen times in the first year alone, it satisfied an aching need to believe in the public school ideal as it was. But a truer harbinger of the future was Alec Waugh's 1917 novel, *The Loom of Youth*, whose tone was picked up in Shane Leslie's *The Oppidan*, published in 1922. The latter told the story of a young Etonian before the war, thrust into a repressive atmosphere at school, his life ruled by strange customs and unwritten laws, a budding intellectual crushed by a philistine world. *Young Woodley*, a 1925 play about a public schoolboy who falls in love with the wife of his headmaster, was banned from the stage until 1928, when it ran for over a year. Ironically, in that same year 1928, *Journey's End* had its premiere and presented a very different perspective on public schools and their products. Replying to criticism that his play had 'too much of the English public schools about it', Sherriff wrote that, 'almost every young officer was a public schoolboy, and if I had left them out of *Journey's End*, there wouldn't have been a play at all'.[44] The balance, however, had truly tipped against the public schools by then, with four or five novels about public school life appearing each year, a very different agenda from the pre-1914 period. Annan, who was at Stowe in the early 1930s, wrote of these works: 'The new hero of the public school novel was the sensitive intellectual who as a pacifist refuses to join the OTC and finds himself in revolt against philistinism and the upper-class official ethos.'[45] David Newsome, the historian and Master of Wellington College (1979–89), made light of such protests: 'Most schools were burdened with some published revelation of the decadence of their lives, jibes at jaded ushers [masters], mockery of hypocritical principles, dark hints of sadism and smutty conduct, unashamed accounts of adolescent romances.'[46]

The new wave was certainly causing widespread dismay. 'The stains have got to be taken off the War Memorial which, for many boys, was now a thing at which they could not look without thinking of one of those pestilential books that had got into their hands', wrote Tubby Clayton in *The Times* in January 1930. He concluded in sadness that 'The one historical ideal of their lives has been smirched.'[47] Staff common rooms became very divided places in the 1920s. Vocal critics of the old order during the war, like Victor Gollancz at Repton, are hard to find, but many teachers nevertheless were in sympathy with the aspirations of the emerging anti-establishment tendency amongst pupils. At Wellington College, a conflict between the old order and the new was mostly about disciplinary procedure, between those who advocated pre-war strictness and formality, and those who wanted a more liberal approach to relations between masters and boys; the historian noted 'the presence of extremists on the staff and the some-what formal manner in which differences of opinion were registered'.[48] Wilfred Jasper Blunt, brother of Anthony, who became a celebrated teacher of art at Eton and Curator at the Watts Gallery, joined Haileybury to teach art in 1923: 'I learned almost immediately that a great barrier stood between those of the staff who had fought in the war and those who had been too old, too sickly or too apathetic. The latter were known to the former as SOBs [Silly Old Buggers] ... .at breakfast we sat in strict order of seniority, the SOBs silent and disapproving behind their copies of *The Times*, the young truculent and garrulous with their *Daily Mail*s near the draughty door at the bottom end'.[49] Similar common room hierarchies were to endure in many public schools right to the end of the century.

At establishment-minded Harrow, 'Masters who returned from the war exerted a profound influence ... Of those arriving between 1919 and 1929, fourteen had been in the forces'.[50] One of these, indeed, the chaplain Geoffrey Woolley, had won the Victoria Cross. Many teachers who had served in the war insisted on being referred to by their rank and liked to wear their decorations on official occasions. Their world was passing before their eyes. As Oliver van Oss, later headmaster of Charterhouse, wrote: 'In September 1930, the senior housemasters –

men in their fifties – had been young men at Oxford and Cambridge before 1900. They had got their Firsts and their Blues in a golden world that had vanished for ever: a world in which the supremacy of England and the public school was unchallenged and seemed certain to endure for ever. That sunlit world had been destroyed in the war. And the survivors, agonizingly aware of their own unworthiness compared with friends who had fallen, were haunted by memories of a land of lost content'.[51]

But some headmasters, scarred by their memories of the Great War, struggled to embrace the new world. One such was Frederick Malim (1921–37) at Wellington College. Malim had been headmaster of Haileybury throughout the war, a school which counted the deaths of nearly six hundred old boys, taking a huge toll of him. Actor Christopher Lee remembers him as humourless and austere throughout his days at Wellington, and how his demeanour affected the whole *timbre* of school life.[52] Malim was to endure the further agony of losing his own son, an RAF pilot, in March 1941. The Sherborne headmaster, Nowell Smith, who had been headmaster since 1909, took leave of absence in the autumn term 1926 because of strain, and then resigned in 1927 because the experience of the war had tested and then contributed to the loss of his Christian faith. His son wrote that, 'at 55 he resigned his headmastership: he had shed his Christian belief and could no longer in conscience preside over a community whose life was centred in the school chapel.'[53]

The long shadow of the Great War continued to affect the public schoolboy. Christopher Everett, a boy at Winchester in the 1940s and later headmaster of Tonbridge, compared the effect of both world wars: 'For those who had been at school in the mid-1940s, the First World War was a stronger presence than the Second. At Winchester, the War Memorial Cloister was a daily feature of our lives. At least five teachers had MCs from the First World War and their outlook – an emphasis on good form, under-statement, self-discipline and good order – was strikingly different from the attitude of young staff returning from the Second World War'. The impact of the Great War on staff who had fought in it had left them with the conviction that the barriers against anarchy and chaos were paper-thin. They recognized the inclinations of the heart but believed that they must be channelled and constrained by decorum of behaviour and rational argument. Christopher Everett particularly recalled his housemaster, a decorated Great War veteran, insisting to him that George Bernard Shaw was a far greater writer than Joseph Conrad.[54]

Day schools were perhaps less stuffy and more open to the new world. At City of London School many young teachers were appointed after 1918. Formality disappeared from the common room, and relations between boys and masters became friendlier.[55] Change also came in the foundation of a number of new boarding schools, boosted by the upsurge in demand for private education, and helped by the availability on the market of many large houses at relatively cheap prices through a combination of the impact of death duties, declining income from farming and families left by the war without heirs. These schools had, if not a more liberal ethos, then certainly a less tradition-bound one. Stowe and Canford were both founded in 1923, Frensham Heights in 1925, Bryanston in 1928 and Gordonstoun, in north-east Scotland, in 1934. At Stowe, headmaster J. F. Roxburgh wanted a school less regimented and dominated by games. Leonard Cheshire, an early pupil, was a member of the League of Nations Club at the school. 'I belonged to a generation which in a hazy kind of way recognised the debt to those who had gone before', he wrote in his memoirs, 'but which rejected war as a means of solving differences between nations and believed that war in Europe was a thing of the past.'[56]

The war had also enhanced the reputation of public schools, not just in the eyes of their traditional clientele, but also among those from different backgrounds, many of them commissioned during the war, and in a new class of what one historian called the 'nouveaux riches'.[57] HMC numbers expanded from 114 schools in 1914 to 151 in 1930, one of the biggest increases in any period of its history, and now including many of those Dominion schools which had made their own significant contribution to the war. Virtually all schools had seen their numbers grow in the war, Trent doubling in size from 144 to 295 and St Paul's going from 594 to 689. This growth continued through the 1920s, Sherborne going from 287 in 1918 to 413 in 1929, and Sedbergh from 326 to 425.[58] Girls' education was blossoming too, with both St George's, Ascot and Benenden founded in 1923. Prosperity was, however, stopped in its tracks by the Depression, with Brighton falling from 601 to 343 between 1927 and 1933, and Lancing, Malvern and Rossall all losing twenty per cent of their boys.[59]

The buoyancy of demand, the need to maintain it and a desire to ground the public schools in the different norms of the interwar years, explains the desire of a limited number of heads to broaden the social base of public schools. Frank Fletcher was paramount in believing it was a loss to the schools 'that their boys come from a limited class, that a large and valuable section of the nation is excluded from them for financial reasons'.[60] In his capacity as Chairman of HMC he met

H. A. L. Fisher, President of the Board of Education, on 3 April 1919. He sought Fisher's support for broadening the base of public school entry, but the plan did not meet with the approval of government. Fletcher's letter to *The Times* in 1935 recounting his quest had an elegiac tone, concluding that the public schools wanted to accept boys from poor backgrounds but that opposition had not come from the schools themselves but from practical and financial problems.[61] But how far most headmasters would have gone to accept such upheaval, which would have had dramatic consequences for the nature of their schools, is far from clear.

Public schools and their alumni continued to help the less fortunate in society through their missions, many of them begun in the Victorian age, such as the Winchester mission in Portsmouth and Wellington's at Walworth in south-east London. The overtly Christian element of Wellington's mission declined after the war, but it brought material assistance to the area and helped develop a social conscience in those boys who participated.[62] Public school officers were also much involved in ex-servicemen's organizations like the British Legion; the daughter of Major George Robertson, a Rossall boy who had won the DSO in the artillery, still has a cigarette box presented to him, inscribed with the words 'with grateful thanks from the disabled soldiers, sailors and airmen, Ashtead, May 21 1930'.[63]

The first wave of dissent in the decade after the war had rocked the public schools. Recognition of the wider human cost of the war created the platform for the inter-war generation to question more fundamentally the public school ethos and its pre-war codes of duty, control and order. As Eton historian Tim Card wrote, 'the old certainties had perished; the young were more willing to question the traditions by which their predecessors had lived – and died.'[64] Yet the status quo won through, not least in the way ranks closed in 1939, when the children of the Great War veterans fought and died because of the failure of the previous generation to establish a lasting peace. The public schools were happy to accept equality in death in the cemeteries and on the memorials of both wars, but they were not yet prepared to open their portals to the common man. The inner structure of school life continued much the same: the public schoolboy of the Edwardian era would have recognized much about his school as far ahead as the 1960s, with a classics-dominated curriculum, compulsory chapel and corps, spartan conditions in dormitories, cubicle toilets, prefectorial powers, fagging, and the same pressures to conform. The real revolution in the public schools was to come only after the 1960s, and when it did, the winds of change were powered in part by memories of and reactions to the

Great War, but also by the more open world consequent on the Second World War and ensuing social changes.

The tenth anniversary of the Armistice and the 1930s

The tenth anniversary ushered in an outpouring of literature about the war and the publication of poetry written during the war. Context is all-important. Suppressed experiences and memories of wartime horrors were coming to the surface, after a decade of forgetting, but were doing so in a very different world to war-torn 1918. The world by 1928 seemed a more settled and peaceful place. The 1925 Locarno Pact had promoted Franco-German reconciliation, the League of Nations was working to foster international cooperation, while the Kellogg-Briand Pact of 1928 sought to renounce war as an instrument of national policy. Even when the international skies began to darken in the early 1930s, the popular mood in Britain remained committed to finding peaceful solutions through disarmament and the League.

November 1928 saw a novel begin serialization in a German news-paper, and it appeared in book form in January 1929. *All Quiet on the Western Front* by Erich Maria Remarque, a German veteran of the war, is told through the eyes of its main character, the nineteen-year-old Paul Bäumer, and recounts the lives and agonies of a group of his friends. Remarque's chilling words in the preface still resonate power-fully: '[The book] will try simply to tell of a generation of men who, even though they may have escaped shells, were destroyed by the war.' The most memorable scene takes place in a shell-hole, where Bäumer kills a man for the first time, with a knife in hand-to-hand combat: he watches in horror as the helpless French soldier take hours to die and then asks forgiveness from his dead body. The book was translated into English in 1929 and given the title by which it is known today, although the literal translation of the German title is 'Nothing New in the West'. Before the end of 1930 the book had sold two and a half million copies in twenty-five languages, and that same year it was made into an Oscar-winning film of the same name in Hollywood. The book was seized on by pacifists as anti-war, though Remarque himself claims in the opening of the novel that he has no political intent but is trying merely to describe.

Journey's End, by R. C. Sherriff (Kingston Grammar School), is the principal British play from the same period, and contains a more nuanced and understated message. It was first put on stage in December 1928, with Laurence Olivier (St Edward's Oxford) in the lead role of Stanhope; Sherriff is believed to have given Olivier his own boots from the front to wear on stage. Some have seen the play as anti-war because the lead characters are all killed at the opening of the German spring offensive. But Sherriff was not being disingenuous when he wrote that his characters were 'simple unquestioning men who fought the war because it seemed the only right and proper thing to do ... It was a play in which not a word was spoken against the war'.[65] Traditions of duty and patriotism still ran deep. One theatre manager had told him his play would never be performed because it had 'no leading lady'.[66] These were the words Sherriff gave to his autobiography published on the fiftieth anniversary of the Armistice. In it he wrote that, though there had been bad times at the front, 'it had been a magnificent, memorable experience'.[67]

The books published around the tenth anniversary similarly display many harrowing scenes, but they are rarely critical of the war, or cynical about its purpose. Sassoon (Marlborough), Graves (Charterhouse) and Blunden (Christ's Hospital) wrote the three best-known memoirs. Sassoon's is a fictionalized autobiography, and its first volume, *Memoirs of a Fox-Hunting Man*, published in 1928, was followed in 1930 by *Memoirs of an Infantry Officer*. It recounts the experiences in the trenches of its narrator, George Sherston, between the spring of 1916 and the summer of 1917, and was immediately greeted as a classic and a faithful account of the reality of life at the front during those years. Graves' *Goodbye to All That*, published in 1929, was purely autobiographical and more explicitly critical, notably of the Battles of Loos and the Somme. Graves had been severely traumatized by the war, and the title of the book expresses his desire to be free of the values of the old world that had embraced the Great War, and celebrates the new mores and freedoms of the interwar years. The book's accuracy was questioned by Sassoon, as it was by Blunden, whose own *Undertones of War* was published in 1928. This is a book written in gentler tones, and describes his fighting on the Somme and at Ypres, which severely traumatized him too. 'A harmless young shepherd in a soldier's coat'[68] is how he describes himself in the book, and he attributes his survival to his small size, which made him 'an inconspicuous target'.[69]

All three writers are angry to different degrees at aspects of the war, especially incompetent staff officers whose thoughtlessness led to futile deaths. But none of them opposed Britain's role in the war or expressed any sense of shame at their own involvement. They remained broadly proud of their own regiments and achievements, and indeed, Graves possibly excepted, of their schools. Sassoon wrote wistfully of Marlborough in *The Old Century*, while Blunden's writings contain many nostalgic references to his schooldays, and he remained devoted to Christ's Hospital all his life.[70] Their education gave these officers a literary grounding as well as the confidence to express themselves in print, a privilege denied the great mass of ordinary soldiers, whose writings about the war are far fewer in number. The public school education then was much narrower in scope than in our own age, but there was more time for reading, and the more talented writers could call upon a formidable array of literary and classical allusions.

A lack of cynicism about the war characterizes a series of lesser-known books produced by public school authors in these years. Charles Carrington (Christ's College, New Zealand) published *A Subaltern's War* in 1929. For Carrington, an Englishman by birth and a teacher at Haileybury throughout the 1920s, the experience of war had been one of deep comradeship and indeed great happiness at times, balancing otherwise unrelieved suffering and fear. He believed the war had to be fought to the very end and that he and his fellow soldiers accepted that there was no alternative but to endure the suffering. In a preface to an edition of the book in 1964 he wrote: 'To me the mood of 1929 with its pacifist emotionalism, its crocodile tears over the dead, and its absurd attempts to make the military commanders the scapegoats of a bellicose human race, seems more irrational than the warlike mood of 1914 when the issues were clear, when men had no doubts about the duty that lay before them.'[71] According to literary critic Paul Fussell, Carrington's view was widely shared by ex-soldiers who wrote to Carrington to express their support.[72]

Charles Douie (Rugby) wrote in similar vein to Carrington in his memoir *The Weary Road*, published also in 1929. His theme was that the war consisted of 'a whole range of experiences, shared and endured by close-knit but constantly changing groups', and he wanted to assert that the natural 'weariness of soldiers should not be interpreted as disillusion'.[73] Like his fellow writers, Douie was deeply affected by the war. Of the fifty-six boys in his house in Rugby when he arrived at the school in 1910, 'no fewer than 23 lost their lives'. But he believed that the cause of the war justified the losses, fought as it was to defend the right of Britain 'to order its own affairs' and to defend the freedoms of its people from 'militarism'.[74] Guy Chapman (Westminster), who became a Professor of Modern History, wrote a fine memoir, *A Passionate Prodigality*, published in 1933. He could not have been clearer about the impact of the war: 'To the years between 1914 and 1918 I owe everything of lasting value in my make-up. For any cost I paid in physical and mental vigour they gave me back a supreme fulfilment I should never otherwise have had'.[75]

Sidney Rogerson (Worksop) published his own short memoir, *Twelve Days on the Somme*, in 1933. It offers a forensic insight into the lives of men during part of the Somme battle, describing their obsession with food, boredom punctuated by terror, and the comforting presence of comrades. His express message was that the soldiers could and did face the ordeal of a battle such as the Somme with resilience, humour, and without loss of morale.[76] He wrote his book in reaction to what he perceived as a besmirching of the war by some contemporary writers. Graham Greenwell (Winchester) had been another very young officer coming straight out from school to the front, like Raleigh in *Journey's End*. In his *An Infant in Arms*, published in 1935, he sees war as an adventure, though he admits that the tribulations at the front were easier for very young men to endure, not having the responsibilities of older officers with families. Reviewers of the book were critical of his upbeat tone, but Blunden wrote in support in the *Observer*: 'To be perfectly fit, to live among pleasant companions, to have responsibility and a clearly defined job – these are great compensations when one is very young.'[77]

This outpouring of literature about the Great War was not balanced at this time by enough scholarly history, largely because the official papers relating to the war were not released until the 1960s. Nevertheless, later historical battle-lines began to be drawn. The official *History of the Great War*, edited by Brigadier-General James Edmonds (KCS Wimbledon), was published in twenty-nine volumes between 1922 and 1949 and has been regarded by some as too lenient towards the generals. On the other side, Basil Liddell Hart (St Paul's), who was close to Lloyd George, published in 1930 a history of the war, *The Real War 1914–18*, which, together with Lloyd George's own memoirs, published in 1936, were heavily critical of Haig and the generals. Winston Churchill, like Lloyd George, had access to official documents denied to mere historians, for his history of the war, *The World Crisis* (1936), but it was seen as self-serving, and was described by Arthur Balfour (Eton), a former Prime Minister, as 'Winston's brilliant autobiography, disguised as a history of the universe.'[78] The most authoritative single-volume history was written by a wounded veteran, Charles Cruttwell (Rugby), Dean of Hertford College, Oxford, and famously satirized by Evelyn Waugh in *Decline and Fall*. Cruttwell's book, *A History of the War 1914–18*, was published in 1934 and has been described as achieving 'an extraordinary objectivity in relation to events which had deeply affected him'.[79] Another official historian was Charles Bean (Clifton), whose twelve-volume *Official History of Australia in the War of 1914–18*, focused more on the experiences of ordinary soldiers and did much to create the Anzac legend.

By 1936 the drumbeat of war from Europe had increasingly caught the popular attention. The memory of the Great War was central to the arguments over appeasement, but the debate over its conduct and purpose was overtaken by the new crisis, and by the British declaration of war on 3 September 1939. Nevertheless, in the tumultuous events of 1939–1940, memories of the Great War did not have the same demoralizing effect on Britain as they had on France. The feeling of 'unfinished business' for Britain is epitomised by Churchill's return, on 3 September 1939, to the same First Lord of the Admiralty's room he had left in 1915, after being blamed for the Gallipoli debacle. Kathleen Hill, his secretary since 1937, recalled the moment: 'He rushed up the steps and flung open the door and there, behind the panelling was a large map showing the disposition of all German ships on the day he had left the Admiralty in 1915.'[80] The Great War then remained in the margins of history, as shocking new horrors emerged at Hiroshima and Auschwitz, only to emerge again in resplendent fury in the 1960s.

The fiftieth anniversary and the 1960s

'As we look back today,' said an editorial in King's Canterbury's magazine in August 1964 about the Great War, 'it seems a conflict conducted by the obstinacy and inflexibility of old men … As the casualties grew with the inadequacy of a command quite unable to fight a modern war, so the soldier in the trenches turned to the negative bitterness and despair that were uppermost in Wilfred Owen's mind … Now on the fiftieth anniversary of the outbreak of war, it would be appropriate for us to consider whether we have learned the lessons … We may only hope that in the event of another crisis the representatives of the nations may not display that lack of statesmanship which forced gigantic conflict on all the nations in Europe'.[81]

Here we have, at the font of the most venerable public school, a complete case for the prosecution. 'The bitter conviction that the men in the trenches fought for no cause, in a war that could not be stopped', as historian Samuel Hynes put it, was becoming accepted wisdom.[82] The 1960s, like the decade from the early 1920s to the early 1930s, saw the zeitgeist turn against authority and the received truths of older generations. Within a few years, the cosy and patriotic verities of films like *The Dam Busters* (1955) had been replaced by the stridency of magazines like *Private Eye* and television programmes like *That Was the Week That Was*. The authority of the Great War veteran, Prime Minister Harold Macmillan, came under full-frontal attack, and with it the credibility of his whole predominantly public school government.

The Profumo scandal in 1963 was proof to many of the moral decadence and decrepitude of this political establishment. The nuclear arms policy which the government had strongly promoted, critics argued, was shown by the Cuban Missile Crisis of 1962 to be high-risk, and the Campaign for Nuclear Disarmament captured many new supporters, notably among the young. The Vietnam War, which spread rapidly from 1964 under President Lyndon Johnson, was another vehicle for anti-American, anti-military and anti-authority radical protest. Vietnam, whose horrors were beamed into every living room by television, for the first time in history, raised fundamental questions about the very nature of war, and whether it could ever be justified. Owen and Sassoon suddenly found a new audience, and became literary heroes to new generations.

Within the public schools, the cool winds of liberation began blowing from the mid-1960s onwards, giving the institutions and their head-masters problems which confronted neither their predecessors nor their successors. Radical youth culture, with its own music and press, greater sexual freedoms, clothes and lifestyle fuelled by the drug culture, spurred young people to challenge and belittle authority. Everything the old guard held dear in schools – the same values (or perhaps more accurately, the same rituals and practices) they had subscribed to during the Great War and years after it – came under attack: the Combined Cadet Force, compulsory chapel, organized games, corporal punishment and fagging. Anything that appeared to constrain personal freedom and expression with a drab conformity came under attack.

The film *If*, the most ferocious attack of the period on the public schools, was first screened in December 1968, against a background of student protests in France, and is still regarded as an iconic moment in the British cinema. This subversive product of the anti-authority culture was written by David Sherwin and John Howlett (both Tonbridge), directed by Lindsay Anderson (Cheltenham), used boys' uniforms from King's Canterbury, and was shot on location at Cheltenham, Aldenham and Uppingham. The most destructive attacks on public schools have often indeed been delivered by those educated within the system. The film's climax comes on Founder's Day, when the rebels arm themselves, set light to the School Hall and open fire on the assembled guests; the headmaster is shot dead and the guest of honour, a General, directs fire back from other boys in the Combined Cadet Force (the successor to the OTC). Extravagant fantasy though the film was, its closing sequence fuels thoughts of why their public school peers of fifty years before had not risen up in such a way against the high command of the Great War. The war may have remained an essential reference point for justifying either continuity or change, but social change in the present is a more potent force than respect for the common ideals of the past, and it is difficult now for younger generations to understand why the conformity and traditionalism in the practices of public schools from 1918 through to the early 1960s were seen as honourable or tolerable by contemporaries.

Divisions over the conduct of the war emerged as early as 1961, when the future Conservative politician and diarist Alan Clark (Eton) published his first book, *The Donkeys*, a study of the Western Front during 1915, above all the battles of Neuve Chapelle and Loos which ended with the dismissal of Sir John French as Commander-in-Chief and his replacement by a scheming Haig, the book's villain. The title was drawn from the expression 'lions led by donkeys', in widespread use to contrast the bravery of the ordinary British soldiers with the doltish commanders who led them. The book was shaped by the military strategist and historian Basil Liddell Hart (St Paul's), who acted as Clark's mentor and corrector of drafts.[83] The book's savage attack on Haig and on the leadership provoked the wrath of many historians, including the Conservatives Robert Blake (Norwich) and Hugh Trevor-Roper (Charterhouse), who was married to Haig's daughter. Historian John Terraine (Stamford), Haig's biographer, was contemptuous, while Michael Howard (Wellington College) dismissed the book as 'worthless'.[84] Historian Richard Holmes (Forest) was one of many to attribute to the book responsibility for conveying an utterly false understanding of the Great War: 'The real problem is that such histories have sold well and continue to do so. They reinforce historical myth by delivering to the reader exactly what they expect to read.'[85] *The Donkeys* became a major inspiration for the 1963 musical (and 1969 film) *Oh! What a Lovely War*. Directed by Joan Littlewood, the former version received its premiere in March 1963, despite protestations from the Haig family. Its savage attack on the war's political and military leadership gained wide acceptance, became the received wisdom of the time, and was given an added authenticity by the use of popular songs from the war.

The year 1961 saw another view of the war emerging in a very different art form. Benjamin Britten (Gresham's) was hard at work that year composing his *War Requiem*, first performed in May 1962 at the consecration of the new Coventry cathedral. This sat adjacent to the fourteenth-century cathedral destroyed in November 1940 during the Second World War by German bombs. Britten was a pacifist, and set nine poems by Wilfred Owen into the Requiem. The contrast between the German aggression and brutality of the Second World War, and the senseless slaughter of the Great War, was evident throughout the composition. On the title page of his score, Britten ghosted Owen's words: 'My subject is war and the pity of war.'

Differences in interpretation became more entrenched when the BBC, in partnership with the Imperial War Museum and the Canadian and Australian Broadcasting Corporations, produced *The Great War* documentary series on television in 1964. Narrated by Michael Redgrave (Clifton), its twenty-six parts made it the largest documentary series ever on British television. The script was written largely by John Terraine, whose staunch defence of Haig had been published in the previous year.[86] Correlli Barnett (Trinity School, Croydon) was another writer who was a well known critic of the 'anti-war' literature of the interwar years, which he argued had been produced by ex-public school temporary officers whose sensibilities were not those of the great majority of participants, and thus presented a distorted view of the reality of war.[87] Terraine and Barnett wanted the series to show off the achievements of the British army and its high command. Liddell Hart was equally clear that it should not, and resigned over the Somme episode, insisting his name be removed from the credits.[88] Liddell Hart had also been a protégé of and researcher for Lloyd George, which Michael Howard believes very largely explains his antipathy to the generals.[89] The ambition of the series – to redress the increasingly popular view of the war given in *The Donkeys* and *Oh! What a Lovely War* – largely failed, with the articulate recollections of the veterans and vivid, often harrowing, film and photographs only enhancing the popular belief about the horrors of the war.

By the end of the 1960s the historians' battle lines had formed very clearly. Lending support to Alan Clark and Liddell Hart was A. J. P. Taylor (Bootham), whose book on the First World War was published in 1963. His parents had been pacifists and sent him to various Quaker schools. Taylor was a savage critic of the conduct of the war, writing of Passchendaele: 'Failure was obvious by the end of the first day to everyone except Haig and his immediate circle ... Third Ypres was the blindest slaughter of a blind war'.[90] Ranged against them were, among others, John Terraine, Correlli Barnett, Richard Holmes and Michael Howard. Hew Strachan (Rugby) was also later to make clear his view that 'this country went to war for good reasons, conscientiously, and the outcome must be seen as a victory.'[91] It has also been suggested that the 'assault' by some historians on the conduct of the Great War was brought about not just by the anti-establishment culture of the 1960s, but also by the fact that the moral and military triumph of 1945 made it more difficult to criticise the conduct of that war.[92]

The 1960s were to prove more enduring in shaping popular conceptions of the Great War than the 1920s had been, and it was the emotional and literary interpretation of the war that was to triumph over that of the military historians. A new wave of memoirs by politicians in the 1960s and 1970s sought to support their embattled view. Eden's *Another World* (1976) was a far more sensitive and thoughtful piece of writing than his earlier and defensive memoirs published after his fall from grace in 1957 as a consequence of the Suez crisis. But Eden's book no more succeeded in changing perceptions of the war than did the writings of Harold Macmillan or his fellow Etonian Oliver Lyttelton, in his 1962 *Memoir* and a later book *From War to Peace* (1968). Ranged against them was a wave of new history books drawing heavily on first-hand accounts of the suffering of ordinary soldiers. In 1972 the Imperial War Museum created its Department of Sound Records, mindful that veterans from the Great War would be fast dying. They thus moved with great speed to interview survivors of all sorts, including those on the Home Front, with the collection being opened to the public in 1977. Again, it was the harrowing experience of ordinary soldiers which made the deepest impression, although Richard Holmes issued a note of caution about such oral history when he wrote that, 'survivors inevitably reflect the past through the prism of the present ... and sometimes played their roles too well, becoming "Veterans, general issue" neatly packed with what we want to hear'.[93]

Lyn MacDonald was one of a series of historians who wrote books drawing on these and other oral archives, including *Somme* and *They Called it Passchendaele*. Martin Middlebrook (Ratcliffe) was another to draw on such testimony in his powerful *The First Day on the Somme*, while John Keegan (King's, Taunton) had published *The Face of Battle* in 1976, which served to illustrate the conditions under which ordinary soldiers fought. Paul Fussell's *The Great War and Modern Memory*, published in 1975, gave powerful support to the emotional and literary interpretation by focusing on the way in which the horrors of war had been portrayed through literature, suggesting that authors had created a new form of writing and language to describe the indescribable. To mark the sixtieth anniversary of the Battle of the Somme, the BBC commissioned a documentary narrated by Leo McKern, which told a powerfully emotional story heavily critical of the generals. Such a view might not be better history than that of the military historians, but it certainly made for more compulsive viewing and reading.

Current views of the Great War
The critical view of the war received a powerful endorsement in *Blackadder Goes Forth*, the fourth and final series of the BBC comedy *Blackadder*, screened in the autumn of 1989. As a parody of public schoolboys' behaviour and alleged public school values, it is perfection.

231

Created by Richard Curtis (Harrow) and grammar school-educated Ben Elton, and produced by John Lloyd (King's Canterbury) it starred Rowan Atkinson (St Bees), Stephen Fry (Uppingham), Hugh Laurie (Eton), and Tony Robinson. The series, and especially the final programme when the actors are killed as they go over the top, has achieved cult status. As Richard Holmes wrote, 'Blackadder's aphorisms become fact ... A well-turned line of script can sometimes carry more weight than all the scholarly footnotes in the world'.[94] Historian Brian Bond observed that when the BBC screened a programme evaluating Haig in 1996, four of the critics took *Blackadder Goes Forth* as 'the historical truth against which to evaluate the programme and Haig's achievements'.[95] It is illustrative to compare *Blackadder* as the most popular television representation of the Great War with the more benign comedy of *Dad's Army* as the evocation of 1939–45, which A. J. P. Taylor called the 'good war'.[96] Moving images can indeed prove the most powerful medium for conveying views about the war, as they had done in 1916 with *The Battle of the Somme*. The Australian film *Gallipoli* (1981), directed by Peter Weir (The Scots College), is a powerful indictment of the British leadership of the war, ignoring the heavy British losses and ridiculing the British command. Its power to reinforce stereotypical views in Australia and New Zealand about the whole Gallipoli campaign is beyond doubt.

The pre-1914 public school system is criticised in *The Old Lie: the Great War and the Public School Ethos*, a powerfully argued book by Peter Parker (Canford). 'It is no disrespect to the dead to regret that many of them fought and died for all the wrong reasons', he writes. 'That men dribbled footballs towards the enemy trenches does not mean that the war was a game. That men died for an ethos does not mean that the ethos was worth dying for.'[97] Much of the great writing that has appeared recently on the war, including Pat Barker's *Regeneration* trilogy, published in the 1990s, *Birdsong* by Sebastian Faulks (Wellington College) and the novel and play *War Horse* by Michael Morpurgo (King's, Canterbury), focuses on the suffering of individuals, and in Morpurgo's case, animals. *Birdsong* now appears on the A-level English syllabus, while GCSE History in schools focuses heavily on the Great War. Not all history teachers have the knowledge or interest to distinguish between different viewpoints, while teachers of English often do more to shape opinion on the war through the study of war poetry and other literary texts.

It is the emotion of the war and its sufferings which deeply affect us, rather than the rational arguments of the historians. One such, Correlli Barnett, believes strongly that the cause was vindicated: 'The war was a tragedy for all participants, but it did end in a victory for democracy over militarist autocracies. The true tragedy lay in that from 1918 through to 1939 the politicians made a muck of the victory handed to them by the soldiers'.[98] Historians will argue the merits of the war for the next hundred years and beyond. What we do know for sure is the continuing truth about the emotion the war still generates. When trips are made to the Western Front, it is cemeteries and memorials which remain longest in visitors' minds, rarely more so than at Thiepval, Tyne Cot or the Menin Gate. The causes for which men may have fought are less memorable and striking than the legacy of pain and the death which ensued.

Human beings, it seems, will always want to identify more with the suffering of fellow men, but the invisible and largely forgotten care and courageous leadership of those men by their young, predominantly public school officers, whose losses were proportionately so high, should not be diminished. These young men, witnesses to the cataclysm which echoed down virtually every other twentieth-century catastrophe, would not have welcomed the polarization of the historical debate which has occurred. We have let ourselves become too mesmerised by the interpretations of the Great War, which are ultimately only ideas and theories. We have spent too little time immersing ourselves in the reality of the lives and experiences of those who participated in the war, who have left behind for us a mass of primary evidence. We have not focused enough on the sacrifices of participants of all kinds, public school and otherwise. During the centenary and beyond, we would do well to immerse ourselves in the experiences of men and women who participated in the Great War, and whose lives were affected by it, rather than in the theorizing of subsequent generations.

Chapter 10

The Lost Generation

'The loss sustained by the war can only be described as the wiping out of a generation.' Thus spoke the Bishop of Worcester when dedicating the war memorial at Malvern College in July 1922: 'Those who are left have to take up a double duty. There remains a great task of recovery, to see that everything is done to make the world better, purer, happier and more united. Those who died had the vision, those who live have the work to do.'[1] This chapter looks at the 'lost generation' from the public schools, those who lost their lives and those whose lives were shattered forever by the war, a generation of men who, in Remarque's words, 'even though they may have escaped the shells, were destroyed by the war.'[2] We know that about 900,000 British and Dominion forces died in the war, that just over two million were wounded – and that three million survived unscathed. We will never know the depth of the scars and suffering that these deaths created for their loved ones in Britain and elsewhere, nor the scale of the family lives disrupted, saddened or otherwise diminished.[3] The empty chair at the table, the tender relationships destroyed forever, the haunting memories, the grieving and the nightmares: these are the unquantifiable legacies. In his haunting contemporary novel *Birdsong*, Sebastian Faulks (Wellington College) evokes this 'unknown loss', when Captain Price reads the roll-call after the company has been in action on the Somme: 'Price hurried from one unanswered name to the next ... Names came pattering into the dusk, bodying out the places of their forebears, the villages and towns where the telegrams would be delivered ... with the children who would have been born, who would have grown or worked or painted, even governed, left ungenerated in their fathers' shattered flesh that lay in stinking shell-holes in the beet-crop soil'.[4] The physical fabric of Britain, unlike that of France and Belgium, might have been largely unscarred by the war. But the toll of human life was beyond comprehension, and the impact on the country at large unfathomable.

'A very fine match' at Lords

The cream of schoolboy cricket assembled at Lord's cricket ground on the morning of Monday, 3 August 1914 for the annual schools' representative match. The 'Lord's Schools' team was picked from the *crème de la crème* – schools like Eton, Harrow, Rugby, Marlborough, Tonbridge and Clifton, Cheltenham and Haileybury – who played an annual fixture at the home of English cricket, and 'The Rest' was made up of players from other public schools, such as, on this occasion, Westminster, Dulwich, Uppingham, Repton, St Paul's and Wellingborough. *The Times* on 4 August said of the teams that 'the players represent the best public school cricket of the day.'[5]

As the teams prepared nervously for their match, spectators in their summer finery filled the stands for two days of cricket pleasure. They had come as much to be seen as to see the cricket. What a spectacle it was. The top cricketers in these public school teams could at that time expect to walk straight into county sides once term had ended. Playing that day were young men of the calibre of Arthur Gilligan (Dulwich) who would captain England in the 1920s, and Jack Bryan (Rugby), later one of those schoolmasters who would effortlessly walk into the Kent side in his holidays.

The first day had gone badly for Lord's Schools and after a poor first innings they were forced to follow on 242 runs behind The Rest. But they rallied powerfully, making 419 in their second innings. Play on the second day was tense. Now The Rest came under pressure, and at several points it looked as if they would lose the game, before they just scrambled home at 7 o'clock that evening, with only two wickets to spare. *Wisden* said that it had been 'a great finish to a very fine match which at the end of the first day promised to be very one-sided.'[6] Not a hint was given of the frantic conversations going on at the same time in the corridors of power across Europe. Yet within five hours of the match ending, the British ultimatum to Germany had expired, and crowds took to the streets outside Lord's and across London in a patriotic frenzy. Twenty-two young cricketers had taken to the field to play in the two-day game. Before the war was over, seven would be dead.

Top scorer in the game was John Howell (Repton), whose 82 in the first innings, and 78 not out in the second, won the match for The Rest. Howell volunteered that same month, but was killed in Flanders on 25 September 1915 aged just twenty. His death was a substantial loss to English cricket: of him it was said at Repton, 'it is doubtful if we have ever had a better batsman than John Howell. None of those who played against him can doubt that had he lived he would have been going in first for England very soon after he left school.'[7] His opening partner that match, Dallas Veitch (Westminster), survived a year longer, before being killed on the Somme in August 1916. The next wicket The Rest lost that day was that of George Heslop, son of the headmaster of Sevenoaks, who had been the star player in the Lancing 1st XI that summer. Heslop captained the school cricket and football teams, and had a place at Cambridge that autumn. His sense of honour decreed that he should defer his place, to enlist instead. He rose swiftly to command a company of 16th Battalion (Public Schools Battalion) the Middlesex Regiment and was proud to be in the first wave of attack on 1 July 1916 at the Somme. He crossed No-Man's-Land at Hawthorn Ridge, close to where the mine had been detonated earlier that day, when his company ran into a wall of machine gun fire. Heslop and so many others fell, his body eventually being recovered a month or two later close to the British front line. His grieving father wrote to a Sevenoaks parent, 'I have just had a long letter from the front telling me of the finding and burial of my boy ... The war is very cruel. By our post yesterday I heard of the deaths of two more old boys. We schoolmasters have suffered'.[8]

Angus Pearson (St Paul's) was a leg-break bowler for The Rest and took an extraordinary five wickets in the first innings, destroying the Lord's Schools on the first day. Probably unknown to Heslop – we will never know – Pearson was fighting very close to him on Hawthorn Ridge, serving with the Royal Dublin Fusiliers. He too was to fall on the morning of 1 July. Rex Sherwell (Tonbridge) was one of the younger boys to play in the match, and remained at school for another year. After he left school in the summer of 1915, he joined the RFC, gaining his wings the following May, and arriving in France on 21 June 1916 to join 25 Squadron. Twelve days later, aged eighteen, and three days into the Somme battle, he was killed. 'It was just the most cruel hard luck', his commanding officer wrote to his parents. 'He had finished his work and had started to descend, well behind our lines, when a chance shell fired by German anti-aircraft guns hit the machine and all was over ... As a fighting squadron we have had very heavy casualties lately. They have all died so gallantly and your boy, in the short time he was with us, showed the same exceptional pluck and grit'.[9]

The last two cricketers to die, Stephen Morgan and George Whitehead, both attended Clifton. Neither excelled in the match, though both were judged to have immense talent. Morgan was killed in May 1915, aged just nineteen, while Whitehead was shot down on 17 October 1918, leading the dawn patrol over Ypres. An Old Cliftonian wrote, 'George Whitehead was a perfect flower of the Public Schools. Intellectually he was far above the average and was as happy with a good book as when he was scoring centuries.'[10]

Other players were severely wounded, with the result that over half the players who took to the field that day were killed or wounded. Don Denton (Wellingborough) made 79 in The Rest's first innings. A strong player, he was in the Northamptonshire side that year, but decided that he had to go off to fight. Following a severe wound, his leg was amputated. Remarkably, he went on to make three further appearances for Northamptonshire, in 1919 and 1920, using his brother as a 'runner'. The Lancashire captain is reputed to have said: 'If any fellow has been to the war and has had his leg off and wants to play, he is good enough for me and can have twenty runners.'[11]

John Barnes (Marlborough), who won the MC and Bar, and Denys Hake (Haileybury), who became headmaster of The King's School, Parramatta in Australia, were others wounded in the war. How many more players were broken or diminished in mind or body is unknown. Unknown too is how the killed and maimed might have contributed to the country had they survived. Sport is a young man's game, as war is largely, and Laurence Binyon's words, 'they shall grow not old', have a particular poignancy for schoolboy sporting prodigies. The romance, especially when they died so young, should not blind us to the waste and squandered lives of so many public schoolboys. The game at Lord's on the very eve of the war epitomizes the whole mystique of the 'lost generation'.

The Lost Generation and the public schools

Britain, her Dominions and allies 'won' the Great War: but Britain never allowed itself truly to celebrate a victory. The shattering scale of loss of three quarters of a million British lives militated against any spirit of triumphalism, and very quickly the idea became widely accepted that a generation had been wiped out, even though, of those who fought, only one in ten soldiers died, and one in five from public schools. As the initial euphoria of the post-war years evaporated, accelerated by government cuts, economic depression and the blackening sky in mainland Europe, the disillusion grew: where was that better world for which some at least thought they had been fighting? As the world tumbled towards another world war, the question was ever increasingly voiced: for what, if anything, did the lost generation die? To American historian Jay Winter, the very term 'lost generation' 'suggests a lack of closure, an unhealed wound in the survivors, a betrayal of trust between the living and the dead, an unbuilt future for their children.'[12] Not all historians, we should note, agree with the idea that Britain was scarred forever by the losses: Correlli Barnett is particularly dismissive, arguing that the Great War crippled Britain psychologically, but in no other way.

The democratic values embodied in the IWGC cemeteries sprouting along the Western Front and other war zones in the 1920s placed a private's identical gravestone alongside that of a general. Arthur Gleason, an American writer, reported a conversation during the war, when another writer asked: 'Do you think working men will ever feel bitter again, now that they have seen their officers leading them and dying for them?'[13] The magazine *John Bull* repeatedly claimed that conflict between the masses and the upper classes had ended in the trenches, as men learned to respect their officers, and officers their men. A cartoon in September 1915 showed a workman and an aristocrat in khaki shaking hands, with the caption reading, 'now we understand each other'.[14] But towards the end of the 1920s, 'war literature' and elite discourse focused on the artists, poets, thinkers and leaders who had perished, uncoupling them from the 'lost generation' of the masses.[15] The view spread that the social, cultural and intellectual elites had suffered particularly grievously, and that therefore the country would never be the same again.

Field Marshal Lord French was one of many to draw attention to the heavy loss of officers: 'we had suffered fearful casualties and the proportion of losses in officers was higher than any other rank and it was going on every day.'[16] The lives of the aristocracy and landed gentry in Britain were indeed forever changed. 'Half the great families of England, heirs of large estates and wealth, perished' wrote C. F. G. Masterman, a former member of Asquith's cabinet.[17] Reginald Pound recorded in his book *The Lost Generation* in 1964 that by the end of 1914, British fatalities included six peers, 16 baronets, six knights, 95 sons of peers, 82 sons of baronets and 84 sons of knights.[18] 'Three Wyndhams, two Grenfells and two Charterises had fallen ...The dowager Countess of Airlie ... lost a son and a son-in-law ... of the great Lord Salisbury's ten grandsons, five were killed in action ...', wrote historian David Cannadine of the war as a whole.[19]

Winter advances several reasons for this disproportionate impact. Enlistment rates were higher among the middle and upper classes, more working-class men failed medical tests for military service or only passed at lower levels required for home duty, and officers were recruited overwhelmingly from the better-off classes until late in the war, amongst whom casualty rates were much higher.[20] He writes: 'The higher up the social scale a man was, the greater were the chances that he would serve from early in the war and that he would do so in a combat unit ... Casualty rates among officers were substantially higher than the men in the ranks and the most dangerous rank in the army, the subaltern, was recruited through much of the war from current pupils or old boys of the public schools and ancient universities'.[21] In the first year of the war six per cent of the rank and file were killed, but fourteen per cent of the officer corps, and 'this continues at a slightly lower level through the war'.[22] This phenomenon was not unique to Britain. Across Europe, officer casualties were much higher than other ranks, and for similar reasons, namely that they led from the front, and their uniforms identified them as particular targets for snipers and machine gunners.[23] 'Attacks would be led by an officer', wrote Peter Parker, 'whose smart uniform set him apart from his men and made him an obvious target for the enemy ...'. The Germans instructed their men to pick off the officers in the belief that without leadership there would be widespread confusion in the ranks.[24] Public school recruits were on average five inches taller than their working class contemporaries in 1914, rendering them healthier and thus more likely to pass medical examinations, but also an easier target for German snipers as their heads were more likely to be exposed above low parapets.[25]

Universities patronized by the elites suffered disproportionately higher casualties. In provincial universities such as Liverpool and Birmingham, the ratio of men killed to those serving was 1 in 8, close to the national average. A smaller proportion of men from these universities served as officers: at Leeds it was only sixty per cent, whereas ninety-seven per cent of Oxford and Cambridge graduates were commissioned.[26] H. A. L. Fisher, President of the Board of Education, said in 1917, 'The chapels of Oxford and Cambridge display long lists of the fallen, and no institutions have suffered greater or more irreparable losses than these ancient shrines of learning and piety.'[27] Fisher, consciously or not, was overlooking the public schools, whose overall casualty rate was as high, or often higher, than both universities.[28] Research into the Eton casualties has shown that the abler one was academically, the greater the chance of being killed. One in four (24.2 per cent) of King's Scholars who fought in the war died, and of the 102 winners of the prestigious Newcastle Prize, 34.3 per cent were to die. Physical prowess seems also to have been a disadvantage. Historians Richard Carr and Bradley Hart have also found that the best rowers at Eton were more at risk of being killed: 15 of the 50 oarsmen who recorded the fastest times at Eton were to die in the war, a rate of 30 per cent,[29] while 26 per cent of Charterhouse 1st XI cricketers between 1901 and 1915 were killed.[30] If this experience was replicated across the public schools, it would support the argument that the brightest and strongest did indeed perish disproportionately.

Winter examined data from 53 public schools; our own research examines data from 192 public schools in Britain and Ireland, and a further 21 in the former Dominions, with the full figures set out in the Appendix. It confirms his 1985 thesis that one public schoolboy died for every five who served. Winter himself pointed out that virtually all books published about the war share 'consistent imprecision over casualties' and he lists thirty-three different estimates of these.[31] Not surprisingly therefore, the accuracy of data gathered by the schools is also open to question: one archivist for instance, who wished to remain anonymous, was puzzled to find names on the school war memorial of individuals who had survived the war. Confusion often surrounded the fate of those who had been recorded as 'missing', and schools had understandable difficulties in the task of record-keeping during the war, finding out information after it, and indeed deciding whether particular deaths were 'war-related'. The IWGC imposed a cut-off date of 31 August 1921 for those who could be claimed to have been killed as a result of the war, insisting that death had to be directly attributable to war-related factors, including wounds, accidents and disease; but the strictness with which public schools interpreted this is open to question. The variation we found in the rates of death could be explained by statistical inconsistencies and errors.

Allowing for such errors, and the fact that some schools could not provide a figure for the number of alumni who served in the war, our conclusions are limited to 164 schools, in England, Wales, Scotland and Ireland, which had an average death rate of between 18 and 19 per cent of those who served. The eight Irish schools separately had an average of 18.1 per cent, with Bangor GS suffering the highest rate with 21.6 per cent and Campbell College 21.2 per cent. The thirteen Scottish public schools we surveyed had a death rate of 19.5 per cent, but Loretto with 25.0 per cent and Fettes with 22.5 per cent are among the highest anywhere. Scotland had a higher volunteering rate, in its general population, than the rest of Britain, with its regiments suffering particularly badly in the battles of 1915.

Dominion school losses were only slightly lower, which is in itself remarkable as all were volunteers, only Canada bringing in conscription very late in the war. Of the 19 schools from Australia, Canada, New Zealand and South Africa, who provided figures, the average death rate is 16.5 per cent. The small sample of two New Zealand schools is highest at 19 per cent, with all the others at 16 per cent. The commitment of public schoolboys from the Dominions is an extraordinary story in itself, and one that deserves to be told at greater length than has been found possible here.

An analysis of fourteen large boarding schools (with 400 or more boys) gives an average death rate of 19.9 per cent of those who served. Fourteen smaller boarding schools (between 200 and 400 boys) have an average rate of 18.2 per cent, and fourteen large English day schools 17.3 per cent. It is difficult to know why this difference should be so, but, interestingly, a book published in 1923 also highlighted it: 'Considerable differences exist among the schools in the proportion of their old boys who served. In many the numbers were equivalent to five or six generations; in some only two or three ... Boarding schools contributed more on average than day schools, possibly because boys from larger boarding schools had great wealth and influence, and could thus risk throwing up their posts in civil life to volunteer'.[32] Some boarding schools also had a longer tradition of cadet corps, supplied more officers to the regular army and applied more peer pressure to volunteer early. The Appendix at the back of the book shows that, in almost all the bigger boarding schools, the number of deaths is greater than the number in the school in 1914, but this does not appear to be true of the wider spectrum of schools.

Our separate analysis of the Rolls of Honour of a varied selection of twenty-eight public schools, who had a total of 6,459 deaths between them, revealed that every year of the war, except 1914, was almost equally deadly.[33] The worst year for public school deaths was 1916, which saw 25.4 per cent of the total, compared to 24.4 per cent in 1917, 22 per cent in 1918 and 20.8 per cent in 1915. Those schools with long-established military traditions that sent large numbers into the professional army, and those with a higher proportion of early volunteers, suffered most in the early phases of the war. Winchester thus lost 37.6 per cent of its total in 1914–15, and Marlborough 31.1 per cent, whereas the figures for RGS Newcastle and Queen's Taunton in that period are 15.8 and 11.5 per cent respectively. Eton lost 192 of its old boys, 17 per cent of its total, before the end of 1914. Lancing, in contrast, had only 7 deaths (out of 163), 4.3 per cent, by the first Christmas.[34]

More men died as second lieutenants than any other rank, nearly a third of all public school deaths: 38 per cent of Sherborne's dead were second lieutenants, whereas at Winchester it was only 25.7 per cent, the latter having a higher proportion than most of senior officers killed – 15 per cent of Wykehamists killed were of the rank of major and above. By contrast, Manchester GS has only four such senior officer casualties in 480 killed. If the war was won by the second lieutenants, then

241

Harrow mourned 124 of them. Big provincial city day schools tended to have a much higher proportion serving as other ranks than the boarding schools: Manchester Grammar School had 153 killed while serving as privates and 222 other non-officer ranks out of a total of 480. By contrast, Marlborough had just 27 in the ranks killed out of 733, Charterhouse 21 out of 687, and Harrow 20 out of 644.

Most striking is the death rate among those who had recently left school. Over 50 per cent of the deaths in the twenty-eight schools were aged 24 or under, nearly half of them in the 18–20 age group. Three quarters of those killed were under the age of thirty. Public school rolls of honour were dominated by those who had been pupils in the fifteen years between 1900 and 1914. Of the fifty-seven boys who entered Radley in the calendar year 1910, twenty-two were to die, constituting 38 per cent of the total;[35] of 42 boys who entered Harrow in just the summer term of 1910, 16 were killed, again 38 per cent.[36] The oldest known public schoolboys to die in action were sixty-eight years old: Lieutenant Henry Webber (Tonbridge), was killed on the Somme on 21 July 1916, and Major Jasper Richardson (Rugby) saw three years of active service before being killed in March 1918 within days of his sixty-ninth birthday.[37] The youngest public schoolboy killed in the army appears to have been Second Lieutenant Cyril Hillier of Cheltenham, who was commissioned straight from school in 1914, was badly wounded in January 1915 and died of his wounds in England, in February 1915, still only seventeen. *The Cheltonian* recorded that 'even in the Crimean War there does not appear to be a younger Cheltonian killed', although in the Royal Navy sixteen-year-old midshipmen from Dartmouth, but some also originally from conventional public schools, perished at Jutland and in other engagements, including Anthony Eden's brother Nicholas.

The most deadly single campaign was the Somme, which accounted for 16 per cent of public school deaths. RBAI lost 15 old boys on the first day, 1 July, over 10 per cent of its total war losses. Passchendaele and the Spring Offensive in 1918 were almost as deadly campaigns, as was Gallipoli, but 90 per cent of public school casualties were on the Western Front. The infantry saw the highest loss of all service branches: 34 per cent of Old Carthusians who served in the infantry were killed, compared to 23 per cent in the RFC, 17 per cent in the engineers and 14 per cent in the artillery.[38] The war, for public schoolboys, was also overwhelmingly the Army's war. Over 91 per cent of the casualties came in the army, with only 6 per cent in the RFC and just 2 per cent in the Royal Navy. Nearly 10 per cent of deaths came from accidents or disease.

Throughout public schools, as in the country at large, the memorials to the fallen of the Great War eclipse in size and grandeur those of the Second World War, reflecting both the different public moods in 1918 and 1945, but also the comparative size of the losses. British forces suffered 384,000 military deaths during the Second World War, and a further 67,000 civilians were killed. Although nearly twice as many British servicemen died during the Great War, a survey of the relative figures, in an admittedly very small number of public schools, do not quite reflect that national statistic. At Eton, 1,157 died in the Great War, compared to 748 during the Second. At Haileybury, the figures are 589 and 314, at Tonbridge, 415 and 301. Brighton College, which expanded considerably during the interwar period, bucks the trend, with 146 killed in the First World War compared to 165 in the Second. The average death rate for nine schools selected and surveyed was 13.4 per cent in the Second World War, roughly in line with the national average, and considerably lower than for the Great War.[39] Public school deaths in 1939–45 were also far less dominated by the army; at Tonbridge, for instance, more died in the RAF than in the army, the greatest toll being in Bomber Command. Deeds of heroism might have been every bit as great in the 1939–45 war, but as we now see, many fewer Victoria Crosses were awarded.

Public School VCs

In the Great War 627 men were awarded the Victoria Cross, of whom 163 are known to have been educated in British and Dominion public schools, twenty-six per cent of the total: in contrast, only 181 VCs were awarded during the Second World War. Over half the Victoria Crosses to have been awarded in history were given in the four years of the Great War. The only 'double' VC was won by Noel Chavasse (Magdalen College School and Liverpool College), although Arthur Martin-Leake (Westminster) added a second VC to the one he won in the Boer War. Both were officers in the RAMC. The army, not surprisingly, dominated the award of the public school VCs, with 137, 18 being awarded to Royal Navy officers and 8 to RFC officers. Four of the army public school VCs were awarded to other ranks (a sergeant, two corporals and a private – Private Robert Cruickshank of Bancroft's School, the lowest-ranked recipient). Two were awarded to generals, Major General Clifford Coffin and Brigadier-General George Grogan, both from Haileybury.[40] At least five were awarded to members of staff at public schools. Twelve VCs were won by public school alumni on the first four days of the Spring Offensive, 21–25 March 1918. At Mons and Le Cateau from 23–26 August 1914 seven were awarded; at the Gallipoli landings on 25 April 1915, and the Zeebrugge Raid 22 April 1918, six were given on each occasion.

Ninety-two different public schools had a VC winner during the war, though some attended more than one school, including Albert Ball, a pupil at both Nottingham HS and Trent. Attempts by the newspapers to publish league tables of awards generally failed, because schools were unwilling to give the press the information they sought. Had such a table existed, the awards given would have reflected the numbers serving from each school, rather than the bravery or the culture of any particular school. Eton thus won thirteen VCs, followed by Harrow with eight, Cheltenham and Haileybury[41] each with six, Wellington, Clifton and Dulwich each with five, then Rugby, Uppingham and Winchester, whose alumni were awarded four VCs each.

Captain Edward Bradbury (Marlborough) was one of the first to win the VC. A thirty-three-year-old professional soldier in the Royal Horse Artillery, he was part of the first cavalry brigade on the morning of 1 September 1914, when his battery was suddenly surprised by a German bombardment and subsequent fierce attack. Bradbury managed to swing three guns into action at only 600 yards range, though two were immediately destroyed by German shells. With his gunner, Bradbury kept the third gun in action, despite intense bombardment. Eventually a shell exploded nearby, blowing off both Bradbury's legs. 'Though the captain knew that death was very near, he thought of his men to the last and begged to be carried away, so that they should not be upset by seeing him, or hearing the cries which he could not restrain', recalled Gunner Darbyshire.[42] Two of his men were awarded VCs for the action, alongside the posthumous award to Bradbury himself.

Major Billy Congreve (Eton) won his VC in July 1916 on the Somme. The son of Major General (later General) Sir Walter Congreve (Harrow), who had won a VC in the Boer War, Billy had won the DSO, the MC and the *Legion d'Honneur* by the time he arrived on the Somme in 1916. His award was for 'sustained gallantry' between 6 and 20 July while serving as Brigade Major of 76 Brigade, particular actions including tending the wounded under heavy fire, positioning himself in exposed positions to direct an attack, and personal reconnaissance of the enemy lines. He fell to a sniper's bullet on 20 July. His father, General Congreve, was in a conference when he was told the news. 'When I told him what had happened, he was absolutely calm to all outward appearance', recalled a fellow officer. 'After a few seconds of silence, he said quite calmly, "He was a good soldier"'. That is all that he allowed to appear. I shall never forget the incident or lose the admiration I felt for the marvellous self-suppression of the "man" in the capacity of the commander.'[43]

Harold Maufe (Uppingham) had suffered the loss of his elder brother on the Somme before he arrived in France. On 4 June 1917, aged only nineteen, Harold was serving near Arras, when he was told about a break in the telephone line between the artillery battery and its forward observation post. Despite a hail of falling shells, Maufe went out and calmly patched up the wires. 'Then he returned and was lying rather done up on the floor when he heard an explosion outside. He ran out and finding some burning boxes near our own cartridges, he pulled them into a shell-hole and dashed across to the shed where the real trouble was – a dump containing gas and HE shells. Finding some fuse boxes alight he went and carried buckets of water and succeeded in saving the HE shells, about 1,000 rounds. In the midst of this the gas shells went up ... [he] never left his job until the wounded had been safely removed ... It was easily the finest piece of work I have known out here', wrote his superior officer, Captain Williams, to his parents.[44] Maufe was to survive the war, but while serving on Home Guard duty in 1942, a trench mortar misfired during an exercise and killed him.

Prime Ministers and the Great War

Prime Minister Stanley Baldwin (Harrow) on occasion sought to explain his governments' limited political success in the inter-war years by reference to the 'absence of men of talent who would have been available for public service had there been no war'.[45] This 'lost generation' legend has been used many times since to explain Britain's difficulties in facing the political and economic challenge of the inter-war years, and her subsequent decline. The idea touched a strong vein in national consciousness. Fifty years later, indeed, in 1986, Ian MacGregor, head of British Steel, remarked that, 'even today we have not fully replaced the dynamism and leadership qualities of the generation that we threw away in the First World War.'[46]

The thinking and actions of all prime ministers in office are affected by their own experiences, and by their understanding of history. The Great War affected Prime Ministers covering a span of seventy years. They responded in different ways, either having their predispositions reinforced, as was the case with Clement Attlee, or forging a fresh outlook altogether, as happened to Harold Macmillan. What is beyond doubt is that the Great War was a formative experience, perhaps *the* formative experience, of them all.

Old Etonian Lord Salisbury's period of office, 1895–1902, was over by the time the Great War broke out, and he died in 1903, but five of his ten male grandchildren were killed in action. Educated at Winchester or Westminster, they were to die in successive years of the war: Lieutenant George Cecil, killed in France in September 1914, Lieutenant Rupert Gascoyne-Cecil, in France in July 1915, Captain Robert Palmer, in Mesopotamia in January 1916, Lieutenant Randle Gascoyne-Cecil, in France in February 1917 and Captain John Gascoyne-Cecil, in August 1918. The Gascoyne-Cecils were three of the four sons of the Bishop of Exeter, and the memorial service for Rupert was held in the church at Hatfield, conducted by his greatest friend, G. K. A. Bell, chaplain to the Archbishop of Canterbury, who spoke of 'one whose love is gentle and pure, whose love of all nature drew all hearts to him.'

Arthur Balfour (Prime Minister 1902–05) was educated at Eton as was his uncle, Lord Salisbury, whom he succeeded. As a bachelor, Balfour lost no children himself in the war, but was very involved in its conduct, as First Lord of the Admiralty when in May 1915 the Conservatives were brought into the Coalition government, and then from December 1916 as Foreign Secretary. Asquith (City of London School, and Prime Minister, 1908–16) was a less effective wartime leader than he had been as a peacetime premier in the years leading up to August 1914. He worried greatly about his sons fighting at the front, the oldest of whom, Raymond, was killed on the Somme in September 1916. The impact of the loss of his beloved boy at such a crucial time politically and militarily was profound.

Andrew Bonar Law (High School of Glasgow) succeeded Balfour as leader of the Conservative Party in 1911. He became Chancellor of the Exchequer in December 1916, and succeeded Lloyd George as Prime Minister in October 1922, serving until May 1923. Two of his sons were killed in the war and he found difficulty managing the loss: 'Night seems to have descended upon him. For the moment he was incapable of work and could only sit despondently gazing into vacancy. All those dark clouds which were never far below the horizon in his thought came rolling up obliterating light and happiness', wrote Conservative historian Robert Blake.[47] His son Richard Law (Shrewsbury) was too young to fight in the war, and wrote in September 1939: 'When one thinks of it, all those who were killed last time, all of those who are going to be killed now, everything wasted through the stubbornness and lack of imagination of a few old men and the shamelessness of a lot of young ones.'[48] Law was a member of Churchill's wartime coalition from 1940, and was with him when he heard the news of Hitler's death.[49] Stanley Baldwin, who succeeded Bonar Law, was Prime Minister until 1929, and again from 1935 to 1937. Baldwin, like his successor, Neville Chamberlain (Rugby), who lost two cousins, was profoundly affected by the losses in the Great War, and the appeasement policy of the 1930s was shaped by the desire of both men to avoid another terrible war.

The next four prime ministers, Churchill, Attlee, Eden and Macmillan, all fought on the Western Front and, in Attlee's case Gallipoli as well. Winston Churchill (Harrow) was Prime Minister from May 1940 to July 1945 and again from 1951 to 1955. A few years younger than Baldwin and Chamberlain, and aged 39 when war broke out, he was the first to see active service in the war; he had taken part in earlier campaigns on the north-west frontier of India and in the Sudan in 1898. On 5 October 1914 he went to Antwerp, which the Belgian government was proposing to evacuate in the face of German attacks, to rally morale, but the city fell on 10 October with the loss of 2,500 men. Churchill then became the main political victim of the failed Dardanelles campaign, of which he was the principal architect. When Asquith formed his all-party Coalition government in May 1915, the Conservatives demanded his demotion from the First Lord of the Admiralty as their price for entry, and he resigned in November 1915. He spent time with the 2nd Battalion Grenadier Guards in France, before being appointed Lieutenant Colonel commanding the 6th Battalion Royal Scots Fusiliers on 1 January 1916. He made some thirty-six forays into No-Man's-Land, and spent part of his time at Ploegsteert in the Ypres Salient. His motive for fighting was in part to rehabilitate his reputation, but he relished being back in the front line and taking part in the action, as he had earlier in his career. He returned to England in March 1916, re-entering the government in July 1917 as Minister of Munitions, a post he held until the end of the war.

Churchill's experience of war was shorter than that of the other three and, unlike Attlee and Macmillan, he suffered no physical wounds. The war nevertheless shaped his thinking in many ways, particularly his reluctance to expose British troops in the Second World War to the same high level of casualties. When General Marshall, chairman of the American Joint Chiefs of Staff, visited London to urge the early opening of a Second Front in northern Europe, Churchill's doctor, Lord Moran, told him: 'It's no use, you are arguing against the casualties on the Somme.'[50]

In May 1944 Churchill took to the House of Commons with him another American, John McCloy, the Assistant Secretary for War, and began talking to him about his early parliamentary career. 'Suddenly,' McCloy recalled, 'he referred to the number of his early contemporaries who had been killed during what he called the hecatombs of World War One'. He went on to say that most of his generation lay dead at

Passchendaele and the Somme and Britain could not afford the loss of another generation.[51]

Clement Attlee had been to Haileybury between 1896 and 1901, an experience he appears to have enjoyed, despite his leadership for twenty years of a Labour Party profoundly hostile to public schools. 'He remained devoted to his school, and kept a close eye on his contemporaries in later life' writes R. C. Whiting.[52] After Oxford, he took the job of resident manager at a boys' club in Stepney supported by Haileybury. When war came in 1914, he was commissioned and saw action at Gallipoli, in Mesopotamia, and in France in 1918. His decision to fight led to a break with his brother Tom, a conscientious objector who spent part of the war in prison. During Gallipoli he fell ill with dysentery, which meant he missed the Battle of Sari Bair, during which many of his comrades were killed. When fit he returned to the Dardanelles and was the penultimate British officer to be evacuated from Suvla Bay. He never blamed Churchill, his long-standing political adversary, for the Gallipoli campaign: rather, it made him admire Churchill, as he believed the campaign had been bold and failed only through errors of strategy on the ground.[53] He finished the war as Major Attlee, a title he continued to use in the 1920s as he worked his way up the ranks of the Labour Party. The war gave him a confidence, an ability to lead and to act decisively and ruthlessly. But he was appalled by the waste of so much young life and he was fired by a desire to build a better Britain for those who had fought and suffered during the war. Attlee's socialism sat oddly with his loyalty to his alma mater. One of his last actions before he left for the front in 1914 was to visit Haileybury to say farewell to his former housemaster. He was back at the school in July 1917 for a concert and was a frequent visitor after the war, according to the visitor books.[54]

Anthony Eden (Prime Minister 1955–57) enjoyed Eton despite never being a star pupil, his housemaster 'Jelly' Churchill describing him as 'thoughtful and steady'. When Eden told him in June 1915 that he wanted to leave Eton at the end of that term, he said he was too young and immature: 'You fool, you fool. You won't be any use in the war. You might be of some use in the house four [rowing]'.[55] Sixty years after the Somme, Eden published an account of his early years, *Another World 1897–1917*, which does not even mention his winning of the MC. He concluded: 'I had entered the holocaust still childish and had emerged tempered by my experience, but with my illusions intact neither shattered nor cynical, to face a changed world.'[56] He was certainly a brave soldier. In August 1916 he led a trench raid in which his platoon sergeant, Harrop, was wounded and bleeding profusely.

He fixed a tourniquet on him in No-Man's-Land, and helped carry him back to safety on a stretcher, despite being under fire. Harrop later recalled of Eden: 'Everyone liked him and he was popularly known as "The Boy". After we'd been in any heavy fighting Mr Eden would see that we were all provided for and made reasonably comfortable before giving thought to his own comfort.'[57] He became the youngest brigade-major in the British Army at the age of just twenty-one, and was only twenty-two when the war ended, after which he went up to Oxford to take a first in Oriental languages at Christ Church. His biographer D. R. Thorpe said of him: 'as a survivor of the 'lost generation', he felt it incumbent on himself to work, in however small a capacity, to create a better world. Idealism not cynicism was the legacy Eden drew from his experiences in war, and this unsentimental sense of responsibility for the welfare of others was always to condition his thinking.'[58]

Harold Macmillan (Prime Minister 1957–1963), unlike Eden, was not happy at Eton; he was plagued by illness and his stay was brief. In later life he was happy to wear his Old Etonian tie, but he never showed much fondness for visiting his old school, even when his son was there. The school merits just a brief mention in his six-volume memoirs. Macmillan was nevertheless an establishment man through and through, who soon after joining up in 1914 secured a transfer to the prestigious Grenadier Guards, where the officers came from the top public schools. Far from a model military figure, he nevertheless had a good war. He acted with courage in the shambles of the Battle of Loos in 1915, his first action, and was then badly wounded on 15 September 1916 in the Guards' attack on the Somme at Ginchy, during which Raymond Asquith and so many of Macmillan's fellow officers and contemporaries were to die. 'I was shot at short range while half crawling, half crouching. The machine gun bullets penetrated my left thigh just below the hip, I afterwards discovered that they had stuck in my pelvis', he later wrote. 'I rolled down into a large shell hole where I lay days ... I had in my pocket Aeschylus's *Prometheus* in Greek. It is a play I knew very well and seemed not inappropriate to my position, so, as there seemed nothing better to do, and I could not move in any direction, I read it intermittently'.[59]

Macmillan was evacuated home and spent the next two years recovering from wounds which were to cause him pain for the rest of his life. Like many fellow officers, he was critical of the generals and staff officers, believing that the main legacy of the war for him was understanding more about the lives of men from very different back-grounds, and gaining the confidence to be able to relate to them, a legacy that informed his commitment to tackling unemployment in the inter-war and post-war years. Like many who served, he experienced 'survivor guilt', which the passing years did nothing to diminish: 'We began to feel a sense of guilt for not having shared the fate of our friends and comrades. We certainly felt some obligation to make some decent use of the life that had been spared to us ... I could not face going back to Oxford. Whenever I went there, it seemed to be 'a city of ghosts'. A certain bitterness began to eat into our hearts at the easy way in which many of our elders seemed to take up again, and play with undiminished zest, the game of politics, "old men lived: the young men died".'[60]

The generation lost

While Siegfried Sassoon was in Craiglockhart hospital in 1917, under the watchful eye of the physician W. H. R. Rivers, he penned the most ironic and bitter poem of the war, 'Does it Matter?', published in his collection *Counter Attack and Other Poems* in 1918. The poem has three verses, each vividly describing a soldier who is suffering from a different injury, and was written as his response to the severe injuries of those he knew, as well as a reaction to his own fear of being blinded in the war. The first stanza runs, 'Does it matter? – losing your legs? .../ For people will always be kind,/And you need not show that you mind/When others come in after hunting/To gobble their muffins and eggs.' He told Robert Ross, his friend and literary critic, about another friend, the pianist Ralph Greaves, who lost an arm shortly before Sassoon wrote the poem.[61] Substantial numbers of young men had suffered amputations during the war. Twenty years after the Armistice, the British government was still paying disability pensions to 8,000 men who had one or both legs amputated and to 3,600 others still alive but with one or both arms amputated.[62]

Many soldiers were severely disfigured as a result of their wounds. Harold Gillies, who had attended a prep school near Rugby before going to Wanganui College in New Zealand and then came back to Caius, Cambridge, was foremost amongst those who worked on facial reconstruction. Many soldiers had parts of their face shot away, losing jaws, missing noses and suffering holes in their cheeks and heads. Gillies pressed the War Office to take such cases seriously and, after the carnage of the first day of the Somme, persuaded the War Office to let him open the Queen's Hospital in Sidcup, Kent, which had a thousand beds, for those involved in facial reconstruction. During the interwar years and after, bystanders would often see men walking the streets with hideously disfigured faces and warped bodies, but living a life of sorts.[63]

In the second stanza of his poem, Sassoon writes, 'Does it matter? – losing your sight?/There's such splendid work for the blind;/And people will always be kind,/As you sit on the terrace remembering/And turning your face to the light.' With such large numbers blinded in the war, as brilliantly depicted by John Singer Sargent in his famous painting *Gassed*, Sassoon's fear of loss of sight was real. In 1938 the government was still paying disability pensions to 2,000 survivors who were totally blind, and to another 8,000 partially blinded men. Much was done for them by the tireless work of Arthur Pearson (Winchester), the newspaper magnate who founded the *Daily Express* and who began his career working on *Tit-bits* magazine. Pearson began losing his sight to glaucoma and later went completely blind. In 1915 he founded the St Dunstan's Home for soldiers blinded by gas attacks or other traumas during the war, with its first base at St Dunstan's Hotel in Regent's Park. Its aim was to provide vocational training rather than charity for invalided servicemen, and thus to enable them to lead productive and independent lives. One of the first residents was Angus Buchanan (Monmouth), who had won the VC on the 5 April 1916 in Mesopotamia, carrying two wounded men back to British lines under heavy machine gun fire. The following year, he was shot in the head by a sniper and blinded, becoming the only VC of the war to have lost his sight. Pearson's was an indomitable spirit, captured in the book he wrote in 1919.[64] His right-hand man was Ian Fraser (Marlborough), who was struck in the head by a German bullet on the Somme on 20 July 1916. When his bandages were removed after he had been sent back to the London General Hospital, it was found that he had lost his sight in both eyes. Hearing about him, Pearson wrote him a letter explaining how he himself had become blind but had made the most of his life. The letter was delivered by a lady whom Fraser later married, and when Pearson died in an accident in 1921, Fraser was chosen to succeed him as chairman of St Dunstan's, a position he held for 52 years. His own autobiography, *Whereas I was Blind*, was written during the Second World War to encourage soldiers who suffered the same fate.[65]

Sassoon's third verse runs, 'Do they matter? – those dreams from the pit?/You can drink and forget and be glad,/And people won't say that you're mad;/For they know that you've fought for your country,/And no one will worry a bit.' To Sassoon's worries about his own mental health, and thoughts about the haunted patients ensconced in Craiglockhart, was added the news that Julian Dadd, who had lost both his brothers in the war, one at Gallipoli and one at Saint Quentin, as well as his voice after being hit in the neck, had suffered a mental breakdown.[66] Dadd served with Sassoon in the Royal Welch Fusiliers and had met him last in December the previous year.

In 1938, an estimated 15,000 men had still been unable to resume normal employment due to head injuries, 25,000 were still suffering from nervous disorders, and a further 3,200 were still committed to mental asylums. These figures considerably underestimate the number of veterans who suffered trauma and unhappiness to the end of their lives emanating from their war experience. Many did not want to talk about it. The government equally did not much want to hear about it. Historian Adrian Gregory writes that, 'the state authorities, particularly the permanent civil service, proved to be generally unsympathetic'. The civil servant with most overall responsibility, Charles Adair Hore, saw his role as being more concerned with protecting the public purse than looking after the rights of disabled servicemen.[67]

Nine hundred thousand soldiers from Britain and her Dominions had been wiped out, some two or three million more had been wounded, and an incalculable number, combatants and civilians, had been scarred by mental and physical trauma, by loss and grief deriving from the war. The numbers affected, whether public school alumni or not, are so vast that the loss can be made more intelligible by focusing on the life of a single individual. This 'narrowed-down' approach is enhanced by the power of the ever-increasing material on the internet, and is used increasingly by schools and by museums and visitor centres along the Western Front.

Wilfred Willett, the St Paul's boy and London medical student, is one such individual. Badly wounded in the head at Ploegsteert Wood, Ypres, in December 1914, he was nursed back to health by the loving attention of his wife Eileen, who had travelled out to France to bring him back. When he realized that he would never be able to pursue his vocation of becoming a doctor, Wilfred fell into deep depression. The once hyper-energetic and warmly sociable student and subaltern became subject to violent mood swings, making life often unbearable for his wife and three children. His close friend Henry Williamson (Colfe's), who had served with him in the London Rifle Brigade at Ploegsteert Wood, and who emerged physically unscathed, could not cope with this shadow of the man he once knew and moved to the far right in the 1930s. Wilfred's response was equally strong: he became a Marxist, writing regular nature articles in the *Daily Worker*, the communist newspaper. The two close friends never spoke again; Henry Williamson's comradely inscription to Wilfred in a copy of *Lone Swallows*, reproduced at the front of this book, was thus not a greeting but a farewell. Wilfred's son, with whom he had a poor relationship, died in

1955 in his early forties: his daughters were affected in different ways by their gloomy and unpredictable upbringing. Wilfred remained desperate to become a writer, something he saw many of his contemporaries achieve, including Williamson, who won the Hawthornden Prize for literature in 1928 with his *Tarka the Otter,* and Eileen would hide for days the manuscripts rejected regularly by publishers. All he could have published was a small number of books on British birds, scant consolation. His was a much diminished life. He died in 1961, whilst still in his sixties, only weeks after his beloved Eileen.

Wilfred was unable ever to free himself from his experiences in those months at the front. His elder daughter suffered particularly from neuroses and anxieties, which in turn affected her children, and they can all be dated back to that day on the 13 December, 1914, when a German sniper fired a bullet into Wilfred's head. The merest fraction of a centimetre in one direction, and he would have been killed outright, while a short distance in the other and the bullet would have missed his head entirely. Had it done so, the likelihood for an officer who joined up so early is that he would have been wounded or killed later in the war. Wilfred Willett was Anthony Seldon's grandfather, his elder daughter Anthony's mother. He and his entire family thus owe their very existence to the minute calculations of that unknown German sniper, and the capricious strength of the passing wind that day a hundred years ago in a once tranquil Belgian wood.

Appendix

List of public schools war statistics

When we started on this book, we asked the archivists of all current HMC schools to answer a questionnaire about their school's history in relation to the Great War. Apart from questions leading to the figures below, we also asked about teachers and support staff who served, decorations awarded, the commemoration of the war, the OTC, and the commemoration and battlefield trips the school undertakes today. In addition, schools were asked for particular source material they might have on old boys killed, poignant stories, and life in the school during the war. This was then followed up by many schools sending in rich source material from magazines, archives and external sources. All of this material has been the bedrock of the book.

The statistics below are those supplied by school archivists. Most of the figures were compiled ninety or more years ago, and have to be taken on trust by the archivists as well as ourselves. All schools have war memorials, in some form or other, where the names of the dead can be found, so schools know, or think they know, how many of their old boys were killed in the Great War. The numbers who served are harder to ascertain, unless someone between 1914 and 1920 kept careful records. One would, however, expect these numbers to be at least three times the size of the school in 1914. Even if there were differences between schools in the numbers volunteering in 1914–15, conscription from 1916 should have meant that all medically fit alumni between the ages of 18 and 40 would be called up. In the figures below there are clear anomalies and differences. The numbers who served are six times the size of the school in 1914 in some schools, and in others two times or less. Similarly, in virtually all the bigger boarding schools the numbers killed are more than, or at least equal to, the size of the school in 1914; in others they represent a much smaller proportion. Since these bigger schools clearly had no monopoly on courage and sacrifice, it is quite possible that smaller schools, struggling with the records during and immediately after the war, have failed to record accurately the numbers who served and even to record alumni who died. Subject to these statistical limitations and a need to treat a few individual school figures with caution, our conclusion is that the death rate across all 185 home and overseas schools, whose statistics below include both numbers who served and numbers killed, is between eighteen and nineteen per cent. These statistics are analysed more fully in Chapter 10.

Finally, a word is needed on the schools included. The first chapter examined the far from straightforward question of what was a public school in 1914, but we have marked HMC members in 1914 in the list below. We have decided to spread the net more widely, and the list contains most current HMC schools, but eighteen did not respond to the request for information, including three who were HMC members in 1914, and some current HMC members, such as Stowe, were founded later.Those HMC members in 1914 which either no longer exist or are not part of HMC today are: Beaumont College, Carlisle GS, Royal Naval Colleges Dartmouth and Osborne, Oxford HS, Owen's School Islington, Newcastle HS (Staffs), Weymouth College, and Wyggeston School. In the list below are 192 schools in the British Isles, another 21 overseas and one public school for girls, Cheltenham Ladies' College.

Key to table below: NK = not known
                       * = HMC member in 1914

Public Schools in England, Scotland, Wales and Ireland

School name	Number of pupils in 1914	Pupils served	Number killed	% killed
Abbotsholme	20	192	30	15.6
Abingdon	111	369	68	18.4
Alleyn's	635	1,863	264	14.2
Ampleforth	130	NK	64	NK
Ardingly	333	1,000	145	14.5
Arnold	186	285	37	13.0
Ashville	80	261	31	11.9
Bablake	320	771	96	12.5
Bancrofts	314	834	168	20.1
Bangor GS	76	176	38	21.6

School name	Number of pupils in 1914	Pupils served	Number killed	% killed
Barnard Castle	270	735	157	21.4
Bedales	158	278	63	22.7
Bedford School*	675	2,200	472	21.5
Bedford Modern	351	1,083	167	15.4
Berkhamsted*	NK	1,233	231	18.7
Birkenhead*	210	553	96	17.4
Bloxham	120	402	76	18.9
Blundells*	240	972	195	20.1
Bootham*	97	419	56	13.4
Bishop's Stortford*	196	456	61	13.4
Bradfield*	172	1,375	279	20.3
Bradford GS*	584	1,150	215	18.7
Brentwood	230	300	59	19.7
Brighton*	280	976	146	15.0
Bristol GS*	331	703	121	17.2
Bromsgrove*	150	427	92	21.5
Bury GS	164	612	97	15.8
Campbell*	155	594	126	21.2
Caterham	162	NK	69	NK
Charterhouse*	579	3,500	687	19.6
Cheadle Hulme	222	375	61	16.3
Cheltenham*	584	3,540	675	19.1
Cheltenham Ladies' College	725	2,000	10	0.5
Chigwell*	80	NK	79	NK
Christ's Hospital*	765	2,058	358	17.4
Christ's Brecon*	120	447	55	12.3
Churchers	78	330	50	15.2
City of London*	708	1,710	291	17.0
Clayesmore	79	NK	39	NK
Clifton*	594	3,063	577	18.8
Clongowes Wood	268	604	95	15.7
ColeraineAcademical Inst.	120	335	64	19.1
Colfe's	260	717	124	17.3
Cranleigh	207	950	172	18.1
Culford	95	284	60	21.1
Dame Allan's	150	652	84	12.9
Daniel Stewart's	457	1,103	215	19.5
Dauntseys	70	209	38	18.2

School name	Number of pupils in 1914	Pupils served	Number killed	% killed
Dean Close*	195	690	128	18.6
Denstone*	90	1,000	163	16.3
Dollar	387	745	161	21.6
Dover College*	NK	827	150	18.1
Downside*	NK	506	109	21.5
Dulwich*	742	3,036	506	16.7
Durham School*	175	536	103	19.2
Eastbourne*	201	879	164	18.7
Edinburgh Academy*	595	1,539	298	19.4
Elizabeth College, Guernsey*	98	662	105	15.9
Ellesmere	191	636	111	17.5
Eltham	124	120	34	28.3
Emanuel	600	801	139	17.4
Epsom*	275	942	154	16.3
Eton*	1,028	5,656	1,157	20.5
Exeter*	129	380	72	18.9
Felsted*	255	1,262	244	19.3
Fettes*	200	1,094	246	22.5
Forest	160	500	98	19.6
Foyle	200	490	72	14.7
Framlingham	300	957	138	14.4
George Watson's	1,209	3,102	605	19.5
George Heriot's	1,400	2,637	411	15.6
Giggleswick*	165	735	122	16.6
Glasgow Academy	681	1,375	327	23.8
Glasgow HS	1,000	2,700	478	17.7
Glenalmond*	119	685	157	22.9
Gresham's*	230	500	106	21.2
Haberdashers' Aske's*	386	NK	106	NK
Haileybury*	475	2,825	589	20.8
Hampton	196	500	75	15.0
Harrow*	504	2,917	644	22.1
Highgate*	532	1,168	221	18.9
Hulme GS	156	227	49	21.6
Hurstpierpoint	174	650	108	16.6
Hymers*	170	NK	117	NK
Ipswich*	160	414	71	17.1
John Lyon	105	200	57	28.5

School name	Number of pupils in 1914	Pupils served	Number killed	% killed
KCS Wimbledon*	294	789	159	20.2
Kelly	60	364	58	15.9
Kent	95	250	51	20.4
KES Bath	212	560	75	13.4
KES Birmingham*	473	1,400	246	17.6
KES Lytham	160	NK	37	NK
KES Southampton	369	450	50	11.1
KES Witley	238	700	96	13.7
King's Bruton	82	282	55	19.5
King's Canterbury*	131	820	150	18.3
King's Chester*	170	415	57	13.7
King's Ely	100	139	24	17.3
King's Gloucester	50	NK	31	NK
King's Macclesfield	190	412	84	20.4
King's Taunton	101	414	82	19.8
King's Worcester*	179	450	86	19.1
Kingston GS	87	222	34	15.3
Kingswood	183	650	116	17.8
King William's IOM*	172	543	136	25.0
Lancaster RGS*	320	399	75	18.8
Lancing*	274	820	163	19.9
Latymer Upper	512	NK	216	NK
Leighton Park	41	149	28	18.8
Liverpool*	294	620	126	20.3
Loretto*	83	592	148	25.0
Loughborough GS	125	315	58	18.4
Magdalen CS*	64	228	47	20.6
Malvern*	424	2,481	457	18.4
Marlborough*	590	3,418	733	21.4
Merchant Taylor's, Northwood*	443	1,820	297	16.3
Merchant Taylor's Crosby*	330	731	155	21.2
Merchiston Castle*	196	851	168	19.7
Manchester GS	1,023	3,506	522	14.9
Methodist Belfast	305	428	80	18.7
Mill Hill*	274	909	193	21.2
Monkton Combe*	78	454	64	14.1
Monmouth*	NK	NK	75	NK
Morrisons	270	426	72	16.9

School name	Number of pupils in 1914	Pupils served	Number killed	% killed
Norwich*	125	278	52	18.7
Nottingham HS*	357	937	189	20.2
Oakham*	90	425	66	15.5
Oundle*	352	1,044	221	21.2
Perse*	189	539	88	16.3
Plymouth*	250	566	106	18.7
Pocklington	47	272	59	21.7
Portsmouth GS*	290	870	129	14.8
QEGS Blackburn	200	560	65	11.6
QEGS Wakefield*	312	403	82	20.3
QEH Bristol	107	300	39	13.0
Queen's Taunton	NK	510	62	12.2
Radley*	213	1,165	225	19.3
Ratcliffe	100	286	55	19.2
Reigate GS	142	306	53	17.3
Repton*	330	1,912	355	18.6
RGS Guildford	228	NK	58	NK
RGS Newcastle*	475	1,114	158	14.2
RGS Worcester*	320	550	89	16.2
Rossall*	295	1,617	293	18.1
Royal Belfast AI	514	703	132	18.8
Royal Hospital School	800	2,750	442	16.1
Rugby*	555	3,244	686	21.1
Ruthin	80	174	39	22.4
Rydal	45	243	63	25.9
Sedbergh*	252	1,260	251	19.9
Sevenoaks	100	350	36	10.3
Sherborne*	267	1,174	221	18.8
Shrewsbury*	386	1,825	321	17.6
Silcoates	89	248	41	16.5
Solihull	150	240	44	18.3
St Alban's*	249	NK	108	NK
St Bees*	304	940	180	19.1
St Benedict's	NK	NK	21	NK
St Columba's	80	389	67	17.2
St Dunstan's	600	977	227	23.2
St Edmund's, Canterbury*	120	330	52	15.8
St Edward's, Oxford*	132	520	114	21.9

School name	Number of pupils in 1914	Pupils served	Number killed	% killed
St George's, Weybridge	NK	NK	52	NK
St John's, Leatherhead*	285	768	158	20.6
St Lawrence, Ramsgate*	211	735	131	17.8
St Paul's*	574	2,917	490	16.8
St Peter's, York*	102	540	68	12.6
Stamford	52	NK	51	NK
Stockport GS	185	NK	52	NK
Stonyhurst*	309	1,012	168	16.6
Strathallan	23	10	3	30.0
Sutton Valence	85	355	50	14.1
Taunton*	700	1,004	165	16.4
The Leys*	124	922	146	15.8
The Oratory	70	428	84	19.6
Tonbridge*	436	2,225	415	18.7
Trent*	144	514	97	18.9
Trinity Croydon	300	NK	130	NK
Truro	145	433	56	12.9
University College School*	352	1,538	247	16.1
Uppingham*	450	2,500	451	18.0
Warwick*	200	410	88	21.5
Wellingborough	300	1,060	177	16.7
Wellington College*	526	3,500	707	20.2
Wellington School	133	377	37	9.8
West Buckland	122	357	54	15.1
Westminster*	308	1,400	222	15.9
Whitgift*	498	1,400	246	17.6
Winchester*	445	2,418	505	20.9
Wolverhampton GS*	319	600	105	17.5
Woodbridge	91	279	60	21.5
Woodhouse Grove	107	NK	56	NK
Worksop	209	420	94	22.4

Commonwealth (Dominion) Public Schools

Appleby Can	NK	27	8	29.6
Diocesan College (Bishop's) SA	216	800	112	14.0
Christ Church GS, Aus	71	20	1	5.0

School name	Number of pupils in 1914	Pupils served	Number killed	% killed
Christ College, NZ	302	661	132	20.0
Geelong GS, Aus	140	444	91	20.5
Hilton, SA	154	371	47	12.7
King's Auckland, NZ	300	600	109	18.2
King's Parramatta, Aus	220	640	101	15.8
Lakefield Preparatory School, Can	40	122	20	16.4
Lawrence, Pakistan	NK	165	25	15.2
Melbourne GS Aus	490	1,370	209	15.3
Michaelhouse, SA	92	195	43	22.1
Scotch College, Vic, Aus	579	1,247	212	17.0
Shore School (SCEGS), Aus	370	880	122	13.9
St Andrew's, SA	290	765	128	16.7
St George's, Zimbabwe	133	190	26	13.7
St John's, Johannesburg, SA	300	299	60	20.1
St Michael's College School, Can	200	340	25	7.4
Sydney GS, Aus	606	1,772	302	17.0
Trinity College School, Can	86	596	123	20.6
Upper Canada College, Can	152	1,089	176	16.2

Notes

Introduction

1. S. Badsey, 'Blackadder Goes Forth and the two Western Fronts Debate' in G. Roberts and P. Taylor, eds., *Television and History*, 2001, pp. 113–25
2. H. Strachan, *Daily Telegraph*, 12 January 2013

Chapter 1 – Public School Men

1. Rex Warner, *English Public Schools*, 1945, p. 33
2. Tonbridge details drawn from *The Tonbridgian*, November 1914; H. Stokoe, ed., *Tonbridge School and the Great War*, 1922; *Tonbridge School Register*, 1900–1965
3. A. Percival, *The Origins of the Headmasters' Conference*, 1969
4. Ibid.
5. HMC List of Members, December 1914
6. Essays by various authors, *Great Public Schools* (1893)
7. J. Honey, *Tom Brown's Universe*, 1977, p. 270. Not until 1912 was the *PSYB* regarded as authoritative by HMC
8. *MCC Cricket Scores and Biographies from 1855–75*, 1877
9. W. Davis, *Into the Silence*, 2012, p. 604
10. R. C. Sherriff, *The English Public Schools in the War*, in Panichas G. A., *Promise of Greatness*, 1968, p. 147
11. Clarendon Commission, 1864
12. Rudyard Kipling, *The Islanders*, 1902
13. G. B. Shaw, *Doctors' Delusions, Crude Criminology and Sham Education*, 1932, p. 346
14. Warner, pp. 33–4
15. Shrewsbury School, 2nd Questionnaire, February 2013
16. A. Tod, *Charterhouse*, 1900, pp. 109–115
17. Manchester Grammar School, 2nd Questionnaire, February 2013
18. King's Canterbury, 2nd Questionnaire, January 2013
19. Sherborne School, 2nd Questionnaire, January 2013
20. A. Meadows and W. Brock, *Topics fit for Gentlemen* in B. Simon and I. Bradley, eds, *The Victorian Public School*, 1975, p. 113
21. Warner, p. 39
22. T. May, *The Victorian Public School*, 2009, p. 31
23. Marlborough College Register 1843–1952, Tonbridge School Register 1861–1945, Radley College Register 1847–1947
24. Manchester Grammar School, 2nd questionnaire, February 2013
25. Marlborough College Register
26. Tonbridge School List, Michaelmas Term, 1913

27. U. Nisbet 'Recollections of Marlborough before the First World War', *The Marlburian*, Summer 1964, p. 25
28. Zillekens, p. 58.
29. Honey, p. 183
30. Sebastian Faulks, *Engleby*, 2007
31. John Betjeman, *Summoned by Bells*, 1960
32. J. Baynes, *Morale: A Study of Men and Courage*, 1967, pp. 208–9
33. Honey, p. 215
34. S. Batten, *A Shining Light*, 2010, p. 40
35. C. Walston, *With a Fine Disregard*, 2006, p. 67
36. Patrick Mileham, *Wellington College*, 2008, p. 54
37. Edinburgh Academy, 2nd Questionnaire, February 2013
38. Robert Graves, *Goodbye to All That*, 1929, p. 42
39. W. Sorley, ed, *The Letters of Charles Sorley*, 1919, p. 54
40. George Orwell, *My Country Left or Right*, S. Orwell and I. Angus (eds.), *The Collected Essays, Journalism and Letters of George Orwell*, 1970, quoted in G. Sheffield *Leadership in the Trenches*, 2000, p. 53
41. Sir C. Harington, *Plumer of Messines*, 1935, p. 295
42. L. Wolff, *In Flanders Fields*, 1959 p. 116
43. John Jolliffe, ed., *Raymond Asquith: Life and Letters*, 1980, p.15
44. Vera Brittain *Testament of Youth*, 1933 , pp. 86–91
45. Antony Quick, *Charterhouse*, p. 98
46. Robert Graves, *Goodbye to All That*, p. 37
47. Rex Warner, *English Public Schools*, 1945, p. 36
48. E. C. Mack, *Public Schools and British Opinion Since 1860*, 1941
49. J. Bickersteth, ed., *The Bickersteth Diaries*, 1995, p. 276
50. Honey, p. 228
51. J. Jolliffe, *Raymond Asquith: Life and Letters*, 1980, p. 236
52. N. Annan, *Our Age*, 1990, p. 43
53. R. C. Sherriff, *Journey's End*, Act One, first performed in London in 1929
54. Henry Newbolt, *Vitaï Lampada*, 1892
55. *Eton College Chronicle*, 1914, p. 642
56. Sir Douglas Haig, *The Rectorial Address Delivered to the Students of Saint Andrews*, 14 May 1919, quoted in Sheffield, p. 44
57. A. Carton de Wiart, *Happy Odyssey*, 1950, quoted in Sheffield, p. 46
58. G. Best, *Militarism and the Victorian Public School* in Simon and Bradley, p. 141
59. Brian Bond, *Survivors of a Kind*, 2008, p. 1
60. M. Edwardes, *Oh to Meet an Army Man*, in J. Gross, ed., *Rudyard Kipling: The Man, His Work and the World*, 1972, quoted in Sheffield, p. 51
61. L. Talbot, ed., *Gilbert Talbot*, 1916, p. 556
62. Quoted in May, p53
63. T. Hinde *Paths of Progress: History of Marlborough College*, 1992, p. 122
64. D. R. Thorpe, *Eden*, 2003, p. 25
65. R. Aldington, *Death of a Hero*, 1929, pp. 285–6
66. *Glenalmond Chronicle 1906*, quoted Simon and Bradley, p. 137
67. *Report of HMC, Bradfield College*, December 1900, pp. 51–4
68. *Report of HMC, Christ's Hospital*, December 1904, pp. 28–46
69. Parliamentary debates, House of Commons 1907, as quoted in Simkins, p. 13
70. M. Magnusson, p. 283
71. Sorley, *The Letters of Charles Sorley*, 1919, p. 16
72. *Fettesian*, July 1914, quoted in McDowell, p. 140
73. J. Riley, *Schoolboys in Uniform: A History of the Sherborne School Cadet Force*, 1989, p. 44

74. P. Burden, *The Lion and the Stars*, 1990, p. 68
75. J. Lewis-Stempel, *Six Weeks*, 2010, p. 12
76. S. Mais, *A Public School in Wartime*, 1916, quoted in P. Parker *The Old Lie*, 1986, p. 65
77. *The Tonbridgian*, December 1913
78. R. Blumenau, *A History of Malvern College*, 1965
79. A. Haig-Brown, *The OTC and the Great War*, 1915, p. 42
80. *The Elizabethan*, June 1914
81. Parker, p. 67
82. Anthony Eden, *Another World*, 1976 , p. 51
83. Recollection by Sir Alfred le Maitre, H. Pyatt, *Fifty Years of Fettes, 1870–1920*, 1931, quoted in McDowell *Carrying On* , p. 141
84. *The Harrovian*, 2 July 1914
85. Eden, p. 66
86. Vera Brittain, *Testament of Youth*, pp. 87,91
87. Campbell College Questionnaire, September 2012
88. *The Tonbridgian*, October 1914
89. Dallas Wynne Willson, *Diary*, quoted in S. Smart, *When Heroes Die*, 2001, p. 15
90. *The Marlburian*, October 1914
91. *The Wellingtonian*, October 1914
92. *The Salopian*, October 1914
93. Smart, p. 21
94. Haig-Brown, p. 71
95. *The Salopian*, October 1914
96. P. Mileham, *Wellington College*, pp. 70–1
97. *The Salopian*, October 1914
98. Haig-Brown, p. 72
99. Eden, p. 66
100. Wynne Willson Diary, quoted in Smart, p. 18
101. C. Wright, *Kent College Centenary Book*, 1985, p. 41
102. Haig-Brown, pp. 102–3
103. Graves, p. 62
104. *Winchester College: Report of the Headmaster*, 1914
105. Arthur Behrend, *Make Me a Soldier*, 1961, pp. 22–5. Quoted in Charles Messenger, *Call to Arms*, 2005, p. 292
106. Major-General D. Wimberley, *Memoirs*, IWM, quoted in C. Moore-Bick, *Playing the Game*, 2011, p. 41
107. U. Nisbet *Diaries and Memories of the Great War*, IWM, quoted in P. Simkins *Kitchener's Army*, p. 222–3
108. *The Times History of the UPS Brigade*, 1917
109. HMC Bulletin number three, Michaelmas term, 1914, p. 130
110. *The Meteor*, 15 October 1914
111. Cyril Alington, *The Salopian*, December 1914
112. A. Gregory, *The Last Great War*, 2008, p. 17
113. Jonathan Smith, *Wilfred and Eileen*, 1975.The author based his novel on Willett's unpublished memoirs
114. Wellingborough School Questionnaire, September 2012
115. Donald Hankey *A Student in Arms* 1916, quoted in Moore-Bick, p. 40
116. F. Malim, *Almae Matres: Recollections of Some Schools at Home and Abroad*, 1948, p. 116
117. U. Nisbet, *Diaries and Memories of the Great War*, IWM, quoted in Simkins, p. 168
118. Robert Graves, *Goodbye to All That*, p. 62
119. Sholto Douglas, *Years of Combat*, 1963, p. 43
120. Arthur Pollard, *Fire-Eater – Memoirs of a VC*, 1932, quoted in Moore-Bick, p. 40

121. Harold Macmillan, *Winds of Change,* 1974, p. 59
122. Guy Chapman, *A Passionate Prodigality,* 1933, p. 13
123. Robert Nichols, quoted in J Lewis-Stempel, *Six Weeks,* p. 30
124. *The Harrovian,* November 1914
125. L. Housman, *War Letters of Fallen Englishmen,* 1930, p. 107
126. Ibid., p. 203
127. Malcolm White to A. E. Kitchin, 11 June 1916, in H Howson ed., *Two Men,* 1919, p. 253
128. Housman, p. 79
129. Ibid., p. 143

Chapter 2 – Into Battle 1914–1916

1. Julian Grenfell, 'Into Battle', May 1915
2. L. Housman, *War Letters of Fallen Englishmen,* 1930, p. 115
3. Richard Holmes, *Tommy,* 2004, p. 120
4. T. Travers, *The Killing Ground,* 1987, p. 5
5. G. Best, *Militarism in the Victorian Public School,* essay in Simon and Bradley, ed., *The Victorian Public School,* 1975, p. 132
6. HMC Bulletin number one, Easter 1911, pp. 96–7
7. S. Robbins, *British Generalship During the Great War,* 2005, p. 11
8. Travers, p. 281ff
9. Barnard Castle and Royal Belfast Academical Institution Questionnaires, January 2013
10. A List of OWs Serving Their Country 1 August–31 December 1914, Wellington College Archival Research Group
11. Stonyhurst Questionnaire, November 2012
12. K. Steward, *Lieutenant Colonel F. C. Briant CMG, CBE, DSO, Gold Coast Regiment and the Short Campaign in Togo, August 11 to August 26 1914*
13. Letter, Sir A. Goodenough to author, 24 March 2013
14. Private papers of Penny Crowe, March 2013, quoted in R. van Emden, *The Soldiers War,* 2008, p. 53
15. *The Marlburian,* November 1914
16. Ibid.
17. *The Harrovian* War Supplement, November 1914
18. Robert Graves to Cyril Hartman, 25 October 1914, quoted in W. Davis, *Into the Silence,* 2012, p. 583
19. J. Dunn, *The War the Infantry Knew,* 1938, p. 101
20. Housman, p. 144
21. Lionel Cohen letter 30 December 1914, private letters held by Jonathan Cohen
22. M. Richardson report, filed in PRO with War diary 1RWF
23. Quoted in J. Archer, 'Brigadier-General R. H. Husey, London Rifle Brigade', in *Stand To,* January 2013
24. G. Cave, Letter, 31 December 1914, Tonbridge School Archive
25. J. Reith, *Wearing Spurs,* 1966, p. 17
26. Holmes, p. 131
27. Archer op. cit.
28. Wilfred Willett, *Memoirs,* IWM 82/1/1, quoted in Joanna Bourke, *Dismembering The Male,* 1996, p. 31
29. Memorials of Rugbeians who Fell in the Great War, 1919
30. *The Treasury,* Rugby School, July 1915
31. H. Stokoe, ed., *Tonbridge School and the Great War,* 1923
32. E. B. Osborn, *The Muse in Arms,* 1917
33. P. Stevens, *The Great War Explained,* p. 27
34. Colonel G. Geddes, IWM Documents, quoted in N. Steel and P. Hart, *Gallipoli,* 1994, p. 93

35. In Memoriam notice on death of Rupert Brooke, Rugby School archives
36. *Wisden Cricketers' Almanac*, 1916
37. P. Blevins, *William Denis Browne*, 2000, quoted on MusicWeb International
38. Bury Grammar School Questionnaire, October 2012
39. Glasgow Academy Roll of Honour
40. Stevens, p. 31
41. *Surrey Mirror*, 15 October 1915
42. Tablet in Eton College Science School. Other information from J. Richardson, R. Egdell, N. and H. Hankins, 'Rutherford, Geiger, Chadwick, Moseley and Cockcroft and Their Role in the Great War', in *Stand To* no 90
43. Stevens, pp. 38–9
44. G. Chapman, *A Passionate Prodigality*, 1933, p. 5
45. W. Sorley, ed., *Letters of Charles Sorley*, 1919, p. 293
46. T. Barnes, *Learning to be a Soldier*, 1969, as quoted in P. Simkins, *Kitchener's Army*, 1988, p. 301
47. Simkins, p. 316
48. G. Talbot, *Winchester College War Memorial Book*, 1919
49. A. Spagnoly, *Salient Points*, 2004, p. 23
50. R. Pound, *The Lost Generation*, 1964, p. 194
51. *The Times*, 7 September 1915
52. *King's Royal Rifle Corps Chronicle*, 1915
53. M. Baring, quoted in Pound, p. 195
54. Letter from R. B. Maclochlen to Woodroffe, copy in Frank Fletcher's scrapbook, Charterhouse Archives
55. H. Macmillan, *Winds of Change*, 1966, p. 77
56. *Eton College Chronicle*, 14 October 1915
57. A. Clark, *The Donkeys*, 1961
58. Douglas Gillespie, letter to father, 24 September 1915, in *Letters from Flanders* 1916, pp. 311–12
59. R. Tompson, quoted in Holmes, p. 212
60. T. and V. Holt, *My Boy Jack: The Search for Kipling's Only Son*, 2007
61. Sorley, p. 311
62. D. Collett, ed., St Dunstan's College Roll of Honour, 1988, pp. 4, 80
63. J. Piggott, *Dulwich College 1616–2008*, 2008, ch 9
64. I. Hay, *All In It: K1 Carries On*, 1917, information supplied by A. Murray, Fettes Archivist, January 2013
65. Letter Vera to Edward Brittain, 14 January 1916, quoted in E. A. Bishop and M. Bostridge, eds., *Letters From a Lost Generation*, 1998
66. Royal Belfast Academical Institution Questionnaire
67. *Statistics of the Military Effort of the British Empire*, 1922, and School Rolls of Honour
68. M. Middlebrook, *The Somme Battlefields*, 1991, p. 247
69. Ibid., p. 79
70. R. Tawney, anonymous article in *Westminster Gazette*, October 1916, quoted in T. Wilson, *The Myriad Faces of War*, 1986, p. 328
71. Holmes, p. 145
72. F. Keeling, *Child Labour in the United Kingdom*, 1914
73. L. Housman, *War Letters of Fallen Englishmen*, 1930, p. 161
74. Charles Moore, 'A brave challenge to the Great War myth', *Daily Telegraph*, 17 June 2013
75. R. Harris, *Billy: The Neville Letters*, 1991, p. 193
76. J. Buxton papers, IWM, quoted in M. Brown, *The IWM Book of the Somme*, 1996, p. 44
77. R. C. Sherriff, *The English Public Schools in the War* in G. Panichas, *Promise of Greatness*, 1968, pp. 147–50

78. Sedbergh School Questionnaire, September 2012
79. J. Bickersteth, ed,.*The Bickersteth Diaries*, 1995, p. 99
80. 2nd Lt Thomas Willey, website for the 'Leeds Pals' www.leeds-pals.com
81. Leeds Pals, Wikipedia
82. Sevenoaks School Questionnaire, September 2012
83. J. Garth, *Tolkien and the Great War*, 2004, p. 183
84. Boswell papers, IWM, www.iwm.org/collections/item/object/1030009123
85. *Oxford Magazine*, November 1916 as quoted in Dom Lucius Graham, ed., *Downside and the Great War*, 1925, p. 150
86. Stephen Hewett, letter to his mother, 3 March 1916, in *A Scholar's Letters from the Front*, 1918, p. 38
87. R. Jenkins, *Asquith*, 1965, p. 413
88. Letter, Winston Churchill to Katharine Asquith, 4 December 1916, copy in Winchester College Archives
89. Lord Chandos, *Memoirs of Lord Chandos*, 1962, p. 66
90. *City of London School Magazine*, December 1916, p. 129
91. Housman, p. 276
92. D. Hankey, *A Student at Arms*, 1917
93. Warwick School Questionnaire, October 2012
94. Graham, p. 110
95. S. Rogerson, *Twelve Days*, 1933, p. 43
96. M. Levett, *Letters of Richard Byrd Levett*, 1917, quoted in T. Card, *Eton Renewed*, 1994, p. 143

Chapter 3 – Ireland and the Dominions

1. War Book of Upper Canada College 1914–19, p.xxii
2. Email to authors from Archivist at Blackrock College, 26 April 2013
3. St Columba's and Clongowes Wood Questionnaires, December 2012
4. *The Clongownian*, November 1916, pp. 6–9
5. P. Costello, *A History of Clongowes Wood College*, 1990, pp. 196–7
6. Ibid., p. 197
7. Campbell College, RBAI & MCB Questionnaires, December 2012
8. Information from Campbell College Archive, K. Haines, November 2012
9. Wylie, Unpublished Memoirs, 1939, National Archives PRO 30/89/1
10. *RBAI School News*, February 1917
11. Ibid., December 1916
12. RBAI memorial website
13. Family correspondence, 1916, Campbell College Archive.
14. *The Clongownian*, May 1917
15. M. Kettle, *The Ways of War*, 1917, p. 71
16. Thomas Kettle, letter to his brother, 8 September 1916, quoted in L. Housman, *War Letters of Fallen Englishmen*, 1930, p. 168
17. T. Kettle, *To My Daughter Betty*, published in *The Ways of War*
18. L. Housman, *War Letters of Fallen Englishmen*, 1930 pp. 225–6
19. William Redmond, Wikipedia entry
20. W. Bate, *Light Blue Down Under*, p. 162
21. King's Parramatta Questionnaire, January 2013
22. Sydney GS Questionnaire, October 2012
23. G. Sheffield, *Leadership in the Trenches*, 2000, p. 168
24. R. Peterson, *Facing the Foe: War Service of Shore Old Boys*, 2006, p. 224
25. J. Kiddle, ed., *War Services of Old Melburnians*, 1923, p. 32
26. Ibid., p. 125
27. Peterson, p. 112

28. Christ's College Questionnaire, October 2012
29. D. Hamilton, *College: 125 Years*, 1996, p. 277
30. Kiddle, p. 140
31. *The King's School Magazine*, December 1915, p. 465
32. Kiddle, p. 85
33. G. Moorhouse, *Hell's Foundations*, 1992, p. 235
34. *The Times*, September 1915
35. Hamilton pp. 279–80
36. K. Inglis, *Charles Bean 1879–1968*, Australian Dictionary of Biography, Volume 7, 1979
37. C. E. W. Bean, *Here, My Son*, 1950, p. 203
38. P. Barton, *The Somme*, 2006, p. 198
39. *The King's School Magazine*, March 1917, p. 25
40. A. Gaunson, *College Street Heroes*, 1998, p. 63
41. Sloman became headmaster of Tonbridge School in 1922
42. First World War Service Record of W. J. McClemans, quoted in P. Edwards and W. Hillman, *A School With a View*, 2010, p. 25
43. *The Mitre*, Volume 1, August 1917, pp. 16–17
44. *The Register*, December 1917
45. F. Ciaran and J. Teal, *The Stained Glass Windows of Christ's College Chapel*, 2001
46. P. Pedersen, *Monash as Military Commander*, 1985, p. 249
47. P. Brendon, *The Decline and Fall of the British Empire*, 2007, p. 284
48. Statistics of the Military Effort of the British Empire, 1922, pp. 758–73
49. *The College Times*, Christmas 1914
50. UCC and TCS Questionnaires, March 2013
51. Lakefield College School Questionnaire, March 2013
52. R. Bradley, *Ridley. A Canadian School*, p. 84
53. Bradley, p. 85
54. Unpublished letter, Mackenzie correspondence, Lakefield Archive
55. Ibid.
56. Quoted by Leo McKern, BBC documentary on the Somme, 1976
57. M. Middlebrook, *The First Day of the Somme*, 1971, p. 189
58. Mackenzie correspondence
59. Stevens, pp. 95–7
60. Brendon, p. 286
61. Mackenzie correspondence
62. *Trinity College School Record*, p. 75
63. A. Barrett, *Michaelhouse 1896–1968*, 1969, p. 53
64. N. Nuttall, *Lift Up Your Hearts*, 1971, p. 30
65. *Diocesan College Magazine*, September 1914
66. *Michaelhouse Chronicle*, September 1914
67. Nuttall, p. 57
68. St George's Questionnaire, September 2012
69. B. Liddell Hart, *The First World War*, 1970, p. 324
70. P. Digby, *Pyramids and Poppies*, 1993, p. 147
71. *Diocesan College Magazine*, December 1916, p. 25
72. E. Bissett, letter home, 21 July 1916, in *St John's College and the War*, February 1917, p. 19
73. M. Poland, *The Boy in You*, 2008, p. 172
74. Fr Eustace Hill, Letters from France, in *St John's College and the War*, February 1917, p. 21
75. Barrett, p. 61
76. Bishops, Hilton, St Andrews, Michaelhouse & St John's questionnaires, November 2012
77. J Gardener, *Bishop's 150*, 1997, p. 255
78. Poland, p. 166

Chapter 4 – School Life during the War

1. W. Adam, 'Naval Interlude', p. 57, MS in Fettes archive, quoted in D McDowell, *Carrying On*, 2012, p. 166
2. E. Partridge, *Rossall in Wartime*, in W. Furness, ed., *Centenary History of Rossall School*, 1944, p. 122
3. D. Finch, *R Patterson: A Life of Great Adventure*, 2000, p. 7
4. M. Hoy, *A Blessing to this Island*, 2006, notes attached to KWIOM Questionnaire, September 2012
5. Trinity Croydon Questionnaire, December 2012
6. D. Wynne Willson, 'Cheerful Yesterdays', unpublished memoir, p. 44, Gresham's School Archives
7. W. Adam, Fettes MS, quoted in McDowell, p. 156
8. B. Handford, *Lancing College: History and Memoirs*, 1986, p. 150
9. A. Douglas-Smith, *City of London School*, 1937, p. 386
10. St Peter's York Questionnaire, January 2013
11. *The Haileyburian*, 26 October 1916
12. Ibid., 28 July 1915
13. R. Hughes, *History of St John's, Leatherhead*, 2001, p. 58
14. R. Blumenau, *History of Malvern College 1865–1965*, 1965, p. 91
15. R. Perry, *Ardingly 1858–1946*, 1951, Ch 10
16. *The Harrovian*, December 1918
17. D. Newsome, *A History of Wellington College*, 1959, p. 279
18. Newspaper cutting dated 15 February 1915, supplied by P. Henderson from King's Canterbury archive
19. Wellington School Questionnaire and supplementary information, November 2012
20. N. Shute, *Slide Rule*, 1954
21. T. Hinde, *Paths of Progress*, 1992, p. 133
22. T. Card, *Eton Renewed*, 1994, p. 135
23. A. Megahey, *History of Cranleigh School*, 1983
24. Douglas-Smith, p. 385
25. R. Croft-Cooke, *The Altar in the Loft*, 1960
26. D. Ballance, *The Buds of Virtue*, 2000, p. 70
27. J. Firth, *Winchester*, 1936, p. 75
28. G. Diggle, unpublished memories of Gresham's, Gresham's School archive
29. C. Isherwood, *Kathleen and Frank*, 1971, as quoted in P. Parker, *The Old Lie*, 1987, p. 260
30. Culford School Questionnaire, January 2013
31. Ruthin School Questionnaire, January 2013
32. Christ's Hospital Questionnaire, January 2013, supplementary information from D. Miller
33. C. Walston, ed., *With a Fine Disregard*, 2006, p. 114
34. *The Radleian*, 15 December 1917
35. Winchester College: Report of the Headmaster, July 1915
36. J. Sargeaunt, *A History of Bedford School*, 1925, p. 222
37. J. Blackie, *Bradfield 1850–1975*, 1977, p. 125
38. C. Scott-Giles, *The History of Emanuel School*, 1947, p. 127
39. I. Macleod, *The Glasgow Academy*, 1997, p. 83
40. *Daily Telegraph*, 19 May 1917, quoted in A. Mumford, *The Manchester Grammar School 1515–1915*, 1919, p. 545
41. Sargeaunt, p. 223
42. St Peter's York Questionnaire, January 2013
43. Macleod, p. 84
44. Blackie, p. 124
45. H. Clarke, *History of Sedbergh 1525–1925*, 1928, p. 210

46. L. Macdonald, *Voices and Images of the Great War*, 1988, p. 126
47. Newsome, p. 287
48. KWIOM Questionnaire, September 2012
49. Head of School Book 1914 and 1915, Harrow School archive
50. A. Waugh, *The Loom of Youth*, 1917, p. 39
51. *The Fettesian*, November 1917
52. R. Hill, *A History of St Edward's*, 1962, p. 174
53. Report of HMC Annual Meeting, London, 22–23 December 1914., pp. 29–30
54. Report of HMC Annual Meeting, Rugby School, 21–22 December 1916, p. 112
55. Kingswood School Questionnaire, February 2013, quote from G. Best, *Continuity and Change: A History of Kingswood School*, 1998
56. Hill, p. 172
57. George Heriot's School Questionnaire and email from F. Simm, Archivist, December 2012
58. Cheltenham Ladies' College Questionnaire, March 2013
59. L. Faithfull, *In the House of my Pilgrimage*, 1924, p. 190
60. *The Paulina*, March 1916
61. Walter Raeburn diary 1915, information provided by David Raeburn, 9 May 2013
62. John Cropton, *The Road to Nowhere*, 1936, p. 155
63. *The Haileyburian*, 15 October 1914
64. Clarke, p. 205
65. T. Hinde, *Paths of Progress*, 1992, p. 129
66. Hill, p. 184. Gabbitas and Thring still exists as an educational agency. One of its roles was to find staff for schools
67. Perry, Ch 10
68. Firth, p. 75
69. Hill, p. 182
70. J. Blatchly, *The Famous Antient Seed-Plot of Learning*, 2003, p. 238
71. St Dunstan's College Questionnaire, December 2012
72. H. Furley, ed., Tonbridge Register, 1861–1945
73. Ballance, p. 65
74. Manchester Grammar School Questionnaire, September 2012, quotation from in MGS Book of Remembrance, 1921
75. Newsome, pp. 288–9
76. Blumenau, p. 89
77. Mumford, p. 542
78. *The Carthusian*, November 1914
79. *The Reptonian*, November 1916
80. Blumenau, p. 90
81. *The Salopian*, 26 October 1918
82. V. Gollancz, *A Year of Grace*, 1950, p. 205
83. D. C. Somervell, unpublished autobiography, Ch 7, Repton School archive
84. Parker, p. 23
85. B. Thomas, *Repton 1557–1957*, 1957
86. Ibid.
87. Somervell, op. cit.
88. War Office letter to G. Fisher, 24 July 1918, as quoted in Somervell
89. Somervell, op. cit.
90. Parker, p. 24
91. Ibid.
92. M. Stannard, *Evelyn Waugh, The Early Years, Volume 1 1903–39*, 1993, p. 45
93. A. Waugh, *The Loom of Youth*, 1917
94. R. Warner, *English Public Schools*, 1945, p. 40

95. T. Seccombe, Preface to *Loom of Youth*, 1917
96. A. Gourlay, *History of Sherborne School*, 1971, p. 207
97. Email to authors from Patrick Francis, Sherborne School, 12 April 2013
98. Sherborne School: Report of Headmaster, 1917
99. Stannard, p. 45
100. Ibid., p. 50
101. W. Hayman, unpublished account of his time at Sherborne 1917–1921, Sherborne School archives
102. *The Cantuarian*, November 1916
103. *The Elizabethan*, July 1917
104. *The Campbellian*, April 1917
105. Handford, p. 152
106. Perry, Ch 10
107. F. Stewart, *Loretto 150*, 1977, p. 177
108. Card, p. 141
109. Harrow, Head of School Book, 1917, Harrow archives
110. E. Partridge, writing in *A Centenary History of Rossall*, 1945, p. 121
111. Blumenau, p. 190
112. Handford, p. 152
113. D. Somervell, ed., *Tonbridge School 1553–1953*, 1953, p. 13
114. G. Diggle, Gresham's School archive
115. Firth, p. 81
116. *The Elizabethan*, February 1918

Chapter 5 – Headmasters and Teachers: the Toll of War

1. S. Bedford, *Aldous Huxley: A Biography*, 1973, as quoted in P. Parker, *The Old Lie*, p. 258
2. D. Newsome, *History of Wellington College*, 1959, p. 289
3. Winchester College: Report of the Headmaster, December 1914
4. Dean Close School Questionnaire, February 2013
5. Sevenoaks School Questionnaire, September 2012
6. L. Faithfull, *In the House of my Pilgrimage*, 1925, p. 183
7. St Lawrence Ramsgate Questionnaire, February 2012
8. *The Meteor*, 27 February 1915
9. Report of the Committee of HMC, October 1915, p. 128
10. Winchester College: Report of the Headmaster, August 1916
11. Report of HMC Annual Meeting, Rugby School, 21–22 December 1916
12. J. Roche, 'The First Half-Century of the Headmasters' Conference', 1972, unpublished PhD thesis, University of Sheffield, HMC Archives, pp. 486–500
13. Haileybury College 2nd Questionnaire, March 2013
14. King's School, Canterbury 2nd Questionnaire, February 2013
15. Winchester College: Report of the Headmaster, 1917
16. Harrow School, Governors' Minute Book, 9 May 1916
17. Winchester College: Report of the Headmaster, 1914
18. Harrow School Governors, Minute Book, 1 February 1915
19. R. Perry, *Ardingly 1858–1946*, 1951, Ch 10
20. Trent College and Rossall School Questionnaires, December 2012
21. St Paul's School and Marlborough College Questionnaires, October 2012
22. Report of HMC Annual Meeting, London, 22–23 December 1915, p. 8
23. Report of HMC Annual Meeting, 1915, p. 23
24. Ibid., pp. 20–33
25. Report of the HMC Committee, Summer 1918, p. 39
26. Report of HMC Annual Meeting, Rugby, 21–22 December 1916, p. 91

27. R. Graves, *Goodbye to All That*, 1929, p. 39
28. Winchester College: Report of Headmaster, 1916
29. The Home Front, Epsom College archives website
30. Report of HMC Annual Meeting, City of London School, 12–13 September 1917, p. 12
31. G. Sherington, *English Education, Social Change and War 1911–20*, 1981, p. 168
32. Interestingly, this became urgent by the late 1930s when some leading boarding schools thought they would not be able to survive at all and mounted a similar delegation
33. F. Fletcher, *Brethren and Companions*, 1936, p. 152, quoted in J. Witheridge, *Frank Fletcher 1870–1954: A Formidable Headmaster*, 2005, p. 193
34. Figures for public school teachers taken from questionnaires submitted by school archivists. For national figures see J. Winter, *The Great War and the British People*, 1985, p. 91
35. Questionnaires submitted by Shrewsbury School, Merchant Taylors' School and Clifton College
36. *The Cholmelian*, November 1914, information from W. Henley-Smith, Highgate School Archivist
37. J. Witheridge, *Frank Fletcher 1870–1954: A Formidable Headmaster*, 2005, p. 155
38. Letter, G. Mallory to A. Benson, 25 April 1915, quoted in W. Davis, *Into the Silence*, 2012, p. 186
39. F. Fletcher, *After Many Days*, 1937, p. 194, quoted in Witheridge, pp. 155–6
40. Witheridge, p. 157
41. Report of HMC Annual Meeting, City of London School, 12–13 September 1917, p. 104
42. Ibid.
43. Winchester College: Report of Headmaster, December 1914
44. J. Hope-Simpson, *Rugby Since Arnold*, 1967, p. 177
45. Governors' Minutes, Manchester Grammar School, 1914, MGS Archives
46. C. Tyerman, *A History of Harrow School*, 2000, p. 444
47. *The Carthusian*, February 1915, p. 414
48. *The Haileyburian* December 1915
49. H. Stokoe, ed., *Tonbridge School in the Great War*, 1922, p. 562
50. George Fletcher to Malcolm White, February 1915, H. Howson, ed., *Two Men*, 1919 , pp. 36–7
51. Email to author from Simon Batten, Bloxham Archivist, 14 November 2012
52. J. Dunn, *The War the Infantry Knew*, 1938, pp. 125–6
53. *Eton Chronicle*, 25 March 1915
54. *The Harrovian*, 3 June 1916
55. G. O'Hanlon, Diaries and Memoir, private papers held in Sherborne School Archives
56. A. Haig-Brown, *The OTC and the Great* War, 1915
57. Christ's Hospital Roll of Honour, 1920, information supplied by D. Miller, Christ's Hospital historian
58. List of First World War Victoria Cross recipients, Wikipedia
59. *London Gazette*, 9 September 1915
60. Captain W. Forshaw VC, 9th Manchesters, www.rubecula.com/Forshaw/index.html
61. *MGS School Magazine*, 1915, p. 213
62. HMC List of Members, 1933
63. Bangor Grammar School Questionnaire, October 2012
64. C. W. Scott-Giles, *The History of Emanuel School*, 1947, p. 199
65. J. Archer, 'H. B. Ryley', in *The Portcullis*, 2011
66. *The Portcullis*, 1918
67. B. Matthews, *By God's Good Grace*, 1984, pp. 144–7
68. Revd C. Alington, *Edward Lyttelton, an Appreciation*, 1943, Ch 5
69. P. Parker, *The Old Lie*, 1987, p. 266
70. T. Card, *Eton Renewed*, p. 137

71. A. Robinson, 'Eton's Great War Scandal', History Today Vol 33 Issue 11, November 1993, p. 18
72. *The Morning Post*, 30 March 1915
73. A. Robinson, 'Eton and the First World War', IWM Review 1993, p. 90
74. *The Times*, 31 March 1915, as quoted in Parker, p. 267
75. Card, p. 138
76. Robinson, *History Today*, p. 14
77. Lord Rosebery to M.R. James, 12 May 1915, Eton College MS 396, quoted in A. Robinson, IWM Review, p. 90
78. Parker, p. 267
79. Robinson, *History Today*, p. 20
80. Parker, p. 267
81. Email to author from D. Sederman, Abbotsholme School historian, 3 May 2013
82. War Office form for 'Application for Exemption on the Ground of Conscientious Objection'
83. Bootham School Questionnaire, October 2012
84. S. Brown, *Bootham School 1823–1973*, 1973, p. 22
85. Leighton Park Questionnaire, October 2012. Supplementary information from J. Allinson, Archivist, January 2013
86. Allinson
87. R. Caddel and A. Flowers, *Basil Bunting: a Northern Life*, 1997
88. *The Leightonian*, November 1916
89. Letters in Frank Fletcher's scrapbook, Charterhouse Archives
90. Matthews, p. 140
91. L. Tanner, *Westminster School*, 1934 , p. 53
92. D. Somervell, *History of Tonbridge School*, 1947, pp. 120–22
93. D. Newsome, *History of Wellington College*, 1959, p. 279
94. Ibid., p. 294
95. H. G. Wells, *The Story of a Great Schoolmaster*, 1924, p. 88
96. Warwick School Questionnaire, October 2012
97. *Memorials of Rugbeians Who Fell in the Great War*, 1923
98. J. Piggott, *Dulwich College: A History 1616–2008*, 2008
99. Letter to author from M. Reader, Headmaster of Wellington School, 21 September 2012
100. S. Smart, *When Heroes Die*, 2001, p. 163
101. Ibid., p. 166
102. Warden Sing correspondence, edited by C. Nathan, St Edward's Archivist
103. Email to author from Simon Smith, Brighton College, 28 May 2013
104. Lilian Faithfull, *In the House of my Pilgrimage*, 1925, p. 189
105. Smart, p. 116
106. W. Ewing, *Pattison of Hebron*, 1931, quoted in D. McDowell, *Carrying On: Fettes College, War and the World*, 2011, p. 177
107. Stokoe, op. cit.

Chapter 6 – The Eternal Bond

1. J. Girling, poems published by his father for private circulation, quoted in P. Mileham, *Wellington College*, 2008, p. 75
2. Mileham, p. 75
3. *The Carthusian*, July 1915, p. 478
4. J. Honey, *Tom Brown's Universe*, 1977, p. 155
5. *The Elean*, January 1917
6. *Eton College Chronicle*, 11 March 1915
7. *The Carthusian*, November 1916, p. 10

8. Information supplied to author by Suzanne Foster, Winchester College Archivist, March 2013
9. *The Harrovian* War Supplement, June 1917
10. *The Breconian*, April 1917
11. *The Cantuarian*, June 1917
12. J. Kiddle, ed., *War Services of Old Melburnians*, p. 142
13. *The Stonyhurst Magazine*, March 1916
14. Vaughan papers, quoted in D. Newsome, *History of Wellington College*, 1959, p. 293
15. *Manchester Grammar School Magazine*, 1917
16. Letters to G. Corner, Wellington School, 1993
17. *Wellington School Magazine*, July 1915
18. T. G. Houston, Letter to Old Boys, Christmas 1916, Coleraine AI archives
19. Extracts from letters in the Warden Sing correspondence, edited by C. Nathan, Archivist at St Edward's
20. M. Charlesworth, *Salopians 1900–1950*, 2000, p. 54
21. H. Macnaghten, *Eton Letters: 1915–18 by a Housemaster*, 1920, p. 60
22. A. Rayner-Wood, *Twenty Years After: The Letters of an Eton Housemaster*, 1939, quoted in P. Parker, *The Old Lie*, p. 208
23. Henry Luxmoore letter to a friend, 22 December 1917, E Coll MS/Luxmoore, quoted in A. Robinson, *Eton and the First World War*, IWM Review, 1993, p. 85
24. *The Shirburnian*, March 1915, p. 4
25. *The Kingswood Magazine*, December 1916
26. *The Haileyburian*, 18 October 1917, p. 602
27. *The Sydneian*, November 1915
28. *The Lyonian*, June 1916, p. 67
29. Letter to T. Bramston from F. Cullinan, November 1916, Winchester College Archive, E/3/5/20
30. A. D. Gillespie, *Letters from Flanders*, 1916, p. 196
31. Ibid., p. 133
32. *The Wykehamist*, December 1915
33. Douglas Gillespie to Montagu Rendall, 14 June 1915, *The Wykehamist*, December 1915
34. D. C. Richter, ed., *Lionel Sotheby's Great War: Diaries and Letters from the Western Front*, 1997, p. 23
35. Ibid., p. 83
36. Ibid., p. 142
37. *The Cantuarian*, August 1916
38. Ibid., November 1917
39. *The Breconian*, December 1916
40. 'Housey' is Christ's Hospital pupils' name for the school, so this is presumably used to mean 'Are you an Old Blue?' Email to author from David Miller, Christ's Hospital Archivist, 22 November 2012
41. *The Blue*, December 1917
42. Paul Jones, letter to his brother 29 April 1917, H. Jones, ed., *War Letters of a Public Schoolboy*, 1918
43. Jones, p. 258
44. Harry Altham, a Reptonian, had taught at Winchester since 1912 and was to win the DSO and MC in the war. He remained at Winchester throughout his teaching career and also became one of the key influences on English cricket as historian, administrator and coach
45. L. Housman, *War Letters of Fallen Englishmen*, 1930, p. 274
46. *The Blue*, June 1917, pp. 162–3
47. Ibid., October 1917, pp. 10–11
48. E. Blunden, *Undertones of War*, 1928, p. 268

49. *The Shirburnian*, March 1915
50. D. Hamilton, *College – A History of Christ's College*, 1996, p. 283
51. Kiddle, p. 202
52. 'A Very Special OW Dinner in 1917', *The Trusty Servant*, November 2007
53. *Eton College Chronicle*, June 1916
54. Marlburian Club website – Bailleul Commemoration Dinner, January 2012
55. *The Radleian*, 20 July 1918
56. *The Campbellian*, July 1915
57. D. Miller,' ComprisHousey', *The Blue*, 2007
58. *The Carthusian*, December 1915, p. 54
59. *Harrow Memorials of the Great War* and *The Harrovian*, 23 October 1915
60. H. Howson, ed., *Two Men*, 1919, preface by C. Alington, p vii
61. Malcolm White, diary entry 4 April 1916, Howson, p. 212
62. Evelyn Southwell, letter to his mother, 27 February 1916, Howson, p. 169
63. Malcolm White letter to Cyril Alington, 27 June 1916, Howson, p. 256
64. Malcolm White letter to Evelyn Southwell, 27 June 1916, Howson, p. 256
65. Evelyn Southwell letter to Hugh Howson, 13 September 1916, Howson, p. 293
66. *The Salopian*, 5 April 1919
67. Julian Bickersteth, letter to his mother 18 October 1916, J. Bickersteth, ed., *The Bickersteth Diaries*, 1995, p. 140
68. L. Talbot, ed., *Gilbert Walter Lyttelton Talbot*, 1916, quoted in J. Firth, *Winchester*, 1936, p. 71
69. C. Messenger, *Call to Arms*, 2005, p. 452
70. Julian Bickersteth letter to his mother, 29 December 1917, Bickersteth, p. 224
71. Letter, 1917, Eric Whitworth papers, Regimental Museum of the Royal Welsh
72. A. Eden, early manuscript draft of *Another World*, quoted in D. R. Thorpe, *Eden*, 2003, p. 30
73. Papers of the Revd E. Crosse, IWM 80/22/1, quoted by J. Archer, *Stand To*, number 88, p. 5
74. Julian Bickersteth letter to his mother, March 1916, Bickersteth, p. 75
75. Ibid., May 1916, Bickersteth, p. 83
76. V. Tanner papers, IWM, quoted in M. Moynihan, ed., *God on our Side*, 1983, p. 144
77. Moynihan, p. 173.
78. R. Holmes, *Tommy*, 2004, p. 518
79. P. Fiennes, *To War with God*, 2011
80. Crosse papers, IWM, quoted in P. Stevens, *The Great War Explained*, p. 81
81. L. Housman, ed., *War Letters of Fallen Englishmen*, 1930, p. 107
82. G. Chapman, *A Passionate Prodigality*, 1933, p. 117
83. *The Stonyhurst War Record*, 1927, Introduction
84. Moynihan, p. 195
85. Ibid., p. 204
86. Private letter, General Hickie to Mr Doyle, Archives of Clongowes Wood
87. G. Sparrow and J. Ross, *On Four Fronts with the Royal Naval Division*, 1918, p. 257
88. Epsom College Archive website
89. *Old Fettesians Who Served in the Great War*, 1920
90. *Radley College Register 1847–1947* and *Tonbridge School Register 1860–1945*
91. Holmes, p. 466
92. G. Keynes, tape recordings, quoted in I. Whitehead, *Doctors in the Great War*, 1999, pp. 156 & 256
93. Whitehead, p. 52
94. H. Somervell, *After Everest*, 1936, pp. 38–40
95. M. Harrison, *The Medical War*, 2010, p. 105
96. S. Sassoon, *The Memoirs of George Sherston*, 1937, p. 56
97. C. S. Myers, 'A Contribution to the Study of Shell-shock', *The Lancet*, 1915, pp. 316–20
98. Lord Moran, *The Anatomy of Courage*, 1945, pxvi

99. Whitehead, p. 185
100. *The Great War*, Epsom College Archive website
101. E. Malet de Carteret, 'Captain H. Ackroyd' in *Stand To*, Sept 1995, p. 30
102. Quoted in P. de la Billière, *Supreme Courage*, 2004, p. 69
103. de la Billière, p. 80
104. D. Wainwright, *Liverpool Gentlemen: A History of Liverpool College*, 1960, p. 215

Chapter 7 – To the End on Land, Sea and Air 1917–1918

1. R. C. Sherriff, 'The English Public Schools in the War' in G. Panichas, *Promise of Greatness*, 1968, p. 147–50
2. R. Tawney, 'Some reflections of a Soldier' in *Nation*, October 1916, quoted in R. Holmes, *Tommy*, 2005, p. 48
3. E. Swinton, *Twenty Years After*, 1920, quoted in Holmes, p. 61.
4. S. Hewett letter to his sister Kathleen, 8 July 1916, in *A Scholar's Letters from the Front*, 1918, p. 112
5. L. Sanders, A *Soldier of England*, 1920, p. 106
6. Lt Col Sir Christopher Lighton Bt, interviewed in July 1992 by Andrew Robinson, quoted by A. Robinson in 'Eton and the First World War', IWM Review, 1993
7. G. Chapman, *A Passionate Prodigality*, 1933, pp. 161–2
8. S. Sassoon, *Memoirs of an Infantry Officer*, 1930, p. 218
9. R. Asquith letter to his wife, 15 March 1916, quoted in J. Jolliffe, *Raymond Asquith: Life and Letters*, 1980, p. 248
10. Arthur Adam to his sister, Barbara (Wootton), 9 July 1916, quoted in L. Housman, *War Letters of Fallen Englishmen*, 1930, p. 22
11. Thomas Arthur Nelson, Notes from Edinburgh Academy Archives, 2012
12. John Buchan, *These for Remembrance*, 1919, p. 11
13. Edward Thomas, *Poems*, 1917
14. Helen Thomas, *World Without End*, 1931, pp. 182–3
15. Edward Thomas, *The Cherry Trees*, May 1916
16. J. Glubb, diary entry 22 April, *Into Battle*, 1977, p. 140
17. J. Neville, *War Letters of a Light Infantryman*, 1930, p. 6
18. R. Rees, *A Schoolmaster at War*, 1936
19. R. C. Sherriff, *The English Public Schools in the War*, in Panichas, pp. 147–50
20. Lionel Cohen letter, 5 December 1914, private letters held by Jonathan Cohen
21. Lyttelton papers, letter posted 4 March 1915, CHAN 8/3, Churchill College, Cambridge, quoted in C. Moore-Bick, *Playing the Game*, 2011, p. 194
22. S. Hewett letter to his mother 3 March 1916, *A Scholar's Letters from the Front*, p. 38
23. R. C. Sherriff, *Journey's End*, 1929
24. A. Spagnoly, *Salient Points Four*, 2004, p. 66
25. Lionel Cohen letter, 15 March 1915
26. Eric Whitworth Papers, Regimental Museum of the Royal Welsh
27. Queen's College Taunton War Memorial, 1919, pp. 52–3
28. Harrow Memorials of the Great War, Vol 3, 1918
29. Private Frank Holding, IWM oral archive, www.iwm.org.uk/collections/item/object/80011703
30. Philip Stevens, *The Great War Explained*, 2012, pp. 93–106
31. Information from Piers Storie-Pugh, Not Forgotten Association, March 2013
32. Arthur Ashford letter, Caterham School Archive
33. J. Dunn, *The War the Infantry Knew*, 1938, p. 418
34. Silcoates School Questionnaire, October 2012
35. B . Wootton, *In a World I Never Made*, 1967
36. J. Winter, *The Great War and the British People*, 1985, p. 82

37. Wootton, op. cit.
38. P. Berry and M. Bostridge, *Vera Brittain, A Life*, 1995, p. 523
39. S. Cooper, *The Final Whistle*, p. 208
40. Captain Henry Smeddle papers, IWM, quoted in M. Brown *The IWM Book of 1918*, 1998, pp. 202–3
41. Royal Aero Club website
42. S. Douglas, *Years of Combat*, 1963, p. 67
43. D. McDowell, *Carrying On*, 2012, p. 236
44. *The Harrovian*, June-December 1915
45. Cooper, pp. 26–35
46. *The Harrovian* War Supplement, June 1915
47. *Eton College Chronicle*, 3 February 1916
48. G. Pitchfork, *The Sowreys*, 2012, p. 32
49. Statistics of the Military Effort of the British Empire, 1922, p. 505
50. *The Haileyburian*, August 1917
51. M. Craze, *A History of Felsted School*, 1955, p. 263
52. *The Shirburnian*, November 1917
53. C. Lewis, *Sagittarius Rising*, 1936, p. 137
54. H. Stokoe, ed., *Tonbridge School and the Great War*, 1923
55. Dom L. Graham, ed., *Downside and the War*, 1925
56. I. Mackersey, *No Empty Chairs*, 2012, p. 67
57. Ibid., p. 69
58. *The Lyonian*, July 1917, p. 54
59. S. Douglas, *Years of Combat*, 1963, pp. 179–80
60. *The Haileyburian*, April 1917, p. 146
61. C. Sharples, 'One of the Youngest Pilots Killed in the Great War', *Stand To* magazine, August 2011, p. 50
62. Information in this paragraph from Eastbourne College archives, October 2012, Michael Partridge, Archivist
63. British Library, LPS/11/75, quoted on www.movinghere.org.uk 'Education of Indian princes in Britain'
64. Information from Eastbourne College archives
65. Robert Gregory, entry in Wikipedia
66. J. Pethica, 'Yeats' Perfect Man', *The Dublin Review*, Summer 2009
67. Lewis, p. 174
68. Albert Ball Letters, Nottingham Public Archives, quoted in P. de la Billière, *Supreme Courage*, 2004, Ch 5
69. Information from J. Sadden, Archivist, Portsmouth GS, December 2012
70. Report of the HMC Annual Conference, Reading, 23/24 December 1913
71. Rolls of honour and service of Charterhouse, Dulwich, Eton, Marlborough and Westminster
72. J. Winter, *The Great War and the British People*, 1986, p. 91
73. Royal Hospital School Questionnaire, January 2013
74. Portsmouth GS and Plymouth College Questionnaires, November 2012
75. *The Cheltonian*, March 1915
76. S. Smart, *When Heroes Die*, 2001, p. 84
77. Graham, op. cit.
78. D. Bardens, *Portrait of a Statesman*, 1956, p. 40
79. Francis Harvey, information from Portsmouth GS archive
80. Norman Holbrook, List of World War One VCs, Wikipedia website
81. R. Pound and G. Harmsworth, *Northcliffe*, 1959, p. 510
82. Cooper, pp. 225–35

83. Captain A. Carpenter VC, *The Blocking of Zeebrugge*, 1921
84. J. Piggott, *Dulwich College 1616–2008*, 2008, Ch 9
85. M. Batey, *Dilly. The Man who Broke Enigma*, 2009
86. Stevens, p. 119.
87. R. C. Sherriff, *No Leading Lady*, 1968
88. David Walsh's research into school rolls of honour, November 2012
89. Graham, op. cit.
90. O. Lyttelton, *Memoirs of Lord Chandos*, 1962, p. 100
91. Wilfrith Elstob, Christ's Hospital archives and List of VCs of World War One, Wikipedia
92. A. Spagnoly, 'A Mother's Pilgrimage', *Stand To*, February 1995
93. E. Dougall, letter to his cousin, 1 April 1918, quoted in R. Snow, *Ten Brave Men and True*, 2012, p. 182
94. Dougall VC citation and chaplain letter, H Stokoe, ed., *Tonbridge School and the Great War*, p. 104
95. R. Holmes, *Tommy*, p. 213
96. John Buchan, *Memory Hold The Door*, 1940, Chapter 8
97. John Buchan, *These for Remembrance*, 1919
98. *Wykehamist War Service Roll*, 1919
99. Malvern College archives and Oxford Dictionary of National Biography
100. Email to author from Brigadier J. Walker, Old Alleynian, 22 January 2013
101. *Statistics of the Military Effort of the British Empire During the Great War*, 1921, p. 252
102. D. Reitz, *Trekking On*, 1933, as quoted in N. Best, *The Greatest Day in History*, 2008, p. 191
103. Mill Hill Roll of Honour
104. G. Whittaker, *The Changing Years*, privately published memoir, 1977, with thanks to Robin Kermode for this information

Chapter 8 – Armistice and Commemoration
1. Email from Elizabeth Owen to author, 29 May 2013
2. Harold Owen, *Journey from Obscurity*, 1963
3. John G. Bennett, *Witness: The Story of a Search*, 1962
4. J. Winter, *Sites of Memory, Sites of Mourning*, 1995, p. 77
5. J. Lellenberg , ed., *Arthur Conan Doyle, a Life in Letters*, 2007, p. 648
6. Winter, pp. 58–61
7. Taunton School Commemoration Service, 27 November 1918
8. J. Bickersteth, ed., *The Bickersteth Diaries*, 1995, p. 296
9. C. Douie, *The Weary Road*, 1929, p. 16
10. J. Dunn, *The War the Infantry Knew*, 1938, p. 567
11. R. Graves, *Goodbye to All That*, 1929, p. 228
12. W. Lewis, ed., *Letters of C S Lewis*, 1966, p. 96
13. H. E. Luxmoore to Christopher Stone, 11 November 1918, quoted in A. Robinson, 'Eton and the First World War', article in IWM Review 1993
14. Padded cushions which were used as satchels for school books but could also be sat on in chapel. Email to author from Terry Rogers, Marlborough Archivist, 10 June 2013
15. T. Hinde, *Paths of Progress*, 1992, p. 134
16. *The Shirburnian*, December 1918, pp. 362–3
17. Sermon preached by Nowell Smith in chapel, 11 November 1923, copy in Sherborne School Archives
18. *The Paulina*, December 1918, p. 7
19. A. Gaunson, *College Street Heroes*, 1998, p. 117
20. M. Poland, *The Boy in You*, 2008, p. 178
21. M. Craze, *History of Felsted School*, 1955, p. 267
22. The Perse questionnaire, December 2012

23. *The Breconian*, December 1918, p. 287
24. *The Silcoatian*, February 1919
25. J. Witheridge, *Frank Fletcher 1870–1954: A Formidable Headmaster*, 2005, p. 165
26. F. Fletcher, *Brethrens and Companions: Charterhouse Chapel Addresses*, 1936, p. 23, as quoted in Witheridge, p. 221
27. P. Longworth, *The Unending Vigil*, 1985, p. 14
28. R. van Emden, *The Quick and the Dead*, 2011, p. 132
29. J. Summers, *Remembered – The History of the Commonwealth War Graves Commission*, 2007, p. 16
30. A. Gregory , *The Last Great War: British Society and the First World War*, 2008, pp. 255–6
31. Summers, p. 17
32. Hansard, House of Commons Debate, 4 May 1920
33. Poland, p. 180
34. Gavin Stamp, *Silent Cities: An Exhibition of the Memorial and Cemetery Architecture of the Great War*, Exhibition catalogue, 1977, p. 5
35. Summers, p. 17
36. S. Sassoon, *Selected Poems*, 1968, p. 57
37. Menin Gate, Wikipedia entry
38. Boys and staff fighting for enemy nations appear to have been few, although some examples have been cited earlier at Abbotsholme, Chigwell and Manchester GS
39. F. Stewart, *Loretto 150*, p. 182
40. *The Radleian*, 28 July 1917
41. Winchester College Headmaster's Report to Warden and Fellows for school year ending July 1915
42. Ibid., August 1916
43. Winter, p. 79
44. *The Gresham*, December 1923, p. 116
45. Bedford School War Memorial booklet, 1928
46. C. Kernot, *British Public Schools War Memorials*, 1927, p. 146
47. Ibid., p. 228
48. Ibid., p. 102
49. Ibid., p. 285
50. Ibid., p. 291
51. Ibid., p. 106
52. Ibid., p. 138
53. Ibid., p. 94
54. Ibid., p. 1
55. J. Piggott, *Dulwich College: A History 1616–2008*, 2008
56. *The Carthusian*, December 1917, p. 164
57. Minutes of Committee of Management of Tonbridge School War Memorial 1918–39
58. Stonyhurst War Memorial, December 1917
59. *The History of the Royal Medical Foundation of Epsom College*, p. 83, Epsom College Website.
60. Letters to George Corner, edited from Wellington School Magazine, Vols V and VI
61. Kernot, p. 69
62. B. Matthews, *By God's Grace*, p. 148
63. Robinson, p. 92
64. Wellington College, Reports of the Master to the Governors 1920–1924
65. Author's analysis of various school questionnaires, March 2013
66. D. McDowell, *Carrying On*, pp. 1, 291
67. Dom Lucius Graham, ed., *Downside and the War 1914–1919*, 1925
68. A. Young, ed., 'War Book of Upper Canada College', 1923
69. Hinde, p. 138

70. Kernot, p. 289
71. N. Pevsner, *Pioneers of Modern Design*, 1949, p. 152
72. Quoted in P. Parker, *The Old Lie*, p. 217
73. Kernot, p. 192
74. C. Stocks, *History of Rossall School*, 1945, p. 126
75. J. Witheridge, *Frank Fletcher*, pp. 182–5
76. J. Firth, *Rendall of Winchester*, 1954, pp. 173–4
77. Baker's design for a memorial cloister at his old school, Tonbridge, was initially approved and then turned down by the governors, probably because of its projected cost
78. Firth, pp. 181–2
79. Ibid., p. 184
80. HM Winchester Report to Warden and Fellows for school year ending August 1924
81. *The Harrovian*, 1919, Issue No 4, p. 10
82. *The Watsonian*, 1919
83. D. Newsome, *A History of Wellington College*, 1959, p. 318
84. Denstone Questionnaire, February 2013
85. With thanks to Simon Smith at Brighton College for this information
86. Kernot, p. 61
87. Winter, p. 107
88. *The Harrovian*, 25 May 1918
89. Sandham Memorial Chapel, entry in Wikipedia
90. *The Magnet*, August 1919
91. McDowell, p. 319
92. Memoir by Miss May Reid, in possession of David Walsh
93. Julian Barnes, *Through the Window*, 2012, p. 83
94. D. Lloyd, *Battlefield Tourism*, 1998, p. 110
95. *The Clavian*, December 1939, p. 123
96. Tubby Clayton, *The Times*, 7 January 1930, as quoted in Lloyd, p. 171

Chapter 9 – The War Becomes History

1. Emails to author from archivists of The Leys, KES Birmingham, Shrewsbury, and, later in this section, Eton, Charterhouse, Bloxham and King's Canterbury
2. George Turner, article in *The Marlburian*, Lent 1966. Turner became Master of Marlborough and Headmaster of Charterhouse
3. Email to author from Peter Henderson, KSC Archivist, April 2013
4. M. Walsh, *Hanging a Rebel: the Life of CRW Nevinson*, 2008, pp. 28–9
5. E. Zillekens, ed., *Charterhouse: A Portrait*, 2011, p. 119
6. Email to author from Simon Batten, Bloxham Archivist, April 2013
7. C. Walston, ed., *With a Fine Disregard*, 2006, p. 126
8. Email to author from Peter Henderson, KSC Archivist April 2013
9. *Collected Poems of Rupert Brooke with a Memoir*, 1923, pxi
10. W. Sorley, ed., *The Letters of Charles Sorley*, 1919, p. 40
11. The Music Master was Percy Godfrey, who wrote these words in a note added to a review of a 1914 concert. Information from P. Henderson, April 1913
12. *The Cantuarian*, November 1916, p. 323
13. Brian Bond, *The Unquiet Western Front*, 2002, p. 13
14. P. Nash to Margaret Nash, 16 November 1917, included in P. Nash , *Outline*, 1949, p. 211
15. P. Nash to Margaret Nevinson, 18 April 1917, quoted in David Boyd Haycock, *A Crisis of Brilliance*, 2009, pp. 263–4
16. Haycock, p. 264
17. Ibid., p. 278
18. J. Stallworthy, *Anthem for Doomed Youth*, 2002, p. 9

19. Ursula Vaughan Williams, *Ralph Vaughan Williams*, 1964
20. Notes on Arthur Bliss, *Artists' Rifles 1914–18*, CD Audiobook
21. *George Watson's College in the First World War*, compilation in George Watson's archive
22. *The Times*, 7 September 1917, quoted in M. Brown, *The IWM Book of the Somme*, 1996, p. 298
23. G. Gliddon, *Somme 1916*, 2006, p. 358
24. H. Page Croft, *Twenty-Two Months Under fire*, 1917, p. 237
25. A. E. Housman, *A Shropshire Lad*, Poem XXIII
26. A. D. Gillespie, *Letters from Flanders*, 1916, p. 70
27. S. Hewett, *A Scholar's Letters from France*, 1918, p. 112, quoted in C. Moore-Bick, *Playing the Game*, 2012, p. 245
28. Gillespie, p. 311. His brother Tom had been killed at La Bassée in October 1914
29. Juliet Nicolson, *The Great Silence*, 2009, p. 142
30. Sherborne School Questionnaire, March 2013
31. *The Gresham*, December 1923, p. 116
32. G. Orwell, *Keep the Aspidistra Flying*, 1936, Ch 3
33. G. Greene, ed., *The Old School Tie*, 1934
34. D. Newsome, *History of Wellington College*, 1959, p. 342
35. N. Annan, *Our Age*, 1990, p. 48
36. Giles and Esmond Romilly, *Out of Bounds*, 1935
37. C. Mackay, *Kelvinside Academy 1878–1978*, 1978, p. 120
38. *The Alleynian*, 1934, quoted in J. Piggott, *Dulwich College: A History 1616–2008*, 2008
39. C. Tyerman, *A History of Harrow School*, 2000, p. 449
40. Annan, p. 35
41. Ibid.
42. Anthony Blunt reminiscence, *The Marlburian*, Lent 1966, p. 32
43. T. Hinde, *Paths of Progress*, 1992, p. 136
44. R. C. Sherriff, 'The English Public Schools in the War', in G. Panichas, ed., *Promise of Greatness*, 1968, p. 134
45. Annan, p. 47
46. Newsome, p. 337
47. *The Times*, 7 January 1930, as quoted in D. Lloyd, *Battlefield Tourism*, 1998, p. 171
48. Newsome, p. 347
49. W. Blunt, *Married to a Single Life: an Autobiography*, 1983, p. 138
50. Tyerman, p. 445
51. A. Quick, *Charterhouse*, 1990, p. 116
52. Christopher Lee in conversation with Anthony Seldon, 22 May 2013
53. S. Nowell-Smith, *The Innocence of Ceremony*, 1989
54. Christopher Everett, letter to author, October 2012
55. A. Douglas-Smith, *City of London School*, 1937, p. 397
56. L. Cheshire, *The Light of Many Suns*, 1985, p. 9
57. B. Gardner, *The Public Schools*, 1973, p. 215
58. Numbers taken from school questionnaires, January 2013
59. Questionnaires from those schools
60. F. Fletcher, *After Many Days*, 1937, p. 278, quoted in J. Witheridge, *Frank Fletcher*, 2005, p. 192
61. *The Times*, 15 April 1935, quoted in Witheridge, p. 193
62. P. Mileham, *Wellington College*, 2008, p. 87
63. Email to David Walsh from Christopher and Billy Everett, 16 June 2013
64. T. Card, *Eton Renewed*, 1994, p. 160
65. R. C. Sherriff, quoted in B. Bond, *The Unquiet Western Front*, 2002, p. 35
66. R. C. Sherriff, *No Leading Lady*, 1968, p. 39ff
67. Ibid., p. 317

68. E. Blunden, *Undertones of* War, 1928, p. 242
69. *Guardian* obituary, 22 January 1974
70. Blunden's pupil at Oxford in 1938–9, Keith Douglas, was also at Christ's Hospital. Blunden nurtured his poetic talents which led to Douglas becoming one of the foremost poets of 1939–45. He was killed in Normandy in June 1944
71. Charles Carrington, *A Subaltern's War*, preface to 1964 edition, p. 16
72. Carrington Papers, IWM, quoted in J. Walker, 'Officers' Memoirs', published in *Stand To* magazine, September 2000, p. 19
73. C. Douie, *The Weary Road*, 1929, pp. 16–17, quoted in Walker, p. 20
74. 'Military Rugby' in C. Walston, *With a Fine Disregard*, 2006, pp. 110–111
75. G. Chapman, quoted in Brian Bond, *Survivors of a Kind*, 1975, pp. 158–9
76. Sidney Rogerson, *Twelve Days on the Somme*, 1933
77. E. Blunden, The *Observer*, 26 May 1935, quoted by Walker, p. 21
78. D. Reynolds, 'Churchill the Historian', *History Today*, Vol 55, 2005
79. H. Strachan, 'Military Rugby', in C. Walston, *With a Fine Disregard*, p. 112
80. M. Gilbert, *Winston Churchill 1922–1939*, 1976, p. 1113
81. *The Cantuarian*, Vol XXX No 3, August 1964, pp. 135–6
82. S. Hynes, *A War Imagined: The First World War and English Culture*, 1990, p. 439
83. Ion Trewin, *Alan Clark*, p. 173
84. Ibid., p. 178
85. Richard Holmes, *Tommy*, pp. xxi-xxii
86. John Terraine, *Douglas Haig: the Educated Soldier*, 1963
87. C. Barnett, *A Military Historian's view of the Literature of the Great War*, Transactions of the Royal Society of Literature 1970, quoted in B. Bond, *The Unquiet Western Front*, p. 27
88. Bond, p. 69
89. Sir Michael Howard in conversation with Anthony Seldon, 10 June 2013
90. A. J. P. Taylor, *The First World War: an Illustrated History*, 1963, pp. 13, 146–8
91. *The Times*, 27 April 2013
92. Sir Michael Howard in conversation with Anthony Seldon, 10 June 2013
93. R. Holmes, *Tommy*, 2004, pxxiii
94. Richard Holmes, *The Western Front*, 1999, p. 17
95. Bond, p. 79
96. I. Beckett, *The Great War 1914–18*, 2001, p. 643
97. Peter Parker, *The Old Lie: The Great War and the Public School Ethos*, 1987, p. 284
98. Correlli Barnett letter to Anthony Seldon, 16 July 2013

Chapter 10 – The Lost Generation

1. Bishop of Worcester, Malvern College, as quoted in C. Kernot, *British Public Schools War Memorials*, 1927, p. 136
2. on the Western Front, preface
3. *Statistics of the Military Effort of the British Empire*, 1922, p. 237
4. Sebastian Faulks, *Birdsong*, 1993, p. 189
5. *The Times*, 4 August 1914
6. *Wisden Cricketers' Almanac*, 1915, p. 321
7. W. Roe, *Public Schools Cricket*, 1951
8. George Heslop letter, September 1917, Sevenoaks School archive
9. H. Stokoe, ed., 'Tonbridge School and the Great War', 1923, p. 295
10. Obituaries, *Wisden*, 1919
11. Don Denton, Cricinfo profile, www.espncricinfo.com and Wellingborough School archives
12. J. Winter, 'The Lost Generation', BBC broadcast, 29 July 2009

13. Arthur Gleason, *Inside the British Isles*, 1917, p36, quoted in Adrian Gregory, *The Last Great War: British Society and the Great War*, 2008, p. 26

14. Gregory, p. 126

15. Winter, op. cit.

16. Lord French, Preface to *The Roll of Honour and the War Record of the Artists' Rifles*, 1922, pp. xi–xxi

17. C. Masterman, *England after the War*, 1922, pp. 31–3

18. R. Pound, *The Lost Generation*, 1964, p. 77

19. David Cannadine, *The Decline and Fall of the British Aristocracy*, 1990, pp. 79–80

20. J. Winter, *London Review of Books*, 5 March 1987

21. J. Winter, *The Great War and the British People*, 1995, pp. 65–6

22. Ibid., p. 86

23. Ibid., p. 85

24. P. Parker, *London Review of Books*, 8 January 1987

25. T. May, *The Victorian Public School*, 2011, p. 58

26. *British Universities and the War: a Record and its Meaning*, 1919, pp. 22, 26, 32. G. Carey, ed., *The War List of the University of Cambridge*, 1920. E. Craig and W. Gibson, eds., *Oxford University Roll of Service*, 1920, quoted in Winter, p. 96

27. *British Universities and the War*, p. xiii

28. Cambridge deaths were 18.0 per cent of those who served, Oxford 19.2 per cent

29. R .Carr and B. Hart, 'Old Etonians, Great War Demographics and the Interpretation of British Eugenics 1914–39', *First World War Studies*, Vol 3 No 2, 2012, pp. 217–239

30. G. Pike letter to author, 17 February 2013

31. Winter, pp. 66–8

32. A. Maclean, *Public Schools and the Great War*, 1923, pp. 7–18

33. The Rolls of Honour analysed were from: Barnard Castle, Bishop's Stortford, Denstone, Downside, Epsom, Fettes, Glasgow Academy, Greshams, Harrow, King's Canterbury, King's Ely, Lancing, Manchester GS, Marlborough, Melbourne GS, Plymouth, Queen's Taunton, RGS Newcastle, RBAI, St John's Leatherhead, Sedbergh, Sherborne, Shrewsbury, Tonbridge, Wellingborough, Wellington School, Westminster, Winchester

34. Gregory, p. 124.

35. Radley College Register 1847–1947.

36. C. Tyerman, *History of Harrow School*, 2000, p. 443

37. C. Walston, *With a Fine Disregard*, 2006, p. 111

38. Charterhouse war statistics, paper in Charterhouse archives, 1975

39. The schools analysed are: Bloxham, Edinburgh Academy, Eton, Fettes, Greshams, King's Canterbury, The Leys, Tonbridge, Winchester

40. List of First World War VCs, Wikipedia. The ranks given are those at the time the award-winning action took place

41. Haileybury's VCs include two from the United Services College, absorbed by the Imperial Service College in 1906 and by Haileybury in 1942

42. R. Holmes, *Riding the Retreat*, 2007, p. 254

43. T. Norman, ed., *Armageddon Road – A VC's Diary*, 1982, quoted in R. van Emden, *The Quick and the Dead*, 2011, p. 122

44. M. Garrs, *Valiant Hearts: Uppingham VCs*, 2010, pp. 42–51

45. J. Winter, letter in *London Review of Books*, 5 March 1987

46. Ian F.W. Beckett, *The Great War: 1914–1918*, 2001, pp. 643–4

47. Robert Blake, quoted in Juliet Nicolson, *The Great Silence*, 2009, p. 146

48. Richard Law to Paul Emrys-Evans, 13 September 1939, British Library, Emrys-Evans Papers

49. Anthony Seldon diary

50. John McCloy, quoted in M. Gilbert, *Winston Churchill 1941–5*, 1986, p. 760

51. Quoted in Beckett, p. 644
52. R. C. Whiting, *Clement Attlee*, Oxford Dictionary of National Biography
53. Francis Beckett, *Clem Attlee: A Biography*, 1997
54. Email to David Walsh from Toby Parker, Haileybury Archivist, 22 May 2013
55. D. R. Thorpe, *Eden*, 2003, p. 28
56. Anthony Eden, *Another World 1897–1917*, 1976, p. 150
57. Thorpe, p. 37
58. Ibid., p. 42
59. Harold Macmillan, *The Winds of Change*, 1966, p. 88
60. Ibid., p. 98
61. Jean Moorcroft-Wilson, *Siegfried Sassoon: The Making of a War Poet.A Biography 1886–1918*, 2002, p. 406
62. Lyn Macdonald, *The Roses of No Man's Land*, 1980, pp. 303–4
63. Sir Harold Gillies, *Trauma*, 2006, pp. 143–56
64. Arthur Pearson, *Victory over Blindness*, 1919
65. Ian Fraser, *Whereas I was Blind; Autobiography*, 1942
66. Moorcroft-Wilson, p. 406
67. Adrian Gregory, *The Last Great War*, 2008, p. 266

Bibliography

1 Primary Sources

1.1 Primary Sources from Schools

1.1.1 School Great War Questionnaires
All schools listed in the Appendix supplied factual information, in Great War **Questionnaires**, about their school in 1914, its record of service in the war, the formation of the OTC, the process of commemoration of the war, their current practice with regard to commemoration and battlefield trips, and other matters. The information contained in these questionnaires will be a resource for future researchers and will be retained in the archives at Tonbridge School.

1.1.2 Headmasters' Conference
Reports of the Committee of the Headmasters' Conference 1914–1929
Reports of Annual Meetings of the Headmasters' Conference 1914–1929

1.1.3 Official Papers in School Archives
Berkhamsted School: Charles Greene's Prefect Book
Charterhouse School: Frank Fletcher's scrapbook
Harrow School: Head of School Book 1914–18
Harrow School: Governors Minute Book 1914–18
Manchester Grammar School: Governors' Minutes 1914–18
Sherborne School: Report of the Headmaster 1917
Tonbridge School: Minutes of Management Committee of the War Memorial 1919–39
Wellington College: Reports of the Headmaster 1919–24
Winchester College: Reports of the Headmaster 1914–24

1.1.4 Unpublished Letters and Memoirs held in School Archives
Bramston, J. T. *Letters*, Winchester College archive
Corner, G. *Letters*, Wellington School archive
Diggle, G. *Unpublished Memoir*, Gresham's school archive
Girling, J. *Poems*, Wellington College archive
Hayman, W. *Unpublished Memoir*, Sherborne School archive

285

Houston, T. *Letters*, Coleraine Academical Institution archive
Luxmoore, H. *Letters*, Eton College archive
Mackenzie, A. *Correspondence* Lakefield College School (Canada) archive
Nathan, C. (ed) *Warden Sing Correspondence*, St Edward's School archive
O'Hanlon, G. *Unpublished War Diary and Memoir*, Sherborne School archive
Somervell, D. *Unpublished Autobiography*, Repton School archive
Wynne Willson, D. *Cheerful Days*, Gresham's School archive

1.1.5 Further source material from the following schools

Abbotsholme School, Alleyn's School, Ardingly College, Bangor GS, Barnard Castle School, Bedford School, Berkhamsted School, Bloxham School, Bootham School, Brighton College, Bury GS, Campbell College, Caterham School, Charterhouse School, Cheltenham College, Cheltenham Ladies College, Chigwell School, Christ Church GS Aus, Christ's College Brecon, Christ's College NZ, Christ's Hospital, City of London School, Clifton College, Clongowes Wood, Coleraine AI, Cranleigh School, Dauntsey's School, Dean Close School, Denstone College, Diocesan College SA, Dover College, Downside School, Dulwich College, Durham School, Eastbourne College, Edinburgh Academy, Eltham College, Emanuel School, Epsom College, Eton College, Fettes College, Geelong GS Aus, George Heriot's College, George Watson's College, Glasgow Academy, Gresham's School, Haileybury College, Harrow School, Highgate School, Hilton College SA, Hurstpierpoint College, Ipswich School, John Lyon School, King's College School Wimbledon, King Edward's School Birmingham, King's School Macclesfield, King's School Canterbury, King's School Ely, King's School Gloucester, King's School Parramatta Aus, King William's College IOM, Lakefield School Canada, Lancing College, Leighton Park School, The Leys, Liverpool College, Loretto School, Magdalen College School, Malvern College, Manchester GS, Marlborough College, Melbourne GS Aus, Merchant Taylors' School London, Merchant Taylors' School Crosby, Merchiston Castle School, Methodist College Belfast, Michaelhouse School SA, Nottingham HS, Oundle School, Perse School, Plymouth College, Pocklington School, Portsmouth GS, Queen's College Taunton, Radley College, Ratcliffe College, Repton School, Ridley College Canada, Rossall School, Royal Belfast AI, RGS Newcastle, Royal Hospital School, Rossall School, Rugby School, St Andrew's College SA, St Dunstan's College, St Edward's School, St John's School Leatherhead, St John's College SA, St Lawrence College, St Paul's School, St Paul's Girls School, St Peter's York, Sedbergh School, Sevenoaks School, Sherborne School, Sydney CEGS (Shore) Aus, Shrewsbury School, Solihull School, Stonyhurst College, Sydney GS Aus, Tonbridge School, Trent College, Trinity College School Canada, Upper Canada College, Uppingham School, Warwick School, Wellingborough School, Wellington College, Wellington School, Westminster School, Whitgift School, Winchester College

1.1.6 School Magazines

The Alleynian (Dulwich), *The Ardinian* (Ardingly), *The Blue* (Christ's Hospital), *The Barrovian* (King William's IOM), *The Breconian*, *The Cantuarian* (King's Canterbury), *The Carthusian*, *The Campbellian*, *The Cheltonian*, *The Cholmelian* (Highgate), *The Chronicle* (Eton), *The City of London School Magazine*, *The Clavian* (Bury GS),

The Clongownian (Clongowes Wood), *College Times* (Upper Canada College) *Diocesan College Magazine* (Bishop's SA), *The Elean* (King's Ely), *The Elizabethan* (Westminster), *The Fettesian, The Gresham, The Haileyburian, The Harrovian, Kings School Magazine* (King's Parramatta), *The Kingswood Magazine, The Leightonian* (Leighton Park), *The Lyonian* (John Lyon School), *The Marlburian, The Meteor* (Rugby), *The Michaelhouse Chronicle, The Mitre* (Christ Church Australia), *The Paulina* (St Paul's Girls), *The Portcullis* (Emanuel), *The Salopian* (Shrewsbury), *The Radleian, The RBAI School News, The Register* (Christ' NZ), *The Reptonian, The Salopian, St Johns College Magazine* (St John's SA), *The School Record* (Trinity College School, Canada), *The Shirburnian, The Silcoatian, The Stonyhurst Magazine, The Sydneian* (Sydney GS), *The Tonbridgian, The Torch-Bearer* (Shore Aus), *The Ulula* (Manchester GS), *The Uppinghamian, The Watsonian, The Wellingburian, The Wellingtonian, The Wellington School Magazine, The Wykehamist*

1.1.7 School War Memorial Books, Registers and Rolls of Honour
Most schools have a roll of honour published within the school in one form or another. Those listed below are the ones we have used. If these are known to have been published externally, the editor, publisher and publication date are recorded.

Barnard Castle *Roll of Honour*
Bedford School *Roll of Honour*
Bishop's Stortford College *Lest we Forget*
Brighton College War Record 1914–19, Brighton 1919
Charterhouse School *Book of Remembrance*
Christ's Hospital *Roll of Honour*
Denstone College *Roll of Honour*
Downside and the War 1914–19, London 1925, Graham, Dom L. (ed)
Eastbourne College *Roll of War Service*
Epsom College *Roll of Honour*
Etonians Who Fought in the Great War, London, 1921, Vaughan E. (ed)
Fettes College *Old Fettesians Who Served During the Great War*
Glasgow Academy Roll of Honour 1914–18, Jackson Wylie, Glasgow, 1923
Harrow Memorials of the Great War, Philip Lee Warner, 1918–21
Hulme Grammar School, Oldham *Roll of Honour*
King's School Canterbury *Roll of Honour*
King's School Ely *Roll of Honour*
Kings School Macclesfield *Roll of Honour*
Lancing College *Roll of Honour*
Loretto School *Roll of Honour*
Manchester Grammar School *Book of Remembrance*
Marlborough College *Register 1843–1952*
Melbourne GS, *War Services Old Melburnians 1914–18*, Melbourne, 1923, Kiddle J. (ed)
Michaelhouse School *Roll of Honour*
Oundle Memorials of the Great War, 1929, King H. (ed)
Queen's College Taunton War Memorial
Plymouth College, *Roll of Honour*
Radley College *Register 1847–1947*

Royal Belfast Academical Institution *Roll of Honour*
Royal Grammar School, Newcastle *Roll of Honour*
Memorials of Rugbeians Who Fell in the Great War, 1919
St Dunstan's College Roll of Honour 1914–19, 1988, Collett D.
St John's School, Leatherhead *Roll of Honour*
Sedbergh School *Roll of Honour*
Sherborne School *Roll of Honour*
Shrewsbury School Roll of Service 1914–18, Wilding & Son, Shrewsbury, 1921
Tonbridge School and the Great War, Whitefriars Press, Tonbridge, 1923, Stokoe H.
    (ed)
Stonyhurst College *The Stonyhurst War Record*, 1927
Tonbridge School *Register 1860–1945*
Wykehamist War Service Roll 1914–19, Wells, Winchester, 1919 Trant Bramston J. (ed)
War Book of Upper Canada College, 1919
Wellingborough School *Roll of Honour*
Westminster School *Roll of Honour*
Winchester College War Memorial Book

Some schools (and individuals) have also created websites encompassing the details to be found in rolls of honour and war supplements. Those which have been used by the authors include the following, although this should not be seen as a definitive list: Epsom, Gresham's, Harrow, King's Canterbury, Lancing, Loretto, Melbourne GS, RBAI

1.2 Published Primary Sources
Asquith, C. *Diaries 1915–18*, Hutchinson, 1968
Bickersteth, J. (ed) *The Bickersteth Diaries*, Leo Cooper, 1995
Bishop, A. (ed) *Vera Brittain's War Diary*, Gollancz, 1981
Bishop, A. and Bostridge, M. (eds) *Letters from a Lost Generation*, NUP, Boston, 1998
Blunden, E. *Undertones of War*, Cobden Sanderson, 1928
Blunt, W. *Married to a Single Life*, Michael Russell, 1983
Brittain, V. *Testament of Youth*, Gollancz, 1933
Brooke, R. *Collected Poems*, Sidgwick & Jackson, 1923
Buchan, J. *These for Remembrance*, Buchan & Enright, 1919
Carrington, C. *Soldier from the Wars Returning*, Pen & Sword, 2006
Chapman, G. *A Passionate Prodigality*, Nicolson & Watson, 1933
Congreve, B. *Armageddon Road – a VC's Diary*, Kimber, 1982
Craster, J. (ed) *Fifteen Rounds a Minute*, MacMillan, 1976
Douglas, S. *Years of Combat*, Collins, 1963
Douie, C. *The Weary Road*, John Murray,1929
Dunn, J. *The War the Infantry Knew*, P. S. King, 1938
Eden, A. *Another World*, Allen Lane, 1976
Edmonds, C. *A Subaltern's War*, Peter Davies, 1929
Faithfull, L. *In the House of my Pilgrimage*, Chatto & Windus, 1924
Fletcher, F. *After Many Days*, Robert Hale, 1937
Fletcher, F. *Brethren and Companions*, Robert Hale, 1936
Gillespie, A. D. *Letters from Flanders*, Smith Elder, 1916

Gleason, A. *Inside the British Isles*, London, 1917

Glubb, J. *Into Battle*, Cassell, 1977

Graves, R. *Goodbye to All That*, Jonathan Cape, 1929

Haig Brown, A. *The OTC and the Great War*, Country Life, 1915

Hankey, D. *A Student at Arms*, Melrose, 1917

Harington, C. *Plumer of Messines*, John Murray, 1935

Harris, R. *Billie – The Nevill Letters*, MacRae, 1991

Hewett, S. *A Scholar's Letters from the Front*, Longmans, 1918

Housman, L. (ed) *War Letters of Fallen Englishmen*, Victor Gollancz, 1930

Howson, H. (ed) *Two Men*, OUP, 1919

Joliffe, J. (ed) *Raymond Asquith: Life and Letters*, Collins, 1980

Jones, P. and Jones, H. *War Letters of a Public Schoolboy*, Cassell, 1918

Kernot, C. *British Public Schools' War Memorials*, Roberts & Newton,1927

Kettle, M. and Kettle, T. *The Ways of War*, Scribner, Dublin, 1917

Levett, M. (ed) *Letters of Richard Byrd Levett*, Spottiswoode,1917

Lewis, C. *Sagittarius Rising*, Peter Davies, 1936

Lyttelton, O. *Memoirs of Lord Chandos*, Bodley Head, 1962

Maclean, A. *The Public Schools and the Great War*, Stanford, 1923

Macmillan, H. *Winds of Change 1914–39*, MacMillan, 1966

Macnaghten H. *Eton Letters: 1915–18 by a Housemaster*, Spottiswoode, 1920

Masterman, C. *England After the War*, 1922

Moran, C. *The Anatomy of Courage*, Constable, 1945

Neville, J. *War Letters of a Light Infantryman*, Sifton, 1930

Osborn, E. *The Muse in Arms*, John Murray, 1917

Owen, H. *Journey from Obscurity*, OUP, 1963

Page Croft, H. *Twenty-Two Months Under Fire*, Murray, 1917

Pearson, A. *Victory over Blindness*, Doran, 1919

Pollard, A. *Fire-Eater: Memoirs of a VC*, Hutchinson, 1932

Rayner-Wood, A. *Twenty Years After*, Spottiswoode, 1939

Rees, R. *A Schoolmaster at War*, Haycock, 1936

Reith, J. *Wearing Spurs*, Hutchinson, 1966

Richter D. *Lionel Sotheby's Great War*, Ohio UP, 1997

Rogerson, S. *Twelve Days*, Barker, 1933

Romilly G. and E. *Out of Bounds*, Hamish Hamilton, 1935

Sanders, L. *A Soldier of England*, Maxwell, 1920

Sassoon, S. *Memoirs of an Infantry Officer*, Faber & Faber, 1930

Sherriff, R. C. *Journey's End*, London, 1928

Sherriff, R. C. *No Leading Lady*, Littlehampton, 1968

Sorley, W. (ed) *The Letters of Charles Sorley*, CUP, 1919

Talbot L. *Gilbert Walter Lyttelton Talbot*, London, 1916

Thomas, E. *Poems*, Nelson, 1920

Thomas, H. *World Without End*, Heinemann, 1931

Times Newspapers *History of the UPS Brigade*, London, 1917

War Office *Statistics of the Military Effort of the British Empire*, HMSO, 1922

Wisden, J. *Cricketers' Almanacs 1915–18*, London

Wootton, B. *In a World I Never Made*, Harper Collins, 1967

1.3 Unpublished Primary Sources

Imperial War Museum Oral History Archive
Raeburn, W. *Unpublished Diary 1914–15*, D. Raeburn
Whittaker, G. *The Changing Years*, 1977
Whitworth, E. *Papers and notebooks*, Regimental Museum of the Royal Welsh

2 Secondary Sources

2.1 School Histories and War Histories

Ballance, D. *The Buds of Virtue*, James & James, 2000
Best, G. *Continuity and Change, Kingswood School through the Ages*, Bath, 1998
Barrett, A. *Michaelhouse 1896–1968*, Pietermaritzburg, 1968
Bate, W. *Light Blue Down Under: History of Geelong GS*, OUP, Australia, 1990
Batten, S. *A Shining Light: Bloxham School*, Third Millennium, 2010
Blackie, J. *Bradfield 1850–1975*, Bradfield, 1976
Blatchly, J. *A Famous Antient Seed-Plot of Learning: A History of Ipswich School*, Ipswich, 2003
Blumenau, R. *A History of Malvern College*, Macmillan, 1965
Bradley, A. *History of Marlborough College*, John Murray, 1927
Bradley, R. *Ridley: A Canadian School*, Canada, 2000
Brown, J. *Independent Witness: 150 Years of Taunton School*, Taunton, 1997
Brown, S. *Bootham School 1823–1973*, Bootham, 1973
Burden, P. *The Lion and the Stars: History of Bablake School*, Coventry, 1990
Card, T. *Eton Renewed*, John Murray, 1994
Charlesworth, M. *Salopians 1900–1950*, Shrewsbury, 2000
Ciaran, F. and Teal, J. *The Stained Glass Windows of Christ's College Chapel*, New Zealand, 2001
Clarke, H. *History of Sedbergh School 1525–1925*, Jackson, 1925
Costello, P. *History of Clongowes Wood College*, Gill & Macmillan, Dublin, 1989
Craze, M. *History of Felsted School*, Cowell, 1955
Douglas Smith, A. *City of London School*, Blackwells, 1937
Edwards, P. and Hillman, W. *A School with a View*, Christ Church GS, Perth, 2010
Firth, J. *Winchester*, Blackie, 1936
Furness, W. *Centenary History of Rossall School*, Gale and Polden, 1944
Gardener, J. *Bishop's 150*, Juta, Cape Town, 1997
Garrs, M. *Valiant Hearts: Uppingham School VCs*, Uppingham, 2010
Gaunson, A. *College Street Heroes*, Sydney Grammar School Press, 1998
Gourlay, A. *History of Sherborne School*, Warrens, 1951
Hamilton, D. *College: History of Christ's College*, Christchurch, 1996
Handford, B. *Lancing College: History and Memoirs*, History Press, 1986
Harding, J. *A Methodist Education: The Leys 1875–1914*, Cambridge, 2012
Hill, D. *For King and Country*, Chameleon, 2003
Hill, R. *History of St Edward's School 1863–1963*, Oxford, 1962
Hinde, T. *Paths of Progress: History of Marlborough College*, James & James, 1992
Hope-Simpson, J. *Rugby Since Arnold*, Macmillan, 1967
Hoy, M. *A Blessing to this Island*, James & James, 2006
Hughes, R. *History of St John's School Leatherhead*, Gresham, 2001

Loynton, J. *A History of Solihull School 1560–2010*, Solihull 2010

MacDonald, H. (ed) *A Hundred Years of Fettes*, Constable,1970

McDowell, D. *Carrying On, Fettes College, War and the World*, Matador, 2012

Mackay, C. *Kelvinside Academy 1878–1978*, 1978

Macleod, I. *The Glasgow Academy: 150 Years*, Glasgow, 1997

Magnusson, M. *The Clacken and the Slate*, Collins, 1974

Malim, F. *Almae Matres: Recollections of Some Schools*, CUP, 1948

Matthews, B. *By God's Grace: History of Uppingham School*, Whitehall, 1984

Megahey, A. *History of Cranleigh School*, London, 1983

Mileham, P. *Wellington College*, Third Millennium, 2008

Mumford, A. *Manchester Grammar School 1515–1915*, Manchester,1919

Nathan, C. (ed) *Cometh the Hour, Cometh the School: St Edward's School, at War*, Oxford, 2004

Newsome, D. *A History of Wellington College*, John Murray, 1959

Nuttall, N. *Lift Up Your Hearts: Hilton College 1872–1972*, Durban, 1971

Orchard, B. *A Look at the Head and the Fifty: Tonbridge School*, James & James, 1991

Perry, R. *Ardingly 1848–1946*, London, 1951

Peterson, R. *Facing the Foe: War Service of Shore Old Boys*, Sydney, 2006

Piggott, J. *Dulwich College: A History 1616–2008*, Dulwich, 2008

Poland, M. *The Boy in You: Biography of St Andrew's College*, Grahamstown, 2008

Riley, J. *History of Sherborne School CCF*, Sherborne, 1989

Scott-Giles, C. *History of Emanuel School 1594–1964*, London, 1947

Smart, S. *When Heroes Die*, Breedon, 2001

Sargeaunt, J. *A History of Bedford School*, Fisher Unwin, 1925

Stewart, F. *Loretto 150*, Edinburgh, 1981

Quick, A. *Charterhouse*, James and James, 1990

Piggott, J. *Dulwich College 1616–2008*, Dulwich, 2008

Somervell, D. *Tonbridge School 1553–1953*, Faber & Faber, 1947

Tanner, L. *Westminster School*, Country Life, 1951

Thomas, B. *Repton 1557–1957*, Repton, 1957

Tod, A. *Charterhouse*, Bell, 1900

Tyerman, C. *A History of Harrow School 1324–1991*, OUP, 2000

Wainwright, D. *Liverpool Gentlemen: A History of Liverpool College*, 1960

Walsh, D. *A Duty to Serve: Tonbridge School and the 1939–45 War*, TMI, 2011

Walston, C. (ed) *With a Fine Disregard: Portrait of Rugby School*, TMI, 2006

Wright, C. *Kent College Centenary Book*, Canterbury, 1985

Zillekens, E. (ed) *Charterhouse: A 400th Anniversary Portrait*, TMI, 2010

2.2 Histories and Biographies

Annan, N. *Our Age*, Weidenfeld and Nicolson, 1990

Barnes, J. *Through the Window*, Vintage, 2012

Barton, P. *The Somme*, Constable, 2006

Baynes, J. *Morale: A Study of Men and Courage*, Leo Cooper, 1967

Bean, C. *Here my Son*, Angus & Robertson, Sydney, 1950

Beckett, I. *The Great War 1914–18*, Pearson, 2001

Berry, P. and Bostridge, M. *Vera Brittain: A Life*, Virago, 2001

Bond, B. *Survivors of a Kind*, Continuum, 2008

Bond, B. *The Unquiet Western Front*, CUP, 2002

Bourke, J. *Dismembering the Male*, Reaktion, 1996

Bradley, I. and Simon, B. (eds) *The Victorian Public School*, Gill & McMillan, 1975

Brendon, P. *The Decline and Fall of the British Empire*, Jonathan Cape, 2007

Brown, M. *The Imperial War Museum Book of the Somme*, Sidgwick & Jackson, 1996

Brown, M. *The Imperial War Museum Book of 1918*, Sidgwick & Jackson, 1998

Cannadine, D. *The Decline and Fall of the British Aristocracy*, Yale UP, 1990

Clark, A. *The Donkeys*, Hutchinson, 1961

Cooper, S. *The Final Whistle*, Spellmount, 2012

Croft Cooke, R. *The Altar in the Loft*, Putnam,1960

Davis, W. *Into the Silence*, Vintage, 2012

de la Billiere, P. *Supreme Courage*, Little Brown, 2004

Digby, P. *Pyramids and Poppies*, Ashanti, South Africa, 1993

Dyer, G. *The Missing of the Somme*, Hamish Hamilton, 1994

Englund, P. *The Beauty and the Sorrow*, Profile, 2011

Ellsworth-Jones, W. *We Will Not Fight*, Aurum, 2008

Ferguson, N. *The Pity of War*, Penguin, 1998

Fiennes, P. *To War with God*, Mainstream, 2011

Foster, R. *Modern Ireland*, Allen Lane, 1988

Fussell, P. *The Great War and Modern Memory*, OUP, 1975

Gardner, B. *The Public Schools*, Hamish Hamilton, 1973

Gardner, B. (ed) *Up the Line to Death: The War Poets 1914–18*, Methuen, 1964

Garth, J. *Tolkien and the Great War*, Harper Collins, 2004

Gilbert, M. *Winston Churchill 1922–39*, Heinemann, 1976

Gliddon, G. *Somme: A Battlefield Companion*, Gliddon Books, 1997

Gollancz, V. *A Year of Grace*, Gollancz, 1950

Gregory, A. *The Last Great War: British Society and the First World War*, CUP, 2008

Harrison, M. *The Medical War*, OUP, 2010

Hibberd, D. *Wilfred Owen*, Weidenfeld & Nicolson, 2002

Hollis, M. *Now All Roads Lead to France*, Faber & Faber, 2011

Honey, J. *Tom Brown's Universe*, Millington,1977

Holmes, R. *Tommy: The British Soldier on the Western Front*, Harper Collins, 2004

Holmes, R. *Riding the Retreat*, Jonathan Cape, 1995

Holt, T. and V. *My Boy Jack: the Search for Kipling's Only Son*, Pen & Sword, 2007

Hurst, S. *The Public Schools Battalion*, Pen & Sword, 2007

Hynes, S. *A War Imagined: the First World War and English Culture*, Bodley Head, 1990

Jenkins, R. *Asquith*, Collins, 1965

Keegan, J. *The First World War*, Random House, 1998

Lewis-Stempel, J. *Six Weeks*, Weidenfeld & Nicolson, 2010

Lloyd, D. *Battlefield Tourism*, Berg, 1998

Macarthur, B. (ed) *For King and Country*, Little Brown, 2008

Macdonald, L. *Voices and Images of the Great War*, Michael Joseph, 1988

Macdonald, L. *The Roses of No Man's Land*, Michael Joseph, 1980

Mack, E. *Public Schools and British Opinion since 1860*, Columbia UP, 1941

Mackersey, I. *No Empty Chairs*, Weidenfeld & Nicolson, 2012

May, T. *The Victorian Public School*, Shire, 2011

Messenger, C. *Call to Arms, the British Army 1914–18*, Weidenfeld & Nicolson, 2005

Middlebrook, M. *The First Day on the Somme*, Allen Lane, 1971

Middlebrook, M. *The Somme Battlefields*, Viking, 1991

Moorcroft Wilson, J. *Siegfried Sassoon: The Making of a War Poet 1886–1918*, Duck, 2002

Moore-Bick, C. *Playing the Game*, Helion, 2011

Moorhouse, G. *Hells Foundations*, Hodder, 1992

Moynihan, M. *God on our Side*, Secker & Warburg, 1983

Nicolson, J. *The Great Silence*, John Murray, 2010

Panichas, G. (ed) *Promise of Greatness*, Cassell, 1968

Parker, P. *The Old Lie*, Constable, 1987

Pitchfork, G. *The Sowreys*, Grub Street, 2012

Pound, R. *The Lost Generation*, Constable, 1964

Robbins, S. *British Generalship during the Great War*, Ashgate, 2005

Roe, W. *Public Schools Cricket*, Parrish, 1951

Seldon, M. *Poppies and Roses: A Story of Courage*, Economic & Literary Books, 1985

Sheffield, G. *Leadership in the Trenches*, Macmillan, 2000

Sheffield, G. *Forgotten Victory*, Headline, 2001

Sherington, G. *English Education, Social Change and War 1911–20*, MUP, 1981

Simkins, P. *Kitchener's Army*, MUP, 1988

Spagnoly, A. *Salient Points Four*, Leo Cooper, 2004

Snow, R. *Ten Brave Men and True*, Menin House, 2012

Stallworthy, J. *Anthem for Doomed Youth*, Constable, 2002

Stannard, M. *Evelyn Waugh: The Early Years*, Norton, 1986

Steel, N. and Hart, P. *Defeat at Gallipoli*, Macmillan, 1994

Stevens, P. *The Great War Explained*, Pen & Sword, 2012

van Emden, R. *The Quick and the Dead*, Bloomsbury, 2011

van Emden, R. *The Soldiers' War*, Bloomsbury, 2008

Taylor, A. J. P. *The First World War*, Hamish Hamilton, 1963

Thorpe, D. *Eden*, Chatto & Windus, 2003

Travers, T. *The Killing Ground*, Pen and Sword, 2009

Walsh, M. *Hanging a Rebel, the Life of C. R. W. Nevinson*, Lutterworth Press, 2008

Warner, R. *English Public Schools*, Collins, 1945

Weintraub, S. *Silent Night*, Simon & Schuster, 2001

Whitehead, I. *Doctors in the Great War*, Pen & Sword, 1999

Wilson, T. *The Myriad Faces of War*, Polity, 1988

Winter, J. *The Great War and the British People*, Macmillan, 1986

Winter, J. *Sites of Memory, Sites of Mourning*, CUP, 1995

Witheridge, J. *Frank Fletcher 1870–1954: A Formidable Headmaster*, Russell, 2005

Wolff, L. *In Flanders Fields*, Longmans, 1959

2.3 Novels

Delderfield, R. F. *To Serve Them All My Days*, Hodder, 1972

Leslie, S. *The Oppidan*, Scribner, 1922

Raymond, E. *Tell England*, Cassell, 1922

Remarque, E. M. *All Quiet on the Western Front*, Little, Brown, 1929

Waugh, A. *The Loom of Youth*, Methuen, 1917

Vachell, H. *The Hill*, London, 1905

2.4 Other Journals

Carr, R. and Hart, B. 'Old Etonians, Great War Demographics and the Interpretation of British Eugenics 1914–39', *First World War Studies*, Vol 3 No 2, p. 217–239, 2012.
Robinson, A. 'Eton and the First World War', IWM Review, 1993
Robinson, A. 'Eton's Great War Scandal', History Today, November 1993
Parker, P. and Winter, J. Letters in *London Review of Books*, 1987

2.5 Unpublished Dissertations

Halstead, T. *The First World War and the Public School Ethos: Study of Uppingham School*, 2012
Roche, J. *The First Half-Century of the Headmasters' Conference*, 1972

2.6 *Stand To*, the Magazine of the Western Front Association

Archer, J. 'Devonshires on the Somme', May and September 2010
Archer, J. 'Brigadier-General R. H. Husey, DSO and Bar, MC', Jan 2013
Long, G. 'Wellington College in 1914', April 2007
Lucas, M. 'R. C. Sherriff, Journey's End and the 9th East Surreys', Jan 2010
Malet de Carteret, E. 'Captain H. Ackroyd VC' , September 1995
Murland, J. 'The Aristocrats' Cemetery at Zillebeke', January 2011
Piuk, V. 'The Marsden-Smedley Memorial', Sept 1994
Richardson, J. 'Rutherford, Geiger, Chadwick, Mosely and Cockcroft', January 2011
Sharples, C. 'One of the Youngest Pilots Killed in the Great War', September 2011
Silk, D. 'Siegfried Sassoon', April 2002
Spagnoly, A. 'A Mother's Pilgrimage', February 1995
Walker, J. 'Officers' Memoirs', Sept 2000

2.7 Websites

ESPN Cricinfo
Leeds Pals 1 July 1916
Music Web International Denis Browne
Royal Aero Club
Wikipedia – List of World War 1 VCs and other entries on various people and places

Public Schools Index

295

Struan Robinson, 207; Hugh Trevor-
Roper, 229; Ralph Vaughan
Williams, 3, 19, 208, 212, 213
Cheadle Hulme, 256
Cheltenham, 27, 39, 135, 188, 217, 228,
235, 244, 256; Lindsay Anderson, 228;
The Cheltonian, 242; Jack Cohen, 161;
John Glubb, 157; Gustav Holst, 212;
Cyril Hillier, 242; L. D. Morse, 172–3
Cheltenham Ladies College, 92, 124, 256;
Lillian Faithfull, 92, 124; Voluntary
Aid Detachment, 92
Chigwell, 93, 256; Albert Harris, 88;
Herr Sommermeier, 93
Christ Church GS, Australia, 260;
William McClemans, 75–6
Christ's College, NZ, 72–3, 76, 144, 260;
J. D. Boys, 74; Guy Bryan-Brown, 76;
casualties, 73, 76; Charles Carrington,
225; Heliopolis dinner, 136; *The
Register*, 74, 76; Noel Ross, 74
Christ's Brecon, 129, 134, 187, 198, 256;
Breconian, 129; Jack Brooker, 134;
A. P. James, 134; John Robinson, 187
Christ's Hospital, 88, 134, 211, 256; *The
Blue*, 135; Edmund Blunden, 135–6,
211, 224, 226; Thomas Boardman,
114; Wilfrith Elstob, 177–8; 'The
Feast of Five', 135; Thomas Flook,
138; Freddie Llewelyn Hughes, 134
Churchers, 256
City of London, 10, 87, 111, 221, 256;
F. R. Dale, 115; Theodore Bayley
Hardy, 145; T. E. Lawrence, 179–80;
Charles Myers, 150; Eric Townsend,
63
Clayesmore, 256
Clifton, 11, 12, 39, 124, 136, 197, 235,
256; Charles Bean, 74–5, 226;
William Birdwood, 40, 179;
casualties, 110; Douglas Haig, 3, 22,
39, 52, 54, 79, 160, 197, 209, 229, 230,
232, 244; Stephen Morgan, 236;
Michael Redgrave, 230; George
Whitehead, 236
Clongowes Wood, 68, 146, 256;
Clongownian Magazine, 68; John
Holland, 70; James Joyce, 68; Tom
Kettle, 68, 70, 71; Michael O'Rahilly,
68; Willie Redmond, 70

Coleraine Academical Inst, 256;
E. G. Houston, 130; W. E. Wylie,
68–9
Colfe's, 256; Henry Williamson, 2, 43,
252–3
Cranleigh, 87, 198, 203, 256
Culford, 88, 256

Dame Allan's, 256
Daniel Stewart's, 256; John Pinkerton,
145
Dauntseys, 89, 256
Dean Close, 143, 256; Joyce Flecker, 104
Denstone, 193, 257; Mothers' Window,
201
Diocesan College (Bishop's), SA, 81, 82,
83–4, 198, 260; Charles 'Oxo' Bull,
84; Louis Esselen, 81; Reg Hands, 84;
Geoffrey Noaks, 84; H. M. Veale, 83;
Henry White, 81
Dollar, 257
Dover College, 105, 257; Arthur
Harrison, 175; Billy Neville, 59
Downside, 27, 141, 167, 197, 257;
casualties, 177; Cecil Daly, 63; John
Esmond, 173; Stephen Hewett, 19,
61, 64, 153, 159, 214
Dulwich, 86, 134, 172, 175, 194, 235, 244,
257; Alleynian Club debate, 194–5;
The Alleynian, 216; Frank Brock, 175;
Humphrey Gilkes, 181; Arthur
Gilligan, 235; Dom Lucius Graham,
197; Paul Jones, 134–5, 163;
R. T. Rees, 158; Henry Smeddle, 163;
George Smith, 123; Francis
Townend, 56; T. G. Treadgold, 123;
P. G. Wodehouse, 56
Durham School, 257; Anthony Bowlby,
149; William Noel Hodgson, 212

Eastbourne, 257; Hardit Singh Malik,
168–9
Edinburgh Academy, 14, 18, 198, 257;
Tommy Nelson, 155–6
Elizabeth College, Guernsey, 257
Ellesmere, 257
Eltham, 257; Fenner Brockway, 120
Emanuel, 89, 116, 257; Harold Ryley, 116
Epsom, 109, 147, 257; Walter Barton, 109,
195; Roland Bradford, 180, 181; John

Glyn Hughes, 151; John Raymond
Smith, 195

Eton, 10, 12, 17, 19, 20, 27, 28, 35, 39, 80,
87, 94, 101, 113, 117–19, 134, 135,
137, 164, 188, 196, 208, 235, 244, 257;
Nigel Anson, 131; Arthur Balfour,
226, 246; Maurice Baring, 53; Francis
Birch, 176; Wilfred Jasper Blunt, 219;
George Butterworth, 21; Julian Byng,
40, 79, 179; Tim Card, 222;
casualties, 62, 239, 241, 243; Alan
Clark, 3, 54, 229, 230; Lionel Cohen,
43, 158, 159; Billy Congreve, 244;
Kingsley Doyle, 184; Anthony Eden,
3, 23, 28, 29, 30, 142, 173–4, 231, 242,
247, 248–9; Nicholas Eden, 173, 242;
Eton Boating Song, 215; *Eton
Chronicle*, 114, 128, 137; Eton
Memorial School, 200; George
Fletcher, 113–14; games debate, 22;
William Gladstone (Soldier), 189;
Prince Henry of Gloucester, 119;
Julian Grenfell, 38, 46, 53, 211;
Alexis de Gunzburg, 42; Stephen
Hobhouse, 21, 120; Edward Hulse,
42; Aldous Huxley, 104; Fourth of
June 1916, 137; Frederick Kelly, 48,
64, 174; Dillwyn Knox, 176; Hugh
Laurie, 232; Christopher Leighton,
154; Dick Levett, 64; Henry
Luxmoore, 131–2, 186; Edward
Lyttelton, 91, 117–19, 177; Oliver
Lyttelton, 62, 158, 177, 231; Harold
Macmillan, 34, 54, 162, 227, 231, 245,
247, 248–9; Hugh Macnaghten, 131;
Henry Moseley, 21, 50; George
Orwell, 19, 215; Herbert Plumer, 19,
40, 51, 179, 193; Edward Foss Prior,
52; Henry Rawlinson, 40, 179;
A. C. Rayner-Wood, 131; Charles
Rolls, 164; Lord Rosebery, 119,
196, 215; John Scudamore, 54;
A. C. Sheepshanks, 52; Cecil Spring-
Rice, 213; Lionel Sotheby, 134

Exeter, 257

Felsted, 11, 143, 167, 187, 257

Fettes, 26, 28, 49, 85, 86, 91, 124–5, 147,
197, 203, 240, 257; Frank Barnwell,
164; Harold Barnwell, 164; James

Hay Beith, 56; John Mackay-
Thompson, 124–5; James Ross, 147

Frensham Heights, 221

Forest, 257; Richard Holmes, 143, 229,
230, 231, 232

Foyle, 257

Framlingham, 257

Geelong GS, Australia, 71, 72, 73, 193,
261; Harold Birt, 198; casualties, 76

George Watson's, 55, 86, 200, 257; Cecil
Coles, 212–13; Sandy Morrison, 55;
Eric Milroy Trophy, 200

George Heriot's, 92, 257

Giggleswick, 257

Glasgow Academy, 11, 49, 89–90, 90,
257; casualties, 49; Walter Barradell-
Smith, 89–90; J. C. Dunn, 161, 185;
Andrew Bonar Law, 246; John Reith,
44;

Glasgow HS, 257

Glenalmond, 24, 257

Gordonstoun, 221

Gresham's, 12, 29, 85, 88, 102, 257;
W. H. Auden, 215; Benjamin Britten,
229; Geoffrey Diggle, 88; J. R. Eccles,
193, 215; Cuthbert Hill, 173; George
Howson, 12, 123; Dallas Wynne
Wilson, 29, 30

Grey College, Bloemfontein, SA, 181

Haberdashers' Aske's, 257

Haileybury, 11–12, 14, 39, 51, 86, 93, 106,
113, 117, 167, 198, 219, 220, 235, 244,
248, 257; Arthur Addison, 51, 57; Sir
Edmund Allenby, 40, 179; Clement
Attlee, 120, 245, 246, 247, 248; Tom
Attlee, 120; Reginald Blomfield, 190,
191, 198, 200; R. F. Bourne, 86;
Thompson Capper, 54; casualties,
243; Clifford Coffin, 243; George
Grogan, 243; *The Haileyburian*, 132;
Denys Hake, 237; Pieter Johnson,
168; Neville Talbot, 52, 144;
H. S. Tindall, 132

Hampton, 257

Harrow, 10, 20, 28, 35, 39, 41, 80, 87, 91,
99, 102, 107, 127, 164, 199, 200,
201–2, 216–17, 219, 235, 244, 257;
Stanley Baldwin, 127, 245, 246;

General Index

304

French, Sir John, 39, 50, 51, 54, 229, 238
Friends' Ambulance Unit, 120, 210
Frost, Robert, 156; *The Road not Taken*, 156
Fry, Stephen, 232
Fuller, J. F. C., 163
Furse, Sir Ralph, 23
Fussell, Paul, 225

Gallipoli, Battle of (1915), 38, 47–50, 64, 73–5, 78, 82, 115, 120, 136, 174, 195, 200, 242, 243, 248, 251; Battle of Krithia, 49; ANZAC Cove, 73; Sari Bair, 248; evacuation from, 50
Gallipoli (1981 film), 4, 232
Gascoyne-Cecil, John, 246
Gascoyne-Cecil, Randle, 246
Gascoyne-Cecil, Rupert, 246
Gater, George, 180, 181
GCSE (General Certificate of Secondary Education), 204
Germany, 28, 29, 32, 33, 176, 235; anti-German sentiment, 36; 93–4, 118–19
Geddes, Guy, 47–8
General Electric Company, 9
George V, HM King, 190, 215
German East Africa, 82
Gethin, Lieutenant., 146
Gibbon, W. D., 115
Gibraltar, 119
Gibson, Guy, 5
Giffard, Edmund, 185
Gilkes, Humphrey, 181
Gill, Eric, 198
Gillespie, Douglas, 54, 64, 133, 214
Gillies, Harold, 250
Gilligan, Arthur, 235
Gilson, Robert Cary, 60–1
Gilson, Rob, 60–1
Gimson, Ernest, 198
Girling, Jack, 126–7; *School Colours*, 126
Gladstone, W. E., 117
Gladstone, W., 189
Glasgow University, 9
Gleason, Arthur, 238
Gloucester, Prince Henry of, 119
Glubb, John, 157
Gollancz, Victor, 96–7, 219; *A Year of Grace*, 96
Gordon, R. E., 134

Gotha bombing raids, 86
Gough, Sir Hubert, 40
Gow, James, 122
Graham, Dom Lucius, 197
Grahame, Gordon, 78
Grant Richards (publisher), 99
Graves, Robert, 18, 20, 31, 34, 41, 108, 183, 185–6, 224; *Goodbye to All That*, 43, 224
Great Britain (government of), 10, 25, 33, 66, 67, 71, 111, 127, 164, 177, 180, 183, 189, 190, 197, 209, 210, 211, 217, 222, 227, 237, 245, 246, 247, 250, 251
Greaves, Ralph, 250
Greene, C. H., 112, 215
Greene, Graham: *The Old School Tie*, 215–16
Greenwell, Graham, 159, 226; *An Infant in Arms*, 226
Greenway, John, 8, 9
Gregory, Adrian, 189, 252
Gregory, Robert, 169–70
Grenfell, Billy 38, 52, 53
Grenfell, Julian, 38, 46, 52, 53; *Into Battle*, 38, 46, 211
Great Public Schools (1893), 12
Great War: impact on Britain, 6; outbreak, 32–7; conclusion, 153–83, historical interpretation, 206–33
The Great War (1964 TV documentary), 230
Grey, Sir Edward 10, 29
Grimwade, George, 74
Grogan, George, 243
Guilford, Monty, 143
Gunzburg, Alexis de, 42
Gurdjieff, J. I., 184
Gurner, Ronald, 52
Gurney, Ivor, 19, 211
Guggenheim, Benjamin, 22

Haig, Sir Douglas, 22, 39, 52, 54, 79, 160, 179, 197, 209, 229, 230, 232, 244
Haig-Brown, Alan, 30, 114; *The OTC and the Great War*, 114
Hake, Denys, 237
Haldane, Lord: 39; reforms, 25
Hale, Edward, 8, 9
Hall, Geoffrey, 73
Hamilton, Duchess of, 123